ROUTLEDGE LIBRARY EDITIONS:
AID

Volume 1

AUSTRALIAN OVERSEAS AID

AUSTRALIAN OVERSEAS AID

Edited by
PHILIP ELDRIDGE, DEAN FORBES AND
DOUG PORTER

Routledge
Taylor & Francis Group
LONDON AND NEW YORK

First published in 1986 by Croom Helm Ltd

This edition first published in 2020
by Routledge
2 Park Square, Milton Park, Abingdon, Oxon OX14 4RN

and by Routledge
52 Vanderbilt Avenue, New York, NY 10017

Routledge is an imprint of the Taylor & Francis Group, an informa business

British Library Cataloguing in Publication Data
A catalogue record for this book is available from the British Library

ISBN: 978-0-367-27806-9 (Set)
ISBN: 978-0-429-32859-6 (Set) (ebk)
ISBN: 978-0-367-34157-2 (Volume 1) (hbk)
ISBN: 978-0-429-32421-5 (Volume 1) (ebk)

Publisher's Note
The publisher has gone to great lengths to ensure the quality of this reprint but points out that some imperfections in the original copies may be apparent.

Disclaimer
The publisher has made every effort to trace copyright holders and would welcome correspondence from those they have been unable to trace.

AUSTRALIAN OVERSEAS AID: FUTURE DIRECTIONS

Edited by

Philip Eldridge, Dean Forbes and Doug Porter

CROOM HELM
SYDNEY: LONDON

Croom Helm Australia Pty Ltd, 64-76 Kippax Street, Surry Hills, NSW 2010
Croom Helm Ltd, Provident House, Burrell Row, Beckenham, Kent BR3 1AT, England

National Library of Australia Cataloguing-in-Publication Data

Australian overseas aid.

Bibliography
Includes index.
ISBN 0 949614 19 X.

1. Economic assistance, Australian — Developing countries. 2. Australia — Economic policy — 1976- . 3. Developing countries — Economic conditions. 4. Committee to Review the Australian Overseas Aid Program.
Australian Overseas Aid Program. I. Eldridge, Philip J. (Philip John), 1935- . II. Forbes, D.K. (Dean Keith), 1949- . III. Porter, Doug, 1953-

338.91'94'01724

Printed in Australia by Southwood Press, Sydney

CONTENTS

LIST OF TABLES AND FIGURES

Tables

Figures

LIST OF ABBREVIATIONS

AAECP	ASEAN-Australia Economic Cooperation Program
AAWL	Australia-Asia Workers Links
ACFOA	Australian Council for Overseas Aid
ACIAR	Australian Centre for International Agricultural Research
ACOA	Australian Clerical Officers Association
ACTU	Australian Council of Trade Unions
ADAA	Australian Development Assistance Agency
ADAB	Australian Development Assistance Bureau
ADB	Asian Development Bank
AFFHC	Australian Freedom From Hunger Campaign
AFSAAP	African Studies Association of Australia and the Pacific
APACE	Appropriate Technology and Community Environment
APCC	Australian Professional Consultants Council
APHEDA	Australian People for Health, Education and Development Abroad
ASEAN	Association of South East Asian Nations
ASPBAE	Asian and South Pacific Bureau of Adult Education
AUIDP	Australian Universities' International Development Program
BINGO	Bilateral Non-governmental Organisation
CAA	Community Aid Abroad
CBA	cost-benefit analysis
CDC	Committee for Development Co-operation
CIDA	Canadian International Development Agency
CRIAD	(Centre for International Relations between Farmers for Development)
CTEC	Commonwealth Tertiary Education Commission

DAC	Development Assistance Committee (of the OECD)
DAOA	Development Assistance Officers Association
deved	development education
DFA	Department of Foreign Affairs
DIFF	Development Import Finance Facility
DIGS	Development Import Grants
DVV	(German Adult Education Association)
EEC	European Economic Community
EFIC	Export Finance Insurance Corporation
EOI	export-oriented industrialisation
FAO	Food and Agriculture Organisation
FFH	Freedom from Hunger
FNSEA	Federation Nationale des Syndicats d'Exploitantes Agricoles
FOB	free on board
FRPL	(Regional Federation of Dairy Producers)
GDP	gross domestic product
GNP	gross national product
HOMDAF	Head of Mission Discretionary Aid Funds
ICAE	International Council for Adult Education
ICARA	International Conference on Assistance to Refugees in Africa
IDA	International Development Agency
IDP	International Development Program
IFC	International Finance Corporation
ILO	International Labour Organisation
IMF	International Monetary Fund
IPF	Indicative Planning Figure

IRDP	Integrated Rural Development Program
ISI	Import Substitution Industrialisation
JCFAD	(Parliamentary) Joint Committee on Foreign Affairs and Defence
JCPA	(Parliamentary) Joint Committee on Public Accounts
LDC	Less Developed Countries
NGO	non-govermmental organisation
NIC	Newly Industrialising Countries
NIDL	New International Division of Labour
NIEO	New International Economic Order
NS IRDP	Northern Samar Integrated Rural Development Project
OAU	Organisation of African Unity
ODA	official development assistance
OECD	Organisation for Economic Co-operation and Development
PADAP	Philippine-Australian Development Assistance Program
PEO	Programme Evaluation Organisation
PEP	Participation and Equity Program
PNG	Papua New Guinea
PSS	Project Subsidy Scheme
PTA	Preferential Trade Area
RCF	Review of Commonwealth Functions (or Lynch Committee)
SADCC	South African Development Co-ordination Conference
SAFCOL	South Australian Fish Cooperative Ltd
SCAAP	Special Commonwealth African Assistance Plan
SOLAGRAL	(Solidarity Farm and Food)
SPC	South Pacific Commission

SPEC	South Pacific Bureau for Economic Cooperation
SPUR	Special Program to Upgrade Resources
SPWP	Special Public Works Programmes
TCDC	technical cooperation between developing countries
UN	United Nations
UNCTAD	United Nations Conference on Trade and Development
UNDP	United Nations Development Programme
UNIDO	United Nations Industrial Development Organisation
WADNA	Women and Development Network of Australia

NOTES ON CONTRIBUTORS

Kaye Bysouth, Community Aid Abroad, 75 Brunswick St, Fitzroy, Victoria 3065. Evaluation Co-ordinator with Community Aid Abroad since 1981 and currently Director of the CAA Development Service. The Development Service is a commercially-run development advisory unit within CAA, which applies the experience gained at the micro level to the identification, planning and implementation of large-scale projects in the areas of health, education, agriculture, community development and management of rural development projects.

Brian Chatterton, 'Riverside', PO Box 82, Lyndoch, South Australia 5351. Member of Parliament. Farmer. South Australian Minister of Agriculture, Fisheries and Forests 1975/9 and 1982/3. Established South Australian Government's dryland farming projects in North Africa and the Middle East. Has been architect of numerous agricultural policies in Australia and currently continues his study of Arab farming and rangeland restoration and management and the application of South Australian farming technology to it. Has published numerous papers on the subject.

Lynne Chatterton, 'Riverside', PO Box 82, Lyndoch, South Australia 5351. Studies and writes about Arab farming and rangeland restoration and management and the application of South Australian farming technology to developing countries. Has had published numerous studies on this subject. Formerly rural policy adviser to South Australian Government, including the setting up of the overseas projects policy and its operation. Has experience in broadcasting — particularly communication with farmers --men and women.

John Connell, Department of Geography, University of Sydney, Sydney, NSW 2006. Currently Senior Lecturer in Geography at Sydney University. Co-author of Migration from Rural Areas (1976), and author of Taim Bilong Mani (1976) and The End of Tradition (1978). Seconded between 1981 and 1983 to be Coordinator of a South Pacific Commission/International Labour Organisation project on migration, employment and development in the South Pacific.

Chris Duke, Department of Continuing Adult Education, University of Warwick, Coventry, UK. Founding Director of Continuing Education, ANU, 1969/85 and founding Director of Open Studies and Professor of Continuing Education, University of Warwick from June 1985. Secretary-General of the Asian and South Pacific Bureau of Adult Education 1974/85. Associate Secretary-General of International Council for Adult Education since 1979. Author of various books and papers on adult, continuing and nonformal education.

Philip Eldridge, Department of Politics, University of Tasmania, GPO Box 252C, Hobart, Tasmania 7001. Senior Lecturer in Political Science, University of Tasmania. Researched and published widely in relation to aid and development issues, with special reference to India, Indonesia, Australia/Indonesia relations and Australian aid policy. His current interests relate to the role of non -government organisations.

Dean Forbes, Department of Human Geography, Research School of Pacific Studies, Australian National University, GPO Box 4, Canberra, ACT 2601. Senior Research Fellow at the Australian National University, recently on leave with the Australian Institute of Urban Studies in Canberra. Author of Petty Commodity Production and Underdevelopment (1981) and The Geography of Underdevelopment (1984). Co -editor of Uneven Development and the Geographical Transfer of Value (1984), and Australian Geographical Studies (1982/6).

Cherry Gertzel, School of Social Sciences, Flinders University, Bedford Park, South Australia 5042. Reader in Politics and Director of the Centre for Development Studies at Flinders University. She has been President of the African Studies Association of Australia and the Pacific since 1982. Her major publications include Government and Politics in Kenya (co-editor, 1969), The Politics of Independent Kenya (1970), Party and Locality in Northern Uganda (1974), and The Dynamics of the One-Party State in Zambia (co-author, 1984).

David Goldsworthy, Department of Politics, Monash University, Clayton, Victoria 3162. Reader in Politics at Monash University. He is Secretary for the African Studies Association of Australia and the Pacific and is a former editor of Australian Outlook. He was President of the Australasian Political Studies Association for 1984/5. His major publications include Colonial Issues in British Politics 1945-61 (1971) and Tom Mboya (1982).

Richard Higgott, Social and Political Theory Programme, Murdoch University, Western Australia 6150. Senior Lecturer in Social and Political Theory, Murdoch University. Author of Political Development Theory (1983) co-editor of Southeast Asia: Essays in The Political Economy of Structural Change and currently editor of Australian Outlook.

Helen Hill, Office of John Langmore M.P., Parliament House, Canberra, ACT, 2601. Founding convenor of Women and Development Group in Canberra, formerly taught sociology and political science at Universities of Melbourne and Monash and the Royal Melbourne Institute of Technology. Carried out research on nonformal education in Fiji, New Caledonia and Micronesia for a PhD at the ANU Centre for Continuing Education. Author of numerous journalistic articles on East Timor, Africa and the South Pacific. Has undertaken consultancy work on programs for out-of-school youth and on nonformal education for women in the Pacific region. Currently on leave from the Australian Development Assistance Bureau.

Juliet Hunt, Department of General Studies, University of New South Wales, Kensington, NSW 2033. Tutor in development studies, currently completing a PhD on the Australian government aid program in the Department of General Studies, University of New South Wales. Formerly Education Officer for Community Aid Abroad in Sydney. Co-author of Foreign News on Sydney Television (1982).

Steven Keen, 16 Mackenzie St, Bondi Junction, NSW 2022. Assistant Director, the Business Union Consultation Unit of the Department of Trade. Editor of Trade - To Whose Advantage? (1980). Formerly economic commentator with the ABC, and Education Officer for the Australian Freedom from Hunger Campaign.

John Langmore, MP, House of Representatives, Parliament of Australia, Canberra, ACT 2601. Formerly lecturer in economics at the University of Papua New Guinea and assistant director, PNG National Planning Office. Coeditor of Alternative Strategies for Papua New Guinea (1973 and 1976) and Wealth, Poverty and Survival: Australia in the World (1983).

Doug Porter, Department of Human Geography, Research School of Pacific Studies, Australian National University, GPO Box 4, Canberra, ACT 2601. Recently completed PhD studies on project evaluation and impact assessment in the South Pacific and the Philippines. Has undertaken assignments for the Australian and New Zealand governments and non-governmental organisations. Co-author of Ethics, Politics, and International Social Science Research (1984) and various articles on development.

Sarah Sargent, 16 Mackenzie St, Bondi Junction, NSW 2022. Since 1976 has worked in United Nations International Audio-Visual Resource Service and then with Australian Freedom from Hunger Campaign and Austcare. From 1980 has researched structural problems and North-South links in Australian agriculture. Author of The Food Makers (1985), and currently the rural writer for the Australian Financial Review.

Michael Taylor, Department of Human Geography, Research School of Pacific Studies, Australian National University, GPO Box 4, Canberra, ACT 2601. Senior Research Fellow at The Australian National University. Co-author of Industrial Organisation and Location (1982). Co-editor of The Geography of Multinationals (1982), and Regional Impacts of Resource Development (1984) and editor of The Geography of Australian Corporate Power (1984).

PREFACE AND ACKNOWLEDGEMENTS

The origins of this volume lay in a chance meeting of the three editors in Canberra in September 1984. The recently published Jackson Report (or, to give its full title, the Report of the Committee to Review the Australian Overseas Aid Program) had caused a stir in the community interested in matters of overseas aid. While the seriousness of the report's commitment to improving the quality of Australian aid was welcomed by the editors, we felt unhappy with the thrust of many of the recommendations. In particular, we were concerned with the Jackson Report's tendency to see aid as primarily a means of accelerating macro-economic growth, at the expense of aid targetted more directly at the poor in developing countries.

More importantly, perhaps, we were anxious that the Jackson Report be not seen as the definitive statement of Australia's future aid program, but as a catalyst to further informed debate on aid options. In this sense the report has been a success, for it has made a significant contribution to the aid debate in Australia, a debate which this volume is intended to continue.

The editors have incurred a number of debts in the production of this volume. In particular we wish to thank Carol McKenzie for her patience and dexterity on the word processor, and Barbara Banks, who assisted with the editorial work and compilation of the bibliography with her usual diligence and good humour. Finally, we wish to thank Chris Kissling for providing the packing and layout program for the text.

INTRODUCTION

Philip Eldridge, Dean Forbes and Doug Porter

In the popular imagination, Australia is a small nation on the southern periphery of a huge and populous continent. Yet it is also a wealthy country, with a Gross Domestic Product (GDP) which in 1982 exceeded the combined GDP of its closest northern neighbours -- Indonesia, Malaysia, Singapore, the Philippines and Papua New Guinea.

Despite its proximity to the developing world, Australia's official aid budget is moderate by OECD standards. Peaking at 0.65 per cent of GNP in 1975, this had fallen back to 0.5 per cent in 1984, and Australia's ranking as an aid donor dropped from fourth to seventh among OECD members. In absolute terms in 1982 it ranked as the ninth largest donor among the 17 industrial country members (World Bank, 1983, pp. 182-3).

The official aid allocation for the 1985/86 is estimated to total $1025.9 million. The lion's share -- $755.1 million, or 73.6 per cent -- is allotted to the bilateral program. Papua New Guinea will receive an estimated $326.4 million of which $302.8 million will go to budget support. Aid to major recipients for projects and training is estimated at $110.9 million and $111.0 million respectively (1985-86 Budget Paper No. 9).

Australian aid is on the brink of some far-reaching changes. First, the current Labor government has continued the previous conservative government's attack on what it perceives to be welfare spending and 'big' government. The aid program is not immune from such cuts, being reduced by 4.9 per cent, in real terms, in the 1985/6 budget.

Secondly, there are clear shifts in the thrust of aid delivery by the major bilateral and multilateral donors. Internationally, powerful and vocal lobbies urge cutbacks in aid spending, 'tied' aid is becoming more prevalent in many countries, and the World Bank is reorienting its loans towards 'structural adjustment' and urges the acceptance of the market economy. Such fundamental shifts will ultimately have an impact on Australian aid policy, both intellectually and in a practical context given the prevalence of co-financing arrangements between the bank and donor countries.

Third, and most importantly as far as this book is concerned, the Committee to Review the Australian Overseas Aid Program presented its report to the Minister for Foreign Affairs in March 1984 (referred to in this volume as the Jackson Report). This was the culmination of a series of critical reviews of the aid program, the most important of which had been the report by the Auditor-General (1981). The Jackson Report was seen by its authors as a radical statement about directions for the aid program over the next decade.

The Foreign Minister's Terms of Reference for the review highlighted the following subjects:

> Equity: consider how Australian aid is distributed in recipient countries, and particularly whether a greater proportion of aid should be provided for the benefit of lower income groups.
>
> Australian interests: examine how the aid program relates to Australia's overall external policies and priorities.
>
> Effectiveness: consider the extent to which there is a need for more effective criteria of economic efficiency in the use of aid in recipient countries.
>
> Multilateral/bilateral aid: consider the desirable balance between bilateral and multilateral aid and the role of international agencies in the delivery of Australia's aid program.
>
> Geographic distribution: consider the geographic distribution of Australian aid programs, and in particular whether more emphasis should be given to the Pacific and South-East Asian region.
>
> Terms of aid: consider and recommend on the terms of Australia's aid, including the scope for introduction of a loans program, and including soft loans, as part of an expanding revolving fund which would be a net addition to the overall aid program.
>
> Australian resources: consider the extent to which Australian resources including skilled people and non-government agencies should be involved in our aid programs.
>
> Administration: assess the effectiveness of the organisation and operation of the Australian administration and delivery of our aid program. (Jackson Report, 1984, p. 245)

The report has been received favourably; it is currently providing the basis for a serious administrative reorganisation of the Australian Development Assistance Bureau (ADAB), intensified staff training, and the formal adoption of country strategies as the basis for the aid program. The report has been praised by economists in the media for its commitment to a market economy, while the 'natural constituency' of the aid program -- supporters of the many non-governmental organisations (NGOs) involved in aid delivery -- were, in general, pleased by the commitment of the report to increased support for NGO activity. But with closer scrutiny there have emerged rumblings of discontent with the direction set by the Jackson Report, particularly its rigid advocacy of a market ideology and a contentious development strategy.

Disquiet and disaffection is reflected in five major themes of this collection. Overall, we attempt to provide constructive criticism of the Jackson Report. But in the first instance this requires that we disperse the aura of infallibility which has surrounded the report. Sustained criticism is in many cases necessary before other interpretations of aid and the development process can be presented. The critical commentary is not, however, orchestrated. The book contains differing interpretations and does not pretend to offer a definitive overall statement on the Australian aid program or aid in general. Indeed, major issues relating to Third World and international social and political structures which have been well canvassed in the literature on development are not, for reasons of both space and context, addressed in any direct sense in the volume. The Jackson Report is a statement both of policy and ideology and the various responses to it are mostly at that level within their particular substantive contexts.

Nevertheless, the book does not represent a sentimental view of the world. Between them, the contributors have years of practical experience implementing, administering, or evaluating many kinds of aid projects, working in developing countries, or researching development issues. Based on this experience, the contributors argue that in many important respects the Jackson Report is either flawed or mistaken in the direction it points for a developmentally effective Australian aid program. Indeed many contributors argue the committee has done a disservice to debate about Australian aid. The polarisation of the growth and equity issue, so prominent in the Jackson Report -- and its alliance with other dichotomies such as realist /idealist, macro/micro, official/community -- is frequently addressed in this volume. All chapters confront the report's growth emphasis; but equally, they argue that in practice, these dichotomies can be sustained only by a selective recall of the evidence, and what protagonists on each side of the divides are saying.

None of the contributors would claim to have reconciled these dichotomies, but the insights of academics, practitioners and activists will hopefully remove some of the barriers constraining constructive debate.

Second, a key attribute of the Jackson Report is an assertion of a largely neo-classical and authoritarian view of world development. In its 'new realism' (see the chapter by Higgott), the Jackson Report is the child of important international and national trends in recent years. In international financial agencies like the World Bank these trends were signalled by the abandonment of the basic needs, equity-oriented development programs of the 1970s in favour of an emphasis on growth oriented, structural adjustment policies. The Jackson Report corresponds with a decline in social democratic political philosophy and resurgent conservative emphasis on confidently espoused 'correct' economic analysis.

The essence of the new realism is implicit also in the Jackson Report's analysis of Australia's position. Australia's problems of economic growth are said to reflect a failure to 'adjust' to the changing fortunes of its neighbours. Within Australia there is the growing influence of technocrats and professionals committed to neo-classical economic philosophies and policies. Despite Australia's status in the region, the new realism encourages the belief that we live in an all-constraining world, and consequently, can have little or no impact on the region. Paradoxically, this 'hard-nosed', pragmatic view of reality in the Jackson Report is sufficiently loose to legitimate diverse ad hoc policy initiatives according to diplomatic convenience.

This book represents an attempt to challenge the assumptions underlying this trend of new realism. The contributors of course recognise this is a difficult task given an unfavourable, if not outright hostile political environment. Yet, tacitly, the contributors reaffirm their belief that rational debate can change ideas and promote community actions and thereby surmount the structures which hinder an equitable and sustainable development process.

The third, fourth, and fifth themes of this book deal with specific aspects of the ethos presented by the Jackson Report. Many contributors conclude the report provides no effective way of reconciling the diplomatic, commercial and humanitarian imperatives impinging on the aid program. Moreover, without a clear hierarchy of objectives, the Jackson Report could ironically result in increased confusion and ad hoc decision-making in the actual practice of development assistance. Yet, even supposing such a hierarchy of objectives had been made explicit, this would not overcome a general disquiet about the committee's scant attention to the linkages between policy and practice. Expressions like 'removing major obstacles', 'political will' and 'professionalism', are bandied around as panaceas for what in fact are pervasive, and often intractable, difficulties in actual practice.

Concern about the links between policy and practice is evident in a fourth theme, namely, the character of the development strategy promoted by the Jackson Report. Disputes about the growth emphasis receive much attention in this book, as does the way in which the report's recommendations about topics as diverse as education, aid management and the Pacific islands, are underpinned by a handy separation of economic and social development. With the Jackson Report we see a return of the old development dictum 'First bake the cake'; in considering equity and basic needs issues, various authors question the largely assumed ingredients of Jackson's cake. They also show that people's previous experience with the way the cake is sliced affect their willingness to participate in its production.

A final theme concerns the new geographic and social distribution of Australian aid proposed by the Jackson Report. At this point concern about the confusion of objectives, about basic needs requirements, diplomatic expediency and the harsh consequences of cost-effectiveness comes to the fore. The social and geographic distribution of Australian aid is, after all, the bottom line of any review of an aid program. On the whole, while contributors acknowledge the need to move from 'shopping lists' to more rational country and program selection criteria, few find the report's rationale logical, or persuasive. The report's assumptions about the Pacific islands capacity to absorb aid, the needs of eastern and southern Africa and South Asia vis-a-vis national self- interest are frequent cases in point.

These five themes, and others linked with them, are pursued in four parts of this volume. The first part of the volume contains three contributions which focus on the general themes and overall context of the Jackson Report.

Philip Eldridge argues that its effect will be to continue past practice whereby several objectives -- diplomatic, trade, humanitarian, etc. — are pursued simultaneously through the aid program. Whereas most contributors see these various goals as in conflict, the Jackson Committee has sought to reconcile them under the all-embracing rubric of 'development'. In defining development, it tries to come to terms with the long-standing debate about the relationship between economic growth, basic human needs and social justice. However, it only succeeds in fudging key choices in its use of the term 'growth with equity', which is applied elastically to a diversity of ad hoc recommendations across the board. Eldridge briefly illustrates these themes with reference to Jackson's recommendations on education, aid administration and the rationale which should apply to regional and country distribution of aid. He concludes by proposing an alternative geographical distribution of aid, and outlining an overall approach he considers to be both more equitable as well as economically and diplomatically feasible.

John Langmore is more sympathetic to the main thrust of the report. He also argues strongly against those who he sees as downgrading the need for aid, at the same time taking the committee to task for failing to make any firm recommendations for increased aid. Langmore's main emphasis is on international economic and financial aspects. He essentially supports the Brandt Report position on Third World demands for a New International Economic Order and attacks the report for its generally negative tone towards the NIEO. Finally, he is critical of Jackson's recommendations for Papua New Guinea, in particular arguing that the current system of general budgetary and program support has been more developmentally effective than a shift to project aid is likely to prove. Langmore also sees project aid as potentially threatening to PNG's control of its overall economic direction.

Richard Higgott does not comment on the content of the report but concentrates rather on the environment in which it has been written. He explains the shift in the World Bank's overall strategy from the pursuit of 'basic needs' in the 1970s to one of 'structural adjustment' in the 1980s. In practice this means a renewed emphasis on economic growth, adjustment of monetary, wages and trade policies in the pursuit of comparative advantage. He highlights the many areas in which, even in its choice of language, the Jackson Report is cast in this mould. Higgott's second major theme concerns the emerging importance of East and Southeast Asia to Australia's economic future and Australia's own changing position in the international division of labour. Taken together, these two underlying trends are shaping an environment unfavourable to the kinds of approaches favoured by most contributors to this volume. Both trends are essential aspects of the 'new realism' so strongly reflected in the Jackson Report. However, Higgott notes that fashions in development thinking change quite frequently and the Jackson Report is in that sense 'a tract for its times'.

Together with Eldridge, Higgott touches on the theme of 'asymmetry' -- an approach which has become increasingly dominant in determining Australian diplomacy, economic relations and policies across the board in dealings with the ASEAN countries. This emphasises Australia's limited bargaining power and relatively greater need of ASEAN than ASEAN has of Australia. Whereas Higgott adopts a generally deterministic outlook on these matters, Eldridge sees more scope for flexibility in Australia's position. In any case, the specific implications of 'asymmetry' for aid are open to question for, as Higgott's analysis suggests, the case for assistance to the ASEAN countries is far more diplomatic than economic.

The second part of the volume deals with the geographical distribution of aid proposed by Jackson and its implications for the regions of the Pacific, South and Southeast Asia and Africa respectively.

John Connell presents a detailed review of aid allocation in the Pacific islands countries. He argues that in situations where prospects for economic growth are limited, and unless marine resources can be more effectively exploited, there is a case for external aid. The report, however, offers no examination of the international and internal political factors which may inhibit development. As with the previous Harries Report (1974) Australian aid has a 'symbolic' and strategic significance; it is a necessary support for the survival and stability of existing political systems. Given diplomatic, strategic and commercial considerations, Connell argues that it is abundantly clear aid is only tenuously related to achieving economic growth or equity. The Jackson Report does nothing to modify this.

Connell is alarmed at how little attention is given in the report to the two established economic bases of most South Pacific economies: agriculture and fishing. Ironically, the report places particular stress on emigration and tourism, which, from the Pacific islands' point of view are 'last resort' sectors. Furthermore the report largely accepts the 'subsistence affluence' myth about Pacific islands countries and consequently does little to acknowledge, or address how Australian aid may assist, the growing poverty and deteriorating health and nutritional status of many Pacific islands people. Noting the report's emphasis on 'outward looking' domestic economic policy, Connell echoes the concerns of many Pacific people over the authoritarian thrust of the committee and their neglect of Pacific beliefs, attitudes and priorities.

Michael Taylor's chapter targets the importance which the Jackson Report attaches to the aid, trade and investment 'trinity', and is particularly critical of the report's propagation of a 'free trade' path to economic development for the small island countries of the South Pacific. His argument centres on an analysis of the recent behaviour of Australian and New Zealand owned firms in Fiji. Taylor suggests that free and undistorted trade does not, and never has existed in the Pacific islands. It is demonstrable that corporations in Fiji seek monopoly power and are concerned with the repatriation of corporate profits. In policies oriented to maximising the well-being of the corporation the interests of the Pacific island micro-states are given low priority. Therefore, Taylor argues, the growth orientation of the Jackson Report's aid advice only helps to reinforce the attempt by large corporations to acquire monopoly power.

Dean Forbes looks at the likely consequences of Jackson's recommendations for the countries of South, East and Southeast Asia, including the Indian Ocean islands, and predicts that they will reinforce the status quo, though with some unintended consequences, such as increasing assistance to Nepal. He notes that whereas the relative allocations of Australian aid have been carefully scaled in accordance with political priorities between the various non-communist countries in the region, in the case of Indo-China the committee pleads inability to allocate any priority on the grounds that political considerations render such decisions impossible. In this context, the Foreign Affairs Minister, Bill Hayden is proving a good deal more willing to move positively. Forbes then compares the criteria advanced by Jackson with those put forward by Community Aid Abroad in its submission to the committee. Although CAA's formula would have resulted in a more equitable, 'needs based' allocation, both approaches produce distortions and random results through unrealistic attempts to quantify criteria of need.

As part of this discussion, Forbes looks at the concept of country programming, which was also discussed earlier by Eldridge. Much hinges on the soundness of this concept, which provides the foundation on which future directions for allocating assistance will be built. In this context Eldridge notes the heavy emphasis on Australia's 'national interest' in the way this concept is being operationalised. If Jackson's recommendations are implemented, inclusion or exclusion and the relative intensity and extensiveness of country programming will clearly be vital to the type and quantity of assistance countries may expect from Australia in the future. Both authors agree that the concept is problematical. Two distinct, though related aspects are liable to become confused in this discussion. Key questions relate to what would be the major components of a country program, how they would relate to each other and what Australia's role would be relative to national planners and international agencies. A second, though subsidiary question relates to how Australia should determine its comparative advantage in selecting countries for country programming. These questions tend to be run together and neither are confronted adequately in the report. Although the need for country programming provides the rationale for categorisation of the countries Jackson proposes, in practice this has been determined on quite other grounds.

Cherry Gertzel and David Goldsworthy make the case for the most obvious losers in the Jackson Report -- the African countries. They begin by delineating key problems and restating the most obvious arguments for assisting Africa, based on needs criteria. Thereafter, though obviously unhappy with Jackson's basic thrust, they offer a framework for continuing bilateral assistance in Africa which is not incompatible with some key arguments in the report. They suggest, for example, that Australia has a potential comparative advantage in dryland agriculture relevant to some areas of eastern and southern Africa, though acknowledging differences in the social context and the pitfalls of technology transfer across cultures. To accomodate the report's emphasis on country programming, Gertzel and Goldsworthy propose that a relatively small number of countries in eastern and southern Africa be selected, where Australia already has a presence, lines of communication are already well established and are likely to prove less difficult than with the Indian Ocean islands, which are given top priority in the report. In the English-speaking Commonwealth countries in that region particularly, some minimum knowledge about the various societies and bureaucracies has been established, often on a more effective footing than in some Asian countries receiving greater measures of Australian support. The authors strongly urge the diplomatic importance of Australia not being seen to be withdrawing support from countries neighbouring South Africa. Finally, they acknowledge that there have been poor bilateral projects in Africa but these are scarcely unique relative to other regions and does not justify withdrawing bilateral assistance from a whole continent. The third part of the volume deals with three topic areas taken up in the report -- education, the role of women and trade -- and a fourth, agricultural aid, which does not feature specifically and is felt to have been treated superficially.

Chris Duke takes up Jackson's themes of 'growth with equity' as applied to education, noting that they reflect more dramatically than in other sectors the dominant trend of 'new realism' among Australian policy-makers discussed by Higgott earlier. Duke notes that Jackson's 'export-oriented' approach will lead to an emphasis on bringing students to Australia rather than helping to build up educational institutions in their own countries, together with a bias towards formal as against non-formal modes of education. As a modest corrective, in such a climate, he proposes a 1:4 ratio should be set between non-formal and formal education spending. Such an approach is perhaps too cautious, as a case can almost certainly be mounted that non-formal education would prove more cost-effective relative to many more institutionalised, capital-intensive programs. Certainly, the Jackson Committee's own proposals in this area have yet to be costed.

This discussion illustrates, among other things, the extent to which development programs constantly entail innovation and adaptation at all levels and how constricting them within the latest trends of orthodoxy emanating from the World Bank and related centres of power can be quite counter-productive on the ground. Paradoxically, the authors of the education chapter in the Jackson Report appear to consider the innovations they propose as the piece de resistance of the whole report. From the standpoint of this analysis, their emphasis on export-oriented education will introduce serious rigidities and distortions into this whole sector.

Helen Hill looks at the apparently positive line taken towards women in the report and details some of its useful and practical suggestions. The Jackson Committee has been commended for its attempt to come to grips with some of the structural obstacles to improving women's lot in the developing world. Hill argues that an adequate treatment of women in development, as with other topics in the report, requires particular attention to such aspects as the division of labour between men and women, income sharing within the family, land reform, and differential access to education. She finds little of this in the report. Moreover, the key beneficiaries of increased attention to women are likely to be those in professional classes rather than poor women in rural areas. Turning to the specific recommendations, Hill argues many of them miss the mark. The Women in Development Fund, reflected in a $50,000 allocation in the 1984/5 Budget, is a problematic recommendation since many of the issues cannot be dealt with through aid projects but require international lobbying and awareness raising. For instance, Hill points to the fact that in the recent East African famine emergency hardly a word was mentioned of women's roles in food production, distribution, and preparation, despite their predominance in agricultural and household labour. This, she concludes, shows how far we are from raising the basic issues.

Steve Keen, in a brief and powerful polemic, mounts a sharp attack on neo-classical economics in general and the theory of comparative advantage in particular. He argues that the success of the so-called 'Newly Industrialising Countries' (NICs) in East and Southeast Asia derives from their public investment programs and the close involvement of their governments in economic planning and their cooperation with private enterprise in export promotion. Redistribution policies, particularly in relation to land reform, were in place before the big push for 'take-off' in the 1960s and 1970s. Far from proving the validity of Jackson-style orthodoxy, the experience of the NICs directly refutes it. Keen concludes that 'trade not aid' is an empty slogan in the light of this experience. He argues that there is no reason why Australian businessmen should not benefit from tied aid, provided that mutual advantage can be demonstrated, compatible with equitable development. To this end, incentives are required to encourage adaptation of Australian technology in ways relevant to the needs of farmers and small enterprises in Third World countries. Several possible examples are offered. In this context, Keen strongly defends the idea of 'economic nationalism' as a justifiable approach for both Australia and neighbouring countries. His use of the term 'mercantilism' is both interesting and controversial in this context.

Brian and Lynne Chatterton criticise the Jackson Report for its failure to focus specifically on agriculture, despite a variety of references to it in the report. They argue that the status of agriculture remains low, with around 10 per cent of total Australian overseas assistance being devoted to agricultural programs of one kind or another. Using case study examples, they identify a persistent pattern in Australian agricultural programs, indicating a professional and research rather than extension and farmer-oriented bias. This results in inappropriate styles of transfer and exchange in every context relating to animals, crops, culture, climate, training and research. The nexus between ADAB, agricultural consultants, higher education and research agencies is as one where vested interests are entrenched and biases against learning from a long history of past mistakes have become institutionalised.

The final section of the volume is concerned both with aid administration in its more specific bureaucratic context and with broader questions of community participation in developmental processes.

Juliet Hunt, while welcoming in principle the report's recommendations to upgrade ADAB, expresses grave doubts about the effectiveness of such efforts, given the overall framework which Jackson proposes. The report, she argues, has done little to resolve either ADAB's inherent weaknesses in policy-making capability or the weak link between policy-making and aid practice noted in the Auditor-General's Report.

In particular, the confusion in defining 'development' and failure to lay down a 'hierarchy of objectives' will undermine the effectiveness of such reforms, with programs being designed to serve conflicting purposes simultaneously. Thus, as the 1981 Auditor-General's Report pointed out, processes for identifying, selecting, designing, operating, monitoring and evaluating programs are subject to similar confusion at every level, which will not be resolved merely by improved upgrading and recruitment, desirable as these may be in themselves. The long-running debate over the status of ADAB vis-a-vis the Department of Foreign Affairs takes place within a similar context and is advanced little further by Jackson's recommendations.

Hunt concludes with a number of specific proposals, including the establishment of 'equity-oriented' programs. She also envisages an 'equity task force' to lay down general guidelines. While clearly sensitive to the obvious dangers of 'tokenism' inherent in such schemes and isolation from mainstream programs, all of which she argues should be informed by equity criteria, even so, Hunt considers that the forces of bureaucratic inertia are so strong that highlighting targets in this way is essential in order to evoke even a minimal response. In this regard, she reflects the pessimistic mood of other authors, such as Chris Duke, in seeking small measures which may salvage something from a generally negative environment.

Kaye Bysouth looks at the contribution which non-governmental organisations (NGOs) might make to the overall development process, both generally and in the narrower aid context. She notes that the report reopens a quite false dichotomy between developmental (or 'real') compared with humanitarian programs, with the latter being seen as essentially peripheral to the 'mainstream' of developmental activity and being largely equated with charity and relief. Juliet Hunt and Dean Forbes had earlier noted that similar kinds of dichotomous thinking influences the committee's criteria of aid effectiveness, which in the language it employs, sits more comfortably with mainline growth than with community or basic needs oriented programs. Having defined the NGOs' role in this way, the report nevertheless advocates a substantial increase in funding to them of some 500-650 per cent in real terms over the next ten years (Jackson Report, 1984, p. 111). Though this may satisfy many NGOs, it is unlikely to lead to satisfactory uses of public funds. Bysouth cites evaluation reports which suggest a decline in the quality of ADAB-supported NGO projects as funding for them has increased -- a process which has accelerated as more NGOs have become involved in overseas development, no doubt attracted by increased funding availability. Such trends call into question the reality of the 'articles of faith' espoused by and attributed to NGOs concerning ideals of participation, self-reliance and commitment to the 'poorest of the poor'.

The chapter ends with some guidelines as to what is required to turn the notion of 'bottom up' development from a slogan into reality. Bysouth concludes that there is a twin need to strengthen the capability of grass-roots organisations to mobilise poor people and to 'link ... local efforts with the macro development activities of the state in order to materially benefit poor groups and usher in a process of accelerated rural development'. This means a shift in attitudes by Australian NGOs which would 'lend legitimacy to the very concept of macro initiatives in community development'. This kind of approach clearly has the potential to overcome a series of philosophical impasses between government and NGOs, in redefining the relationship between 'growth' and 'equity' and in dissolving many sterile debates about the usefulness of infrastructure assistance. However, it is unlikely to be easily accepted either by 'orthodox' economists or, at the other end of the spectrum, those who see inherent contradictions between the efforts of community groups and the interests of the state.

Sarah Sargent, echoing some of the concerns expressed earlier in the Chattertons' chapter, urges the need to involve the Australian rural community in development education programs. She cites a number of European examples where, following the establishment of contacts between European and Asian or African farmers, the former have learned greater respect for the technology of the latter and become active lobbyists against dumping of food surpluses and the conversion of Third World land from food to cash crop production. Sargent sees parallel 'North-South cause-effect' relations between Australia and Third World countries and similar opportunities for involving Australian farmers. Unfortunately, the latter are apparently dismissed as uniformly reactionary by Australian mainstream NGOs, who make no efforts to reach them. However, in recent years, some informal action groups, albeit city based, have become involved in issues relating to food production and processing, employment conditions and trade between Australia and the Third World.

Doug Porter, in contrast with most critics of the Jackson Report, is sceptical of proposals for upgrading ADAB's 'professionalism' and technical sophistication. He questions the validity of the concept of professionalism and sees it as linked to the ethos of infallibility and 'realism' which emanates generally from the report. The notion of professionalism is obviously open to various kinds of interpretation. However, certain styles of 'professionalism' all too commonly provide a framework for avoiding difficult social and political questions. They can also provide a cloak of authority for ad hoc, 'seat of the pants' judgements which must be made every day in operational situations and for which standard 'cost-benefit' and other well-worn techniques cannot provide a substitute. Mr Hayden has stressed the need for a 'judicious mix' of equity and growth in Australia's aid program. In the Jackson Report, where it is assumed that the 'right mix' is a managerial problem, this is to be operationalised by professionals weilding a battery of sophisticated techniques. But Porter argues this will do little in practice to overcome the particular problems of development projects. These problems are not amenable to technocratic solution, but require new understandings of the practitioners' role and increased participation of target groups in aid projects.

Given the heavy philosophical biases which permeate the Jackson Report's various policy recommendations, it has been necessary to spend much energy in countering these and in particular urging that community and equity-oriented goals should be given greater emphasis. Equally, the need for establishing a clear 'hierarchy of objectives' as between various purposes ostensibly served by aid programs has been stressed. The Jackson Committee insists, in its responses to critics, that Australian aid is necessarily multi-purpose, whereas this volume reflects the viewpoint of practitioners on the ground that multi-purpose aid programs are a formula for confusion. Even so, merely laying down a hierarchy of objectives which emphasise goals of equitable development will not in itself ensure that these will actually be implemented on the ground. Such a statement of priorities could be described as a necessary but not a sufficient condition to achieve this.

We could well understand if, at the end of reading this book, practitioners who are trying to cope with the daily complexities of their immediate field of activity were to feel a sense of frustration that, for the most part, their specific problems are not addressed in any detail — though equally, we suggest, they might well resent efforts to do so by those remote from their immediate concerns. Which brings us to the basic purpose of the volume, which is to lay the foundation for just such a 'nuts and bolts' approach to the design and implementation of programs and the reshaping of structures in ways which will place values of equity and community participation in the forefront.

Many kinds of expertise will be required for such a task. However, there is a role to be played by all kinds of people at all levels, whether as consultants to particular programs; as non-government activists; as administrators or professionals; as individuals with experience of particular countries; as academics arguing about the theoretical underpinnings of aid programs; as politicians or simply as concerned individuals or groups in the community who want to see aid funds directed in ways which will benefit the poor.

All these contexts are ultimately related to each other and, if this book serves to demonstrate that point in a variety of small ways it will have performed a valuable purpose. To understand this point, however, it is necessary to transcend the various false dichotomies discussed earlier, and in particular to bridge the gap between policy and philosophy on the one hand and operational practice in the village, market place, embassy or planning agency on the other. In a sense this book has concentrated on the essentially negative task of removing a series of obstructions to such a process which have been thrown up by the Jackson Report. Nevertheless, we believe we have at least pointed the way to the more fundamental constructive task which lies ahead.

If there is a real dichotomy it is between what those near the centres of power in government and academia see as possible, let alone desirable and those aware of specific areas of need and concerned for justice in the Third World see as essential. While procedures are being laid down for incorporating 'community concerns' into the government's overall consensus strategy in the aid field --for example in the evolution of country programs -- the message is being conveyed loud and clear from many powerful quarters to NGOs and other critics that the debate over philosophy is over and they had best formulate their proposals in as practical and detailed form as possible. Certainly, the 'end of ideology' in the Australian aid debate cannot be decreed by fiat in this way or meekly accepted, even though styles of language and discourse may change up to a point. Nevertheless, it places more onus on those seeking change to spell out more concrete proposals and operational strategies which can prove viable in a generally unfavourable intellectual, political and bureaucratic environment.

In this context, the response of the Parliamentary Joint Committee on Foreign Affairs and Defence to the Jackson Report in May 1985 holds out some measure of hope to those willing to work hard at this level. Though largely endorsing the report's specific proposals, its treatment of themes relating to the philosophy of development is more even-handed. Most importantly, at the operational level, the committee concluded that decisions on the most effective use of Australia aid, regardless of whether it is for infrastructural development or for basic needs projects, will have to be on a case by case basis in the context of a comprehensive country programming (JCFAD, 1985).

Finally, there is a sense in which the Jackson Report has gained official acceptance because no alternative exists in quite the same authoritative and tangible form. Nevertheless, the problems raised in this volume and many others besides will not simply disappear as will become increasingly evident as experience is gained in 'implementing' the Jackson Report.

GENERAL ISSUES IN AID POLICY

1 PHILOSOPHY AND STRATEGY OF THE JACKSON REPORT: TOWARDS AN ALTERNATIVE PERSPECTIVE

Philip Eldridge

A common response to the Jackson Report has been that while the scope and detail of its analysis will contribute usefully to the evolution of Australian aid policy, it is flawed by serious inconsistencies in its assessments of goals and priorities. It is intended in this paper to highlight these apparent contradictions, to place them in an overall context in relation to competing pressures to which Australian aid is subject and to argue that alternative approaches to those currently prevailing are both feasible and desirable. This will entail going beyond the frame of reference of the report itself to more general diplomatic considerations. Particular attention will be paid to the regional distribution of aid proposed by Jackson.

There are, of course, dangers in overestimating the significance of Australia's aid contribution. It is assumed that aid cannot have more than a marginal impact on most countries' overall development, which is mainly determined by their internal plans and structures, linked to the international context in which they operate. Nevertheless, aid can influence the way these each evolve and in that context the Jackson Report provides significant pointers to some emerging directions in Australian foreign policy and related fields.

Hopes had been expressed in many quarters that the appointment of the Jackson Committee would provide the occasion for some major re-thinking about the direction of Australia's aid program. However, despite some important proposals for change, continuities with previous long-standing policy priorities remain strong. In particular, the importance of diplomatic objectives dominates the whole tenor of discussion and practical recommendations throughout the report, though not surprisingly, given that three out of six members were economists, together with the strong economic orientation of the Foreign Affairs Minister, Mr Hayden, the committee has worked hard to produce a developmental rationale for determining aid priorities and practices. Even so, its reasoning is frequently stretched and contorted in order to accord with established diplomatic priorities, which have been defined more tightly in terms of Australian interests in the neighbouring Asia/Pacific region. At the same time, the report comes down quite strongly in favour of the orthodox, growth model of development -- an outcome which was predicted by many more long-standing critics of Australia's aid program as soon as the composition of the committee was known.

In releasing the report in June 1984, the Minister for Foreign Affairs, Mr Hayden, foreshadowed a period of twelve months' community debate before firm policy decisions would be taken, except with respect to recommendations considered 'non-controversial' (the determination of which is obviously an arbitrary exercise in itself). There are, nevertheless, grounds for scepticism, in the light of some items included in the 1984/5 Aid Budget and other actions, that decisions have already been pre-empted in certain key areas of policy.[1] This has not improved the environment in which discussion of the report has taken place. In the short time since its release, debate on its findings has tended to polarise and become somewhat acrimonious. There is also a danger that discussion will become bogged down in relatively arid philosophical controversy. While it is unlikely that basic differences can be bridged between the Jackson Committee and its critics, it is nevertheless important to analyse the goals and assumptions underlying the report in order to both understand what the various participants in this debate are saying and to properly evaluate specific policy recommendations.

ASSUMPTIONS AND PHILOSOPHY OF THE REPORT

Two key, distinct but interlocking themes are evident in this context. The first relates to the committee's recognition that Australian aid is designed to serve several goals simultaneously and its efforts to reconcile these goals. Discussion here will focus, as in a variety of contexts throughout this volume, on the report's basic failure to order any 'hierarchy of objectives' as between developmental, trade, diplomatic and other goals pursued within the framework of aid programs. The second relates to the committee's underlying philosophy of development, particularly the relationship between pursuit of economic growth and equity objectives.

The committee's own philosophy is indicated more explicitly with respect to the second than the first aspect but in the case of both must be largely inferred from their treatment of specific policy contexts. The strategy offered in the report should be understood in relation to the political context in which it was written and the known views of key committee members on a range of issues impinging on aid. Their high profile at public forums and seminars following the report's release indicates that they have no intention that it shall be allowed to gather dust. To that end, its language has been carefully framed in order to persuade policy-makers of the pragmatism of the proposed approach. The net result has been to rationalise diplomatic objectives in developmental terms, while offering sufficient incentives to gain an adequate balance of support from the various domestic aid constituencies.

From its inception in the early 1950s, Australian aid policy has sought to serve several objectives, notably strategic, diplomatic, trade, employment of Australian expertise and institutional resources as well as humanitarian purposes. In its opening paragraph the report states that:

> Aid is given primarily for humanitarian reasons to alleviate poverty through economic and social development. It is the response of the wealthy industrial countries to the needs of hundreds of millions of people who live harsh and materially meagre lives. Aid also complements strategic economic and foreign policy interests, and by helping developing countries to grow, it provides economic opportunities for Australia. (Jackson Report, 1984, p. 3)

Obviously, this passage is open to conflicting interpretations with respect to both the priority accorded to developmental relative to other goals and to the committee's concepts of development. With respect to the former, the report lists, without ordering, the major interest groups supporting various goals and approaches. It then reviews what it considers to be Australia's 'broader interests' in relation to stability in the Asia/Pacific region and 'maintenance of its good standing as a member of the world community', concluding that 'It is important that aid decisions are closely integrated with foreign policy, without jeopardising development objectives'. The report is optimistic that the diverse goals which aid supports can be reconciled with each other and with the interests of people in recipient countries, asserting that 'The faster development takes place, the better Australian strategic and economic interests will be served' (Jackson Report, 1984, pp. 22-3).

The committee's approach appears to reflect the current Hawke Labor government's emphasis on 'consensus'. In any case, insofar as the potential for conflict between competing aid goals is acknowledged, little guidance is offered as to how these should be resolved. However, the following passage signals that greatest weight should be placed on foreign policy aspects:

> When several objectives of aid policy are consistent, decisions on which projects to undertake are relatively straightforward. However, conflicts can never be altogether eliminated. For example, humanitarian principles suggest that aid should go to the poorest people and those countries which have the greatest difficulties in stimulating development. But many of these countries are in Central and West Africa where Australia's foreign policy interest is modest. Strategic interests, on the other hand, suggest that aid should be concentrated on countries closer to home, in South-East Asia and the Pacific. (Jackson Report, 1984, p. 24)

This emphasis emerges very strongly in the report's specific recommendations in relation to regional distribution of aid.[2]

Those who urge the need to define a 'hierarchy of objectives', which would stress the primacy of developmental goals, risk incurring accusations of political naivete on two somewhat contradictory grounds. The first relates to a broad set of conventional wisdoms about Australia's role in the Asia/Pacific region, stressing the importance of goodwill with neighbouring countries and the need for policy-making in all contexts, including aid, to serve or at least not conflict with this overriding objective. This aspect will be discussed later in the chapter. The second argues that, by their nature, governments inevitably pursue multiple objectives, balancing them as circumstances demand. So demands for firm, logically consistent statements of priorities are not in accordance with the 'hard' political and bureaucratic 'facts of life'. From these two, seemingly self-evident propositions, it is a short step to inferring that the diversity of *ad hoc* recommendations which emerge from the report should be accepted by all sensible and reasonable people.

The quest for consensus in official formulations of aid goals can be best understood by focusing on the concept of 'development'. In Jackson, as in most advisory reports and official statements, orthodox notions of development have for a long time provided the rhetorical link which serves to reconcile purposes which commonsense and the factual situation on the ground would suggest are in basic conflict. According to this kind of perspective, for example, it is possible to see road -building programs in militarily sensitive areas of the Philippines as assisting poor people in less accessible rural areas, maintaining good relations with a friendly government and even promoting human rights through the all-embracing benefits of development. It is argued that by raising all-round living standards, development benefits everyone through higher incomes, increased trade, stability and goodwill. Further, by taking the steam out of revolutionary demands and thereby the pressure off governments considered repressive by Australian standards, it is implied that more liberal political regimes may eventually emerge. In a word, development taken in regular doses, is the surest prescription for curing the ills of rich and poor countries alike. The major instrument for achieving development, not surprisingly, turns out to be economic growth.

Of course, not all this is said directly in the Jackson Report -- though most of it was made fairly explicit earlier in the Harries Report on *Australia and the Third World*. But it represents the inevitable outcome of attempting to stretch the meaning of 'development' to accord with the multiple purpose objectives of official aid policy and to accommodate the conflicting pressures impinging on politicians and bureaucrats in Canberra. Jackson's specific contribution here, in line with the Hawke government's general strategy of 'consensus', has been to integrate the three major 'mandates' -- diplomatic and strategic, economic and trade interests plus humanitarian and community concerns (which Jackson claims Australian aid programs are designed to serve) into an overall trilogy which will lay the foundation for defining Australia's 'national interest', subsumed within the all-embracing framework of 'development'.

The Jackson Report defines development as 'the way in which the quality of human life and society is improved' and as integrally linked to both growth and equity (Jackson Report, 1984, p. 59). Fierce controversy has raged over many years about the interpretation of this concept. The dominant model, stressing economic growth linked to 'modernisation' programs in all spheres, has been attacked both by 'reformists' who emphasise distributive justice and the 'basic needs' of the poor majority, and Marxist and other heterogeneous radicals who focus on more basic structural barriers to 'development' of a kind capable of transforming the condition of the masses. Many other contributors to this debate would see popular participation in decision-making and social justice --concepts which the report deals with very perfunctorily -- as basic goals in their own right.

One may further discern a tendency throughout the report to mentally separate 'humanitarian' from 'developmental' activity. Thus, types of aid which support 'development' are seen as representing a rational, effective use of resources, while 'humanitarian' assistance is viewed as a form of charity. This kind of dichotomous thinking permeates the committee's analysis in many specific policy contexts. For example, the role of non-governmental organisations (NGOs) is seen as one of complementing official 'development-oriented' programs and filling in gaps with small-scale local programs for disadvantaged groups plus disaster relief. Similarly the role of NGOs in 'development education' within Australia is seen as one of mobilising support for the official aid program plus some fund-raising on their own behalf, while the main responsibility for education about development per se would rest within the formal education system and with ADAB itself.

The report ignores the radical critique entirely, as do official reports and commentary generally -- with the exception of the Harries Report which takes to task those who seek to use aid policy, (through the subversive use of the 'basic needs' approach) to '... turn the flank of Third World elites' and to 'divide them from the people they govern' (Harries Report, 1979, p. 156). This is not the place to rehearse the complexities of dependency (sometimes labelled 'radical' or 'neo -Marxist') theories of development. However, despite its practical and theoretical weaknesses, the major merit of this line of approach lies in its emphasis on institutional and structural features of development. The net result of totally excluding such perspectives from consideration is a policy-making environment in which formulation of aid goals and programs takes no critical account of the real context within which these must operate. While one would scarcely expect official recommendations or policy statements to advocate revolution, some basic awareness of structural dimensions by policy-makers could at least render discussion of aid issues less anodyne and the conception of programs more concrete and sharply focused.

Nevertheless, in comparison with the Harries Report, which accords humanitarian goals a very low priority and dismisses the idea of 'basic needs' with contempt, the Jackson Committee at least attempts to take issues relating to equity seriously, even though its conclusions do not differ significantly from Harries. Development is defined in terms of both growth and equity, though without assigning any weight to either or indicating how they are to be integrated in any operational context. Scrutiny of relevant passages indicates that the committee accords clear priority to growth, in the sense of 'growth first, distribution later', where any clash occurs between these two objectives (Jackson Report, 1984, pp. 3-4, 59-61). The report sees the role of foreign aid as one of removing 'bottlenecks' and providing infrastructure to service growth, rejecting the arguments of critics who emphasise direct targeting of services to the poorest groups.

Throughout the report, the concept of equity has been lumped together as 'growth with equity' so that it loses any distinctive operational force unrelated to growth. In the same way, 'social development' is merged with development. The effect of such semantic sleights of hand is to allow more or less indiscriminate application of the label of 'growth with equity' to any policy proposals which the committee chooses to advance.

Given the report's rejection of any kind of basic needs emphasis, the net outcome resembles conventional 'trickle-down' theories. To greatly oversimplify a very complex theoretical and policy debate, the report seems to have produced its own variant of classic economic arguments that it is first necessary to produce a cake before it can be distributed. Extending this analogy, it may be objected that the content and quality of the cake is also important and may not prove equally digestible to rich and poor consumers. In contrast with the conventional model, a basic needs strategy would allow the overall rate of growth to be derived from the composition of a country's development program. This in practice determines whether what is produced is usable by and accessible to the poor majority, which in turn depends on the prevailing distribution of ownership, control, income and wealth.

In the light of gross inequalities prevailing in most developing countries, there must inevitably be competition for scarce resources such that growth and equity objectives often conflict. Thus where food producing land is acquired for airports, highways, power schemes, tourist or other forms of urban-oriented development, cost-benefit calculations are rarely made with reference to net income or employment gains and losses to the poor, let alone to questions of community identity affecting the quality of life. Equally, design and location of projects critically affect their accessibility and utility to poor people in every field.

As an example, in the design of health programs, the relative weight placed on primary health care in the form of extension workers, health posts and clean drinking water at village level is crucial in determining their impact on the poor. While such efforts need to be supported by adequate infrastructure, expertise and services from higher levels of government, these must be appropriate to the village situation. Unfortunately, such services and infrastructure have primarily been directed towards servicing urban needs. Similar propositions can be advanced in all major fields of development.

While the report appears sympathetic to such arguments in principle, in practice it fails to spell out the extent to which conflicts of interest require hard choices in distinguishing patterns of growth compatible with equity objectives from those which are in sharp opposition. Further, it is too little appreciated that serious pursuit of equity objectives requires that these be built into the design and implementation of programs from the outset.

These twin themes of ambivalence in defining development and in ordering priorities between developmental and other goals of aid policy, which permeate the entire report, will be drawn out in a variety of detailed contexts in other chapters. In the next sections, a few examples illustrating the way in which the report persistently fudges (or endeavours to integrate, according to one's viewpoint) these key concepts will be offered in relation to education and aid administration, followed by some canvassing of issues relating to geographical distribution of aid. Special attention will be paid to diplomatic aspects. In the concluding section, it will be argued that these must be confronted specifically, if any serious shift is to be effected in favour of emphasising equity-oriented goals in Australian aid policy.

EDUCATION AND TRAINING

The committee's dominant concerns are perhaps most dramatically expressed in relation to education. A substantially increased share of the aid budget is recommended on the grounds that education and training are central to development and prerequisites to overcoming deficiencies in every other field of activity.

In general, there is a disjunction between the developmental rationale offered by Jackson and the means proposed to achieve it. The report urges that access to education complements the need for food, clothing, shelter and health, is an essential investment in human resources, a prerequisite to lifting productivity in all major basic needs sectors, deserving support from donors on both growth and equity grounds (Jackson Report, 1984, pp. 87-8). At the same time, the committee asserts that 'Education should be regarded as an export industry in which institutions are encouraged to compete for students and funds' (Jackson Report, 1984, p. 87). It recommends that a large number of 'merit scholarships' be allocated for open competition by developing country students. Australian tertiary institutions are to be encouraged to adapt their post-graduate courses and procedures in order to compete with other Western countries, notably the USA, in attracting overseas students. Apart from some general oversight by ADAB, the shaping of such courses is to be left to the educational market place.

Despite emphasis on the importance of joint planning and consultation with developing country institutions, the thrust of such policies would seem to institutionalise biases against local training and research or collaboration with third countries, for which developmentally sound arguments can often be made. No guidelines are offered as to how equity considerations will be built into the design of courses or the selection of students for training in Australia. It seems to be assumed that developmental benefits are transmitted in some way to all students from all developing countries. This is implicit in the recommendation that subisidies to private students, entailed in not charging visa entry fees on a full cost basis, be counted as part of the aid program. This view has been adopted in the 1984/5 aid budget (1984-85 Budget Paper No. 9, p. 11).

As the committee points out, about 80 per cent of overseas post -secondary students in Australia come from Malaysia, Singapore and Hong Kong (Jackson Report, 1984, pp. 91-2). Though categorised by the World Bank as 'upper middle income' countries,[3] these are the only Asian countries sending undergraduate students overseas in large numbers. The cultural and developmental impact of such policies have long been questioned but unfortunately the merits of such arguments have recently been clouded by the furore over immigration policy in Australia.

The Malaysian government sends large numbers of sponsored students, both through its own and ADAB schemes, but at the same time is anxious that entry fees into Australia be kept down in order to relieve pressures on their own education system from large numbers of non-Malay students. However, Malaysia's Prime Minister, Dr Mahathir, has expressed willingness to consider sending students abroad only in their final year, if foreign universities will cooperate in upgrading Malaysian institutions to cater at lower levels, while the Australian Vice-Chancellors' Committee has commented that ASEAN's longer term educational interests are better served by Australian assistance in supporting the development of ASEAN educational institutions (Morrison Report, 1984, pp. 250, 252). Far poorer countries such as India and Indonesia have long ago adopted national policies based on undergraduate education at home, with overseas training being sought predominantly in post-graduate, professional and vocational courses.

Jackson's recommendations in the educational field should be read in conjunction with the Goldring Report (1984) on overseas students in Australia and the Joint Committee on Foreign Affairs and Defence Report on Australia and ASEAN: Challenges and Opportunities (referred to as the Morrison Report, after the name of its Chairman, Hon. W.L. Morrison MHR). While Goldring questions the educational wisdom and equity of Jackson's market-oriented approach, Morrison is more concerned at prospects of a 'backlash' from Malaysia, similar to that which disrupted their trade relations with Britain. Whatever policies are finally adopted, political pressures seem likely to dictate that a substantial slice of Australia's aid budget will continue to be earmarked for educational assistance to Malaysia for reasons which have little or nothing to do with equity criteria.

Despite different nuances in approach between Jackson and Morrison, the latter report in many ways makes explicit the major new thrust being proposed in Australia/ASEAN relations whereby a major upgrading of educational and cultural relations will provide the cutting edge for an expanded Australian business thrust in the ASEAN region. In that context, what appears mildly idiosyncratic in Jackson must be seen as part of a more extensive agenda for integrating all major fields of policy into overall relations with ASEAN. Thus Morrison argues that 'if Australia is to be able to develop its service industries' involvement in the ASEAN region, the degree to which such involvement is likely to be welcomed will be influenced by the degree to which Australia is seen as politically interested in and sympathetic towards ASEAN interests' (Morrison Report, 1984, p. 263).

Finally, the Jackson Committee can reasonably be accused of recommending that aid funds be channelled to fields in which it has a professional stake, since three of its members are involved in higher education. This contrasts with its stern injunctions to the business sector not to seek aid funds in order to expand markets or investment opportunities. Its recommendation that development education should be expanded primarily within the formal education system is open to similar objections, in the light of the allocation of $600,000 in the 1984/5 Budget to a 'Development Studies and Research Fund' (1984-85 Budget Paper No.9, p. 13).

AID ADMINISTRATION

Recommendations for a significant upgrading of ADAB's management capability have been widely welcomed as long overdue after nearly a decade of cost-cutting, despite growth in the number and variety of programs. Glaring deficiencies in procedures for identifying, selecting, designing, operating, monitoring and evaluating projects had been identified by the Auditor-General's Report in 1981 (Auditor-General, 1981), in a professional and systematic review of aid administration.

Two issues are relevant in this context to understanding the relationship between diplomatic and developmental forces motivating Australian aid policy-making and implementation. The first relates to the impact of ADAB's various operating procedures on day-to-day dealings and overall relations with host governments. The second relates to the perennial issue of the relationship between the agency or bureau administering aid and the Department of Foreign Affairs.

In relation to the first question, I have argued elsewhere that there is a conflict, in both a conceptual and practical sense, between developmental and diplomatic goals, with the former stressing social or economic outcomes and the latter harmony and goodwill deriving from aid programs (Eldridge, 1983, pp. 12-3). Concern for developmental objectives involves a willingness to ask awkward questions and prod bureaucracies in order to achieve results, while diplomats generally strive to avoid the type of low level conflict which can easily result from a too single-minded pursuit of developmental goals, even when the governments concerned are in complete agreement over a program's basic objectives. This logic can be applied irrespective of the specific developmental approach being advanced though, in practice, a whole series of trade-offs occur, with diplomatic objectives being rationalised in developmental terms and vice versa.

The language of the Jackson Report indicates a strong developmental emphasis in the management and operation of aid programs, with a crash program of upgrading and recruitment being proposed to this end. As will be argued later in this volume by Juliet Hunt, the committee's concepts of professionalism, rationality and aid effectiveness reflect its own ideologically biased notions of development and equally fail to resolve the present confusion over basic objectives which should guide Australia's overall aid effort. Here, the influence of diplomatic considerations underlying the committee's thinking on aid administration is illustrated in its very thin discussion of the Auditor-General's findings. The thrust of that report was that confusion over basic objectives characterised every sphere of ADAB activity, with the intervention of political, diplomatic and business interests being identifiable at each stage of the aid process. These arguments have been either misunderstood or ignored by Jackson.

The report considers five possible forms of administrative arrangement for determining ADAB's relationship <u>vis-a-vis</u> Foreign Affairs, ranging from a slight variation in current arrangements to the establishment of an independent Department of Overseas Aid (Jackson Report, 1984, pp. 237-42). It then narrows down the choice to one between becoming either a separate bureau within Foreign Affairs, with the Director's position being made a statutory appointment and reporting directly to the Minister, or establishing the aid authority as a separate agency responsible to the Minister. In terms of all the key criteria which the committee identifies -- consistency with aid objectives, appropriateness in aid delivery, accountability and development of a high level of professionalism and status -- it found in favour of an independent agency but in the end opted for the more cautious alternative. This suggests that the unhappy experience of the Australian Development Assistance Agency in the 1975/6 period[4] had placed a high premium on organisational stability, which the new government was not willing to challenge. It seems that the committee calculated that the Department of Foreign Affairs was unlikely to accept the more radical option and would be in a position to again undermine such an arrangement, particularly at field level where all operational staff are subject to control by the Ambassador.

The net result is likely to be some marginal increase in ADAB autonomy and a more even balance of bureaucratic power <u>vis-a-vis</u> Foreign Affairs. However, some degree of mutual dependence seems inevitable and even desirable, if for no other reason than that ADAB depends on the strength of Foreign Affairs, in Cabinet to maintain the level of the aid budget. This, remarkably, increased slightly in real terms over the otherwise lean years of the Fraser government (Eldridge, 1983, p. 3, Table 1) -- a testimony to the priority attached to the diplomatic role of aid in relations with developing countries by Australian governments of all political colours.

RATIONALISING DIVERSITY

Running through the committee's analysis is a concern to rationalise the unwieldy spread of aid across sectors, programs and countries (cf. especially, Jackson Report, 1984, Chapter 9). Such rationalisation is widely accepted as long overdue. However, efforts have been concentrated almost entirely on geographical rationalisation, without seriously attempting to determine priorities between the multiplicity of interests and purposes outlined earlier, which are arguably the major cause of diffusion and inefficiency. Such contradictions are viewed benignly for the most part in the report, while harsh principles of cost effectiveness are applied to more geographically 'distant' countries -- most of which are among the world's poorest -- that are considered too difficult or inconvenient to support. Yet there is no reason to suppose that Australia could not support programs in a great variety of countries, if attacking poverty was clearly established as the primary goal of aid policy. Indeed, Sweden and the Netherlands, which pursue primarily 'basic needs' oriented policies across a significant range of countries and sectors, are regarded internationally as among the most efficient in aid delivery.

Rationale for Country Selection

The report proposes that programs be designed within a framework of 'country programming', relating projects to overall plans for each country. Country managers would be grouped together in regions and be responsible for preparing forward-rolling programs as part of an agreed long-term strategy. It is argued that such planning can only take place against a background of detailed knowledge of a country's social system, economy and institutions. To achieve these objectives, Australia should concentrate efforts on fewer countries. The following four categories of countries are proposed to determine eligibility for various types of assistance (Jackson Report, 1984, pp. 140-2):

1. Papua New Guinea, South Pacific and Indian Ocean islands which should be eligible for all forms of support.

2. Southeast Asia and small South Asian countries (Burma, Nepal, Bhutan and Sri Lanka). While country programming should play a major role, project aid should be limited to priority sectors and areas of special Australian expertise.

3. China and the larger South Asian countries. While the largest concentrations of poverty are to be found in these countries, it is argued that the impact of Australia's aid can only be modest. Country programming should only be undertaken at a very general level, while sectors of concentration should be carefully selected.

4. Other developing countries, which will not be subject to country programming and consequently receive no new bilateral project assistance. Such countries, which include the entire African continent, will still be eligible to receive food aid, technical and research cooperation, import credits, multilateral and non-government assistance, though as indicated in earlier discussion, there is some doubt as to whether project support ratios for NGOs will in future be structured according to the proposed 'eligibility framework'. If that proves to be the case, many agencies are likely to accord greater priority to the South Pacific, the Indian Ocean and Southeast Asia at the expense of South Asia and Africa.

Subsequent discussion is based on the premise that the concept of country programming would represent a vast improvement on the present practice of selecting projects from 'shopping lists' provided by countries requesting aid. It will be argued that while the committee's rationale for 'country programming' is generally well founded, its criteria for determining priorities between countries are opportunist and inconsistent. Nevertheless, the concept itself is not free from ambiguity and needs further refining.

A plain reading of the Jackson Report would suggest that what is intended is a more systematic attempt to integrate assessments of countries' overall development, plans and needs with Australian capability (or 'comparative advantage') to assist in particular areas. Stated thus, while there will obviously be differences about the ordering of priorities and many other details, the principle is hard to fault. One could go further and urge that while the case for such country programming is particularly cogent in relation to bilateral projects, arguably all forms of assistance ought to be fitted within the framework of some overall program. Indeed, the committee makes precisely this point in relation to multilateral assistance, though without indicating how this is to be achieved. Also, the line between 'projects' and other forms of developmental activity is in practice a fine one.

In that context, a case can be made that single projects in more distant regions could be fitted into a framework of country programming depending on the quality of information available from other international agencies and relevant country sources and providing one can be confident about the effectiveness of relevant institutions on the ground. In any case, whether Australia supports one or thirty projects in a country, it is still bound in the end to fit these into that country's national plans. Therefore, the 'shopping list' aspect will never be entirely eliminated, however sophisticated country programming may become.

More important questions centre on whether Australia can make useful and legitimate inputs into such planning processes. A sense had begun to emerge that it may be possible to engage in models of dialogue, compatible with recipient countries' national sovereignty, which could shift their overall development programs, however marginally, in a more equity-oriented direction. However, the way in which the concept of country programming is now evolving will change the frame of reference significantly to place primary emphasis on defining Australia's interests vis-a-vis specific countries. In line with the threefold 'mandate' mentioned earlier, Australia's diplomatic trade and community concerns will be spelt out in specially commissioned papers. These will then be integrated into a statement of national interest and aligned with statistical analyses, evaluation of the country's plans, and general progress to develop a 'country strategy'. Within this framework, surveys of selected sectors, with special reference to Australian capabilities, will provide the basis for identifying specific programs which will make up the overall country program.

The internal mechanisms for achieving a balance of viewpoints and reconciling conflicting interests and perspectives are as yet unclear. Further, the processes whereby interested groups can both make inputs and participate in evaluating the overall country program have yet to be defined. Key elements in this process seem likely to remain confined within ADAB and the Department of Foreign Affairs, while the full program statement is unlikely to be publicly available, for the usual combination of diplomatic and bureaucratic reasons.

Pacific and Indian Ocean Island States

The committee's rationale in relation to this region is less than convincing. It is acknowledged that:

> The region receives the most aid, per capita, in the world although compared with other regions the need for aid is marginal. Even where poverty exists in statistical terms, the quality of life is high. However, although the islands are not of major significance economically, they will provide increasing, albeit modest, commercial and trading opportunities for Australia. Strategically, the location of these island nations gives them special significance. (Jackson Report, 1984, p. 167)

The report notes that the small island states of the Indian Ocean face similar development problems to those of the South Pacific and ADAB should develop special expertise to assist them in the light of their special characteristics. This seems an odd comment, since the current existence of special Australian expertise is proposed as one of the major criteria for selecting countries in the first place.

From Tonga to Mauritius, one could scarcely imagine a more geographically dispersed selection of territories, in terms of administration costs per unit of aid delivered and the committee's own country programming principles, though grouping of islands for development cooperation could, as the committee suggests, rationalise aid flows to some extent. More worryingly, no account seems to have been taken of the islands' limited capacity to absorb large inflows of resources from outside. The same may be said of some of the smaller South Asian countries, such as Bhutan and Nepal, which the report places in the second priority group alongside the ASEAN countries.

South and Southeast Asia

The report places the large and very poor South Asian countries -- India, Pakistan and Bangladesh in the third priority category, for reasons which appear highly unconvincing. For example, it is acknowledged that India, once the major recipient of Australian aid, 'by most of the criteria that determine the allocation of aid ... should rank higher in Australia's aid program than it does' (Jackson Report, 1984, p. 196). Diplomatic as well as developmental factors point in this direction, the report argues, notably India's prominent role among both the Commonwealth and non-aligned group of countries. Despite India's many problems and slow pace of development, long-term commercial opportunities for Australia are also envisaged in view of India's large internal market and industrial base. One is therefore puzzled as to why India is placed in only the third category. Perhaps this is explained in the comment that:

> The contribution of Australian aid to investment and growth in South -East Asia has been very small. In South Asia, it ... is almost indiscernible. The lesson is clear: the volume of Australian aid will not be a major factor in the growth of these regions. However, by working at the margin of the overall development effort in areas where Australia has special skills, Australian aid can have a tangible impact. (Jackson Report, 1984, p. 187)

A not overly cynical interpretation of this last comment would be that since our aid efforts can only have marginal impact, choices should be made on other, notably trade and diplomatic grounds of national self -interest. In the case of the larger and poorer countries, the attitude that any assistance can only be seen as a 'drop in the bucket' particularly colours official thinking and reinforces arguments for avoiding more than token involvement in their development planning.

Indonesia is given high priority, not on grounds of poverty but due to its diplomatic importance, along with other ASEAN countries. Nevertheless, the committee is at pains to offer a developmental rationale for continuing concentration in the ASEAN region, noting that there are still many poor people even in 'middle income' countries. This appears to conflict with earlier insistence that aid should be directed towards overall growth programs rather than to specifically disadvantaged groups. The existence of poor people is thus invoked, as it were, to justify active involvement in countries where Australia is considered to have important trade, diplomatic and other interests.

Underlying pressures for linking aid to trade and investment promotion are most evident in the context of expanding Australia/ASEAN relations, notably from such lobby groups as the ASEAN-Australia Business Council and related bilateral business organisations (Morrison Report, 1984, p. 195). The influence of such groups is evident in many of the activities generated by the ASEAN-Australia Economic Cooperation Program (AAECP). This program has grown from an initial outlay of $5 million in 1974 to an overall commitment in 1984 of $56.5 million. AAECP supports ASEAN regional programs, additional to and distinct from bilateral programs, covering food handling and processing, agricultural, population and energy projects plus a growing range of trade promotion and investment programs, exchange visits, economic research and joint feasibility studies (ADAB, 1984a, pp. 113-7).

Assistance to Africa

As has been argued in a later chapter, a good case can be mounted on a variety of both developmental and diplomatic grounds for selecting a small number of African countries in which to concentrate assistance, in line with the country programming principles proposed by Jackson. Apart from the extreme poverty of most African countries, it can be argued that the quality of Australian aid could be significantly improved by an active Australian presence in a few selected African countries. Work under drought conditions could greatly enhance our experience in dryland agriculture, irrigation and water supply -- often claimed as areas of special Australian expertise. The experience of developing new forms of appropriate technology under African conditions could no doubt be adapted to aid programs in other countries and prove an invaluable asset in Australia itself. While the report recommends that Australia should still join in co-financing arrangements with other countries and international agencies assisting Africa, the potential benefits outlined above could only be derived from direct involvement on the ground. In general, Australia's contribution to international understanding of problems facing the world's poorest regions would be greatly enhanced by active cooperation in Africa.

It is not entirely clear how far Australian NGOs will be encouraged to fill gaps left by the withdrawal of official aid. Confusion is likely to arise from the way in which incentives to cooperate with official policies are manipulated in the report. Currently, most aid funds are channelled through the Project Subsidy Scheme. Levels of support for approved projects range from ratios of 1:1 to 3:1 for projects in the Pacific. Jackson recommends that:

> The ratio of ADAB to agency funding should be increased with a ceiling of 9:1. The highest ratios should be applied to projects in Category One countries or activities in the poorest countries. Projects having complementarities with the official program should also attract higher ratios. (Jackson Report, 1984, p. 109)

This statement is ambivalent as to whether NGO programs in low category countries, which are often among the world's poorest, will be encouraged or discouraged under this formula, depending on how the last sentence is interpreted.

POSSIBLE ALTERNATIVE APPROACHES

Criticisms of Jackson in this paper have focused on (1) the interpretation of 'growth with equity' in ways which give inadequate weight to the poor majority in recipient countries; (2) parallel downgrading of poverty criteria in selection of countries; (3) frequent setting aside of the committee's own stated developmental criteria in favour of diplomatic, trade and other considerations; (4) failure to define basic objectives, resulting in inadequate identification of the major causes of administrative confusion and ineffectiveness. This has led to highly selective proposals for rationalising aid programs at the expense of poor countries and poor people.

Such judgements are equally normative as those of the committee. However, in order to make any impact, critics will need, over time, to spell out some alternatives and to clarify their own assumptions. A general outline is offered in the remaining pages of what such an alternative approach might look like.

It is not my intention to argue that diplomatic factors can be ignored. Since diplomacy is an international expression of politics, this would be almost as unrealistic as saying that aid and development can ever be non-political. Political choices need to be made in each context. It is the nature of those choices which is in question. Moreover, efforts to change aid policy are only likely to succeed if linked to broader efforts to restructure Australia's foreign relations.

Clearly, some of the prescriptions suggested earlier are based on diplomatic as well as developmental judgements. For example, an Australian commitment to East and Southern Africa can be justified both as assisting the world's poorer countries and at the same time in signalling support for countries bordering South Africa who are facing increasing pressures. This approach makes good sense both morally and diplomatically, in terms of giving Australia some increased standing in the African continent and therefore in the Third World as a whole.

This last aspect was pointed out by the Harries Committee (Harries Report, 1979, p.119) and generally accepted by the Fraser government. The thrust of that report was that ASEAN countries should form the core of Australian policy towards the Third World, in that they could both influence and be influenced by the perceptions of the rest of the Third World towards Australia. It is doubtful if the Fraser government fully accepted that particular perspective, though they certainly built upon the ideas of the Harries Report to expand aid to an increasing range of countries. It is that concept of geographically expanded participation in Third World development which the Jackson Committee has sought to dismantle. This general trend can be linked to negative sentiments towards the Commonwealth apparently held by both Mr Hayden and Mr Hawke and their determination to shift Australia's centre of gravity towards East Asia and the Pacific. By contrast, those concerned to avoid undue dependence on the ASEAN countries would point to a need to strengthen relations with South Asia and Africa by way of achieving a better overall balance in Australia's external relations, with the Commonwealth potentially giving greater substance to such regional links.

It seems that the growing stress being placed on relations with the ASEAN countries and the need to harmonise Australia's policies in every field substantially in accordance with the wishes of their governments, is emerging as a major roadblock to any substantial redirection of our aid towards poorer countries. In another chapter, Richard Higgott has argued that this trend is due to the pressure of strong external forces substantially outside Australia's control. In fact, the case for 'asymmetry' in bargaining power between Australia and ASEAN countries was first stated in the early 1970s in relation to Indonesia and was argued on geo-political rather than economic grounds, long before many of the current economic and international ideological trends were in evidence. Subsequently, 'asymmetry' has been regularly -- and often quite opportunistically -- invoked to advocate a wide range of policy initiatives and as a tool with which to beat all kinds of critics over the head. More recently, explanations of Australia/ASEAN relations in terms of 'asymmetry' have been rendered more plausible by analyses of the 'economic determinist' variety, whether from a neo-classical or traditional Marxist standpoint, supported by the kind of economic data advanced by Higgott.

Such arguments may or may not stand the test of time, as Higgott himself has suggested, and would in any case require a separate paper to deal with adequately. To those unwilling to accept this scenario, the search for alternatives becomes ever more pressing. However, the 'asymmetry factor' will evidently remain dominant at least in the immediate future. Therefore, in practical political terms, in order to achieve a shift in favour of poorer countries or even to re-direct assistance to poorer groups within neighbouring countries, it seems necessary to show that either overall Australian policy goals vis-a-vis the ASEAN countries are compatible with the kinds of shift in aid priorities advocated by most contributors to this volume or alternatively that they can be achieved by other means outside the aid program.

In principle, the last approach seems quite feasible, using a combination of commercial, cultural and non-aid budgetary policies, although diplomatic efforts will be required to assure ASEAN countries that cuts in aid funds do not signal any downgrading of relations. Indeed, if Higgott's economic assessments are correct, they offer impressive support to arguments usually advanced on equity grounds that ASEAN countries have little need for aid. Further, if Australia is becoming 'irrelevant' to ASEAN countries, it is hard to see why they would be concerned if it were phased out. Only if aid is seen as 'tribute money' in lieu of good diplomatic relations do threats that Australia will be ignored as 'peripheral', 'white trash' and so forth, emanating from various lobby groups, make any sense in the aid context.

Potential conflict with the ASEAN countries over such a shift in emphasis could be substantially defused by greater liberalisation of trade arrangements. Indeed, the ASEAN countries, particularly Singapore and Malaysia, have indicated that they see access to Australian markets as far more important to their development than aid programs. The problem here is that aid has been used increasingly to compensate for rigidities in Australian domestic and tariff policies. If trade liberalisation proves too difficult in the Australian domestic political context, 'soft loan' arrangements could be considered as an interim arrangement. However, loan aid is not seen in the report as a desirable way of reducing subsidies to groups and countries well able to afford some measure of repayment (Jackson Report, 1984, pp. 72-3). In any case, an important first step would be to transfer programs deemed necessary on political or commercial grounds but which cannot be justified in equitable developmental terms to a framework of operation outside the aid budget.

Among ASEAN countries, Indonesia's claims on aid resources are most obvious on grounds of overall poverty, although the Philippines and Thailand evidence wide disparities in income distribution reflected in low levels of nutrition and health among significant sections of their population. While there is a need for Australian aid in all these countries, far greater selectivity is required in choice of programs. Even then, doubts remain about prospects for success of basic needs oriented programs in view of the political structures in those countries, especially in the Philippines.

In the broader context, the diplomatic and strategic imperatives underlying current policies are indeed very powerful. Yet in a world of burgeoning communications and shrinking distances, the emerging geo-political determinism shaping Australia's sense of its place in the world seems myopic in the extreme. The ASEAN countries seem to set no such narrow regional constraints in shaping their own external relations. Interestingly, the Jackson Report has not been entirely overawed by 'asymmetry' arguments in the aid context and only places ASEAN countries in the second priority category. Though suspect in developmental terms, Jackson's efforts to shift priorities towards the Pacific and Indian Ocean islands may possibly represent an important first step in diffusing the current excessive emphasis on ASEAN.

What are the diplomatic implications of shifting Australian aid in a 'basic needs' direction? As this approach requires redesigning of infrastructure and more specific targeting of programs towards poorer groups, perennial questions arise about the propriety of linking aid with intervention in host countries' internal planning and management processes. However, such questions apply also to more orthodox models of development espoused by Jackson. Aid programs can be implemented only by mutual agreement and, in terms of diplomatic convention at least, must be initiated by requests from host countries. In practice, potential donors have opportunities to propose new or expanded programs at any stage in the process. Dialogue over possible new directions can usually be legitimised in terms of the host country's official developmental goals. Problems of intervention can thus often be exaggerated by those opposing change.

While some measure of assistance to the Pacific and Indian Ocean islands is justified on both diplomatic and developmental grounds, the committee's own analysis indicates that potential benefits from aid are at this stage marginal, while serious doubts remain about the islands' absorptive capacity. This would seem to justify reversing the priorities in Jackson's proposed 'eligibility framework' and channelling most assistance to the islands through multilateral, regional and NGO programs.

Committee members have responded to critics that since some 60 per cent of the aid budget is locked into assisting Papua New Guinea and multilateral (international and regional) programs, apparently with little protest from NGO lobby groups, little scope exists for redirecting assistance to the poorest countries of South Asia and Africa. This is at least partly true, unless serious efforts are made to raise the total aid budget nearer to the UN target of 0.7 per cent of GNP.[5] Committee members have claimed that they were instructed to work within the existing budgetary framework, though this is not apparent from their formal terms of reference. In any case, with optimistic growth scenarios, they have been able to project substantial increases in favoured sectors without assuming changes in aid as a proportion of GNP.

While aid to PNG is planned to reduce slowly, it seems to be widely accepted that Australia has special long-term obligations to assist that country in completing the process of de-colonisation. Whatever model of development is applied, PNG is by most standards still a very poor country and this priority therefore poses no inconsistency with the general thesis being advanced.[6]

Given such constraints, a range of strategies are possible in order to free some resources for additional assistance to the major poverty areas of South Asia and Africa. These include elimination or drastic reduction of the DIFF 'mixed credit' scheme, pruning of the rapidly growing ASEAN-Australia Economic Cooperation Program, more selective use of funds for educational and training assistance, including a more sceptical view of the expanding research sector, and more careful appraisal of multilateral programs. In the latter context, Jackson proposes a substantial shift away from UN programs in favour of the World Bank and its regional affiliates. While this shift is justified on efficiency grounds, an element of ideological preference can also be detected, in line with the committee's general leaning towards neo-classical economic philosophies. Above all, major scope exists for pruning or drastically redesigning infrastructure programs in more equity-oriented directions.

In general, the problem of limited resources can be made more manageable by closer integration with other countries and international agencies in both the identification and implementation of programs. This is necessary to overcome what might be called the 'drop in the bucket' view of the whole aid process, which represents a common perception in relevant opinion-forming circles in business and government and is in evidence in many parts of the Jackson Report itself. Unfortunately, such a cooperative approach does not fit with a long-established bias in Australian aid programs in favour of building up a visible Australian presence, which is seen as being best achieved by concentrating on small or medium-sized centres. This is no doubt an important consideration in Australia's emerging emphasis on the Pacific and Indian Ocean islands.

In the end, probably the most serious obstacle to such a shift in direction is the interlocking set of conventional wisdoms which now seems to be operating with increasingly less flexibility in all major spheres of policy relating to the Asia/Pacific region, and which particularly overshadows discussion of human rights and development issues. These conventional wisdoms are reflected in large measure in the work of the Jackson Committee, though linked to its own peculiar and not always consistent notions of aid effectiveness and rationality. These latter evidenced in a somewhat less than dispassionate search for special areas of expertise, local spheres of influence or at least some small spaces where a visible Australian presence can be established. Such attitudes militate against re-distribution of aid towards countries of greatest need and inhibits any contribution which Australia might make in the search for strategies of international cooperation which might effectively shift the bias of world development towards a more just international order.

NOTES

1. Notable examples are the running down of bilateral projects and aid personnel in Africa, the increase in the Development Import Finance Facility (DIFF) Scheme from $10 to $16 million in authorised funds (ADAB sources and 1984-85 Budget Paper No. 9, p. 4) and the inclusion of notional subsidies to private overseas students in the aid budget. The geographical emphasis on the Asia/Pacific region is also apparent in the ALP's 1984 platform relating to overseas aid and international relations (ALP, 1984, pp. 89-90).

2. cf. 'eligibility framework' proposed in the Jackson Report, 1984, pp. 140-2.

3. cf. annual World Bank reports.

4. For a succinct 'inside' account of this experience, cf. Viviani and Wilenski, 1979.

5. Currently Australia devotes a little under 0.5 per cent of GNP to overseas assistance ... cf. 1984-85 Budget Paper No. 9, pp. 20-1.

6. According to World Bank, 1983, p. 148, Table 1, despite a GNP of 840 US dollars per capita in 1981, life expectancy in PNG was 51 years and adult literacy only 32 per cent.

2 SOME INTERNATIONAL ECONOMIC DIMENSIONS OF THE JACKSON REPORT: A CRITICAL ASSESSMENT AND A VOTE FOR SELECTIVE SUPPORT

John Langmore

The Jackson Report is a pleasure to read. The structure is logical, the prose lucid and the presentation easy to follow, beginning with a chapter summarising the argument and recommendations, with a precis at the head of each chapter, and with highlighted inserts of tables, diagrams or additional information presented in the style of the World Bank's annual World Development Report. The benefit from the appointment of editorial staff seems evident. A high standard is set for other reports to government.

This chapter will discuss five principal issues. These are: development strategy within developing countries; global economic relations; international finance; the quantity of Australian aid; and aid to Papua New Guinea. On each of these centrally important subjects the committee has over-simplified by neglecting important aspects of the issue or presenting only part of an ongoing debate with the effect of distorting the conclusions.

Nevertheless, these criticisms do not undermine the value of many of the report's other conclusions which have been cogently argued and presented. It is important that these should be speedily accepted and implemented by the government. These include introduction of indicative forward budgeting on a five-year, rolling plan basis; clarifying the geographic focus of aid to give priority to the Asia/Pacific region; increased emphasis on the role of women, education and research (though $5 million for non-agricultural research is still too modest); additional support for voluntary agencies; continuation of aid in grant rather than loan form; increased discretionary aid funds for heads of diplomatic missions; and posting more aid personnel overseas. Above all, the committee has rightly stressed the need for upgrading ADAB professionalism and strengthening its management systems.

First a comment on why aid is given. The committee identifies accurately Australians' motivations for giving aid. It is refreshing to read the rationale for aid described first in humanitarian terms and only second in self-interested strategic and economic terms. This is the reality for the majority of people who actively support aid, but it is a reality which bureaucrats and politicians have shied away from recognising publicly for 30 years.

Politicians, in particular, have generally sought to justify aid principally in terms of Australia's narrow national interest rather than disinterested concern about poverty and injustice. Yet Christians and secular humanists are the active aid organisers and lobbyists in Australia, not sectional interest groups. Those concerned individuals working through voluntary aid organisations, churches, political parties and unions are responsible for maintaining pressure on governments to increase aid.

Commercial interest groups have been only peripherally interested in aid, and then only in ensuring that they benefit from consultancies and contracts, not in increasing the overall level. Diplomats and aid administrators have advocated increased aid, but some other public servants, particularly in the Treasury and the Department of Finance, have bitterly opposed aid. I remember John Stone, the former Secretary of the Treasury, complaining about a quarter of a million dollars given to Bangladesh for flood relief on the grounds that it would be wasted! P.T. Bauer is an academic leader of this style of opinion.[1] Advocating aid to developing countries is, of course, in Australia's broad, long-term national interest. The degree of economic interdependence between countries is increasing, and so economic growth of countries in our region contributes to our growth as well through trade, investment and opportunities for the provision of financial services and professional consultancies. Aid can also assist in maintaining orderly, balanced development, and so increase political stability by reducing poverty. This is not an argument for supporting the present Philippines government or other repressive regimes. Quite the reverse -- it is an argument for concentrating aid in countries committed to equitable development strategies, such as Papua New Guinea and the smaller Pacific island states. Strategy within developing countries is one of the issues dealt with in a skewed way in the report.

DEVELOPMENT STRATEGY

Economic growth or basic human needs are presented as the polar choices in setting development strategy. While recognising that 'In some circumstances poverty alleviation and a contribution to economic growth can be effectively combined' the committee recommends that Australian aid should concentrate on removing major constraints to development through capital-intensive inputs (Jackson Report, 1984, p. 4).

From one point of view this emphasis is a useful corrective to simplistic critiques from people who perceive aid to be inevitably neo-colonial, supportive of repressive regimes or having an inequitable impact. Several statements have been made in recent years by spokesmen for Community Aid Abroad, for example, which have virtually argued that official aid is counterproductive to development. Theresa Hayter is an academic noted for such views.[2] These views were also expressed at a seminar on the Jackson Report in Canberra in various ways and with various degrees of intensity. The Jackson Committee was attacked for opposing attention to basic human needs.

Obviously there is considerable scope for debate about the growth /basic needs issue and each person's judgement will be influenced by his or her own experience. It seems to me first, that the quantity of aid is important and should be increased and, second, that the conflict between growth and basic human needs is less than suggested by both the committee and its critics.

Given that 80 per cent of the world's population receive only 20 per cent of the world's income, there must be potential benefit in redistributing income from the rich to the poor countries. It is to be expected that many factors could reduce the value of such transfers but surely ways can be found of avoiding or at least reducing these problems. On these grounds neither the Community Aid Abroad/Hayter critique nor the Stone/Bauer critique are plausible.

My own experience of the use of aid from ten years working in Papua New Guinea sharply reinforces this prima facie conclusion. Between 1945 and 1975 steadily increasing Australian aid to Papua New Guinea made possible the spread of health and education services, and the expansion of income-earning opportunities in both wage employment and self-employment. Choices for most people increased, though so did the severity of new social and economic problems. Many of those problems were to do with the nature of economic development rather than being a direct consequence of aid, but the great majority of Papua New Guineans would probably say they were glad that their country had received Australian aid.

Papua New Guinean experience also points vividly to the importance of achieving a balance between capital intensive infrastructure projects and support for basic human needs. The Jackson Report has echoes of a debate which took place in PNG in the late sixties and early seventies about growth versus development. The colonial Australian government set out to maximise the growth rate of national income. Since this included the incomes of expatriate Australians whose salaries were many times that of indigenous Papua New Guineans, and since much of Australian aid was used for employing expatriates, the direct benefit to Papua New Guineans of large increases in national income from rapid economic growth was greatly reduced. However, when after self-government the income maximising goal was expressed as the income of Papua New Guineans, development was immediately redefined as an aim which included both growth and distributional objectives.

This is a special case with which to illustrate the growth versus basic human needs debate but it is an illuminating one. For implicit in the Australian colonial goal was a view about the type of society which should develop, and this inevitably involved greater inequalities in the distribution of income. Explicit in the strategies of the independent Papua New Guinea was the goal of widespread, equitable development. If the simple growth maximising goal had been continued there would have been more reliance on capital-intensive projects. By concentrating on incomes of Papua New Guineans, highest priority was put on agricultural extension and local roads, health centres and schools.

The committee appears to have overemphasised the place which capital-intensive projects should have in Australian aid. There are many kinds of constraint on development of which lack of highways, electricity and harbours are some. Lack of a convenient water supply for villagers is also a severe constraint on the time they have for productive activity because so much time is spent carrying water. The same is true of basic health services or primary education.

This debate can easily degenerate into simply semantic dispute. The central issue is how can Australian aid be most effective in both supporting basic human needs and in encouraging growth of income in the particular places to which it is allocated. The composition of growth is the determining factor. So the extent to which Australian aid can be given for projects which will both meet basic human needs and contribute to economic growth was probably underestimated by the committee. This is a matter of emphasis. In contrast, the committee's view of international economic relations was severely distorted and simplistic.

GLOBAL ECONOMIC RELATIONS

Economic relations between countries -- other than relations concerning aid --do not have a central place in the report nor should they have had, given the committee's terms of reference. However, the committee could not forbear from making an attack on the New International Economic Order (NIEO) proposals (Jackson Report, 1984, p. 44). Its comments provide the context for other parts of the report and, therefore, cannot be left unchallenged. The basis for attack is conventionally neo-classical, that 'the "new international economic order" foundered largely because it did not have a sound analytical foundation' (Jackson Report, 1984, p. 44). By this it is meant that developing countries proposed to intervene in the working of the market through such devices as commodity price stabilisation schemes which neo-classical economists believe will reduce efficiency.

The committee's analysis fails to recognise the severe imperfections in international markets which prevent them working efficiently and which maintain the economic power of the already wealthy. Commodity markets, for example, are variously distorted by obligations, cartels, transnational corporate power and collusion, monopsonies (buyers' monopolies such as Japanese coordination in buying Australian coal and iron ore), national market organisations, import restrictions, export subsidies, dumping and other imperfections.

Not only are most commodity markets imperfectly competitive, but there is asymmetry in the way the markets for primary commodities and manufactured goods work. Whereas markets for primary and mineral commodities are more strongly influenced by supply and demand conditions, prices of goods and services of industrial countries are commonly set by large corporations in industries where concentration has grown strongly in the post-war period.

The effect of an international recession, such as that at the beginning of the eighties, is to depress commodity prices as a result of falling demand but to leave prices of industrial output relatively stable; the fall in demand being largely absorbed through either higher stocks or lower utilisation of capacity. Further, the administered prices of the industrial corporations can be managed to the extent allowed by their complete or partially monopolistic positions.

Even if commodity prices boom, this affects the industrialised countries as an increasing cost which producers simply pass on through their administered prices, thus quickly offsetting any short-term deterioration in their terms of trade. So whatever happens to the international business cycle, producers of commodities tend to lose through a persistent deterioration in their terms of trade.

The very existence of gross inequity in the distribution of wealth and income represents a massive distortion in market power, regardless of complications caused by all these market imperfections. There are also other severe imperfections involving, for example, the gross inequities in the control of technology and in the operation of the international financial system.

For a few years commodity producers were encouraged to think that they might be able to break out of this bind by the success of the Organisation of Petroleum Exporting Countries (OPEC) in setting oil prices. The NIEO proposals included not only the integrated program for commodities mentioned by the committee but also reduced protection in the North against Southern manufactured exports; international monetary reform; codes of conduct for technology transfer and transnational corporations; and reform of international institutions to provide greater equity for Southern representatives.

The NIEO proposals foundered not because of their analytical bases but because of the unwillingness of the wealthy Western countries to concede a skerrick of their overwhelming economic power. Sir Shridath Ramphal, Secretary-General of the Commonwealth Secretariat, wrote in November 1984 that little had been achieved in the ten years since the NIEO proposals were formulated for three reasons:

> First, because of the judgement of Northern governments that they have been able to overcome the perceived threat from OPEC and commodity exporters in general without having to concede major shifts in economic power. Second, because the sense of insecurity induced by the debt crises has been allayed through the piecemeal solutions

> so far devised. Third, because of the changes in the intellectual climate in the North, with the ascendence of economic gurus of a distinctly anti-Third World (and, of course, anti-aid) school. (Ramphal, 1984, p. 12)

Fortunately, the committee was free of the more extreme forms of this reactionary anti-aid theorising, but it acquiesced uncritically to a model of the style taught to many first year economics students and which is notable for the unreality of its simplifying assumptions.

One senses, by little slips in various parts of the report, that this may be partly because of an unselfconsciously Western world view, one which perhaps lacks experience in, and empathy with, developing countries. Much of the report avoids this, but it pops out occasionally such as in the sentence which describes aid as 'the response of the wealthy industrial countries to the needs of the poor ' neglecting the most generous donors of all, the Arab OPEC countries (Jackson Report, 1984 p. 3). The absence of references to books and articles by writers from developing countries stands out. A conservative Western-owned journal, such as The Economist, is recommended, but the journals South and The New Internationalist, which are sympathetic to developing countries are omitted. The emphasis on increasing project aid to Papua New Guinea implies that Australians are better able to manage public expenditure in PNG than Papua New Guineans, a point to which we will return shortly.

The committee's view of the international economy was not crucial to most of its recommendations, but it is disappointing that the simplistic anti-Southern model is perpetuated in the report. This was, however, possibly responsible for one gaping omission from the discussion -- international financial policy.

INTERNATIONAL FINANCE

Official development assistance -- aid -- is a smaller part of the total financial receipts of developing countries than private lending through the international capital markets in the form of bank lending and the issue of bonds. Comprehensive, detailed discussion of these private financial flows would have been beyond the committee's terms of reference, but the overlapping issues relating to multilateral aid through the international financial institutions were explicitly referred to the committee, which was asked to 'consider the desirable balance between bilateral and multilateral aid and the role of international agencies in the delivery of Australia's aid program' (Jackson Report, 1984, p. 245).

The issue which the committee completely omitted, and which would have been within its terms of reference, was Australian policy relating to the international financial institutions such as the World Bank group and the International Monetary Fund (IMF). In 1983/4 $200 million or almost 25 per cent of Australia's aid was distributed through mutilateral organisations, about half of this through the World Bank, Asian Development Bank and the International Fund for Agricultural Development. Yet there is no description of the policies of those institutions, nor a serious evaluation of their performance in relation to their goals, let alone an assessment of their goals and strategies.

An even more serious omission is the issue of the inconsistency between Australia's policies in different forms. For example, Australia was a strong opponent of an issue of special drawing rights in 1983, and equally strongly opposed the holding of a conference on the international monetary system. Yet both proposals were supported by an expert committee established by the Commonwealth Secretariat of which Australia was a member, and by the meeting of Commonwealth Finance Ministers (Commonwealth Secretariat, 1983). Both proposals could make significant improvements in developing countries' access to funds and reduce the imbalance in the power of North and South in the international financial system. Australia's stand on these issues is reported to be more hard line than that of even the Reagan administration.

The inconsistency occurs in part because direct aid policy is prepared in the Department of Foreign Affairs while Treasury has control of international financial policy. There has been no significant public discussion of international financial policy, so the government has not been encouraged to debate the issues. The lack of discussion in this report is an opportunity lost. Perhaps there should be a parliamentary inquiry into the issue.

The issues are profoundly important. There have been widespread fears for the stability of the international financial system because of the perceived danger of default by large developing country borrowers. In fact, the danger of default by large corporations is far greater because they are larger borrowers. The international financial institutions are being constrained from taking effective action in a critical situation by an outdated mandate and inadequate resources (Ramphal, 1984, p. 12). Yet Australia has not only failed to consider change, it has been amongst the chief resisters of reform.

The committee neglects even to mention, let alone to discuss, the proposals for introducing automaticity into international financial transfers, that is, for international taxation. Many proposals have been made over the years -- for the issue of special drawing rights to developing countries only; for taxation of the resources of the seabed; for a special income tax on the rich countries; for taxation of commodities entering world trade (see the Brandt Report, 1980, for example). It is difficult to see development assistance reaching the United Nations' target and being sustained at that level without some form of international taxation.

The analogy of the evolution of domestic social welfare policy appears to apply well. In the same way as care for the poor grew from the voluntary concern amongst humane groups, through gradually increasing state involvement in the provision of welfare services, to social security payments by right, so the world has passed through the stage where voluntarism is an adequate basis for development assistance, and is now reaching the stage where international transfers of development assistance must become obligatory. The committee not only did not mention this issue, but was passive about the issue of the quantity of aid.

THE QUANTITY OF AID

The committee is bland and uncommitted about the quantity of aid: 'It would be undesirable to prescribe precise target dates and ratios, but equally Australia's aid effort should not slip back' (Jackson Report, 1984, p. 4). The discusion of volume targets is limited in two paragraphs, and argues only that 'it is highly desirable that Australia maintain its position in relation to other donors -- that is, about midway in the aid league table -- and that it should not allow the share of GNP allocated to aid to fall' (Jackson Report, 1984, p. 45).

A volume target without a date is no target at all. Such real politik is at odds with the motivation for aid so effectively described at the beginning of the report. It is one of the clearest arguments for expediency I have ever read. This means that, on a crucial issue, the committee has adopted an expedient approach, failing to address a question directed at it. Perhaps they were trying to provide excuses in advance to Ministers for failing to reach the goals in the Labor platform.

The committee was asked to 'take into account the Government's platform on aid'. Yet there is no evidence in the report that the committee even read the platform. If it had it would have found references to aid and development in both the foreign affairs and economic sections. The foreign affairs section describes Labor's approach to development cooperation as:

> based upon an unequivocal commitment to achieve the UN target of 0.7 per cent of gross national product for official development assistance with an immediate target of 0.5 per cent by 1985 and an eventual target of 1.0 per cent. (ALP, 1982, p. 72)

The economic section is even more ambitious:

> In view of the global extremes of wealth and poverty and of the entrenched injustice in the present international economic system, and recognising that the well-being and security of all peoples depends on changing that system - a Labor Government will increase overseas development assistance with the aim of achieving community support for the target of 0.7 per cent of GNP within five years of attaining office. (ALP, 1982, p. 46)

This section was drafted personally by Bob Hawke when he was chairman of the national economic policy platform committee.

Decisions about the quantity of aid are essentially political and therefore the committee should have relied more closely on the platform at this point than any other. Other parts of the report are also directly contrary to the platform. For example, the platform promises that Labor's approach to development cooperation will be based on 'the progressive concepts of development contained in the Brandt Report' (ALP, 1984, p. 89), yet the committee explicitly rejects the Brandt strategy as discussed above in the section on the NIEO. The committee should not have been required to blindly adopt the platform framework if it believed it to be technically misjudged and that is why this point was not brought out in that context. Its error in international development strategy was its technical misjudgement, its simplistic model of the global economy, though this undoubtedly arose from an ideological position substantially different from that of the writers of the platform. In the context of the quantity of aid its misjudgement was in refusing to take the Labor government at its word.

Perhaps the committee believed that the government's moderately expansionary fiscal policies, combined with the intense competition for funds for all other types of expenditure, would make movement towards the aid target of 0.7 per cent of GNP difficult. If it did, it was correct, but it should then have discussed how support for that target could have been achieved. Mr Hawke drafted the economic section very carefully: a Labor government will aim to achieve community support for the target of 0.7 per cent of GNP within five years of attaining office. The government's task is, therefore, to lead public opinion; not just to be moulded by it.

This implies that a major program of public education to mobilise public opinion is required, for the available evidence suggests that the public is satisfied with the current level of aid. One survey of community attitudes to aid, quoted in the report, is inadequate because there was no direct question about the amount of aid. Only the extent of support for the principle of assisting developing countries was tested: answers to that question indicate that 65 per cent of Australians support assisting developing countries.

Another opinion poll taken in 1978 by the Sydney Morning Herald was directly on the quantity of aid. Public opinion in Australia then favoured maintaining aid at existing levels. This poll concluded that 44 per cent of respondents wanted aid left as it was, 26 per cent wanted it increased, and 25 per cent supported cuts. The same poll asked respondents would they personally make additional sacrifices in favour of poor countries, 48 per cent said 'yes' and 48 per cent said 'no'. Some 51 per cent of capital city residents answered affirmatively. These results, while disappointing, at least do not suggest there would necessarily have been an outcry if real aid was increased.

Another indication of the extent of public support for aid is the level of contributions to voluntary aid organisations. In 1982 Australians gave an average of $US2 per head to aid groups, putting us twelfth behind, amongst others, the Norwegians who gave $US9 a head, the Netherlands $US8, Germany $US6, and the US $US6 (Jackson Report, 1984, p. 104). I doubt if these figures are strictly comparable because the encouragement given to non-governmental aid organisations is much greater in some countries than others. (It would be interesting to know how much difference tax deductability of donations to voluntary aid agencies in Australia has made to their total receipts.) The figures do suggest, though, that support for voluntary aid groups is relatively low in Australia. Therefore, concerted and sustained public education on the value and uses of aid is essential.

Dr Stuart Harris, who was recently appointed Secretary of the Department of Foreign Affairs, wrote several years ago that:

> ... The Brandt Report was designed to influence political leaders in the developed world. To a large extent, however, the views of the political leadership are influenced and constrained by public opinion. The report will contribute to educating the public but it could at best make only a small contribution. It does make a strong case for substantial action by the North, but without a more aware public opinion, the scope for its influence on the political leaders of the nations, as well as on those in Australia, will be limited. The countries most active in the development arena, such as Holland and Sweden, also maintain a large program of public education ... There seems to be a Catch 22 situation - without public pressure, political leaders are not persuaded, but without the persuasion they will not fund the education program and therefore the public reaction will be limited. (Harris, 1980)

The committee recognised this, but proposed that only $1 million a year be allocated to the task. This is quite inadequate. The government spent three-quarters of a million dollars recently on a publicity campaign about the 'Accord' which lasted for only three weeks, indicating how inadequate would be $1 million spread over a whole year for a comprehensive sustained public education campaign covering all media repeatedly. The voluntary agencies do most of the public education at present. One cost effective method of widening public education would be enlarging their funds for that task. The role of the voluntary agencies in focusing attention on the shocking consequences of drought and the collapse of the food distribution system in Ethiopia is a dramatic illustration of the point -- though more public education should emphasise the achievements of aid rather than concentrating on heart-rending pictures of distress which provide a justification only for crisis relief. One of the places on which education about the benefits of sustained aid could appropriately concentrate is Papua New Guinea, for it has been the largest recipient of Australian aid throughout the last 40 years.

PAPUA NEW GUINEA

The committee's principal recommendation about aid to PNG is that the aid relationship be 'normalised' by reducing, and eventually phasing out, budget support and replacing it with bilateral technical assistance, project aid, co-financing and other forms of specific program support. Acceptance of this whole proposal would involve a regressive return to neo-colonial structures, and as well would probably be wasteful.

The argument for the proposed change is superficial, paternalistic and riddled with platitudes. For example, the section begins by noting that 'Australia's budget support has been very important to Papua New Guinea, particularly in the difficult period since the early 1980s' (Jackson Report, 1984, p. 161). Having already noted that Australia's aid program provides almost 30 per cent of PNG's central government revenues, the comment is redundant. It is also misleading because Australian aid has been falling as a proportion of total revenues throughout the last decade, and so was obviously even more important in the difficult period of the seventies. The lack of a table showing the extent of PNG's reduction in dependence on Australian aid as well as the incompleteness of the whole discussion suggest lack of homework.

The reductions in real aid to PNG during the last decade are one influential cause for the slower rate of economic growth there during the last ten years, a fact which the committee does not even seem to recognise. There is no serious analysis of the causes for the slower growth. The implication that it was because of a lack of commitment to growth by the government neglects not only the cuts in real aid, but also fluctuating and generally low commodity prices and the rapidity of political, administrative, economic and social change. The PNG government has been struggling for economic growth and development since self-government in 1972, as even a cursory reading of Strategies for Nationhood (Papua New Guinea, 1974) and the National Development Strategy (Papua New Guinea, 1976) will show.

The committee seems to have accepted the view that because 'budget support grants do not require detailed accountability, Papua New Guinea has not used Australian funds as effectively as it would if similar levels of aid had been provided for specific projects' (Jackson Report, 1984, p. 161). No evidence is presented. The only substantial case of project aid from Australia to PNG of which I am aware is the upgrading of Nadzab Airport, which is an under-utilised white elephant. In any case the PNG government is accountable to its electors. Accountability to Australia can be achieved in many ways. Ten years ago a PNG negotiating group (of which I was a member) proposed to an Australian aid mission that a PNG section be established in ADAA (the Australian Development Assistance Agency, as it was then - see Chapter 12) which would keep in close contact with what was happening in PNG, that regular dialogue take place in discussions between the countries, and that the Auditor General's office in PNG be strengthened to maintain scrutiny of honesty in administration. It is a comment on ADAB, the successor to ADAA, not on the capacities of PNG officials, that these suggestions have still not been fully implemented.

The reductions in real Australian aid to PNG during the last ten years have kept strong pressure on the government to maintain fiscal discipline. The high cost of government -- which is due to Australian colonial policy -- is being reduced (Langmore, 1972).

A rapid shift from budget support to project aid as recommended could well exacerbate rather than ease these problems. Negotiation of project aid adds substantially to the administrative complexity of establishing a project. Scarce managerial personnel would have to be diverted to the process of negotiation when they would be more productively employed in planning and managing the project itself. The committee recognises that the proposed changes would impose strains on aid administration in Australia and that they are inherently paternalistic. 'There would be an undesirable tendency for responsibility and decision making to be taken over by Australian officials' (Jackson Report, 1984, p. 162). In any case the proposed rate of introduction of project aid is faster than PNG could feasibly cope with.

The committee suggests that strains would be imposed on the PNG budget, but this might well not be so, for if the net effect is simply to increase the proportion of a declining real level of aid which is allocated through projects there will be no net effect on total PNG public expenditure. For example, if Australia decided to fund a road between Port Moresby and Lae which the PNG government would have built anyway, then the allocation for road construction in the PNG budget would be reduced by the amount of the Australian grant. All that would have happened is that managerial control of the project would have been transferred from Papua New Guineans to Australians -- a regressive change.

Is not a more mature approach to continue with budget support and to increase information flows and dialogue between Australia and PNG, and to strengthen the capacity for internal scrutiny within PNG? If this process led to the identification of structural or managerial problems then there could well be value in Australia offering appropriate forms of technical assistance, such as skilled personnel or training programs, to enable PNG to cope with the problem. This would involve real development without loss of independence, and for both Australia and PNG this could well be more cost-effective. Such an approach would be based not on paternalism but on justice -- on the principle espoused earlier in this chapter of regular transfer of resources from rich to developing nations to reduce unacceptable inequalities in living standards.

CONCLUSION

This chapter has identified a number of inadequacies in the Jackson Report. These include an undue polarisation between growth-centred development strategy and the basic needs approach; a trite dismissal of NIEO strategies; a failure to consider Australia's relationship to international financial institutions; far too little consideration of the quantity of aid; and a quite inadequate and ill-informed discussion and recommendations about aid to PNG. Yet the majority of the committee's recommendations should be implemented swiftly. The quantity of funds allocated to aid justifies spending a relatively small amount in upgrading administration. If this occurs, the result of the Jackson Report could be to considerably improve the effectiveness of Australian aid.

NOTES

1. P.T. Bauer is an extremely reactionary critic of aid (see Bauer, 1971).

2. Theresa Hayter wrote a cynical review of aid a decade ago (see Hayter, 1971).

3 STRUCTURAL ADJUSTMENT AND THE JACKSON REPORT: THE NEXUS BETWEEN DEVELOPMENT THEORY AND AUSTRALIAN FOREIGN POLICY

Richard Higgott

INTRODUCTION

The Jackson Report has certainly achieved the quantity of publicity, if not always of the quality wished, that the Minister of Foreign Affairs had hoped for when he tabled it in Parliament in early 1984. This collection of essays, along with other recent works, is a product of this demand for analysis and critique. As these provide fairly comprehensive discussion of the contents and recommendations of the report, this chapter will neither attempt to duplicate such efforts nor to quibble with many of the report's obviously sensible recommendations. Indeed, it is less a chapter on the Jackson Report than one on development theory and policy designed to complement the other 'Jackson specific' chapters in this collection. Its major aim is to establish the broader intellectual and historical context in which a report such as Jackson's needs to be located, and from which suggestions about the relationship between the report's central assumptions and political practice can be made.

This chapter will argue that Jackson's essence is founded on two sets of assumptions. The first of these relates to the debate over Third World development and underdevelopment -- specifically with regard to strategies for the eradication of poverty. The second set of assumptions relates to Australia's role in world affairs -- particularly the question of Australia's relations with the Third World and most notably with its immediate regional neighbours.

The chapter is suggestive in intent, not accusative. It will argue that whilst the two issue areas identified are themselves fields of immense intellectual conflict, the Jackson Report is founded on quite specific, and relatively narrow aspects of these debates -- and its recommendations are the logical outcome of intellectual assumptions deriving from them.

As a precautionary note, it should be noted that it is impossible to prove, in a one to one relationship, the linkage between a general idea set and specific policy initiatives. Observers of Jackson have not, for example, been privy to meetings of the committee. However, it may be suggested more modestly that policy recommendations emanate not from a vacuum, but from specific intellectual, socio-economic and cultural contexts. In short, Jackson as a report on the nature of Australian aid to developing countries is the product of a particular moment in development thinking on the one hand, and thinking on Australia's perception of its global position on the other. It is the reflection of a dominant set of assumptions about growth and development, and how they relate to Australia at this point in time.

Just what are the specifics of these dominant assumptions? At the first level, that of development thinking, the Jackson Report reflects the current orthodoxy in development thinking, which I will tackle in the next section of this chapter under the subheading of 'From Basic Needs to Structural Adjustment' and which I will suggest is epitomised in current World Bank development policy. This approach enables us to be more sophisticated in the analysis of the report's policy recommendations than by simply referring to the report as functioning in a 'neo-classical' economic paradigm (cf. e.g. Stent, 1985).

Stent observed, for example, that the three professional economists on the committee all operated within this dominant paradigm of economics and also pointed to the fact that all three have, at various times, worked for the World Bank. This may be relevant at one level, but at another level we should ask whether it is necessary to personalise analysis in this way? Rather, a comparison of the current orthodoxy in development thinking with the ideas about development espoused in Jackson is likely to prove more enlightening. As David Ricci has noted:

> No scientist sees paradigmatic bundles of ideas carried around like mental baggage. He simply absorbs some ideas, and unless he reads Kuhn's book, he uses them without impact on his perception and curiosity. (Ricci, 1977, p. 22)

In considering Australia's role in the global economic and political order, the report -- at the second level -- reflects the current preoccupation with examining how Australia must adjust to being a member of a rapidly developing (in absolute GNP terms at least) and increasingly competitive Asia/Pacific community. Again it is less important to speculate on the extent to which the interests of various members of the committee influenced the report, than to analyse the degree to which the report reflects these currently fashionable concerns. Accordingly, the next two sections are devoted to analysing these dominant assumptions.

FROM BASIC NEEDS TO STRUCTURAL ADJUSTMENT

Much has been written of late about the intellectual origins, processes of development, transformations and subsequent processes of decline of various theories of development and underdevelopment. What emerges from such analysis is the essentially infant and uncertain stage of development studies. Ideas rise and decline in popularity with a life expectancy measured in single figure time spans, as do trends in policy emanating from such 'ideas' (Higgott, 1983). Such processes cannot be described here. The most recent history of international development thinking is, however, very important for an understanding of the Jackson Report. We can most accurately trace it by looking at the shift that has come about over the last four or five years as the World Bank has abandoned its 'basic needs' strategies of the 1970s in favour of an emphasis on 'structural adjustment' policies in the 1980s. An understanding of this process helps us locate the Jackson Report in its intellectual context.

As explained in two quite recent World Bank publications (World Bank, 1981a,b), such policies superficially appear logical and rational. But in a wider context they become much more contentious -- with important implications for the recommendations of aid documents such as Jackson. The move from basic needs to structural adjustment strategies is, I shall suggest, symptomatic of the passing of the international welfare state or Keynesian approach to development at the expense of what we might broadly call the 'neo-classical' resurgence in keeping with the Friedmanite philosophies so popular of late in the major industrial powers and which Jackson, by its argument and recommendations, would appear to support. These shifts are themselves a response to a variety of factors, notably the growth of neo-conservative political thinking and world recession (see respectively, Steinfels, 1979; Parboni, 1981). Most importantly, for purposes of this discussion, is the major structural change of the last decade in the international division of labour which has, in turn, influenced the nature of development policies, with heavy stress on the promotion of Export-Oriented Industrialisation strategies (EOI) in the Third World (see Higgott, 1984). As I will shortly show, the Jackson Report is quite clearly an intellectual child of such changes.

Too much has been written about basic needs strategies to warrant a detailed discussion here. It is sufficient for us simply to appreciate their origins in the reaction to the inadequacies of economic development theory as it passed from its growth-oriented phase of the late 1950s and early 1960s into a period of self-doubt in the late 1960s and early 1970s. The failure of Third World societies to 'take off' and of a 'trickle -down' of benefits to the poor to occur, brought about a move towards basic needs strategies. These strategies were pioneered in or around the policy-making circles of the World Bank, and adopted and articulated by its then president, Robert McNamara, in 1973. While such strategies have to be seen in part as an attempt to head off the more radical demands for a New International Economic Order (NIEO), that began to emanate from Third World leaders about the same time, there is no reason to doubt that basic needs strategies were taken seriously in official quarters - as even staunch critics of the World Bank like Teresa Hayter (1981) have acknowledged.

In essence, basic needs strategies were not introduced to supplant growth theory but to supplement it by the commitment of funds to the poorer sections of the community that were in many cases, particularly in the rural areas (see Lipton, 1977) becoming worse off despite a wider process of aggregate national growth in the Third World. Thus by means of deliberate intervention into the policy process, basic needs strategies would focus on the 'human needs' of the poorest sections of the community with regard to nutrition, basic education, health, sanitation, water supply and housing (Streeten and Burki, 1978; Hicks and Streeten, 1979). Further, the best way to facilitate such a process would be by implementing 'redistribution with growth' strategies as advocated in the 1974 World Bank-sponsored publication of the same title (Chenery, et al., 1974).

While these strategies had come about during the pessimistic period following the failure of the first United Nations Development Decade, it was not yet a period of what we might call unbridled cynicism in which the major industrial powers had abandoned their basic commitment to an essentially Keynesian philosophy towards international development. Recession in the West was still in its early stages in the mid-1970s. As late as 1980, Robert McNamara was still arguing to the Board of Governors of the World Bank that spending on the social sector should be increased (Hayter, 1981, p. 90). Similarly, the theme of the World Bank's World Development Report 1980 was 'Poverty and Human Development' and reports such as that of the Brandt Commission were still making their appearance (Brandt Report, 1980).

The turn of the decade did, however, see fundamental philosophical changes in official development thinking, as a consequence of which basic needs strategies have largely been superseded after their short lifespan. The actual passing of basic needs, and also many of its major supporters at the World Bank -- Robert McNamara, Mahbub Ul Haq and Paul Streeten -- are not of themselves major events. Nor is this shift of priorities at the World Bank, from direct attacks on poverty under McNamara to the advocacy of policy related to economic efficiency, a contested event (see, for example, Far Eastern Economic Review, 27 September 1984, p. 66). It is, however, symptomatic of the decline in policy circles of what Robert Cox (1979) has called the 'social democratic' or Keynesian/welfare state approach to international development, epitomised by the hostile reception meted out to the Brandt Report (1980) in a variety of influential circles. Brandt was seen by the new orthodoxy as the advocate of developmental strategies that would simply throw good money after bad. In sharp contrast to Brandt, and underpinned by monetarist philosophical influences, development strategy in the policy-making circles of the major western powers, especially the USA and the UK, and the international agencies is now fiercely 'supply side' (Anon., 1982). These intellectual influences, adopted as guidelines for government policy in many industrial countries, need no elaboration. They also have implications for development theorising that have found their way into the Jackson Report.

At the theoretical level, the '... goddess of growth ... is returned ... to her pedestal' as Mahbub Ul Haq (Righter, 1982) suggested on his resignation from the World Bank. In short, basic needs has given way to growth strategies and the vehicle for their implementation -- structural adjustment policies. These two issues are related but distinct. The former is the wider theoretical construct, the latter is the resultant policy formulation. If we consider the wider theoretical issue first then we can see that the resurgence of growth theory has been accompanied by, or can in fact be seen as the outcome of, the revival in the fortunes of the theory of comparative advantage and the growing attraction of export-oriented industrialisation strategies.

Theories of comparative advantage are the antithesis of such an approach. Unlike theories of 'unequal exchange' and dependency (Emmanuel, 1972 and Amin, 1978), they see trade for the Third World in positive-sum, not zero-sum terms. It is, however, easy to see why such a theory as unequal exchange should have gained popularity in that pessimistic period at the end of the first UN development decade. Not only did it go a long way towards providing an explanation for the poor performance of Third World economies, it also provided the basis for radical policy prescription -- to wit the dismantling of the existing inegalitarian international economic order and the establishment of a new one more beneficial to the Third World. In this context, the important point is the way that 'comparative advantage' and 'unequal exchange' tended to 'square off' at each other on either side of the study of development and underdevelopment. While it might have seemed for a short time, that dependency theory had dealt comparative advantage a knockout blow, it was in fact only out for an 'eight' count and has come back strongly in the later rounds over the last few years. There are several reasons for this revival worthy of brief mention.

The earlier notions of comparative advantage which paid almost exclusive attention to the importance of labour when determining the nature of a comparative advantage a country might possess have now been added to, so that factors such as land, resources, capital, and most importantly, political will are also taken into greater consideration. Particularly influential in development policy, or at least illustrative of it in recent years, has been World Bank Research Publications such as those of Hollis Chenery, Structural Change and Development Policy (1979). These modifications, accompanied by the successful trading activities of the Newly Industrialising Countries (NICs), especially of East and Southeast Asia, and the growing body of critiques of the dependencia school in the late 1970s (for a discussion see Higgott, 1981) have seen comparative advantage restored to a central philosophical position in economic development theory and a crucial role in economic development policy.

A corollary of the revival of the fortunes of comparative advantage (it is difficult to know whether it is a cause or effect) has been the perceived successes of export-oriented industrialisation strategies in a number of Latin American and Asian countries over the last few years. EOI strategies have taken over from Import Substitution Industrialisation (ISI) (see Leaver, 1985) strategies as the policy option amongst policy

-makers in the major financial institutions and many planning ministries around the Third World. As part of this process, basic needs strategies have been largely jettisoned as we can see in the following discussion of current World Bank policy. If World Bank strategy can be taken as the orthodoxy in development thinking then growth through trade is the orthodoxy of the 1980s (World Bank, 1981a, p. 5). The way such strategies are to be brought about is through the implementation of structural adjustment policies. In this context national adjustment at the state or sub-state level in the Third World is seen as much more important than global adjustment, or more plainly, movement towards a New International Economic Order.

Arguments for a New International Economic Order might have had currency in a situation where notions of 'unequal exchange' were influential, but in a situation where the utility of comparative advantage is reasserted (rhetorically if not always empirically) demands for a radical restructuring of the economic order can be pushed to one side. The prevailing 'Establishment' perspective (Cox, 1979) on the NIEO, epitomised by the treatment of the Brandt Report and the futility of the Cancun North /South discussions in 1981, is one that sees no fundamental problems with the world economic order that cannot be put right by the freeing up of trade. What we need, it is argued, is an overhaul of the existing order, or what the Trilateral Commission -- the apotheosis of the Establishment perspective, would see as a Renovated International Economic Order (Sklar, 1980). Such a Renovation of the International Economic Order can best be brought about by the implementation of structural adjustment at both a global and a national level.

'Adjustment' is basically a codeword for a variety of overlapping actions such as practising fiscal responsibility, controlling inflation, controlling the money supply, producing reform (very often a euphemism for devaluation), having a reasonable balance of payments ratio, or to paraphrase the World Bank -- restoring the external accounts of developing countries. There are, of course, other aspects of an adjustment package -- especially diminishing the role of parastatals and encouraging the private sector as well as the introduction of a variety of austerity measures geared to cutting down public expenditure (see World Bank, 1981a, p. 4).

The economic philosophy underpinning structural adjustment is, of course, 'supply side' whereas the basic needs approaches of the previous decade were 'demand side' or consumption oriented. To take the argument one stage further structural adjustment means, in the words of Bela Balassa, an economist closely associated with recent World Bank policy:

> that ... growth objectives will need to be given greater weight as compared to income distributional objectives ... further ... policies to alleviate poverty should give emphasis to measures that raise the productivity of the poor rather than increase consumption through the provision of public services or governmental subsidies. (Balassa, 1982, p. 23)

In simple terms structural adjustment is really about developing countries 'putting their economic houses in order' in a manner similar to the desire which seems to preoccupy many Western governments in the 1980s. The rationale of adjustment is its supposed facilitation of export led growth.

The World Development Report, 1981 points to several countries that are model exponents of these policies. Of middle income countries, South Korea is the one above all, though not the only one, that has achieved '... spectacular results through export led growth' (World Bank, 1981a, p. 67). Of the primary producing nations with agriculturally based economies, Ivory Coast and Thailand are prime examples of a fairly successful process of diversifying exports to earn foreign exchange for investment in the development of manufacturing industries (World Bank, 1981a, p. 71). (These same countries are similarly singled out in Jackson (Jackson Report, 1984, p. 28 .) In general terms, 'outward' oriented economies are applauded by the World Development Report, 1981 for having been the most successful of the last decade in responding to dislocations such as those caused by rapid increases in the cost of energy. Consequently, the World Bank's 'Policy Lessons' for the 1980s are geared towards adjustment for outward oriented strategies. Its loans policy is undergoing a considerable change from the second half of the 1970s with less emphasis given to project lending in the pursuit of basic needs. Instead 'structural adjustment lending' will see funds:

> ... applied towards productive investments which enhance the country's capacity to produce exports and curb imports. For this reason, the uses to which external finance are put required careful monitoring emphasis added . (World Bank, 1981a)

In 1980 the Philippines, by way of brief example, received one of the World Bank's first Structural Adjustment Loans (it has just received its third). This $US600 million loan was geared towards securing the 'reform' of the Philippine tariff structure in the form of an overall reduction of protection from the average rate of 42 per cent in 1978 to 28 per cent in 1985 and the 'rehabilitation' of selected Philippine industries. Particularly it was aimed at increasing international competitiveness through the improvement of managerial and technical assistance, the injection of capital and the establishment of trading corporations to improve export potential (Hill, 1982). Further evidence of World Bank policy and thinking on these issues can be gleaned from the policy recommendations in its report on Accelerated Development for Africa (World Bank, 1981b).

The preceding discussion is a fairly straightforward and largely uncontentious account of what we might call the current orthodoxy — export-oriented growth strategies, carried out by the implementation of structural adjustment policies. Important for this collection of essays, is the need to recognise that this orthodoxy has been central to the intellectual climate in which the Jackson Report was written. A reading of the report provides ample evidence to support an assertion of the orthodoxy's influence over its structure. A student of comparative literature skilled in textual and discourse analysis would have no problem supporting such a view -- even down to the degree in which the format of the report mirrors the World Development Reports with their different coloured 'boxes' and inserts, and, more significantly, the way in which the bibliographical guides provided in the report are extremely dependent on reference to World Bank sources and those of authors such as Peter Bauer who fall into Stent's neo-classical mould.

Most important, however, is the debate over the merits of basic needs strategies versus growth strategies. Jackson adopts the World Bank line that growth strategies must prevail. As the Jackson Report (1984, p. 5) points out:

> Views differ widely on whether aid should be directed to providing basic needs for the most disadvantaged groups or whether it should be used to promote economic growth. In some circumstances, poverty alleviation and a contribution to economic growth can be effectively combined. However, in the main, Australian government aid funds and skills are most effective when applied to removing major constraints to development. This often involves capital intensive inputs.

On this question, as in other parts of the report (paragraphs 4.3 and 4.4 on p. 60), the report plumps for capital intensive, infrastructural aid rather than aid which might seek '... to assist the poor directly' (Jackson Report, 1984, p. 60). It is not my task to debate the respective merits of basic needs and growth strategies (see, for example, Lipton, 1977; Hicks, 1980; Hicks and Streeten, 1979; Streeten and Burki, 1978), but rather, as indicated earlier, to locate Jackson. Stent's (1985) analysis of Jackson (as do other chapters in this volume) provides the necessary empirical support to emphasise the priority of growth strategies at the expense of basic needs strategies. Further support is also provided by a committee member, Professor Lim, in his recent attempt to answer the challenge that the report is purely growth oriented (Lim, 1985). Notwithstanding his intentions, Lim's discussion of the underlying framework of Jackson adopts a view of economic growth entirely consistent with that outlined as the current orthodoxy in this chapter.

Perhaps nowhere is the influence of the current orthodoxy on Jackson better illustrated, however, than in two specific similarities. First, the choice of 'model' developing countries is the same in World Bank publications as it is in the Jackson Report. Compare, for example, the World Development Report, 1981 discussion of the policies of the Asian NICs (World Bank, 1981a, p. 71) with the discussion in Chapter two of the Jackson Report. Secondly, note the box on 'Factors on Development' (Jackson Report, 1984, p. 30), particularly in the emphasis on 'political will', 'stability' and the pursuit of appropriate fiscal policies -- which mirror World Bank structural adjustment policies. It is also in this context that it exhibits the classic weakness of much of this strategic orientation for development -- the Jackson Report has no theory of society and/or politics to go with what it considers to be rational, self evident-economic policy. I have discussed in some detail elsewhere (Higgott, 1983, 1984, 1985a; Higgott et al., 1985) how the implementation of such policies can have a very severe impact on socio-political stability and, as an outcome, can lead to the resort by governments to repressive political action to preserve their position. This tendency has also been noted by other students of the implementation of structural adjustment policies in the Third World (Bello et al. 1982; Robison, forthcoming, Chapter 11). And indeed, even the World Bank (1981a, p. 5) is prepared to acknowledge, albeit obliquely, the degree to which it is the '... human development programs which are obviously at risk at a time of budgetary stringency'. Structural adjustment emphasis on productivity and growth takes funds away from those sectors of public spending which have no immediate returns but which were at the core of the basic needs strategy. Education and health policy are two areas which have only an intangible relationship with productivity but which are high cost areas offering instant prospects of 'savings' -- especially salaries. All structural adjustment policies inevitably rein in on public sector spending -- as the World Development Report acknowledges:

> There is no reason to single out social programs for cuts during an adjustment period. In many cases, however, budgetary constraints will force cuts in spending, and a share of this burden will fall on human development programs. (World Bank, 1981a, p. 98)

The Jackson Report makes similar acknowledgement, supporting the assertion in this chapter of the strong influence of current development orthodoxy on it.

In summarising this section we can say that current orthodoxy emphasises growth through trade and the role of aid as supportive of this strategy. Jackson, again like the World Bank, recognises that the role of aid in development is only a secondary factor, at best. This assertion, of course, would not be challenged in many quarters, irrespective of ideological persuasion. But where aid is used, the orthodoxy argues, it should be to support growth-inducing strategies through the implementation of structural adjustment policies in selected sectors of an LDC's economy. Structural adjustment lending by the World Bank is another layer of conditionality above and beyond the macro-economic policy advice already given to borrowers by the World Bank.

The Jackson Report does not, of course, hint at conditionality and I am not suggesting that Australian aid could operate in a manner commensurate with that of the World Bank. The asymmetries of influence are so obvious as to need merely noting here. Rather I am suggesting that in its philosophical approach, and in specific recommendations -- especially when we consider such issues as the sectoral focus for aid-giving -- then the influences of World Bank thinking on the Jackson Report are fairly clear. This section has also been at pains to stress that whilst such approaches to development may be in the ascendency in the current intellectual climate they are, nevertheless, essentially contested in other areas of the development studies community. As

David Lim is prepared to concede '... the report adopted a strategy for development not universally accepted' (emphasis added) (Lim, 1985, p. 19). For the purposes of this chapter the appropriateness of the course of action adopted is less important than its establishment.

THE ENVIRONMENTAL LOCATION OF THE JACKSON REPORT

Having briefly identified the Jackson Report as an intellectual child of the current orthodoxy in development thinking, there is now a second important dimension we must consider. This section will relate the Jackson Report to an emerging, powerful and influential view of Australia in the international political and economic environment. Unlike the 'developmental' dimensions of the report which are widely dispersed, the environmental imperatives within which the Australian aid program operates is quite neatly defined in the report's chapter entitled 'The Changing World and Australia'. The essence of the structural adjustment model advocated as development strategy for developing countries is, ironically, also implicit in the report's analysis of Australia's position in the global economic order outlined in Chapter 2. As the chapter highlights from the outset:

> Australia's economic performance since World War II has not been as good as that of other industrial countries. Despite rich natural resources, growth has been low and inflation and unemployment have risen. In part, this has been caused by a failure to adjust emphasis added to changes in the world around Australia. Meanwhile the composition of Australian society has been altering through immigration, which in recent years has included a significant proportion from Asia. This has produced a greater realism emphasis added in Australia's attitude to Asian countries, although much ambivalence remains. In Asia there is increasing impatience with traditional Australian attitudes. (Jackson Report, 1984, p. 26)

In that one introductory paragraph the Jackson Report captures the imperatives of contemporary Australian foreign policy. These represent what we might call the impetus for a 'new realist' perspective on Australia's international economic relations. The older realist tradition, which emphasised Australia as the 'lucky country' in economic terms and also provided for it a politico-cum-ideological position within the Western camp in the context of post-World War II superpower confrontation (see Indyk, 1985), has changed relatively slowly. However, the economic elements have undergone a sea-change in the post-World War II era.

The new realism now accepts the paramountcy for Australia's economic future of its economic location in the middle of a rapidly growing Asia/Pacific region characterised by the increasing economic power of the regional NICs, the growth of trade as a percentage of regional GDP, the growth in importance of inter-regional trade (Drysdale, 1984), and the relatively poor performance of Australia within these overall changes.

There is a growing belief that Australia's traditionally high standards of living and relative national economic power are being dissipated. The Australian media abounds with cliches, alluding to the 'death of the lucky country' or the 'land of lost opportunities', and statistics showing the country's plight. Further, and this is often seen as most disturbing to a somewhat smug Australian population, it is suggested that by the end of the millenium several of Australia's regional neighbours in the Asia/Pacific region such as Singapore and South Korea will have climbed above it on a GNP per capita wealth table that has seen Australia fall from first place in 1900 to outside the top 20 nations in 1980.

In this context it is worth noting that two members of the Jackson Committee have been particularly influential in highlighting this 'new realism' in Australia's international economic position in general (see H Hughes, 1983) and in the regional economic context in particular (see McCawley, 1983, 1984a,b). Professor Hughes has been particularly vociferous in warning against Australia's slipping position. There is not, I think, a little irony in the fact that the remedies she suggests -- particularly the need for Australia to adjust its economy in a way that gets its competitive exporting 'act' together -- are very similar to the remedies suggested to LDCs in the literature of the current development orthodoxy.

Whilst we need to keep a sense of proportion concerning the growth of the Asia/Pacific economy -- it has not swamped Europe and North America, but rather is joining it as a third force at this stage (see Madigan, 1984) -- we have to be a lot more sanguine about Australia's relative position. Australia's post-World War II growth has been amongst the slowest of the world's developed countries and whilst our regional trade may have grown in absolute terms our relative penetration of the Asia/Pacific region has declined. Similarly, trade has declined as a share of GDP at a time when it has been growing in the region overall. Finally, Australian trade has grown more slowly than world trade. Between 1939 and 1975, for example, our share of world trade has dropped from 2.5 per cent to 1.25 per cent of world total in an era when growth through trade has been the order of the day for many of our regional neighbours in the Asia/Pacific region (for a discussion see Madigan, 1984; Krause, 1984, p. 278-81).

Australia is, ironically given its traditional inward looking and protectionist nature, an open and vulnerable economy undergoing a process of 'marginalisation' within the context of what we might call the New International Division of Labour (NIDL) (see Higgott, forthcoming, for a full exposition of this process). This process of marginalisation contrasts sharply with that of the rapid process of incorporation of many of Australia's regional neighbours --but not necessarily for many of the world's truly poorest states (Higgott, 1985b). One example of this marginalisation can be seen in Australia's unfortunate specialisation in export commodities with a low value added component unable to hold their overall share of world trade. To add to this dilemma, Australia is faring badly in absolute as well as relative terms. For example, whilst world agricultural production grew at the rate of 4.2 per cent per annum between 1971 and 1981, Australian agriculture managed an increase of only 0.8 per cent. The figures for manufacturing over the same period were 6.7 per cent and 2.2 per cent, respectively. Only in mining was the trend reversed with Australia growing at an annual rate of 7.6 per cent in contrast to world growth of 1.4 per cent (Krause, 1984, p. 281).

The disparities in the rates of Asian and Australian growth are well known and the implications of this emerging pattern are becoming clearer. There is a growing asymmetry of need between Australia and its regional neighbours. Much more important to the growing economies of the Asian region than a healthy relationship with Australia, with a market of only 15.5 million people, is an increased trading relationship with the faster growing markets of Europe and North America. Prime Minister Lee of Singapore has shown a noticeable lack of reticence in pointing out Australia's increasing irrelevance to Asian countries in the formulation of their economic and trading policies. And as Lee also points out '... economics do, in the long run, decide politics' (cited in Johnson, 1984, p. 62).

Australia in the past has been cushioned by its income from resource exports but will in the long run need to restructure the 'mix' of its exports if it is to get a greater share of world trade. This is easier said than done. As it is widely acknowledged in all sectors of the policy -making community in Australia, the country has a fairly poor track record when it comes to the possession of an efficient outward-oriented manufacturing sector quick to innovate and adjust to changes in market requirements in international trade. Yet it has been those states of the Asia/Pacific region that have been successful in the process of export -oriented industrialisation that have fared best in NIDL. Australia has undergone a process of gradual marginalisation.

The authors of the Jackson Report may not utilise the terminology employed by analysts of the New International Division of Labour (see inter alia, Fröbel et al., 1980; Ruggie, 1983) but in their writings they have recognised the symptoms regularly enough. Whatever nomenclature is used there can be little doubt, however, of the influence on the Jackson Report's recommendations of a recognition of Australia's contemporary international economic position. Both implicitly and explicitly, the Jackson Report recognises Australia's regional strategic priorities. The ranking of the four groups of LDCs in the Jackson Report recommendations was influenced overwhelmingly by the 'new realism' of Australia's position in the international economic order. As Lim noted, ranking was done 'largely in order of their ... the LDCs ... importance to the strategic interests of Australia' (Lim, 1985, p. 10).

Again it is not my purpose in this chapter to analyse the rectitude of this ranking process. Both Eldridge (1985, p. 29) and Stent (1985, p. 37) have suggested that foreign policy rather than developmental priorities have been the major concerns. Further argument will no doubt be presented in this volume to suggest Australian aid may well possess greater developmental capacity in areas largely forgotten in the report, such as Africa, than in our more immediate neighbourhood of Southeast Asia for example. For the purposes of this chapter, the important point to note is the degree to which the Jackson Report has been greatly influenced by those prevailing priorities in Australian policy-making circles that assert not only its general international economic position but specifically, in the fashion of the Morrison Report, Australia and ASEAN: Challenges and Opportunities, that:

> While Australia will be affected by developments in other regions of the world, and by the global interests of the superpowers, no other part of the world promises to be of more consistent importance to Australia than the region of East and Southeast Asia. (Morrison Report, 1984, p. ix)

At this stage such a statement is more a reflection of what pundits perceive 'must inevitably be' rather than 'what is'. In 1982, ASEAN GNP was $US202 billion in contrast to the $US156 billion of Australia. But based on extrapolations from ASEAN growth figures for the period from 1979 to 1983 (relatively low growth rates at the height of the global recession), ASEAN GNP is expected to be $US2000 billion by 2000, nine times greater than the $US220 billion estimate for Australia. The debate over how this relationship may or may not evolve is far too complex for treatment here (but see Higgott, forthcoming). What we can say, however, is that there would appear to be an asymmetry of need emerging in the immediate regional relationship that is reflective of the wider process of marginalisation in the international economic order that also afflicts Australia. As it is evolving, Australia is going to need the region much more than -- as both Bob Hawke and Lee Kuan Yew readily admit -- it will need Australia.

A brief example will perhaps emphasise this point. If we accept the extremely small base from which the partnership began, then the growth in the trading relationship between Australia and ASEAN has not been insignificant. An 8 per cent growth rate per annum saw the volume of Australian trade with ASEAN grow from $487 million in 1972/3 to $3.43 billion in 1983/4. More importantly, Australian exports to ASEAN have grown at a faster rate than Australian exports overall -- 15 per cent per annum as opposed to 11.4 per cent per annum between 1978/9 and 1983/4. During the same period ASEAN imports to Australia grew at 14 per cent per annum. Currently, ASEAN as a group -- albeit that most trade takes place at a bilateral level -- is now Australia's fourth largest trading partner providing just over 5 per cent of Australian imports and taking about 9 per cent of Australia's exports. When we look at the relationship from the other side of the glass a somewhat different picture emerges. Australia's importance to ASEAN is marginal. It is a market for only 2.6 per cent of ASEAN exports and a provider of only 3 per cent of ASEAN's imports. Further, these figures, recorded for 1981 have undergone a decline in the short-term. The figures for 1983 are 1.7 and 2.5 respectively (Morrison Report, 1984, p. 133).

The policy recommendations that flow from a reading of Australia's international economic relations suggestive of the process of marginalisation --in both wide and narrow regional contexts -- are very similar to those recommended in the Jackson Report for LDCs, and which emanate from the current orthodoxy in the manner outlined in this chapter's previous section. In essence, the resultant policy options are the pursuit of export-oriented growth strategies brought about by the implementation of domestic structural adjustment geared towards allowing states to exploit their comparative advantage (whatever it may be). This approach has become widely accepted in Australian government, academic and other circles nowadays (see, inter alia, Hayden, 1983a; Ferris, 1984; Drysdale, 1984; Walsh, 1984). To the extent that Jackson sees aid as fostering our regional relationships it is more a document in foreign policy analysis than it is a tract in development. But as Eldridge (1983), has noted in a previous discussion of Australian aid policy, it is not unusual for foreign policy imperatives to prevail in any conflict with development needs.

CONCLUSION

This chapter has analysed only tangentially the contents of the Jackson Report -- detailed analysis is a task left to others in this volume. Its prime concern has been to locate Jackson in its intellectual and politico-economic contexts. It has done this by examining the two related elements indicated in the chapter's sub-title: 'The Nexus Between Development Theory and Foreign Policy'. On the one hand it has been suggested that the Jackson Report is the intellectual child of what I have called the 'dominant orthodoxy' in development theory. This description has been preferred to that of a 'paradigm' (be it neo-classical or whatever) since the notion of an orthodoxy conveys a greater sense of temporal uncertainty and much less of a sense of scientific authority than does the notion of a paradigm.

On the other hand, it has also been argued that the Jackson Report is a document that reflects what I have called the 'new realism' in the analysis of Australia's position in the global economic order. The nexus between these two sets of assumptions is to be found quite clearly in the policy implications that flow from them. The strategy to be pursued in developing the LDCs, and in retrieving Australia's international economic position is the same -- export-led growth secured through structural adjustment policies. The aims of this chapter have been only secondarily to question the strengths and weaknesses of those approaches to either development in LDCs (but see Higgott, 1984) or Australia (but see Higgott, forthcoming). Its primary intention has been to suggest the assumptions which locate the Jackson Report as a tract for its time.

ACKNOWLEDGEMENTS

The author would like to acknowledge the Australian Geographical Studies for permission to reproduce sections of an article published in the April 1984 edition (see Higgott, 1984).

GEOGRAPHICAL DISTRIBUTION OF AID

4 SMALL STATES, LARGE AID: THE BENEFITS OF BENEVOLENCE IN THE SOUTH PACIFIC

John Connell

> 'I think Australia is helping us because it is a rich country and not because it has respect for us'. (Ratu Sir Kamisese Mara, Prime Minister of Fiji, The Age, 18 April 1977)

> 'Ole Pasifikiwei immersed himself totally in the supreme task of development through foreign aid, relishing the twists and turns of international funding games. He has since shelved his original sense of self-respect and has assumed another, more attuned to his new, permanent role as a first-rate, expert beggar'.(Hau'ofa, 1983, p. 93)

Papua New Guinea (PNG) and the South Pacific island states are small, relatively isolated and remote from world markets and from each other. They are dependent and unusually open economies and, especially in Melanesia, are dominated by limited monetisation, agriculturally-based subsistence systems and considerable cultural diversity. Most have limited natural resources and skilled manpower and each experience the diseconomies of small-scale; this has contributed to limited import substitution, economic instability and inflexibility. Compared with many parts of Africa and Asia, per capita incomes (when subsistence production is incorporated) are not low but some basic needs, including health, nutrition and education, are sometimes poorly satisfied. In situations where the prospects for sustained economic growth appear slight, unless marine resources can be more effectively exploited, there appears to be a case for external assistance. Indeed, the small states of the South Pacific region (as defined by the South Pacific Commission's area of interest) increasingly tend to look towards foreign aid and investment as a means of solving economic problems to a rather greater extent than in most other parts of the world. Most countries in the South Pacific have, at one time or another, demanded greater aid levels, demands that often appear as 'loud complaints' (Shaw, 1982, p. 99) and, especially in the case of Papua New Guinea (e.g. Namaliu, 1984), renewed demands for continued high aid levels exemplified response to the Jackson Report. There has been little or no opposition to the principle of aid despite the consistent rhetoric of self-reliance enshrined in national development plans.

Australian aid to the South Pacific region is likely to increase in the future. For most countries aid remains essential to ensure economic viability (if not greater self-reliance); financial weakness following declining Australian aid would lead to a greater dependence on other aid sources. Moreover, the weight of precedent precludes significant reduction in aid without presenting the appearance of a political snub to the countries concerned. Underlying this is the perception of the necessity for peaceful change in the South Pacific, a situation that is likely to be sustained and encouraged by greater aid levels, although the components of that aid are crucial to the trajectory of change. At higher per capita income levels, with greater local financial resources, and with economic policies which also enable mobilisation of foreign exchange, the necessity for aid declines. However, even if these conditions occur (and there is little general indication that they will), a pattern of extensive foreign ownership of the economy, combined with high personal consumption expenditure on imported goods and services may reduce 'surpluses' retained for investment in the national economy and so perpetuate the need for aid, even at fairly high national income levels (Demas, 1975, p. 196). These conditions currently prevail in the South Pacific and are accentuated by trade dependence, remittances and a reliance on overseas technical and managerial expertise. What role might Australian aid play then in contributing to economic growth and development in the region?

THE NECESSITY FOR AID ?

The Jackson Report starts with the question 'Why Give Aid?', and whilst assessing the primacy of humanitarian goals, notes that 'Assistance for development is not wholly altruistic. Development promises greater world security and economic prosperity and it is in Australia's strategic and commercial interests to foster it. Australians generally agree that the overall aims of foreign aid are to achieve humanitarian, strategic and commercial goals' (Jackson Report, 1984, p. 19). The balance between this trilogy of objectives is of particular interest in the context of the smaller states of the Pacific region. The committee goes on to argue that:

> The faster development takes place the better Australian strategic and economic interests will be served. As development programs succeed, the need for aid will decline and ultimately disappear. (Jackson Report, 1984, p. 23)

Already the balance has shifted towards more obviously Australian interests whilst no evidence is presented to suggest that the need for aid will eventually disappear. It is the contention of this chapter that, in the context of the South Pacific, this cannot be demonstrated but also that aid is likely to increase and thus enhance some aspects of dependence, a dependence that will serve Australian strategic and, to a lesser extent, economic interests. Given the emphasis on commercial and strategic objectives the report does not assess the case for not giving aid. Although the bibliography to the chapter on 'Why Give Aid' refers to books (Bauer, 1971, 1981; Lappé et al., 1980), each of which in different ways, argues that aid is counter-productive, the issues they and others raise are not discussed. Broadly these objections to aid are five-fold. First, aid may obstruct progress towards lessening the development gap, by supporting repressive governments and elites rather than contributing to the solution of complex national and international issues. Secondly, the transfer of capital to poor countries tends to draw resources away from the poor, either to elites in the recipient countries or to the donor countries or groups within them (Hayter, 1971; Payer, 1974; Weissman, 1975; Feder, 1983; Schuftan, 1983). Whilst the Jackson Report refers to Lipton's (1977) emphasis on the need to help poor people directly (Jackson Report, 1984, p. 25) nowhere is this adequately elaborated. Thirdly, the content of aid (which might include food aid, tertiary technological training or large-scale capital projects) may encourage and perpetuate particular forms of dependence, including the 'brain-drain', and by conflicting with national priorities, reduce the possibility of interdependent or self-reliant development. Fourthly, servicing development projects may draw domestic resources away from locally-defined long-term development priorities. Fifthly, tied aid may reduce the demands for exports from poor countries and contribute to a worsened trade imbalance (Streeten, 1968). Overall the problems attached to foreign aid have been well summarised:

> The present levels of assistance are only of marginal significance for the developing countries and come with so many project conditions, foreign consultants, inappropriate technology and irritating debt problems that they sap the initiative and freedom of action of the developing world. (Ul Haq, 1976, p. 46)

None of these issues are discussed in any detail yet all concern the South Pacific where aid for many countries is high both in total and per capita terms. Aid is simply assumed to be necessary.

THE GEOGRAPHY OF AID

Overall aid flows into the region are exceptionally high by global standards, especially for the New Zealand associated states of Niue and Tokelau and the American and French territories. A high proportion of this aid is direct budgetary support. By contrast, per capita aid levels are low for Fiji, PNG (although PNG receives the highest aid in absolute terms), Solomon Islands, Tonga and Western Samoa (Table 4.1). In nine countries aid is equivalent to at least 50 per cent of income and in twelve is equivalent to over 50 per cent of government expenditure (Sevele, 1984, p. 22). Whilst France and the USA account for 50 per cent of all aid to the region, this was almost entirely restricted to their dependent territories; the USA, for example, currently operates no bilateral aid program to independent states in the region although dis-

Table 4.1 The South Pacific

Aid to the South Pacific	Estimated Population (mid-1982)	Per-centage Urban	Popula-tion Growth Rate	Land Area (sq. kms)	Popula-tion density (person per sq. km.)	Exports by(1) Category (1981 Percentages) Agric.	Fish.	Minerals	Per Capita Income (1981) $A	Aid 1982 (U.S. $m)	Per Capita aid 1982 (U.S.$2)	Austra-lian Bilateral aid (1982-83 $Am)	Australian Bilateral aid as Percentage of all aid (1982)
American Samoa	33.900	34	1.9	197	172	-	99	-	3440	31.8 (1980)	980 (1980)	-	-
Cook Islands	16.900	22	-1.8	240	70	51	-	6	980	10.4	581	0.69	5.0
Fiji*	658.000	38	2.0	18.272	36	67	7	4	1700	35.4	56	12.04	44.0
French Polynesia	158.800	51	2.2	3.265	47	19	15	-	6290	173.2	1169	0.01	-
Kiribati*	61.200	29	2.2	690	89	90	10	-	380	15.1	258	2.03	18.0
Nauru*	8.400	100	2.8	21	400	-	-	100	..	-	-	-	-
New Caledonia	144.000	53	1.3	19.103	8	..	..	77	5880	158.7	1138	-	-
Niue	3.150	..	-3.5	259	12	33	-	-	960	4.4	1294	0.03	4.0
Papua New Guinea*	3.126.600	13	2.2	462.243	7	36	5	53	710	3189.0	102	274.95	97.0
Solomon Islands*	243.000	8	3.4	28.530	9	59	38	..	550	28.4	126	8.08	25.0
Tokelau	1.580	..	0.1	11	144	100	-	-	480	1.9	1188	-	-
Tonga*	98.000	26	0.2	700	140	76	..	-	530	17.3	177	4.01	34.0
Tuvalu*	7.700	28	2.0	26	296	85	-	-	480	6.2	827	1.01	14.0
Vanuatu*	125.000	12	3.7	11.800	11	43	-	-	640	26.0	221	5.09	18.0
Wallis and Futuna	11.900	..	5.0	255	47	100	-	-	805	6.6 (1980)	608 (1980)	-	-
Western Samoa	157.000	20	0.7	2.935	53	72	-	-	720	22.9	146	7.02	25.0

Source: Connell, 1983; Sevele, 1984.

1. .. Not 100 per cent because of re-exports and manufactured goods (Kiribati data is from 1980).

cussions have recently been concluded that are likely to result in a bilateral aid program for Fiji. By contrast, aid flows from New Zealand and the UK are more diversified, although both retain a particular bias towards former colonies; contrasts between Australian and New Zealand aid flows (Table 4.2) are readily apparent. West Germany, Japan and The Netherlands are now entering the region as significant donor countries, and there are increasing flows from the Asian Development Bank (ADB), the European Economic Community (EEC) and the United Nations Development Programme (UNDP). A further recent trend is for several of the more established donors to extend their traditional range of assisted countries (Sevele, 1984, pp. 24-5). In recent years there has been a real increase in aid to the region and a greater diversification both of aid donors and the geographical extent of their assistance. Australian dominance of bilateral aid distribution in the region has fallen slightly from 29 per cent in 1978 to 27 per cent in 1980 (although these figures include American 'aid' to the Trust Territory of the Pacific Islands) whilst multilateral aid to countries has more than doubled in that period (although only accounting for 5 per cent of all aid). Australian aid policy is crucial.

The most striking feature of Australian government aid distribution is its geographical concentration in the South Pacific region; in 1979 some 68 per cent of all Australian bilateral development assistance went to this region, including 61 per cent to PNG. This PNG proportion has since been reduced to 36 per cent in 1983/4 and the Jackson Report proposes further reductions (Jackson Report, 1984, p. 160) ; a further 14 per cent has been allocated to the remainder of the South Pacific region. By contrast, of the much smaller assistance given by non-governmental organisations (NGOs), relatively little is given to the South Pacific region; in 1979, the only year for which accurate information exists, some 8 per cent of all ACFOA (Australian Council for Overseas Aid) aid went to the region, including 3 per cent to PNG (Percival, 1981, p. 35) whereas 61 per cent went to Asia and especially India and Thailand (Jackson Report, 1984, p. 37). Thus voluntary agencies tend to direct their aid more widely and towards countries of 'greatest need' whereas the geographical focus of government aid is much more concentrated.

PNG's primacy is a function of its special relationship with Australia, a relationship earlier explained by the Minister for Foreign Affairs, first, as a newly independent nation with former dependent status and, second, as the nearest neighbour to Australia, elaborated as:

> Australia's interest in Papua New Guinea will be sustained. Our incentive to have a stable and prosperous and friendly neighbour is a permanent one. (ADAB, 1980 cited by Percival, 1981, p. 40)

Stability and prosperity would ensure the protection and vitality of Australia's trading interests, and of those many Australians remaining in PNG (Jackson Report, 1984, p. 41). As the Jackson Report records: 'No other donor country allocates as large a proportion of its total aid to a single recipient nation' (Jackson Report, 1984, p. 146). Any special relationship

Table 4.2 Bilateral Aid to the South Pacific Region: Australia and New Zealand

	$Am Australia 1982-83	$NZm New Zealand 1983-84
Cook Islands	0.69	11.34
Fiji	12.47	4.87
French Polynesia	0.10	-
Kiribati	2.29	0.68
Nauru	0.01	-
New Caledonia	-	-
Niue	0.25	6.03
Papua New Guinea	274.95	3.35
Solomon Islands	8.83	1.46
Tokelau	-	2.70
Tonga	4.15	4.32
T.T.P.I.	0.02	-
Tuvalu	1.15	0.73
Vanuatu	5.88	1.54
Western Samoa	7.21	6.14
Regional	5.68	6.05
Total Pacific	323.68	49.21
Total Bilateral Aid	552.44	59.93

Sources: ADAB, 1984b, pp.180-236; Development, 7, 1984, p.28

with the remainder of the South Pacific region has not been hitherto spelled out; thus Percival (1981, p. 41) attributes the significant increase in aid levels in the late 1970s to increased awareness of the regions strategic significance (cf. Commonwealth of Australia, 1978, p. 12). In the past this was a response to increased Soviet and Chinese presence in the area (Fry, 1977; Herr, 1977). Whilst the activities of these countries in the region are minimal their presence is nevertheless novel and potentially increasing. This has also prompted similar American and New Zealand responses.

The primary objection to aid, that it may support repressive governments and elites and hence hinder development, is scarcely valid in the South Pacific. Although there has been some discussion of the extent of corruption in PNG, and several indications of the emergence of elites in a number of countries, the independent states of the South

Pacific are generally stable and functioning democracies, with ideologies in favour of competition, free enterprise, opposition to communism (as most crudely understood) and without significant military establishments. They are, therefore, the kinds of states most favoured by metropolitan social democracies. These factors are mentioned: '... the South Pacific states have important advantages. Transition to independence has mostly been peaceful: they are committed to democratic and representative government; and they are politically very stable. As yet, there is no poverty in the region' (Jackson Report, 1984, p. 175). In what context these are 'advantages' is not stressed but they are discussed only in terms of economic expectations. There is no attempt to assess a situation where the stability of states, in a region of significant social stratification (primarily in Polynesia), may maintain or enhance inequalities. The internal political factors that may inhibit development are not reviewed; ensuring the survival of the system is more crucial.

The South Pacific states have benefited from the 'small-country bias' that marks the aid-giving policies of most donor nations, including Australia (cf. De Vries, 1975; Eisen, 1973). This bias is particularly apparent for Australia, because of the high proportion of aid to PNG, although NGO funds show no bias towards small countries (Percival, 1981, p. 56). De Vries (1975) has argued that this bias in distribution partially follows a greater need by small states for aid because of diseconomies of scale and limits to domestic diversification. Small South Pacific island states have little possibility of achieving economies of scale in transport, communications or administration (cf. Ingram, 1979, p. 4). Isolation and shipping costs restrict overseas investment, and local industry is restricted by market size, transport and limited local resources, hence necessitating significant import dependency. Capital is difficult to obtain from major financial institutions, such as IMF and the Asian Development Bank, which are geared to providing large loans on competitive markets to larger nations with greater prospects of economic growth.

Other explanations for the small country bias are, first, that small countries have more interest in building effective donor-recipient relationships which 'may be significant to donors seeking to build political alliances through aid relationships' (Percival, 1981, p. 49). Secondly, aid given to small states assumes a much higher 'visibility' than in large states, especially where that aid comes from a very limited number of donor countries. Thirdly, donor agencies (especially NGOs) believe they can more effectively evaluate the effects of aid in small states (cf. Eisen, 1973, p. 2). The Jackson Report clearly spells out the reasons why small South Pacific states receive disproportionate aid allocations, and notes that:

> Small states carry the same voting weight in the United Nations as large states, so the strategic and political imperatives of aid tend to favour small countries. (Jackson Report, 1984, p. 42)

Australia has obviously been strongly influenced by these considerations especially 'in its own backyard' (cf. Percival, 1981, p. 57). Other countries are also aware of these issues (see Connell, 1985b); hence the bias towards small states that results from their economic and locational disadvantages and administrative problems (De Vries, 1975) is here reinforced by political and strategic objectives. In its approach to the South Pacific region, the Jackson Report does not depart far from the Harries Report which noted that the principal reasons for Australian interest in the region were because of its 'symbolic significance' and for security (Harries Report, 1979, p. 117).

There is a case to be made for significant levels of aid to the South Pacific region; the Jackson Report argues the case on the basis of strategic and commercial interests. A stronger case might have been made on the basis of inadequate basic needs and the existence of poverty, which the Jackson Report does not recognise (Jackson Report, 1984, p. 175), or the particular technical problems of development and financial management in very small states. What is abundantly clear is that aid allocations 'are not purely based on altruistic assessments of need' (Percival, 1981, p. 59) and are only tenuously related to the possibility of achieving local economic growth and development. Economic aspects of aid are framed in the context of Australian interests rather than the achievements of regional economic growth which would indirectly contribute to Australian economic growth.

The report's trilogy of objectives for Australian aid has contributed to a particular focus on Papua New Guinea and the small island states of the South Pacific; these countries and, with less emphasis, the small island states of the Indian Ocean are located in a 'Category One' entitling them to eligibility for a diversity of aid assistance, including possible budget support (as in the case of Papua New Guinea). The report does not consider dependent territories of France, the United Kingdom and the United States. Overall the focus within the report is on the independent states, particularly the largest and the smallest. The reasons for a particular focus on the South Pacific are established at several points in the report, and most directly in the Executive Summary: 'Australia's political interests and special relationship with Papua New Guinea indicate that the main country focus should be on Papua New Guinea and the small island nations of the Pacific and Indian Oceans' (Jackson Report, 1984, p. 6). The 'special relationship' with PNG is subsequently referred to repeatedly (Jackson Report, 1984, pp. 7, 140, 145), but elaborated only once and then briefly, as having 'strong political and strategic considerations' (Jackson Report, 1984, p. 145). The rationale for a particular focus on the South Pacific is similarly elaborated (Jackson Report, 1984, pp. 8, 167). Overwhelmingly, the central focus for Australian interest in the region, and especially the small states, is expressed here as a strategic and, secondarily, a commercial concern. Humanitarian objectives are rarely apparent. The report thus re-emphasises the existing geographical focus of Australian aid, rejects new initiatives and suggests an even greater focus on the 'backyard'.

THE FORM OF AID

The Jackson Report identifies some of the areas in which, it is argued, aid will contribute most directly to economic growth. Economic growth issues are emphasised in the chapter on the small island states whereas, for PNG, where aid is budget support and cannot therefore be targeted towards projects or sectors, but where there is greater growth potential, the report has identified particular welfare needs that should be tackled by the PNG government. For the small South Pacific states the actual targets for project aid are not clearly indicated. The report expresses a commitment to economic growth through the expansion of exports and through private sector development, but is aware of considerable problems:

> Exports have to be expanded. Population and employment problems, oversized administration and public services, all need attention. Only a few of the Islands are likely to achieve economic self-sufficiency before the end of the century. (Jackson Report, 1984, p. 176)

Albeit noting that the many different states have different goals and strategies, and that ADAB is preparing country-specific strategy papers, the report never goes beyond such generalisation. What is alarming is how little attention is given to two established economic bases of most South Pacific economies, agriculture and fishing. The report does emphasise the role of cash crops:

> Traditional agriculture such as livestock, copra and fisheries could be improved by more economic holdings, small processing plants, better marketing and planning for bulk transport. Cash crops could increase export earnings, but careful planning is needed to obtain maximum returns in regional markets. Possibilities include coffee, cocoa, palm oil, tropical fruits, vegetables, pepper, vanilla and certain new crops, such as tropical fruits and flowers. Such crops can also provide a minimum of import substitution. (Jackson Report, 1984, pp. 175-6)

This statement is quoted at length, not because it makes any contribution to substantial debate on strategies of agricultural development in the region, but because it is the only statement in the chapter on the small South Pacific states. Whilst noting that 'food consumption has become heavily weighted towards processed foods, particularly canned fish' (Jackson Report, 1984, p. 175), other than the above, there is no mention of fisheries in the report. Given that for the smaller states, such as Kiribati and Tuvalu, the only real prospects for increased income generation within the country are from fisheries, this is an alarming omission.

In sharp contrast to the lack of any adequate discussion of agriculture and fisheries, the report places particular stress on tourism and emigration. Indeed tourism is singled out as an area where there are real prospects, despite local opposition (Jackson Report, 1984, pp. 175-6).

The many arguments against tourism are not discussed and the 'social benefits' (Jackson Report, 1984, p. 175) that few local observers have noted, are not identified. Thus what is most remarkable about the chapter on the small states is that it singles out as a growth sector, one which has belatedly become a 'last resort' for these states against real cultural inhibitions, where foreign ownership of the infrastructure is extremely high and the market fluctuating and seasonal, but largely ignores the potential contribution of those sectors of the economy where there are possibilities for both local ownership, economic growth and increased food production. For PNG the report reviews the structure of the economy, noting the maintained significance of the subsistence sector, the emergence of substantial inequalities, and 'the sluggish growth performances' (Jackson Report, 1984, p. 154). The report records the long-established, and now largely ignored, 'eight aims', which reflect 'far sighted policy priorities' being oriented towards 'equitable growth' (Jackson Report, 1984, p. 155); this is virtually the only favourable mention of equity in the report which subsequently notes that 'the cost of the emphasis placed on equity and stability was a neglect of growth-oriented policies in rural areas, particularly in agriculture and agriculture-related service sectors' (Jackson Report, 1984, p. 155). The report then goes on to stress the virtues of agricultural development, in a manner quite absent from the chapter on small states where only cash crop production is considered:

> Food crops in particular deserve higher priority. In contrast to many developing countries that now give higher priority to food crops the subsistence food sector in PNG has been neglected ... However, despite the interest in rural development and equity there is no clear policy for the development of food crops. (Jackson Report, 1984, p. 156)

There is little in this important argument that is not valid for the rest of the South Pacific region. Again there is no reference to fisheries. There is also no analysis of the potential contribution of mining, manufacturing and tourism.

Whilst the chapter on the small states only hints at the need for population policies, although the review elsewhere notes 'the urgency of population issues in Papua New Guinea and other South Pacific countries' (Jackson Report, 1984, p. 62), the PNG section elaborates on this theme, concluding that 'It seems surprising that the Government of PNG has no population policy' (Jackson Report, 1984, p. 156). This is an important concern, especially since PNG has abandoned its previous (limited) commitment to reducing the rate of population growth. Similar opposition to the development of a population policy is apparent elsewhere in the Pacific, especially in the Solomon Islands (Connell, 1983), and the need for new initiatives is increasingly critical. The report also stresses the serious shortage of skilled workers, and notes that 'in the short-term, less skill-intensive patterns of social and economic development should be planned' (Jackson Report, 1984, p. 165). The necessity for a greater level of participation of women in government and business (Jackson Report, 1984, p. 157) is emphasised;

again these are issues that are also relevant in the smaller states. In each of these areas the need for more appropriate human resources policies is increasingly apparent and the report has wisely drawn attention to them.

Whilst focusing on the particular importance of the small Pacific states the review makes the surprising initial statement:

> The region receives the most aid, per capita, in the world although compared with other regions the need for aid is marginal. Even where poverty exists in statistical terms, the quality of life is high. (Jackson Report, 1984, p. 167)

Perhaps the most relevant paragraph (10.33) in both the regional chapters is that on basic needs which, for PNG at least, notes that child malnutrition is a problem, and that low-cost community education programs, alongside more emphasis on subsistence food production, the development of a population policy and more female participation in development would contribute towards resolving these problems (Jackson Report, 1984, pp. 156-8). Subsequently, the report also notes the need for more attention to be given to primary and vocational education, rather than secondary and tertiary education (Jackson Report, 1984, pp. 164-5), although its main thrust is for development-related tertiary education to be undertaken in Australia. All these issues could equally be stressed for all parts of the region, and since these are not issues that are currently the topics of significant debate at the highest levels there, the report's concern is thus particularly appropriate. Yet, apart from such passing references, welfare objectives of aid delivery are scarcely mentioned. The two chapters emphasise strategies directed towards achieving economic growth based on the underlying theme of the review that 'Aid alone cannot achieve development. Domestic policies of developing countries are the critical component of growth with equity' (Jackson Report, 1984, p. 3). This is a reflection of a major World Bank theme in development, the need for Redistribution with Growth (Chenery et al., 1974); here, significantly, the primacy of growth has been restored even for small countries where external constraints on internal decision -making are enormous.

Had the committee sought to establish a basis for a more humanitarian perspective on aid distribution in the region it would not have been difficult to achieve. The report singles out Kiribati and Tuvalu as extreme cases where even massive inputs of aid would be unlikely to achieve economic growth (Jackson Report, 1984, p. 8). They could equally have stressed that these and other states, most obviously Papua New Guinea, have real problems in meeting basic needs of the national population. It is useful to establish the significance of some of these needs in contrast to the perspective of 'subsistence affluence' that the committee have chosen to adopt uncritically, although its principal proponent has revised and limited his earlier perspectives (Fisk, 1982).

There is much evidence that in some contexts levels of welfare are neither adequate nor improving; for example, in Melanesia, there is currently a resurgence of malaria, in part because of the limited allocation of resources to preventive measures. In PNG there is also a resurgence of yaws especially in areas of poor nutrition. In the past decade cholera epidemics have claimed many lives in both Truk (Federated States of Micronesia) and Kiribati. In terms of nutrition the PNG National Nutrition Survey of 1978 found that 38 per cent of children could be classified as malnourished (Lambert, 1978); there is good evidence that nutritional status is least adequate where access to government services is poorest (Townsend, 1982, p. 79), and 'reports of food shortages are becoming increasingly common' (Harvey, 1982, p. 73). In Kiribati recent figures suggest that more than 10 per cent of pre-school children are malnourished and 'night-blindness' has become widespread in Tarawa (Connell, 1985a). More widely in the South Pacific there has been an epidemic increase in nutritional disorders and nutrition-related non-communicable diseases such as obesity, iron-deficiency anaemia, cardiovascular disease, hypertension, diabetes, gout and hyper-uricaemia, bowel and intestinal cancers and disease (Thaman, 1983). The rapidly increasing body of literature describing health and nutrition problems in the South Pacific region has been extensively reviewed (e.g. Kripps, 1982; Thaman, 1982, 1983; R Taylor, 1983; Zimmet et al., 1983) and a series of strategies for prevention, control and cure have been recommended, which could be implemented through appropriate forms of external assistance.

Basic problems of limited resources are often exacerbated by natural hazards, and vulnerability, in some contexts (Campbell, 1984; Currey, 1980), is actually worsening. In some areas, such as Kiribati, the level of access to basic amenities, such as sanitary provision or adequate water supplies, is extremely low (Love, 1982). In PNG especially, access to primary education is limited and in 1979 the proportion of children aged seven to twelve attending school was 59 per cent (Weeks and Guthrie, 1982, p. 26); in low-income urban areas of Port Moresby the proportion is no more than 31 per cent (Morauta, cited by Weeks, 1984). These are not isolated instances of deprivation and disadvantage, chosen selectively from more positive evaluations, nor are they the conclusions of obscure reports, rather they are objective statements about situations where basic needs are inadequately satisfied and, in many cases, where the prospects of national economic growth contributing to an improvement in that situation are poor.

Inevitably, the report does not stress how Australian aid might contribute most to resolving these problems, even where they are discussed in the case of PNG, although it does note the widely held view that aid would have been used most effectively if it had been tied to particular projects, specifically noting that training and technical assistance has been limited because of this (Jackson Report, 1984, p. 161). The report further accurately notes that PNG strongly prefers budgetary aid, a situation which has discouraged recourse to other concessional sources of finance to the extent that 'on occasions, PNG has actually been reluctant to accept offers of aid from other donors because the conditions under which the aid was offered were not sufficiently generous' (Jackson Report, 1984, p. 161). But the nettle has not been grasped here, although for other regions the report stresses the value of project aid (see Connell, 1985b).

The most novel and thus striking feature of the report is its particular emphasis on the needs of small states: 'Australia should develop special expertise in the economic development of small island states and associated regional issues to improve aid delivery to such countries' (Jackson Report, 1984, p. 8). Kiribati and Tuvalu are singled out as countries with unusual and particular needs, giving them a significance hitherto, and still, denied to all other states except Papua New Guinea and perhaps Indonesia:

> Kiribati with a population of 60,000 and Tuvalu with a population of 8,000 have special problems. Their remote and minute land areas are heavily populated. They depend very much on remittances from their emigrants and on foreign aid. Their long-term development prospects are discouraging. In view of structural problems which are beyond their control and beyond the reach of aid, Australia should make available limited opportunities for immigration from Kiribati and Tuvalu. (Jackson Report, 1984, p. 8)

Disappointingly, the main body of the text scarcely extends on this summary; the report does however note that Australia 'must identify the limits on development and learn from past mistakes. Some responses by Australia should go beyond traditional ideas of aid' (Jackson Report, 1984, p. 181) by establishing an immigration quota for the two countries. To single out two more countries, for which Australia should go beyond 'traditional ideas of aid' is radical; to subsequently state that Australia should establish a special immigration quota for them is almost revolutionary. It is tantalising, therefore, that the Jackson Report expands on the policy and its selectivity no further.

The report singles out Tuvalu as having 'a unique combination of minute size, tiny population and an almost total lack of resources. It is a state without internal economic viability, and it will have to remain dependent on remittances and aid' (Jackson Report, 1984, p. 117); it is also identified as having additional problems of land shortage, urban drift and high youth unemployment (Jackson Report, 1984, p. 171). Kiribati is seen as exemplifying the problems of distance and communications; 'the country consists of islands with a total land area of 690 square kilometres spread over a sea area of 3.5 million square kilometres and remote from the nearest developed country market' (Jackson Report, 1984, p. 171). Although the review identifies no other specific problems in Kiribati those listed for Tuvalu are equally serious there.

In a number of areas of basic needs, including health, nutrition and unemployment, both countries fare less well than many others in the region and, although the report reiterates that 'by global standards poverty is not evident in the region' (Jackson Report, 1984, p. 168), there is evidence that, by most conventional definitions, it is increasingly apparent, especially in Kiribati. At the same time the opportunities for improving basic needs, achieving economic growth and minimising poverty are unusually restricted and actively worsening (Connell, 1984, 1985a,b). All the evidence suggests that the serious development problems experienced in Kiribati and Tuvalu cannot adequately be met by internal policies, or regional cooperation, and that higher levels of aid will only marginally contribute to economic growth (as opposed to improved welfare). This is certainly the case in Niue which has one of the highest levels of per capita aid in the world and also one of the highest incidences of emigration.

Underlying this shift towards a policy which conflicts with present immigration policy (irrespective of aid policies) are a number of factors which may continue to give it political acceptability. First, because of the limited prospects for economic growth in Kiribati and Tuvalu most aid to these two countries has been for social infrastructure; emigration might reduce the costs of basic needs provision in the long term. Second, a policy allowing increased migration to Australia would enable 'aid' funds to be expended in Australia. Thirdly, migration to Australia would be likely to be of economic benefit to Australia and, through remittances, to Kiribati and Tuvalu. But these are trivial reasons; its political acceptability may well depend on the strategic benefits to be gained from the further subversion of Kiribati and Tuvalu, through international migration, into the Australian political economy, a situation roughly parallel to that already existing for American Samoa and New Zealand associated territories. The strategic situation of these two independent states, both former colonies of the United Kingdom and now in a Central Pacific power vacuum, prompted Australia to establish a High Commission in Kiribati in 1981 and may also have influenced the Jackson Committee to choose this unusual policy which has massive implications for other small states in the region which have previously requested migration rights in Australia.

AID AND ABSORPTION

Outside PNG, Australia's bilateral aid program for the South Pacific recognises particular problems of manpower, development, communications and transport, energy resources, rural development and the improved utilisation of natural resources (ADAB, 1984d, pp. 39-40). There is a $300 million indicative planning figure for aid to the region over the five year period from 1983 to 1988; this is quite unlike other regional aid programs, where there is a one year commitment, and is intended to give island governments greater flexibility in situations where aid absorption is often difficult. A second initiative in the region is the provision of a reserve fund for multi-country projects such as recent projects on opthalmology, hydrography and family planning. Thirdly, provision has been made for assistance through a small grants scheme, whereby Australian overseas missions have increased powers and finance for appraisal, approval and monitoring of small projects including village self-help activities. Fourthly, the South Pacific program has been willing to meet the local costs of projects and, in certain cases, their running costs, the financing of development banks (see below), joint venture funding and direct assistance to states in the preparation of proposals for assistance (Ingram, 1980, p. x; 1983 p. 105). Fifthly, at the start of 1984, a Pacific Regional Team was established in Sydney to respond more directly and quickly to requests for advice and assistance in areas such as agricultural development, manpower planning and engineering. In all these areas Australian approaches to aid delivery have both been moulded towards the needs of very small states and demonstrate much greater innovatory capability than is suggested in the Jackson Report; in this area the organisation of aid delivery is in advance of its review.

Many of the priority projects requiring funding in the South Pacific are small but cannot be implemented by ADAB without involving the equivalent amount of work for much larger projects. To ease the absorptive capacity of recipient countries, since 1976 grants have been made to national development banks, initially those of Fiji, Western Samoa and Tonga (SSCFAD, 1977, pp. 738-9), and later those of the smaller countries which subsequently established banks. This policy has a range of important advantages notably that bank loans can reach more disadvantaged groups, especially in rural areas, and can also contribute to the improvement of local infrastructure (Cole, 1983a,b; Connell, 1985b).

A further innovative element of the Australian aid program since the mid-1970s is the bilateral subsidising of NGO projects, under particular conditions, including that they contribute to locally determined needs, complement national development plans, have wider application and contribute to the needs of the disadvantaged (ADAB, 1983). These BINGO schemes have emphasised training and social welfare programs, and have thus contributed more directly to basic needs provision than other areas of the aid program. Especially in the South Pacific region there have, therefore, been deliberate, innovative and sensible attempts to direct aid resources to local needs, through national institutions.

In recent years increased emphasis has been given to aid for health, education and the provision of social infrastructure and, within the South Pacific, Australian aid policy:

> lays stress on making health care, nutrition, basic sanitation, maternal and child health, family planning, vaccinations, preventative medicine and health education universally accessible to individuals and families in the community at a cost the country can afford to maintain. It emphasises the need for development of human technologies based on scientifically sound methods which are socially acceptable and are appropriate to the communities conditions. (ADAB, 1980 cited by Percival, 1981, p. 74)

Projects such as paramedical clinical teams, sewerage and domestic water supply projects, vaccine production and disease control, population control projects and nutritional projects have been supported. Despite the intended policy orientation, available evidence indicates that relatively small proportions of Australian aid into the region go directly to social development rather than to physical infrastructure. Of the 1982/3 allocation to the South Pacific some $15.8 million (35 per cent) was for public utility provision, $12.7 million (28 per cent) for education, $6.6 million (15 per cent) for economic planning and public administration, $4.5 million (10 per cent) for agriculture, fisheries and forestry and only $536,000 (1.2 per cent) for health (ADAB, 1984b). The infrastructure bias, especially for transport provision, is apparent (see ADAB, 1984d, pp. 41-72) and the program has been criticised for this technological bias, in general (e.g. Allen et al., 1983; Brookfield, 1977; Brown, 1983) and in the specific case of water supply schemes in the Solomon Islands (Roughan, 1983) and Kiribati, because of their orientation, the limited 'spread effects' of physical infrastructure and high maintenance costs.

There is little information available on the success, in any sense, of aid projects in the region or of effective evaluations of similar projects undertaken by other donors. Available evaluations do demonstrate a degree of continued dependence for recurrent costs, urban bias in aid allocation, exacerbated by limited local skilled manpower, so that a number of potentially viable and appropriate projects have been disappointing (McDonald et al., 1982, p. 38). This situation has been noted by each of the two country submissions to the report (Cook Islands, 1983; Tuvalu, 1983). Samana (1984) has drawn attention to the perceived technical failure of aid projects in PNG, whilst ADAB in-house reviews have questioned the economic justification for projects, often because of their limited integration into the local and national economy (notably cattle development schemes), the management capability of local project managers and governments, and the limited extent over which economic (and social) benefits are extended. The faults are not necessarily those of the aid donors (cf. Hoadley, 1981) although the lessons have been learnt by some donors who have consequently put greater stress on rural, redistributive and welfare issues. No aid projects are without flaws; indeed, almost by definition, aid projects are likely to be either marginal to the most pressing development problems or beyond local management and maintenance capabilities.

Most Australian government aid (outside PNG) is administered in grant form, mainly to specific projects; ADAB defines the purpose of funds within the recipient country thus effectively tying their use. There has however been some slight decline in the proportion of untied aid which, by 1982/3, was 65 per cent (although most of this was direct budgetary support to PNG and support for multilateral institution), to allow local purchase of goods. This has been a very slow transition despite consistent demands from within the region to untie Australian aid (eg. Cook Islands, 1983; SPEC, 1983) to avoid the supply of inadequate, inappropriate and expensive imported equipment, especially where this necessitates heavy maintenance costs or much skilled labour. In the case of PNG, where Australia provides budgetary aid, absorptive capacity is a more complex issue, and local debate principally revolves around the nature of dependence (Connell, 1985b). The probability of the 'aid weariness' that befell overall global aid in the 1970s, due primarily to limited growth and to the limited accountability of recipients for aid funds, has also prompted greater pressures for more project aid, and hence greater accountability, and for a general increase in the monitoring and accountability of aid projects (e.g. Cole, 1983b; FFH, 1983; D Healey, 1983). In the case of PNG especially, this is likely to lead to a greater degree of Australian tied project aid, a situation welcomed by some (eg. Australia Department of Trade, 1983, p. 12). The arguments against project aid (and aid tying) are made on the grounds of national pride, sense of independence and maintenance of the flexibility that enables PNG to make its own choices (Garnaut, 1981, p. 182; cf. Wilkinson, 1976; Conroy, 1982; Allan and Hinchliffe, 1982). Space precludes the adequate consideration of this important argument (see Connell, 1985b).

The Australian Minister of Foreign Affairs, Mr Hayden, has noted that 'for our part, we must be extremely fussy about who benefits from our aid programs' (Hayden, 1983a, p. 122). The ability to absorb aid increases the likelihood of receiving it; this situation may occur in Fiji and perhaps elsewhere. The absorptive capacity of small Pacific states is necessarily limited and their particular needs are thus rather different from those of larger states; both Japan and West Germany are reported to have experienced problems in giving aid because of problems in reconciling their own guidelines with regional needs (Baker, in SSCFAD, 1979, p. 1308; cf. Conroy, 1982, p. 96). By contrast not only has the Australian aid program generally attempted to meet the specific problems of small states but, of all Australia's regional programs, the South Pacific program has been in many ways the most innovative.

Aid given to multilateral organisations by Australia is also directed towards the South Pacific region. Major United Nations agencies, organisations such as the Asian Development Bank, and two regional organisations, the South Pacific Commission (SPC) and the South Pacific Bureau for Economic Cooperation (SPEC) are all partly funded by Australia. Multilateral organisations have some advantages in that their activities minimise overtones of charity and interventionism, they have the ability to mobilise capital and expertise beyond the capacity of individual donors and they can coordinate aid from both multilateral and bilateral sources (Percival, 1981, pp. 76-7) but Australian multilateral contributions have lagged behind those of some other donors accounting for, in 1980/1, some 19 per cent of total Australian aid, although by 1983/4 that proportion had risen to 24 per cent. The extent to which international institutions contribute to development in the South Pacific region is reviewed elsewhere (Connell, 1985b), suggesting that the regional organisations are more capable of assisting those small countries that are without the expertise or administrative capacity to properly elaborate requests, evaluate or implement projects and can, therefore, reduce absorptive and manpower problems. In its establishment of the Pacific Regional Team, which should increase the possibilities for funding and assisting such organisations, ADAB once again appears to be in advance of a report which attaches little value to small organisations.

CONCLUSION

It is scarcely more than a decade since the Australian Development Assistance Agency (ADAA) was established by the Whitlam Labor government (see Chapter 12); characteristically it was heralded by the Prime Minister, Mr Gough Whitlam, in terms that had little to do with foreign policy and strategic interests: 'the Government will look to the agency for the development of innovative policies responsive to the needs for economic self-reliance and social justice in developing countries ...' (Whitlam, cited by Percival, 1981, p. 19). Under this and the subsequent Fraser Liberal government (despite the absorption of ADAB into the Department of Foreign Affairs) the ADAB commitment to social justice was largely maintained and renewed (eg. ADAB, 1981, pp. 15-16; Percival, 1981, p. 62). Although this commitment has not always been translated into more effective aid projects, ADAB has consistently attempted to develop innovative programs to serve the special needs of the small states of the region and to address aid to issues of welfare and equity. Over the past decade Australian aid in the South Pacific has been increasingly innovative, and has attempted to assist in stimulating economic self-reliance and social justice, even though these attempts have sometimes fallen on stony ground. These innovations are not reflected in the Jackson report which paints a much more conventional picture of aid distribution through emphasising economic growth, in situations where growth is difficult to achieve and absorptive capacity is poor. In doing so the report minimises increasing poverty problems and thus the necessity for basic needs provision. This conventional neo-classical approach stems very much from the orientation of Helen Hughes:

> Perhaps the strongest lesson of the development experience of the last 30 years is that no matter how well or ill countries are endowed naturally ... their economic performance depends primarily on their commitment to growth and the appropriateness of the policy framework they evolve to implement their growth strategy. (Blazic-Metzner and Hughes, 1982, p. 85)

Even if this were 'a prevailing orthodoxy' (Taylor, 1984a, p. 26) and in global terms this is far from the case (Stewart, 1985) the weight of evidence for most of the South Pacific, much of it submitted to the review, suggests that it is largely irrelevant simply because significant economic growth is improbable. The report's view that Kiribati and Tuvalu have 'structural problems which are beyond their control and beyond the reach of aid' (Jackson Report, 1984, p. 8) has a greater regional relevance.

Underlying this conservative economic orientation is a narrowly focused political perspective:

> Successive Australian governments have seen the South Pacific region as having fundamental strategic and political importance to Australia. Australia needs to communicate across the region with its allies and trading partners, to move freely in the region, and to have access to its ports and facilities. Above all Australia wants a region which is independent, cohesive and free of super-power rivalries. Political or economic crises that destabilise the region would be most unfortunate. (Jackson Report, 1984, p. 170)

There is nothing in this bald and opportunistic statement that smacks of either mutual respect, genuine assessment of development potential and problems or the role of aid in contributing to self-reliance. The limited response to consistent themes recurring in regional submissions, including those from countries, even suggests that the report was designed more to convert many of those individuals and groups who made submissions rather than consider and respond to those submissions. A prominent South Pacific islander argues that aid:

> perpetuates the feelings of superiority and inferiority fostered initially during the period of colonialism, helps to maintain paternalism in the relationships between communities and between sections of communities, contributes to the erosion of the sense of self -respect that people have of themselves as individuals or as groups, and leads to all kinds of cynical and corrupt practices. (Hau'ofa, 1985, p. 2)

The Jackson Report cannot escape such criticism. In a situation where none of the committeemembers had extensive expertise in the region, where their visits to the region were little more than tokenism and where the report was intended to be an advisory document rather than a policy blueprint these limitations are unfortunate.

Whilst self-interest is essential to the national policies of a democratic state, as much in foreign affairs as in other aspects of policy, it should not produce this minimal emphasis on welfare (and its contribution to economic growth). There is no question of the strategic significance of the South Pacific region to Australia but the extent that this has here influenced potential aid-giving strategies is surely too great. Policies which are beneficial to Australian interests are inherently less likely to be beneficial than policies oriented to the (diverse) interests and needs of the South Pacific states.

The political and strategic influences on the proposals of the Jackson Committee are apparent throughout the report, but nowhere more so than in its rationalisation of the aid bias to small countries (Jackson Report, 1984, p. 46), the constant reiteration of the 'special relationship' with PNG, the consideration of New Caledonia as being important only if France withdraws (Jackson Report, 1984, p. 171) and the novel approach to the needs and incorporation of Kiribati and Tuvalu. Were Australian economic interests of greater concern in the region, blatant political interests might have been less in evidence (although the absence of a humanitarian perspective on the basic needs of Pacific islanders does suggest that even this may not be so). Nonetheless, the drawing of the

South Pacific on to a global stage, in association with domestic economic difficulties, has necessarily led to the growing strategic significance of the region for several metropolitan countries; this is now widely perceived and may result, as elsewhere (Wood and Smith, 1984), in aid policy becoming competitive rather than constructive.

For the South Pacific states the significance of aid rests on its role of contributing to development, that is some combination of economic growth and needs provision. Economic growth is essential and even PNG, the largest country in the region, and with the most varied natural resources, has an economic growth rate akin to those of the bottom half of sub-Saharan African countries; the population growth rate is as high as those countries and such social indicators as life expectancy, education level and access to health facilities arennnso similar to those countries. This lack of growth is reflected in a lack of equity and increased inequality in income distribution and access to education, health facilities and jobs (Hughes, 1984). In these circumstances the then PNG Minister for Foreign Affairs and Trade, Mr Rabbie Namaliu, has stated that, alongside the decline in the real value of Australian aid, the PNG Government has been capable only of 'continuing to maintain, and even to make modest provision for extending, services to the people' (Namaliu, 1984). Elsewhere, whilst incomes and services may be distributed more equitably, the prospects for economic growth are extremely poor; Howlett has gone so far as to argue:

> that 'economic development' is a spurious concept for the Pacific ... Opportunities for achieving real self-reliance through structural transformation are minimal. 'Economic development' is patently the wrong measure for the Pacific. The development effort to date, assisted substantially by aid, has achieved little in reducing economic dependence, in stabilising production and markets, in reducing or averting social crises, or in bringing about a degree of balance between population and resources in the islands, although improvements in material welfare have been achieved. Firmer recognition is needed that island socio -economies have inherent and enduring limitations. (Howlett, 1983, p. 1)

This situation implies that aid should be channelled into those few areas where there are limited but real prospects of economic growth (notably in agriculture and fisheries), that aid directed towards social services provision and maintenance will be necessary to maintain welfare at current standards in a number of countries and contribute to economic growth (see Connell, 1985b) and that aid must be tailored to the individual needs of small states, each of which experience a particular series of problems and possibilities. Support for regional institutions, such as the South Pacific Bureau for Economic Cooperation SPEC (and the Pacific Forum and Forum Fisheries Agency) , the South Pacific Commission (SPC), the Pacific Islands Development Program and the University of the South Pacific, would both encourage a sense of collective identity in the region (cf. Harries Report, 1979, p. 117) and increase the amount of aid that might be channelled through those multilateral agencies that have extensive expertise in the region. This would not remove serious national concern over foreign influence and the tying of aid (Namaliu, 1984, p. 3), but it would be a step in the right direction; historical accident, strategic and commercial interests are likely to result in more serious biases and more overwhelming external ties. The perspectives from the South Pacific are thus very different from the perspective from Canberra.

Critical to actual Australian aid policy has been the acceptance of the view that:

> It is essential for a fruitful aid relationship that it be based upon the principal of mutual respect and that the precise development goals sought through the aid program are mutually understood and acceptable. (Ingram, 1983, p. 103)

When those goals are articulated in the Jackson Report in primarily strategic and commercial terms, and where they follow similar and earlier statements in the Harries Report (1975), the criticism that has been expressed in some parts of the region (eg. Namaliu, 1984; Hau'ofa, 1985), and which follows similar earlier sentiments (eg. A Hughes, 1983), is expected and indeed essential. The Solomon Islands Secretary of Finance, Mr Tony Hughes, notes the package of 'assistance' that may be offered by donor nations, the difficulties in evaluating, let alone rejecting, comprehensive assistance and concludes:

> The objective of the offeror sic may be military, political, commercial or generally 'strategic'; but for sure the 1980s will see the South Pacific island states being wooed, bribed and bullied as outside influences try to persuade them to cash in large parts of the independence we planned and worked for in the 1960s and 1970s. (A Hughes, 1983, p. 259)

Likewise, Herr (1984, p. 36) notes that 'the nation-destroying effects of aid dependency loom so large over the South Pacific at the moment that it is impossible to suggest that more aid will provide any automatic advantage to the South Pacific or to the prospective donors'. The content of aid is critical, hence regional concerns over the authoritarian thrust of the report, with its neglect of expressed Pacific beliefs, attitudes and priorities, are substantial.

For the South Pacific the 'strings' that are attached to aid are strategic and commercial; few would dispute valid Australian interests in both these objectives, though there is obvious scope for debate on the extent and content of that interest. What is disappointing about the Jackson Report is that it scarcely seeks to review, let alone impose, the kinds of 'strings' that are more appropriate, that is that aid be tied to projects that seek to ensure national economic growth and/or contribute to greater individual and collective welfare and social justice. And 'equity' was the first topic scheduled for the review.

If aid is to contribute to the reduction of uneven development, there is little to suggest that, in the case of the South Pacific, implementation of the recommendations of the Jackson Report will assist. The only exceptions are in the case of Kiribati and Tuvalu where those exceptionally poor states may be unwilling and inadvertent benefactors of Australia's (and other's) strategic interests. Yet here, too, 'aid to Governments of "poor countries" is one thing, aid to poor people of these countries another' (Seers, 1980, p. 255). By the report's focus on the supposed longer-term interests of nations, and its exclusion of any consideration of the nature of the state (and hence political force), the shorter-term and subnational interests have largely been lost. Thus an advisory report on aid, tabled for subsequent parliamentary debate (when issues of trade and defence will be raised), turns out to have already incorporated these concerns before the debate has begun; in a review of aid, poverty and development should surely have had priority rather than equal status with other foreign policy objectives I contend, along with John White, that, 'the central case for aid is increasingly a moral one, the obligation of the rich to help the poor in such ways as are open to them' (White, 1974, p. 21). Although this is echoed in the report: 'there is widespread agreement that development in the sense of the alleviation of poverty should be the principal objective of aid' (Jackson Report, 1984, p. 59), a view shared by the electorate, this central moral imperative is here subsumed into issues of Australian security and economics; that aid and foreign policy initiative might focus on the poor whilst also serving other interests is scarcely acknowledged even for countries where economic growth is improbable. Pragmatism may triumph over principles but a review should not start from that point. In an age of doubt and confusion it is perhaps not surprising that there is no moral passion here; nor is there a proper sense of humility in the face of often irreconcilable objectives and major, long-term development constraints in countries with quite different, and diverse, cultures from those of Australia. Whilst the review wisely notes that, 'Development is a risky and difficult process' (Jackson Report, 1984, p. 134) this truism seems otherwise forgotten.

ACKNOWLEDGEMENTS

I am indebted to Doug Porter for his comments on an earlier version of this chapter. The present chapter is a shorter version of a longer working paper (Connell, 1985b).

5 IDEOLOGY, AID AND THE PACIFIC MICROSTATES

Michael Taylor

The giving of aid and the reasons for giving aid are nowhere more hotly disputed issues than in Australia following publication of the Jackson Committee's review of Australia's overseas aid program. National self -interest together with humanitarian, moral and ethical reasons are the motives usually proffered in support of aid-giving. However, the OECD now recognises a third and major cause for aid-giving, the maintenance of a viable global system, which coincidentally favours the interests of its DAC (Development Assistance Committee) members. This is obviously the motivation that underpins the Jackson Report. However, in presenting its views and recommendations (which are certainly not the views of many of those who made submissions to it) the Jackson Committee also advocates implicitly, and sometimes explicitly, a particular view of the functioning of national economies within a global system. Unashamedly, the report espouses a dogmatised, free-trade view of the world which links trade, aid and investment within a mythically competitive market framework as the only possible way of achieving the economic efficiency from which social equity can flow. That such simplified and simplistic Utopias have not, do not and will not exist, is only too evident from the report itself which constantly refers to distortions of competition and the competitive ethic which it links to subsidy, protectionism, inefficiency, high costs, lack of exports, the absence of economies of scale and sluggish growth.

The concern of this chapter is that the application of such an unrealistic and simplistic model to the functioning of the small island economies of the Pacific is not just inappropriate but potentially damaging. The Pacific islands may appear insignificant in a global context, but international interest in the functioning of these economies is growing, and, when Papua New Guinea is included, these islands currently receive 59 per cent of Australia's bilateral aid. The model is inappropriate in the sense that it presupposes that lying subsumed within all non-socialist societies is a market economy which is distorted only by the actions of governments. It is potentially damaging in the sense that it prescribes only one way of achieving self-sustaining economic growth and that is through the adoption of outward-looking economic policies promoting export-led growth. Korea and Singapore are raised as models of this form of development but the role of US aid following the Korean War and the massive entrepot function of Singapore created by colonialism, for example, are conveniently forgotten. But the model is potentially damaging in a second and more specific sense in terms of Australian aid. Aid, it is argued, should foster the adoption of policies in recipient countries which create open, export-oriented economies. In other words, a form of blind economism should be a guiding principle in most aid-giving situations and Australia's aid, trade and foreign direct investment should be shackled unquestioningly to the prevailing orthodoxy of the world's most powerful international development agencies -- an orthodoxy which has become nothing more than dogma.

This same dogma, as it is presented in the report of the Jackson Committee, sees trade as being more important than aid for both donors and recipients since, according to the tenets of the model, trade fosters growth and raises incomes by enhancing countries' comparative advantages and improving the internal allocation of resources (Jackson Report, 1984, p. 115). Thus, while a free market is said to benefit all countries (Jackson Report, 1984, p. 34), government protectionism is judged to harm growth by limiting market access, with the corollary that sluggish growth occurs everywhere (Jackson Report, 1984, pp. 115-16). This is also the World Bank's view which maintains that '... price distortions are introduced by governments directly or indirectly in the pursuit of some social or economic objective' and that these are more important than, '... distortions ... caused by monopolistic tendencies in the private sector' (World Bank, 1983, p. 57). The report makes it clear that, in its view, countries with outward-looking policies, which have promoted trade, are the ones that have achieved the fastest growth, have generated the most jobs and have increased wages more than countries that have not adopted those policies (Jackson Report, 1984, pp. 118-19). Only replication of the experience of the NICs, therefore, can bring growth and development.

The model is then extended to embrace private direct foreign investment. Australian enterprises are first chastised for being introverted, protectionist, and uncompetitive, with competitive bidding for aid projects administered through international agencies (which are said to be efficient but which have been criticised elsewhere for being anything but even-handed in the awarding of contracts!) being essential to their education in the 'school of hard-knocks'. For recipient countries, however, private direct investment, especially through joint ventures, is seen as a boon to development, bringing the often cited, but rarely proved, advantages of finance, technology, management, on-the-job training and access to world markets (Jackson Report, 1984, p. 126).

Aid, in the report, is then the junior partner in the trinity — a pump-primer for growth and development. Its purpose in this model is to remove development constraints and not simply to alleviate poverty

(Jackson Report, 1984, p. 59). The implication of the report is that aid is some form of necessary economic evil which can be used to get the developing economies of the Pacific on the 'right' free-trade tracks and transformed into miniature Hong Kongs and Singapores as has been inferred elsewhere (Blazic-Metzner and Hughes, 1982; Hughes, 1984). To quote the report, 'The faster development takes place, the better Australian strategic and economic interests will be served. As development programs succeed, the need for aid will decline and ultimately disappear' (Jackson Report, 1984, p. 23).

For Pacific island states, this model of the world means that current expectations of living standards and public service are too high (Jackson Report, 1984, p. 175). Sectors of future comparative advantage have to be identified and encouraged, and aid should encourage private sector development through development banks. The report suggests that private direct foreign investment in the islands should increase and the development of exports should be encouraged, but not exports entirely dependent upon duty free access to Australia and New Zealand (Jackson Report, 1984, pp. 126, 176, 182). However, a major constraint to development is seen as the size of the public bureaucracies in the island states which the authors of the report consider to be sufficiently large to inhibit private sector development (Jackson Report, 1984, p. 174).

Most of these propositions are open to question. First, the proposition that free markets have ever existed, especially in the 1980s, is open to debate. Second, the presupposition that outward-looking policies favouring export-oriented industrialisation are the exclusive causes of growth is questionable. Indeed, there is a very real possibility that overzealous export promotion by some NICs may have been a cause of neo-protectionism which flourishes today. Furthermore, the contention that distortion of economies is the result of government action alone and not the result of monopoly manipulation by private enterprise must be questioned strenuously. The implication that the operations of multinationals (crudely reified as private foreign direct investment) are benign in home and host countries alike is a demonstrable fallacy. Finally, the implicit assumption that the glibly labelled 'once-and-for-all' costs of structural adjustment in national economies in any way falls short of total social dislocation is a moot point.

This chapter examines, in the context of the Pacific islands and especially Fiji, two of the principal propositions that underpin the ideology upon which the Jackson Report is founded. The first proposition is that free and undistorted trade is possible for the small states of the Pacific. Instead, it is argued here that the very form of island economies is distorted and always has been distorted from the time of first colonisation and the superimposition of commercialism on a subsistence society. The current economies of countries like Fiji and PNG represent cumulative distortion frequently orchestrated by commercial organisations which sought privilege, power and subsidy as a means of generating revenue and profits rather than a quest for some figment called 'efficiency'. Such cumulative distortion means that no free market economy lies thinly cloaked in the island states. The second proposition that is examined is that the operations of multinationals in the island states are benign. The argument is the same. Foreign capital, in the shape of multinationals, seeks mainly monopoly power and transferable revenues that benefit the corporations and not necessarily either home or host countries. The sun-seeking entrepreneurs from Australia and New Zealand that the report sees as setting up benevolent businesses in return for cheap access to tropical island paradises are too thin on the ground to be treated seriously.

CORPORATIONS AND TRADE IN THE ISLAND ECONOMIES

From the outset of discussion, there is a fundamental problem in defining what is meant by a Pacific island economy. There has certainly been much discussion of their smallness and openness (Dommen, 1980; Hughes, 1984; Jalan, 1982; Selwyn, 1975). However, using IMF definitions they barely warrant being called independent economies at all. The opening sections of the balance of payment statistics published by the International Monetary Fund (IMF, 1983, p. xiii), for example, define an economy as 'being comprised of the economic entities that have a closer association with a given territory than with any other territory'.

Within the individual countries of the South Pacific an outstanding feature of their economies is the dominance of foreign-owned companies (Winkler, 1982; Taylor, 1984a), and data for Fiji and Papua New Guinea presented in Table 5.1 demonstrate this point clearly. A very strong inference that must be drawn from this table is that even the larger Pacific island economies (in their formal as opposed to subsistence sectors) are comprised of 'entities' which primarily owe allegience 'elsewhere' rather than to the island microstates themselves. These are economies dominated and, it can be argued, distorted by the activities of foreign capital and companies to which government, in effect, plays only second fiddle.

Indeed, from the very beginning of colonial rule, corporate interests have manipulated the island economies. The shipping services of Burns Philp and Co. Ltd at the beginning of the present century were either subsidised or not supplied, and frequently they were subsidised by both governments in Australia and Missionary Societies (Buckley and Klugman, 1981). Moreover, it was commercial interests that brought settlement and plantation development in the first instance in the New Hebrides (Vanuatu) and German New Guinea (Scarr, 1967). As such the very 'coconut overlay', to use Brookfield's (1973) term, can be interpreted as commercialism hand-in-hand with colonialism rather than the development of some economic comparative advantage also see Fieldhouse (1978) dealing with Lever Brothers operations in the Pacific . It is arguable that coconut plantations would never have been developed as extensively as they were had not the Germans sought colonies, had not

Table 5.1: Foreign control in Fiji and Papua New Guinea

		Fiji (a) % foreign	Papua New Guinea(b) % foreign
1.	Agriculture	56.2	96
2.	Mining and quarrying	99.6	100(c)
3.	Manufacturing	85.6	86
4.	Electricity, gas, water	100.0	n.d.
5.	Construction	28.9	92
6.	Wholesale, retail, restaurants	84.9	) 89
7.	Hotels, etc.	81.8	)
8.	Transport, communication, stage	77.8	89
9.	Banking and finance	93.2	) 88
10.	Real estate, business services	34.5	)
11.	Community, social, personal services	27.4	90
12.	Not classified	87.6	n.d.

Notes:

n.d. = no data
(a) per cent turnover (1980) of all companies with foreign equity
(b) per cent value of shares (1974) held by foreigners
(c) excludes Bougainville Copper Ltd.

Sources: Carstairs and Prasad (1981); Donaldson and Turner (1978).

Australian, French and British adventurers sought to exploit the islands and force colonial annexation in their wake and had not subsidised shipping services, through Burns Philp and Nord-Deutcher Lloyd, for example, and the subsidised competition that went on between these companies, created unrealistic transport networks. Indeed the very processes of monetisation and commercialisation of island economies were company-based processes right down to the smoking parties the Germans organised for the natives in New Guinea to create demand for trade goods which could be satisfied only through the provision by the natives of wage labour which the Germans so earnestly desired.

Notwithstanding tariffs and government subsidies, it can be argued that the distortion of prices in the modern island economies is principally a function of corporate power, not government power, which results in countries like Fiji receiving too little for their exports and paying too much for their imports. The case, unfortunately, can only be argued anecdotally as corporate manipulation remains removed from the public gaze while agencies such as the World Bank (1983, pp. 57-63) expend great energy in pointing the bone at government policy-makers rather than corporate policy-makers.

The production of sugar is the foundation of the Fiji economy. In the mid 1970s, however, New Zealand bought its sugar from Fiji very cheaply paying only $NZ 113 per tonne in 1974. As Bellam (1980) pointed out, this deal meant that refined sugar went into the New Zealand market at less than half the price that prevailed in the UK at that time. This undervaluation of Fiji's exports arose from a long-term inter-governmental agreement on trade which allowed the New Zealand Minister of Trade and Industry to boast that New Zealand would have cheap sugar for a decade.

Much more evidence exists for corporate manipulation of import prices, with Fiji being made to pay above the odds. For example, Australasian multinationals holding distribution franchises have forced the supply of soap powder into the Fiji market to be directed through Australia rather than allow the international manufacturer of the product involved to import directly into Fiji from lower cost sources in Asia (Taylor, 1983). In the context of maize imports, actual prices have been cited in the Fiji Parliament. In this instance New Zealand maize that could be bought in Fiji at $NZ185 per tonne, FOB, was quoted for supply through the General Foods group at $195 per tonne while the same maize was going to Papua New Guinea at only $NZ163 per tonne. As Nand stated in the Fiji Parliament, 'All I can say is that for 10,000 tonnes of maize, this would amount to well over $200,000 finding its way into the pockets of some representative of the conglomerate in New Zealand' (Nand, 1983, p. 1296).

It is not just prices for island imports and exports that are manipulated by foreign-owned companies, even the volume of imports may be affected. The strongest evidence of this practice comes from the operation of produce importers in New Zealand. Thus, Howie (1973, p. 65) accused the Fruit Distributors Co. in New Zealand of operating a '...deliberate policy of restrictive imports of bananas from the Pacific (notably Fiji and the Cooks)'. Bellam (1980) has expanded upon this point more recently showing how corporate interests in New Zealand have served to restrict the volume of trade in primary produce between the island states and New Zealand and how they have also inflated import prices into New Zealand.

In the context of 'duty-free' shopping and the sale of tourist goods in Fiji, detailed information on the manipulation of wholesale prices to the disadvantage of local Fiji retailers has been presented by Britton (1979). Virtually all Fiji's tourist goods are manufactured outside Fiji except for a few simple articles held in artisan shops (about 0.4 per cent of inventories). The importing industry is highly concentrated with Fiji's 19 duty-free importing companies handling 87 per cent of a sample of 140 brand name articles familiar to Australian and New Zealand tourists. Isolation, distance and a small market have the effect of increasing the prices of these goods to some extent. However, most goods are only available in Fiji through subsidiaries of manufacturers or designated distribution agents. As Britton (1979, p. 311) has remarked:

> ... they have considerable commercial leverage with manufacturers due to their location in the larger regional markets of Australia, Singapore, Hong Kong and New Zealand. This market position enables them to acquire distribution rights to subsidiary regional markets in the South Pacific.

With this leverage metropolitan distributing companies can attempt to ensure that duty-free shopping in Fiji does not become too attractive to tourists. Indeed, Britton (1979, p. 313) has maintained that Australian companies such as Morris Hedstrom Ltd, Burns Philp (South Seas) Co. Ltd, Prouds (Fiji) Ltd, Philips Electric (Fiji) Ltd, Hagermeyers Ltd, Farebrothers Co. Ltd and Hardy's (Fiji) Ltd;

> ...have determined wholesale costs in Fiji which preclude Fiji retailers from offering goods to Australian tourists at prices significantly below those prevailing on Australian domestic markets. In some cases, Fiji's wholesale prices (including importers' mark-ups) are above Australian retail prices.

Intense competition in the Fiji retail sector, and especially amongst duty-free dealers, which has been intensified by the contraction of tourism since the heady days of the mid 1970s, has precluded the mounting of any concerted effort to redress this form of import price manipulation.

By and large, multinationals operating in countries like Fiji are not searching for export platforms from which they can attack new markets but are looking simply for markets for their established products and services. This point has been well made for Australian-based companies by Bennett et al. (1981) (Table 5.2). Producing for, or distributing to, overseas markets dominates Australian companies' objectives in overseas investment. By no stretch of the imagination can the Pacific region be seen as an area where export bases would be established. Australian capital, at least, sees only Asian locations in such a light. Thus, in the context of the Pacific microstates a gulf exists between economists' prescriptions and businessmen's perceptions and predispositions.

Even where exports currently exist there will always be tension between corporate interests and microstate aspirations owing to the smallness of these economies. Take for example the hypothetical proposition floated by Burns Philp's chief executive that:

> ...if two countries have a demand for both biscuits and soap, is it not better that one sets up a biscuit factory and the other a soap factory and each allows duty free access to the products of the other. (Pacific Islands Monthly, 1982, April, p. 45)

That this company has both biscuit-making and soap-making interests is immaterial. What is important is that 'One man's rationalisation becomes another man's balance of payments problem, employment problem, development problem and sovereignty issue' (Taylor, 1984a, p. 41).

Table 5.2: The Principal Objectives of Australian Companies Investing Abroad

	Region of investment		
	Pacific % respondents	Asia(a) % respondents	Elsewhere % respondents
Manufacturing for export	3.0	10.4	0.8
Manufacturing for the local market	39.4)	47.8)	38.5)
	) 75.8	) 76.1	)72.9
Distribution of Australian products and services	36.4)	28.3)	34.4)
Other (including no answer)	21.2	13.4	26.2

Note: (a) excluding Japan

Source: Bennett et al. (1981) Table 3.

The rapid expansion of franchising which is evident globally as well as in the Pacific islands also creates problems in the economies of small island microstates. When a global corporation franchises, for example, a Fiji-based company to produce its brand products to serve a broad South Pacific regional market, apparent export-led growth is created in Fiji. The very success of this development can, from Fiji's point of view, also be its undoing. If the franchise expands sufficiently exports to another micro state, it is possible that the global corporation might be encouraged to franchise yet another company in that second state to supply that demand. The second country then obtains import substitution and the prospect of export-led growth, while for Fiji there is a loss of exports and even a loss of jobs. This is no more than a hypothetical example but it shows quite clearly how corporate rationality can fly in the face of national economic planning strategies.

CORPORATIONS AND MONOPOLY POWER

That foreign capital dominates the Pacific island economies is indisputable and, as might be expected, the role of this foreign investment is far from benign. Foreign-ownership in these economies is also highly concentrated and in Fiji 60 per cent of the turnover of foreign companies is from Australian-based companies. What is more, within Fiji the subsidiaries of two Australian companies, WR Carpenter Holdings Ltdl WR Carpenter (South Pacific) Ltd and Burns Philp and Co Ltd Burns Philp (South Seas) Ltd , are of overwhelming significance exercising near monopoly control in aspects of retailing, agriculture, manufacturing, transport and services to the extent that the many arms that these businesses have has led to their being labelled economic octopuses (Rokotuivuna et al., 1973). Notwithstanding the tendency for foreign capital to withdraw from the Pacific Islands in the late 1970s and 1980s (Taylor, 1984a), these companies are still of massive significance within the Fiji economy. The dimensions of the Burns Philp octopus in Fiji in 1982 is demonstrated in Figure 5.1.

There has been much criticism of the operations of these companies from the point of view that they are exploitive, monopolistic and even oligopolistic (Rokotuivuna et al., 1973; Commonwealth of Australia, 1978; Utrecht, 1984; Howard and Chand, 1984). Notwithstanding the programs of localisation they have followed in recent years these criticisms persist. Memories are long. The way that two local organisations in Fiji, Nirajan Bros and the Suva Co-operative Association, lost franchises for the sale of Datsun cars and 'Maxwell House' tea and coffee respectively to Australian monopoly concerns is a case in point (Howie, 1973). More recent takeover activity involving the Wattie group in New Zealand only reinforces those criticisms.

Wattie Industries Ltd was created in New Zealand in 1971 following the merger of J. Wattie Canneries Ltd, General Foods Corporation (NZ) Ltd and Cropper-NRM Ltd. The group is involved in cereal milling, feed milling, ice creams, snack foods, frozen foods, poultry raising, trading, Kentucky Fried Chicken, refrigerated transport and so on. It has been engaged in a large number of takeovers to eliminate competition. To consolidate its animal feed exports to Fiji the Wattie group bought 34 per cent of the shares of Crest Mills (Fiji) Ltd and Crest Hatcheries (Fiji) Ltd, which were themselves Australian-based, in 1981 (Wattie Industries Ltd Annual Report, 1981; Nand, 1983). In July 1981, Fiji's largest locally-owned chicken producing and processing company, Chutes Chicken (Fiji) Ltd, was also taken over in its entirety by the group, in part financed by money borrowed from the Fiji Development Bank. The takeover was opposed in Fiji but no local investors could be found that were willing or able to buy out Chutes Chicken Ltd.

The result for Fiji is that a major portion of the country's poultry industry is now in the hands of one foreign-owned organisation. The corporation, Wattie Industries Ltd, is vertically integrated and so oligopolistic power runs through feed importing, feed production, poultry growing and processing. An estimate of this power is provided in Table 5.3. The hatchery stage of poultry production is still in local, Fijian hands with Crest Hatcheries only producing 10 per cent of all day-old chicks. From the growing stage onwards Crest's magnified oligopolistic power is now felt. Crest Mills Ltd has 42 per cent of stock feed market and is the route through which NRM Ltd in New Zealand can export grain into Fiji. Watties' enlarged interests in poultry growing give it 27 per cent of that particular market in Fiji but that is only the portion of the market that is directly controlled. Other growers of chicks in Fiji are contracted to the major companies, like Chutes and Crest, who supply them with day-old chicks. These major companies collect the grown chicks and pay the growers a contract price less the cost

Table 5.3: The Oligopolistic Position of Wattie Industries Ltd Interest in the Fiji Poultry Meat Industry

Stage of production	Wattie Industries Ltd interests	% market share	production
Hatcheries	Crest Hatchery (Fiji) (Ltd)	10	8000-9000 chicks per week
Feed millers	Crest Mills (Fiji) Ltd	42	15,000 tonnes capacity per year
Growing	Chutes Chicken Ltd) Crest Mills (Fiji) Ltd)	27	787,500 birds per year
Processing	Chutes Chicken Ltd Crest Mills (Fiji) Ltd	43.0) 19.5) 62.5	1655 tonnes in 1981
Marketing	Atomistic retail structure General Foods holds Kentucky Fried Chicken franchise		retail margin $F0.60 per bird

Source: Confidential.

of the day-old chicks and the poultry feed. Therefore, at the processing stage, the Chutes/Crest combine products over 1600 tonnes of poultry meat each year which represents almost two-thirds of total output in Fiji. At the retailing end, the company operates refrigerated distribution to an atomistic retail structure. However, it is also significant that, within the Wattie stable, the General Foods Corporation of New Zealand Ltd, which has poultry production interests in New Zealand and Thailand, also holds the Kentucky Fried Chicken franchise in Fiji and opened its first store in Suva in July 1982 (Keith-Reid, 1982).

It has been suggested in government circles in Fiji that the foreign -owned oligopolistic structure of the poultry meat industry will tend to adversely affect pricing for the least advantaged and still locally-owned group in the industry -- the contract growers. They are now simply subordinated subcontractors as are other local companies in furniture making and clothes making in Fiji (Taylor, 1984b). The same vertically integrated multinational structure has been felt by some to have additional ramifications. First, it allows the oligopolist to out-price its competitors while second, and most importantly, it invites transfer pricing on imports, putting tax revenue in Fiji at risk (confidential sources).

But this example of Wattie Industries Ltd in Fiji does not end with the poultry industry. A second arm of this corporate empire is Tip Top Ice Cream producing frozen foods and ice cream from imported New Zealand milk powder and here, too, the quest for monopoly is apparent. At the beginning of 1982 three companies (including Lees Ice Cream and Katos Ice Cream) were in competition with Tip Top and Tip Top was

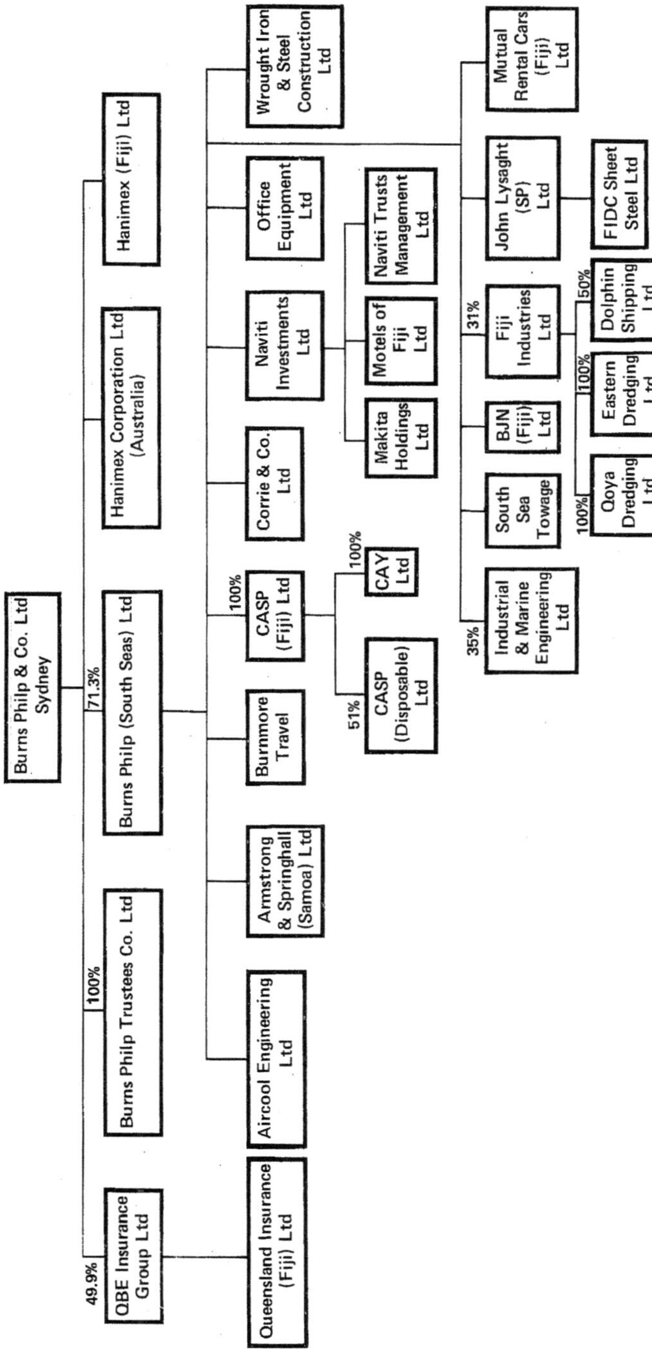

Figure 5.1: Burns Philp Penetration of the Fiji Economy, 1982

losing market share. By adopting tactics taught in New Zealand, two of the competitors were forced from the scene leaving, as a company newsletter remarked, only one more to go (General Foods Corporation, 1982).

What is shown by these examples is that while important multinationals in countries like Fiji are actively seeking oligopolistic power and control, governments and local business are often too small and indecisive to institute and police any effective countermeasures. Instead, multinational corporations are free to transfer to other countries, including tax havens, the value they create in Pacific island microstates (i.e. fractions of revenue and profits channelled through intra-corporate transfers). In effect, multinationals can establish syphoning mechanisms that allow income or value to be transferred from 'peripheral' to 'core' regions.

An estimate of the magnitude of such value transfers from the periphery has been made recently using data for Fiji (Taylor, 1984b). Cast within a business organisations framework, this analysis recognises a large number of intra-organisational flows that were possible between a parent and subsidiary in the same corporation (Plasschaert, 1979; Robbins and Stobaugh, 1973). The first flow refers to intra-firm trade and payments for goods, with firms charging themselves 'non-neutral' as opposed to 'arms length' prices. Two, more rigid, channels for value transfer are equity and investment while a more flexible conduit for the transfer of earnings is the payment of dividends. Loans to subsidiaries and the payment of interest on those loans are also convenient and flexible routes of retrieving income created in subsidiaries. However, fees charged for services provided by the parent are perhaps the most manipulable conduit available to the multinational enterprise. These fees divide into three sets: fees for intangible property (including royalties and patents), fees for services (including management and accounting), and fees for indivisible head office overheads. Finally, the timing of payments can be modified to the advantage of the organisation as a whole rather than the individual subsidiary. A range of payments can be either anticipated or delayed including management fees, royalties and even trade credits.

In addition, three inter-organisational conduits exist for the transfer of value: trade, trade credit and payments for intangible property (royalties, patents and so on). The trade and intangible property conduits reflect the dominance and subordination of companies in commercial relationships which are cemented in contractual arrangements, subcontracting, franchising and licensing. The trade credit conduit recognises the temporal dimension of this subordination amongst autonomous enterprises as, for example, it is well known that small firms have great difficulty in managing the trade credit they are forced to give to larger, dominant companies (Davis and Yeomans, 1974).

Balance of payments figures and trading loss estimates can be assigned to these channels or conduits for value transfer, and this has been attempted for Fiji in Table 5.4. The estimates are crude, espec-

Table 5.4: The Corporate Transfer of Value into and out of Fiji, 1980 ($F 000)

	Receipts	Payments	Net flow in(+)out(-)
1. Equity contributions			
(i) overseas investment in Fiji (incl. real estate)	5923	1859	+4064
(ii) Fiji investment overseas	328	2133	-1805
2. Loans	4259	6480	-2221
3. Dividends	n.d.	9841	-8352(a)
4. Interest on overseas loans (private)	n.d.	5405	-3879(a)
5. Fees for intangible property (commissions, patents, royalties, copy-right, brokerage and estimated reinsurance)	922	5785	-4863
6. Fees for services			
(i) operating expenses	15598	n.a.	+15598
(ii) expenses of offices agencies and counterparts overseas	n.a.	7238	-7238
(iii) non residents transfers to meet commitments and expenses overseas	8061	10617	-2556
7. Trade	n.a.	n.a.	-17300(b)
Total Transfer			-28552

Notes:

(a) estimates from Carstairs and Prasad (1981), Table 11.
(b) Taylor (1984b), Table 8.2.
n.a. = not applicable
n.d. = no data

Source: Unpublished data supplied by Bureau of Statistics, Fiji, and reproduced in Carstairs and Prasad (1981), Appendix 4; Taylor (1984b).

ially those for trade. The estimates are also very conservative being derived from official statistics. Indeed, they can be considered as minimum estimates of the flow of funds out of Fiji that can be attributed to the dominance and manipulation of foreign capital within that economy. Many caveats must be attached to the data. Notwithstanding the limitations of the analysis, the bottom line is still that over $F28 million is syphoned out of Fiji by multinationals through their dominance in the functioning of the economy. That figure represents in excess of 2 per cent of GNP or approximately $F45 per head of population. It is, in effect, a tax on the population for the priviledge of foreign direct investment.

CONCLUSION

Underscoring the Jackson Report on Australia's overseas aid program is a particular ideology which links trade, aid and foreign investment within a free market framework as the only sound way to achieve economic development. Currently, those three facets of the development formula are seen as 'distorted' by government policies and protectionist attitudes in the business community. The prescription of the report is simple, too simple. Remove the so-called distortions (the shackles) and achieve unlimited growth in the largest and smallest economies alike.

The contention here is that this prescription misreads the motives and aspirations of corporate organisations. Their aims, at least in the Pacific islands, are principally to monopolise and manipulate. In many instances, their reputations are poor and they have not been enhanced by recent takeovers, withdrawals of investment, reductions of transport services and so-called rationalisation strategies. The visibility of Australian investment in the Pacific means that Australia receives most of this criticism. But this is not new (Commonwealth of Australia, 1978).

Now, the Jackson Report would see aid linked to, or at least directly associated with, foreign direct investment. There is no quicker way to tar an aid program with the same brush as the actions of multi- national corporations. This can only do the image of Australian aid un- told harm in the Pacific. Corporations, including the state-owned airlines of the metropolitan countries bordering the Pacific have, or at least are perceived to have, undermined the sovereignty of some newly independent Pacific states through the commercial power they are able to wield (Taylor and Kissling, 1983). Australian commercial interests are all too frequently blind to island sensitivities. There is, therefore, a very real need to see Australian aid completely divorced from the foreign direct investment issue, and even the trade issue, if it is to have credibility in the islands arena.

There is also the concern that the report's prescription for growth and development may not be the only outcome of the forces they would set in train in the islands. The role of corporations in the trade, aid, investment trinity is far from benign. It is quite possible in the light of the discussion in this paper, that aid targeted according to the free trade path to development may stimulate only enhanced economic extraction and value transfer from the Pacific's fragile microstate economies as the corporations gain enhanced monopoly power and local enterprise becomes subordinated and locked into subcontract relationship with them. Any aid policy must guard carefully against being associated with the economic dominance and the value extraction associated newly independent states no matter what their size. An aid policy associated in any way with commercial interests can never be neutral.

NOTES

1 WR Carpenter Holdings is owned by another Australian comany, Griffin Holdings.

6 AUSTRALIA'S OFFICIAL BILATERAL AID TO ASIA

Dean Forbes

The 'near north', as one of my dimly remembered school textbooks labelled Asia, has, for most practical purposes, never been near to the core of public policy formation or public debate in Australia. Therefore, despite Australia's geographic proximity to the 'developing countries', official development assistance has often suffered as a consequence of being an adjunct of diplomacy and foreign policy. Inevitably, this has detracted from the effectiveness of aid. As Viviani and Wilenski (1979, p. 93) commented prior to the formation of the Australian Development Assistance Agency in 1972: 'Diplomatic officers of the department of Foreign Affairs regarded a posting to the aid branch virtually as a black mark in their careers'.

Successive official reviews of the Australian Development Assistance Bureau (ADAB) and Australia's official development assistance (ODA) by the Auditor-General (1981), the Joint Parliamentary Committee on Public Accounts (JCPA, 1982) and the Jackson Report (1984) have done much to establish the importance of a properly administered program of aid. Yet there remains confusion about the aims of Australia's aid program. Some would argue that diplomatic goals still predominate, much against the wishes of the public supporters of the non-governmental aid organisations who propose that humanitarian concerns should be pre-eminent (Eldridge, 1983). The Jackson Report, while not ignoring Australia's diplomatic, strategic and business interests, clearly stated that the purpose of aid 'is primarily for humanitarian reasons to alleviate poverty through economic and social development' (Jackson Report, 1984, p. 3).

However, having defined the goals we must ask 'How do we achieve them?', 'What are the optimal directions for Australian aid?', and 'How do we assess our achievements?'. While I agree with the goals set by the Jackson Report, there is room for debate on the means of bringing them about.

This chapter discusses some types of aid policy decisions which stem from the Jackson Report's recommendations on Australian bilateral aid to Asia. The first part briefly summarises recent trends in Australian aid to Asia and the report's chief recommendations on future aid to

Asia; the second part examines the logic of inter-country allocations of aid, and the third the current question of human rights and aid policy; the fourth part looks at the concept of country-programming in aid, especially the Jackson Report's advocacy of 'aid-for-growth', and the authoritarian overtones of this rationale; and the concluding part of the chapter sets out some alternatives to the report's recommendations on these issues.

TRENDS IN BILATERAL AID TO ASIA

Table 6.1 summarises Australian official bilateral development assistance to select Asian countries since 1978/9.[1] The region as a whole received 26.4 per cent of Australian bilateral aid in 1978/9, and a slightly smaller proportion -- 25.2 per cent -- in the estimates for 1983/4. In 1978/9 money values, Australian bilateral aid increased by 3.2 per cent in the five years from 1978/9, but the Asian share decreased in real terms by 1.6 per cent. On a country-by-country basis, the major increases in Australian aid went to Laos, Mauritius, the Philippines, the Maldives and Bhutan, three of which were low-income countries by World Bank definitions. The main losers were India, South Korea, Malaysia, Bangaldesh and Burma. Paradoxically, India, Bangladesh and Burma are also classified by the World Bank as low-income countries.

There are three different measures of country-share of Australian bilateral aid presented in Table 6.1. In total terms Indonesia is the main recipient, followed by Bangladesh, the Philippines and Thailand. Together they account for two thirds of the Asian allocation, even though in real terms Indonesia's share of Australian aid has declined in the past five years. Altogether six of the top ten Asian recipients of Australian aid were 'low-income' countries, and only one of the top four.

Examining aid distribution measured by cents per capita reveals a strong skew towards small Asian countries. The main recipients were the Maldives, Seychelles, Sri Lanka, Laos and Bhutan, all of which, with the exception of the Seychelles, are low-income countries. Bunched around the middle range with per capita receipts over 22 cents are the Southeast Asian countries and Bangladesh. Right at the bottom are the large South Asian countries -- India (0.3 cents per capita), Pakistan and Nepal -- and China (0.4 cents per capita). A similar pattern emerges from looking at Australian aid relative to GNP (measured by cents of aid per $100 GNP). The island states (Mauritius, Seychelles, Maldives) do best, followed by Sri Lanka, Bangladesh and Burma, and then, considerably lower down the list, the rest of Southeast Asia, Nepal and Pakistan. Australian aid to India and China is only a miniscule proportion of GNP.

The current geographic distribution of Australian aid within Asia reflects an accumulation of circumstances and motivations. Aid to

Table 6.1: Australian Official Bilateral Development Assistance to Select Asian Countries, 1978/9 - 1983/4

	78/9 ($000)	83/4[1] ($000)	Real change[2] 1978/9 - 1983/4 %	1982/3 Cents per capita	1981/2 Cents per $100 GNP	'Low-income countries'[3]
Maldives	303	865	+ 85.5	271.4	53.4	x
Mauritius	781	2,298	+ 91.2	2.2	494.7	
Seychelles	256	449	+ 14.1	106.2	230.7	
Indonesia	36,000	49,074	- 11.4	22.8	4.8	
Malaysia	4,863	4,397	- 41.2	39.3	3.1	
Philippines	6,493	17,339	+ 85.5	29.0	3.7	
Singapore	703	1,362	+ 25.9	39.6	1.3	
Thailand	10,220	16,294	+ 3.6	27.2	2.6	
Burma	8,045	10,076	- 18.6	35.6	15.5	x
Laos	797	2,524	+105.7	46.8		x
Bhutan	233	559	+ 55.8	41.2		x
Nepal	1,026	2,176	+ 37.8	9.6	5.4	x
Sri Lanka	4,368	6,780	+ 0.9	56.8	26.2	x
South Korea	350	233	- 56.9	0.5	0.0	
Bangladesh	20,296	21,605	- 30.8	22.2	20.8	x
India	3,862	2,304	- 61.1	0.3	0.1	x
Pakistan	4,719	7,892	+ 8.7	7.9	4.1	x
China	-	10,156	-	0.4	0.2	x
Total bilateral aid	391,566	621,600	+ 3.2	-	-	

1 Estimates only
2 Using 1978/9 values
3 World Bank definition

Sources: ADAB, 1984a

Singapore and, to a lesser extent, South Korea is partly an historical inheritance, for neither country has a pressing need for development assistance. In contrast, the growth of aid to China, the Philippines and Thailand (though, curiously in real terms bilateral aid to the ASEAN countries as a whole declined by 1.3 per cent in the five years prior to 1983/4) might reasonably be attributed to the growing diplomatic significance of these countries for Australia. How else could one account for the increased significance of the Indian Ocean islands in the Australian aid program, except by reference to their strategic significance?

Yet, underlying this complex tangle of motivations, humanitarian concerns continue to play a role. Half of the top ten Asian aid recipients, by each of the measures used, were low-income countries, and low-income countries received in total 41.5 per cent of the Australian bilateral aid to Asia. However, they accounted for 86.6 per cent of the population, and this does not include low-income Asian countries such as Vietnam and Afghanistan which were not included in the calculations. Even removing China and India from the totals, the remaining low-income Asian countries had 43.8 per cent of the population but received only 33.6 per cent of the Australian aid going to Asia.

Many more factors need to be taken into account before much could be made of these figures, including the type of aid, the absorptive capacity of Asian recipients in the sectors in which Australia specialises, and whether Australia is able to supply the development assistance that is required. Nevertheless, there appears to be a prima facie case for further investigation of whether the current distribution of aid within Asia is an appropriate one for Australia. The overriding reasons for the geographic allocation seem to be political and humanitarian, in that order (cf Eldridge, 1983).

The Jackson Committee took the view that the distribution of Australian aid was too fragmented, and felt that it should be focused on fewer countries:

> This fragmentation has made it difficult to undertake any systematic form of sector or program specialisation within the Australian aid program. Minute amounts of aid, unless given in areas of vital interest to the recipient, amount only to tokenism and do not serve either aid or foreign policy interests. Dispersal has also exacerbated ADAB's problems of administering the aid program in a professional way. (Jackson Report, 1984, p. 139)

There is a potential for confusion in this argument. In fact the committee urges geographic concentration within the Australian aid program, not sectoral concentration. Australia is urged to develop sectoral specialities according to its comparative advantage, but this does not necessarily imply a greater concentration. Already there is a strong concentration in the Australian aid program around agriculture and infrastructure development, which the report recognises as excessive. Therefore, the Jackson Report is urging a greater geographic concentration, and a greater sectoral dispersal of development assistance.

The Jackson Report recommends the implementation of an 'eligibility framework' for rationalising the geographic distribution of aid (Table 6.2). Asian countries are distributed through three of the four categories.[2] The only Asian countries in Category 1 are the Indian Ocean island states; Southeast Asian and smaller South Asian countries are in Category 2; while Category 3 comprises the large South Asian countries and China. All categories are eligible for the general aid instruments,[3] and all but the large Asian countries will be the subject of country programs with forward-rolling budgets. Project aid is to be distributed across all sectors in Category 1 countries, in selected sectors in Category 2 countries, and 'narrowly focused' in Category 3 countries.

Table 6.2: Future Aid Categories Relevant to Asian Countries

	Category	General aid instruments	Projects	Country Programs	Countries included
Indian Ocean island states	1	Yes	In all sectors	Detailed	Maldives, Mauritius, Comoros Seychelles
Southeast Asia	2	Yes	In selected sectors only	Detailed	Indonesia, Philippines, Thailand, Malaysia Laos
South Asia	2	Yes	In selected sectors only	Detailed	Burma, Bhutan, Nepal, Sri Lanka
Large Asian countries	3	Yes	Narrowly focused	In broad terms	Bangladesh, India, Pakistan, China

Source: Jackson Report, 1984, p. 141

Who wins and who loses from this eligibility framework? Keeping in mind that Australian aid is a relatively minor contribution to development assistance in almost all these countries, it is nevertheless clear that some Asian countries are going to do much better than others. First, the Indian Ocean Island states, which are already well provided with Australian aid (Table 6.1), are going to continue to be at the forefront. This will prove something of a bonanza for the Comoros, though it is a puzzle to those who are concerned at the downgrading of Australian aid to the rest of Africa (see Chapter 7 in this volume). Of all the recommendations in the Jackson Report the decision to include the Indian Ocean islands (with the exception of the Maldives) in Category 1 is the most bemusing.

Nepal is another Asian country that might expect to gain substantially from its inclusion in Category 2. By comparison with its neighbouring 'small' Asian countries its per capita share of Australian aid has been modest, although it has been growing (Table 6.1). The remaining Southeast Asian and small Asian countries in Category 2 all stand to gain from their recognition of priority status within the aid program, but the increases will probably be marginal. It may, however, serve to arrest an apparent decline in aid to Indonesia, Malaysia and Burma.

There are three principal potential losers from the eligibility framework. First, within Asia, Bangladesh has been the second most important recipient of aid after Indonesia. Bangladesh was included in Category 3, along with India, Pakistan and China, because it was thought Australia's impact was minor relative to larger national and multilateral aid agencies and, therefore, it was better to focus on smaller countries where the Australian impact was greater. Secondly, India, Pakistan and China -- on a per capita basis small recipients of Australian aid — cannot expect a much greater input. The rapid growth of aid to China in recent years, however, suggests it may well continue to improve its share of Australian aid despite the eligibility framework. Thirdly, a number of countries -- principally Vietnam, Kampuchea and Afghanistan — were not considered in the eligibility framework. Australian aid to these countries is at present very small; the Jackson Report believes the resumption of normal levels of Australian aid to them is a political decision and, therefore, leaves them out of serious calculations.

THE GEOGRAPHIC DISTRIBUTION OF AID TO ASIA

This part of the chapter examines the logic for deciding how to distribute the one quarter or so of bilateral aid funds allocated to Asia. It is tackled at two levels; what is the criteria for the distribution as a whole? and which issues effect particular sets of bilateral relations? Politics and human rights issues are examined more closely.

It has been made clear that the primary purpose of aid, according to the Jackson Report, is humanitarian. That is, its principal goal is to alleviate poverty through economic and social development. However, tagged on to the end of this is a caveat:

> Aid also complements strategic, economic and foreign policy interests, and by helping developing countries to grow, it provides economic opportunities for Australia. (Jackson Report, 1984, p. 3)

This statement bears a close resemblance to the sentiments of the Minister for Foreign Affairs, Mr Hayden, in an article written prior to Labor achieving government:

> development assistance should go to those who most need it and it should be consistent with our own interests. (Hayden, 1983a, p. 117)

Once tied, the knot which binds humanitarian and other interests is hard to unravel. Even if we accept that aid will, if not complement, at least not contradict foreign policy,[4] we are left with the question of how to balance humanitarian and non-humanitarian ends.

The Jackson Committee considered five principal criteria in determining the eligibility requirements for geographical allocation of Australian aid. These were humanitarian concerns, Australia's comparative advantage, recipient country requirements, 'regional responsibilities and traditional links; and Australia's strategic and economic interests' (Jackson

Report, 1984, p. 139). Other factors, such as the ability of the potential recipient to absorb aid, were also taken into account. Yet how did the stated aims of the aid program measure up against the outcome in the substance of the Jackson Report?

The Jackson Report has been very strongly criticised on these grounds. The Community Aid Abroad view is this:

> there is no vision in the Report of what an effective aid program based on humanitarian principles would look like ... the humanitarian principle is used as a justification for the assistance program but Australian skills, economic prospects and issues of political and strategic importance are the basis on which the report rests. (Omedei, 1984, p. 5)

The complaint that the substance of the Jackson Report betrays its own principal goals in favour of the politically expedient is a most serious criticism.

On balance, the politics of aid distribution within the report strongly outweighs the commitment to humanitarian ends. The disproportionate focus on small island countries within Asia, with the possible exception of the Maldives, can only be justified in strategic and foreign policy terms. Similarly, the distinction between small Asian and large Asian countries cannot be explained in terms of humanitarian criteria. All these countries are 'low-income countries' in World Bank terms. Most Australian aid will continue to be project aid thereby minimising the dangers of diffuseness. The only reason for differentiating between large and small Asian countries is the visibility of Australian aid provision, surely a political and not a humanitarian factor. And finally, the strong commitment to the ASEAN countries cannot be divorced from Australian foreign policy. All the ASEAN countries are now 'middle-income' countries. It is true that most have large numbers still in poverty, but the rapid growth rates of the economy are by the Jackson Report's own logic sure to reduce the problems of the poor. Once again, the principal reason for the focus of Australian aid, therefore, must be foreign policy issues.

Although the Jackson Report put humanitarian principles to the front of its argument for the geographic rationalisation of aid, the non-humanitarian political and strategic interests figured prominently in the rationalisation proposals made in the report. There are three main objections to this position. First, it is confused and confusing. Either humanitarian purposes are predominant or they are not -- you simply cannot have your cake and eat it too. Secondly, there is an inherent danger in such a complex mix of humanitarian and political ends, not least of which is the problem of being just too clever and hence confusing to countries in the region. Thirdly, the value of an aid program is seriously undermined when it is used to achieve foreign policy ends.

Humanitarian concerns should figure as the most important reason for Australian aid delivery. Moreover, specific country requirements and Australia's comparative advantage need also be taken into account. However, there are considerable problems, as the Jackson Report demonstrates, in translating these humanitarian goals into a practical framework for allocating aid between countries. The Joint Parliamentary Committee of Public Accounts reasoned:

> If Australian aid were entirely altruistic, the majority would go to Africa, Latin America and the Indian sub-continent. If allocated on entirely 'political' grounds, South-East Asia would be the chief recipient. (JCPA, 1982, p. 14).

On a different tack, the Brandt Report argues that aid flows should be a form of international taxation, in which donor funds are provided on a sliding scale based on national income (Brandt Report, 1980, p. 274). The Community Aid Abroad (CAA) submission to the Jackson Committee argued for a geographical allocation of aid based on a pre-determined formula. The CAA submission put forward the need for a 'logical framework' for the aid program, though also noting the key role of aid staff 'professionalism', 'commitment' and 'determination'. An 'objective' formula for selecting aid recipients was devised, which could also identify appropriate levels of activity, projects, sectors and channels for aid delivery. The formula was as follows: Aid priority = need x effective absorptive capacity x geo/cultural proximity. Detailed definitions of these concepts, the variables upon which they are based, data sources and the mathematical formula are all specified in the submission and do not need to be repeated here (CAA, 1983, pp. 12-21).

The product of the formula was an alternative list of the fifteen top priority countries for the Australian government aid program (Table 6.3). Principal beneficiaries, due to the weighting of population within the measure of needs, included India and China, while Vietnam and Nepal were also in a considerably improved position. Major losers, according to the formula, included the Philippines, Egypt, Sri Lanka and Malaysia. Smaller losses in ranked priority included Thailand and Tanzania, and to a lesser extent, Indonesia, Bangladesh and Pakistan.

It would be possible to quibble with the details of the calculation. For instance, the formula ignores Australian specialities in aid delivery, aggregate per capita income is poorly correlated with income distribution, 'needs' are crudely defined, and 'emotional rapport' and 'cultural proximity' are incapable of being sensibly measured. Yet these could be adjusted and improved.

More importantly, however, it is not clear that use of a formula ensures a more humanitarian aid distribution than, say, a periodic assessment of available information guided by a well-defined set of objectives. Moreover, the rigidities that a distribution formula creates, the unilateral nature of the calculation, and the spurious guise of 'objectivity' which surrounds it, are potentially harmful. The indicative allocation of

Table 6.3: Current and Ideal Priorities for Australian Government Aid According to CAA Formula

Current Priority	Ideal Priority
Papua New Guinea	Papua New Guinea
Indonesia	India
Bangladesh	China
Philippines	Indonesia
Pakistan	Bangladesh
Burma	Burma
Thailand	Pakistan
Tanzania	Vietnam
Egypt	Nepal
Sri Lanka	Sudan
Malaysia	Ethiopia
Kenya	Kampuchea
Ethiopia	Mozambique
Sudan	Tahiland
Kampuchea	Tanzania

Source: CAA, 1983, p. 20

aid to a country is, after all, only the first in a series of steps (choosing sectors, regions, projects, etc.), all of which require a prioritising of available options and matching of donor strengths and recipient needs. These are not decisions which can be made by recourse to a formula. Each needs to be negotiated on its merits, and subjected to past evaluations of project success, and clearly spelled out objectives and guidelines. This is the intention of the country programming of aid, which will be taken up later in this chapter.

AID TO VIETNAM

Perhaps one of the most difficult aid decisions which faces a government is the pressure to withdraw aid as a protest against some sort of political action, particularly that which violates the very ambiguous concept of 'human rights'. The seriousness of the 'crime' has not always been perceived with consistency. Indonesia's invasion of East Timor in 1975, for instance, had few repercussions for the Australian aid program, whereas Vietnam's invasion of Kampuchea led to a complete halt of bilateral assistance. More recently, problems with the Marcos regime in the Philippines have generated many calls for the halting of Australian military aid to the Philippines, but no response has been forthcoming from the government. This is not the place to canvass the rights and wrongs of these decisions, but it underlines the point that Australia deals with a disparate group of countries. Each of these countries needs to be considered on its merits when it comes to an aid program, but there should be some consistency in the Australian outlook, and this outlook should not be determined solely by foreign policy considerations.

Rather than attempt a definition of human rights, I will confine the discussion to the issue of Australian assistance to Vietnam. Australian aid to Vietnam was formally suspended in January 1979. At the time of the cutoff, Australian aid went to four projects -- a Thai Binh cattle project, the Moc Chau dairy processing plant, a WHO anti-venereal disease program, and an Australian-based student training program. Aid to Vietnam in 1977/8 was valued at $4.4 million. According to the government of the day, the suspension of aid was due to the marked upsurge in Vietnamese refugees in 1978 (when almost 89,000 left the country, compared to 15,500 the year before) and the invasion of Kampuchea in December of that year. Australia was not alone in its actions. China had suspended its large aid program (around $260 million per year) in 1978, and a number of key West European donors and Japan cancelled or phased down their aid to Vietnam in 1979.

The Jackson Report dodges the question of resumption of aid to Vietnam entirely, dismissing it as a political issue for the government to decide. In other words, it is another case of allowing a foreign policy issue to override the humanitarian purpose of aid. Like the politics of aid to the Indian Ocean island states, the Jackson Report has come down on the side of the status quo; in this context a decision not to comment on an aid issue is as much a political statement as the decision to comment.

The government itself has taken a much bolder stance on the issue of aid to Vietnam than the Jackson Report. Since halting official assistance in 1979, it has permitted Australian NGOs to develop small projects in Vietnam. Furthermore, in Bangkok in November 1983, the Foreign Minister announced that disaster assistance would be provided to Vietnam following the devastating typhoons which hit the central coastal area in the middle of 1983. Finally, in recent months Australian assistance to a multilateral agency has been used to bring Vietnamese students to Australia to study at the Canberra College of Advanced Education. Formal bilateral aid to Vietnam may not have resumed, but there is ample evidence of a steady growth of indirect assistance by the Australian government.

Recently, a segment of the Vietnamese community in Australia has demonstrated strong opposition to the formal resumption of aid ties. At the same time, a number within the Australian Labor Party are openly committed to the resumption of bilateral assistance to the Thai Binh and Moc Chau projects, and have included this in the Party's platform. A dissenting report signed by Labor members in the Report from the Senate Joint Committee on Foreign Affairs and Defence (Beazley, et al., 1981, p. 93) expressed a similar view, though, not unexpectedly for a committee of this nature, one of the principal reasons for the resumption of aid was to reduce Vietnamese dependence on the Soviet Union.[5]

According to the hierarchy of objectives outlined in the Jackson Report, humanitarianism is the prime reason for giving aid. There can be no dispute that Vietnam is in desperate need of aid, nor that the

Vietnamese government recognises this. During his visit to Australia in 1984, the Vietnamese Foreign Minister, Mr Nguyen Co Thach, stopped short of formally requesting aid from Australia. In the last few months, however, Prime Minister Pham Van Dong has again reiterated the basic message: the food situation in Vietnam remains serious and economic problems enormous. He added, 'Vietnam is waiting for all the aid which outsiders can provide' (Indochina Chronology, 1984, p. 4).

There are two main barriers to the resumption of Australian bilateral assistance to Vietnam. First, and most importantly, the ASEAN states, China and the USA clearly frown upon any move in this direction. Second, there is some uncertainty of the implications of resumption for domestic Australian politics, given the recent active protests within the Vietnamese community against resumption, together with the absence of a vocal pro-Vietnam lobby. Yet, as John Langmore has argued in Chapter 2, governments should take an active role in aid policy, rather than passively responding to the whims of the electorate. It is disappointing that the Jackson Report did not tackle the issue of Australian aid to Vietnam. If it had done so it would have been an important demonstration of the report's stated intention to pursue the humanitarian goals of the aid program.

COUNTRY PROGRAMMING

Once the aid budget is split and the bilateral allocation determined,[6] an approximate country allocation can then be decided by recourse to an eligibility framework, formula, or defined set of guidelines, as discussed earlier in the chapter. The Australian aid program has often been criticised because the selection of programs and projects within a country seemed to be done on an ad hoc basis. Recipient governments were expected to provide a 'shopping-list' from which the donor chose the projects which it felt best suited its purse, experience etc. In actual fact informal negotiations often took place beforehand in order to ensure the 'shopping-list' contained the correct projects. No government willingly loses face by putting up projects that are bound to be refused.

The country program is a frequently canvassed alternative. As the Auditor-General (1981, p. v) recommended:

> ADAB should put more emphasis on the planning and development of country programs for Australia's principal aid recipients, derived from assessment of Australia's bilateral relations with and appreciation of the development needs and priorities of those countries.

ADAB was in the process of developing country policy and strategy papers at the time of the release of the Jackson Report, which enthusiastically endorsed the concept of 'country managers' and the country program as the principal organisational mechanism for the bilateral program. The report envisages an initial analysis of a recipient country's situation, followed by the formulation, in consultation with the recipient, of a forward -rolling program of aid, concentrating on those sub-sectors and regions which best match donor capability and recipient need (Jackson Report, 1984, p. 135).

Thus far, there is little to object to in the concept of the country program. The intention to overcome the ad hoc nature of program and project selection is entirely appropriate, and the concept fits well with the eligibility framework outlined in the report. As was detailed in Table 6.2, countries in Categories 1, 2 and 3 are eligible for detailed country programs, while those in Category 4 will be restricted to broad strategies.

Some might justifiably complain that the concept of a country program builds an additional rigidity into a potentially flexible system of aid disbursement. The report pre-empts this criticism on a country basis by arguing that the Head of Mission Discretionary Aid Fund is the appropriate mechanism for ensuring flexibility. More serious, perhaps, is the rigidity in the inter-country allocation, for lack of a country program for a place like Vietnam may provide an excuse for not increasing aid to that particular country. Given the long lead time necessary to draft and gain approval by donor and recipient, the country program may prove cumbersome, particularly for those countries on the margins of the aid program.

There are two strategies that can be adopted in a country program. The first-best strategy is for those countries with 'appropriate' policies — i.e. policies which favour a high growth rate through the promotion of trade and an open economy as the report suggests is evident in East and Southeast Asia (but see Chapter 5 by Taylor and Chapter 10 by Keen). Here Australian aid will be directed towards overcoming the obstacles to development such as poor physical infrastructure, which the committee believes, 'often have higher benefits for the poor , even in the short run, than projects which seek to assist the poor directly' (Jackson Report, 1984, p. 60).

The second-best strategy is for those countries with poor policies. It is not always clear which countries fall into this category, but it applies to most socialist states, as well as those countries with low growth rates or those in which equity goals feature prominently in national plans, such as India and Papua New Guinea. In fact, the report equates poor policies with low growth rates, and good policies with high growth rates, in breathtakingly simplistic fashion. The purpose of Australian aid for countries with poor policies is to supplement welfare investment, for instance through basic needs strategies, but welfare spending is considered a second-best strategy.

This separation of economic growth and social development strategies is a distortion of the growth-with-equity model the report espouses. First, arguments for aid expenditure targetting the poor directly through basic needs and employment generation strategies cannot simply be dismissed as welfare spending. Strategies of investment in health, education, food supply, housing, water, sanitation and so on contribute to economic growth through increasing the productivity of labour and increasing the capital stock. Generating productive employment among the poor assists in the more efficient use of factor endowments (Mikesell, 1983, pp. 34-7; Forbes, 1985).

Secondly, the report places great faith in the 'trickle-down' effect, or to be more precise, the ability for gains in national economic growth rates to be converted into real improvements in the well-being of the poorest sections of the community. The degree to which 'trickle-down' operates in a developing country is perhaps the most hotly disputed issue in development studies over the past 15 years. It is generally accepted that income inequality increases in the early stages of development, in line with the Kuznet's curve, but the evidence about shifts in income for the poor (and, indeed, the accuracy of the income distribution data these observations are based upon) need to be treated with a great deal of caution. Mikesell's (1983) recent review of the relationship between growth and poverty was inconclusive. While there is no a priori reason for a conflict between growth rates and meeting basic human needs, there is no certainty that high growth rates in the poorest countries (the middle-income countries are another matter) will result in the reduction of absolute poverty (Mikesell, 1983, pp. 28-33).

There are other criticisms of this separation of growth and social development strategies. In the Southeast and East Asian context it is all very well to argue the need to postpone basic consumption-oriented infrastructure development until economies can afford to pay for these investments themselves. However, rapid city growth means both the unit costs and total costs of providing this infrastructure are likely to escalate at a greater rate than the ability of cities (and even nations as a whole) to pay for them. Postponing such desperately needed services as a piped safe water supply and sanitation facilities not only prolongs hardship and nullifies attempts to improve public health, with all this means for labour productivity, but it means Asian cities will be saddled with the huge burden of providing infrastructure to massive unserviced populations.

The ultimate test of the country program strategy is whether it will improve the aid which Australia is able to deliver. On balance, the answer to this should be yes, but with certain provisos. It is still unclear to what extent the Australian public will have access to the country programs in the formative stage. NGOs have been invited to prepare certain contextual material (e.g. on social development background) but this falls short of an open discussion of donor and recipient requirements.

Finally, the homogeneity which a country program might well encourage may not always be welcome, particularly when it contains an evaluation of a country's development strategy (Jackson Report, 1984, p. 134). The major multilateral aid agencies find it hard to resist lecturing recipient countries on the 'correct' policies for development. There are many thinly veiled comments in the Jackson Report characterised by a similarly authoritarian stance, particularly in the section on Papua New Guinea (Jackson Report, 1984, pp. 145-66). Country programs must not be permitted to become a vehicle for forcing an 'open economy', growth-first ideology upon recipient countries.

CONCLUSION

This chapter has looked at four aspects of Australia's bilateral aid to Asia:

1. The current pattern of disbursements within the Asian region, the eligibility framework for future aid allocation proposed in the Jackson Report, and the potential consequences of the implementation of the framework.

2. The Jackson Report's logic for its recommended inter-country distribution of aid, alternative formulations of this problem, and the need to adhere to a clear hierarchy of objectives for the aid program.

3. The problems of particular countries, such as Vietnam, where humanitarian objectives within the Jackson Report are dumped in favour of a spurious political 'neutrality'.

4. The importance of country programming, different types of country strategies that have been discussed, and the problems of separating economic and social development.

The aim of the chapter has been to assess critically some of the major issues affecting the pattern of distribution of aid to Asia. Three main conclusions can be drawn. First, despite claims that the document presents radical new departures for the aid program, many of its arguments are a restatement of the status quo. The eligibility framework, it is argued, is a case in point, and so too the contentious issue of aid to Vietnam. Secondly, the Jackson Report frequently inverts its own proclaimed hierarchy of objectives, placing diplomatic goals well ahead of humanitarian goals in determining aid disbursements. Thirdly, the strategy advocated in the report oversimplifies the development process, underemphasising the importance of social investment, particularly of the basic needs type, in development.

NOTES

1. Mauritius and the Seychelles are not normally included in Asia. I have done so because together with Comoros and the Maldives they are included in Category 1 in the Jackson Report, and thus provide a useful contract with the better known Asian countries.

2. The fourth category -- the lowest priority -- includes countries in Africa, the Middle East, Latin America and the Caribbean.

3. General aid instruments include the whole range of training and technical assistance programs, support for voluntary and multilateral agencies, the Development Import Finance Facility and so on.

4. One might, of course, seriously question why this area of international economic policy should be so closely tied to the political, when in other areas such as trade a more pragmatic view seems often to predominate. Australia's attitude to South Africa is a case in point. Sporting links -- or in other words trade in a specialised service -- is an exception to the rule in Australia's case.

5. For a more detailed argument in favour of the resumption of aid to Vietnam see Alliband (1984a, 1984b).

6. Mention should be made here of the various regional programs such as the ASEAN-Australia Economic Cooperation Program (AAECP). The AAECP was launched in Bangkok in 1974 with a budget of $5 million. Disbursements in 1984/5 are estimated at $14.3 million, and the total financial commitment over the life of the program so far is $70.6 million.

7 AUSTRALIAN AID TO AFRICA

Cherry Gertzel and David Goldsworthy

Sub-Saharan Africa, with 21 of the world's 33 poorest developing countries, is indisputably the region of the Third World that in the mid-eighties stands in greatest need. By virtually all the economic indicators, the region holds:

> the largest concentration of the poorest countries in the world... Alone among the regions of the world, famine and disease are endemic in this area... few countries have as high a percentage of their population living at such low levels of subsistence and health as the majority of African countries... Many have failed to establish any foundation for economic development, or to reduce the numbers living in absolute poverty. (Jackson Report, 1984, p. 201)

Average *per capita* income levels for sub-Saharan Africa (excluding, here and throughout, South Africa), stood at $US411 at the end of the 1970s. The average annual growth in GNP *per capita* had fallen from 1.3 per cent in the 1960s to 0.8 per cent in the 1970s; the corresponding figures for all developing countries were 3.5 per cent and 2.7 per cent. Life expectancy stands now at 49 years compared with 58 in Asia and 63 in Latin America. Africa's problems are rendered all the more acute in that its population growth rates are very high — around 3 per cent, with parts of Africa today registering the highest population growth rates in the world -- while at the same time, African agricultural output is in long-term decline. During the 1970s, food output per head declined by 0.9 per cent, and the rate of decline is accelerating. Moreover, as is very well known, the longest and most widespread drought of the century is currently turning vast areas of arable land to dust. Famine has struck in Ethiopia, Chad, the Sudan, Somalia and Mozambique. According to the FAO, on current trends Africa will provide for only half its food needs by the year 2020 (see World Bank, 1981b, statistical tables).

The World Bank has recognised that Africa's development crisis cannot be overcome without massive international support. It is true that the bank has placed substantial blame for Africa's present plight on African policy-makers themselves, arguing that there can be no development without domestic policy reforms. Nevertheless, it has also insisted on the need for massive external support -- a matter on which there is now global consensus. Thus, in September 1984, the bank's 147 member-states (including, of course, Australia) acknowledged the enormity of the African crisis by endorsing a bank program that would direct an additional $US2 billion a year (to be raised from the member-states) into sub-Saharan Africa (The Age, 25 September 1984, p. 9). Within the Australian community itself there is a considerable and growing recognition of Africa's need, and a desire to help that was clearly demonstrated in the last months of 1984 when voluntary agencies raised some $18 million for famine relief. The question, however, is not whether Africa needs aid; that is beyond argument. The question here is what role Australia can best play.

To begin with the fundamentals: an assistance program for Africa must comprise both humanitarian relief and developmental aid. It is important to be clear about the distinction. Relief offered in times of emergency and disaster is a vital element of the relationship between rich and poor countries, reflecting the essentially humanitarian concern to alleviate suffering. But it cannot provide long-term solutions. Developmental aid is concerned to reduce poverty in ways that tackle not only its effects (e.g. hunger) but also its causes (e.g. low agricultural productivity and, in turn, the causes of that); and in ways that increase the capacities of poor countries and communities to work for their own future economic and social improvement. It is essential that the aid programs of wealthy countries such as Australia look to the goals of long-term development, as well as to the immediate problems of emergency relief. No doubt this could be said of Australia's aid to almost any region, but the urgency of the dual task is nowhere greater than in critically impoverished Africa.

Of course aid programs as at present perceived have other objectives, including the political, strategic and commercial self-interest of the donor. Whether such objectives can be legitimately identified with an aid program is increasingly, however, a question at issue. More and more the evidence suggests the difficulty of doing so, since what is appropriate for the eradication of poverty in the Third World will not necessarily benefit the donor state in any immediate political or economic sense. Especially in relation to a continent as needy as Africa, donor self-interest must be accepted as subsidiary to the main humanitarian and developmental purposes, to be pursued, if at all, only in ways that complement, rather than conflict with, these basic purposes.

It is with this hierarchy of objectives in mind that we shall comment later on the analysis and recommendations of the Jackson Report, and proffer an alternative set of guidelines for aid to Africa. First, however, we need to note the present policy base, and the main characteristics of the current Australian program in Africa.

AUSTRALIA'S CURRENT AID PROGRAM TO AFRICA

Virtually negligible until the middle 1970s, Australia's aid program in Africa grew steadily during the next few years in consequence of agreements made at successive Commonwealth conferences: the Uganda rehabilitation conference following the fall of Amin in 1979, the Zimcord conference at the time of Zimbabwe's independence in 1980, the establishment of the Southern African Development Co-ordination Conference (SADCC) in 1980, the two International Conferences on Assistance to Refugees in Africa (ICARA I and II) in 1981 and 1984, and other stimuli.

In money terms, Australia's bilateral aid to Africa rose from $7 million in 1976/7 (2 per cent of the total bilateral aid expenditure) to $56.2 million in 1982/3 (10.2 per cent). Bilateral aid in the latter year was distributed among 26 African countries. The major recipients were Tanzania ($9.0 million), Egypt ($7.2 million), Kenya ($6.8 million), Uganda ($4.7 million), Ethiopia ($4.3 million), Sudan ($3.5 million), Mauritius ($2.8 million) and Zambia ($2.7 million).

In all these countries food aid was by far the largest component of Australian aid, as it was in the African aid program as a whole (totalling $40.4 million in value, and comprising some 60 per cent of Australia's food aid world-wide in 1982/3). The food aid to Egypt was a case apart; it was given largely in order to stimulate the commercial sales of much larger quantities of Australian cereals to that country.[1] In drought-stricken sub-Saharan Africa, however, it was given as emergency relief. Australian aid to African refugees, amounting to some $36 million in value between 1978 and 1982 and still continuing, is in a similar category, directed towards short-term relief rather than long-term development.

The 1982/3 expenditure also included $8.2 million for training aid and other forms of staffing and technical assistance. Development Import Grants accounted for $2.7 million, and capital projects assistance for $3.1 million. This last figure clearly indicates the very modest scale of Australian project aid in Africa. In mid-1982 there were just 29 Australian projects in Africa and the Middle East combined, compared with 158 in the South Pacific. Seven African countries received project funding in 1982/3, but only one of them, Tanzania, received funding of more than $1 million.

Other aspects of the year's program included small contributions made through multilateral agencies for Namibia, reflecting Australia's role as a member of the UN Council for Namibia; contributions to international financial institutions such as the IDA (International Development Agency, the World Bank's soft-loans agency) which, in turn, provide aid to Africa; and support for the work of Australian (and some international) non-governmental organisations (NGOs) operating in Africa. In addition, and especially after the establishment of the Australian Centre for International Agricultural Research (ACIAR) in 1982, Australia has mounted an agricultural research effort that is limited in scope but high in calibre.

In sum, this is a small-scale program spread over many countries. It is dominated by programs of food aid and refugee aid which are humanitarian in their objectives but not developmental in their effects. Directly developmental forms of aid to Africa -- in particular, training, research and project aid -- amounted in dollar value to only about 3 per cent of Australia's total bilateral aid bill in 1982/3.

The programs for the years immediately preceding and following 1982/3 were broadly similar, suggesting that, by then, a certain pattern had become established. The 1984/5 budget estimates, however, would seem to be modifying the pattern in some ways. It is stated in the relevant budget document that:

> An important recommendation of the Jackson report calls for greater focus in Australian aid both by geographic region and in terms of economic sectors. Budgetary constraints this year have served to reinforce this direction by concentrating aid more on our own immediate region. (Budget Paper No. 9, 1984, p. 1)

By attributing this greater regional concentration to budgetary constraints rather than to policy decisions, the government has avoided appearing to pre-empt public and parliamentary discussion of Jackson's policy recommendations. But the effect, for 1984/5 at least, is the same. Whether, in consequence, total aid to Africa has been cut in money terms cannot be deduced from the crude budget figures, though there have been some general reductions that are likely to affect Africa: the expenditure for refugee and disaster relief is down from $23.2 million in 1983/4 to a projected $14.3 million in 1984/5, and the provision of funds to the IDA is down from $70.1 million to $60.0 million. On the other hand, the provision for food aid has risen from $102.9 million to a proposed $111.9 million; but a high proportion of this is apparently destined for countries in Southeast Asia.

By early 1985 it was clear enough that the year's program for Arica was being geared much more to relief than to development. Between mid -1984 and January 1985, the government committed $33 million of emergency assistance in response to the Ethiopian calamity. But project aid has languished. No new projects in Africa are being planned. Australia has now pulled out of one of its two most important projects in Africa, the Singida water supply scheme in Tanzania, and is visibly unenthusiastic about the other, the Magarini settlement project in Kenya (that Australia remains in Magarini at all is partly due, it seems, to Kenyan diplomatic pressure applied at the highest level). In fact, no bilateral initiatives of any kind are currently in the pipeline for Africa. Staffing Assistance Scheme commitments are running out in most countries. No new Development Import Grants are planned. Expenditure under the Zimcord agreement will largely end in 1986/7. We understand further that there is at present no official programming basis for forward planning of the Australian bilateral program in Africa, and that Africa has had last priority in determining annual appropriations for the geographical spread of bilateral aid. It can hardly be said, then, that the Australian Government has been actively exploring the possibility of developmental aid (as distinct from humanitarian relief) in this massively needy continent.

Jackson, as we shall see in a moment, did recommend some restructuring of aid to Africa -- but not a 'reduction of the Australian commitment' (Jackson Report, 1984, p. 9). It is very much to be hoped that the trends of 1984/5 do not signal the beginning of such a reduction -- whether initiated by decision or by default.

THE JACKSON REPORT ON AFRICA

The Jackson Report recognises that many of the poorest countries are in sub-Saharan Africa, and that 'their plight cannot be ignored' (Jackson Report, 1984, p. 6). Africa is directly disadvantaged, however, by the report's key recommendation that the Australian aid program should be given a firmer geographic and sectoral definition which narrows the geographic focus for bilateral aid principally to Southeast Asia and the Pacific, and which aims to concentrate on fewer, larger projects. Africa is placed in Category 4 of the eligibility framework. The report is careful to point out that this does not mean that all Australian aid to Africa should be withdrawn. African states should continue to be eligible for training, technical assistance and research, especially in areas of Australian comparative advantage and expertise such as dryland farming and forestry. Development Import Finance Facility funds should continue to be provided. Head of Mission Discretionary Aid Funds (HOMDAF) should be increased, especially for assisting small-scale, grass-roots social programs; and the work of voluntary agencies should continue to be supported. Food aid, 'preferably with development objectives', should continue at present levels, while relief contributions should continue to assist victims of natural or man-made disasters (Jackson Report, 1984, pp. 142, 204).

Nevertheless, the aid program should be restructured in important ways. As a Category 4 region, Africa should no longer be eligible for Australian project aid (although Australia might co-finance some projects with international financial agencies). Nor should African states be eligible for Development Import Grants; and country programming should not be undertaken. The report argues that Australia ' cannot do everything and cannot help everybody', and that project aid activities outside the Asia/Pacific area would 'impose an excessive load on Australian administative resources' (Jackson Report, 1984, p. 204). Generally:

> Australia cannot mount substantial and effective aid programs in distant countries as well as meeting its considerable commitments in its own region. Its humanitarian obligation to the world's poor should not lead to a dispersal of its aid effort so wide that the effectiveness of Australian aid is substantially reduced. Australia's aid to Africa... should take into account the substantial programs already undertaken there by other donors. (Jackson Report, 1984, p. 199)

COMMENTARY

We are pleased to note the report's positive view of several aspects of Australia's existing aid effort in Africa. There can be no question, for example, of the high potential value of Australia's agricultural expertise, given the topographical, climatic and other similarities between the semi-arid tropical zones of various parts of Australia and Africa; Australia stands virtually alone among the DAC (Development Assistance Committee of the OECD) donor countries in this respect. Many others, including Africans, have commented already on this point; for example:

> The Organisation of African Unity has called an emergency conference of drought-affected countries and has asked that Australian experts attend to advise on fighting drought. Dr Peter Onu, interim secretary-general of the OAU, said yesterday it was 'absolutely necessary' to get experts from countries like Australia which had experienced drought to discuss the problem. (The Age, 15 November 1984, p. 9)

It is good to note, therefore, that there is no suggestion that Australia should do other than maintain its assistance by way of agricultural training and research. Post-Jackson, several Australian training institutions have offered courses in such areas as crop fertilisation and storage, and some important ACIAR research programs, totalling some $4.5 million in value, are in train. These programs entail long-term collaborative research in Kenya, Nigeria, Zambia, Zimbabwe and Burundi, and deal with the improvement of non-irrigated crop and forage production, the ecology and epidemiology of ticks on African livestock, the use of Australian hardwoods for fuel and agroforestry, and the management of nitrogen fixation using casuarina trees. (For details of research programs see Lee, 1984, and ACIAR, 1983.) It is to be hoped that the ACIAR contribution can be steadily expanded, to embrace further areas of relevant Australian expertise in soil and pasture management, domestication of plants, animal health and nutrition, and so on.

That the range of relevant Australian expertise for both research and training is indeed very wide has now been amply demonstrated in Dr Helen Newton-Turner's ACFOA report Australian Agricultural Aid to Africa - Appropriate Expertise (Newton-Turner, 1985). Having performed the service of identifying Australian skills, this document has helped move the discussion among interested parties on to the deeper problems of how these skills might be adapted and applied, with due sensitivity to the social framework of African agriculture. To these ends, it is of course important that a good deal of Australian research and training should be done in Africa, in association with African ministries and institutes and key international bodies such as the International Livestock Centre for Africa in Addis Ababa. We will return to this theme in a later section.

We welcome, too, the report's recommendation for continuing government support of voluntary agency work; as an example we might mention the program of primary health care being developed by Community Aid Abroad (CAA) in Somalia (see JCFAD, 1983, pp. 71-4). The recommendation for increased HOMDAF assistance is perhaps more controversial. HOMDAF assistance could well be of use if it were indeed to be channelled to the kinds of grass-roots programs the report mentions, and there might be circumstances -- e.g. in South Africa — where this would be the only way in which Australian funding could reach such programs. But since HOMDAF is discretionary it is also unaccountable, and, as a general principle, we would prefer to see aid moneys publicly committed.

We take issue most strongly, however, with the two important recommendations that project aid in Africa should be phased out completely and that there should be no country programming at all for Africa. While we would not dispute that 'Australia cannot do everything and cannot help everybody', it appears to us that the movement from this commonsense position to the conclusion that there should be neither project aid nor country programming for Africa depends upon some very questionable arguments. These are:

1. that Australia lacks the resources, and especially the administrative capacity, to carry out worthwhile bilateral programs of project aid in Africa. Administration and delivery of aid is all the more difficult in that Africa is a long way from Australia;

2. that since Africa is heavily aided by multilateral agencies and by major European and North American donor states, Australia can withdraw its very small-scale project aid in good conscience;

3. that in terms of Australia's own interests, Africa is not important. Australia's political, strategic and economic interests require rather a concentration of attention on the East Asian[2] and Pacific regions.

Before asserting the positive case for project aid and country programming for Africa, we would like to comment on each of these arguments.

The Argument About Administrative and Geographical Problems

The administrative and geographical constraints upon Australian agencies in the effective delivery of aid programs in Africa are real enough. Such constraints have not, however, applied only in Africa. They apply also in the other regions in which Australia has been active in aid programs, including the South Pacific. The two most authoritative reports on the Australian overseas aid program prior to Jackson made this very clear. The Auditor-General's report of 1981 demonstrated that ADAB's administrative problems extended over the whole of the program, in all regions. It pointed out, in addition, that ADAB's administrative inability to evaluate the likely macro-economic efforts of Australian development assistance applied particularly in the island countries of the South Pacific and the Indian Ocean (Auditor-General, 1981, p. 71). Evidence to the JCPA similarly makes it clear that ineffective communication, ignorance of local conditions and the lack of administrative capacity are problems that have bedevilled ADAB in the administration of projects in regions other than Africa; in the Zamboanga project in the Philippines, for example, as well as the Magarini project in Kenya. The Jackson Report itself acknowledges this (e.g. Jackson Report, 1984, pp. 220-1).

In fact, the administrative and geographical problems in Africa can be --and often are -- overstated. In many respects, Eastern and Southern Africa are a good deal less difficult to service than many of the small ocean states. There are direct air links between Australia and Southern Africa, and good air communications from there to the rest of sub-Saharan Africa. Electronic and mail communications between Australia and Africa are satisfactory. Some of the island states which the Jackson Report places in Category 1 -- the Seychelles and the Comoros -- are most conveniently reached by way of mainland Africa, which, partly for reasons of distance, has been placed in Category 4. As for the administrative frameworks of recipient countries, it is worth stressing that the bureaucracies of Commonwealth Africa are derived from the Whitehall model and the language of administration is English. In these respects Commonwealth African countries have a good deal more in common with Australia than do many of the ASEAN, Oceanic and East Asian states ranked higher in the eligibility framework. In speaking of the 'disproportionate burden' placed on hard-pressed recipient-country administrators who must 'become familiar with Australian procedures' (Jackson Report, 1984, p. 204), the report is once again making a point which applies rather less closely to several of the African states than it does in other culture areas.

While we are agreed, then, that rationalisation of the Australian program is necessary in the interests of more effective aid delivery, we do not agree that arguments about geographical and administrative difficulties tell more strongly against Africa than other recipient regions. In our view they tell less strongly. Certainly they do not provide sufficient grounds for the relegation of Africa to Category 4.

Underlying the argument here is the question of whether rationalisation of the aid program is best conceived in geographical terms anyway. Many have argued that it would make better sense to rationalise the objectives of the program. If it were clearly established that the primary objective is to attack poverty, with the donor's political and commercial self-interest ranking as secondary, then a great deal of confusion and inefficiency could be eliminated. But, as Eldridge points out, contradictions over objectives are generally left unresolved in the report. At the same time, the report applies:

> harsh principles of cost effectiveness... to more geographically 'distant' countries - most of which are among the world's poorest - that are considered too difficult or inconvenient to support. Yet there is no reason to suppose that Australia could not support programs in a great variety of countries, if attacking poverty was clearly established as the primary goal of aid policy. Indeed, countries such as Sweden and the Netherlands, which pursue more directly 'basic needs' oriented policies across a significant range of countries and sectors, are regarded internationally as among the most efficient in aid delivery. (Eldridge, 1984, pp. 6-7)

The 'Drop in the Bucket' Argument

It is true that the major international donors are aiding Africa on a massive scale, and that Australian aid is very small by comparison. But the fact that a contribution to a major task is relatively small is not a good reason for making it even smaller. If it were, then the same argument should be applied to Australia's aid to the Asian countries, where Australian aid is equally a very small part of the total aid flows (see Jackson Report, 1984, Boxes 12.3 and 12.4, pp. 193-4).

Australia's aid to Africa is indeed so small that to reduce it further would bring into question her commitment to the previously-mentioned global consensus -- that the needs of Africa are of paramount concern for the entire international aid effort. At this time, when Africa faces the worst drought conditions of the century, it is particularly difficult to justify a decision to restrict rather than increase assistance. Whether we like it or not, Africa will continue to be in critical need of assistance for at least the next twenty years. How we respond to this long-term African need must be seen as a major test of Australia's commitment to global justice and development.

The important question to be asked about the aid of both the major and the minor donors in Africa is not so much how large it is in money terms, but how appropriate and relevant it is in relation to African needs. In the past, much of the large-scale international aid to Africa has failed either to promote development or to reach the people and sections in greatest need. The argument that Australia's aid is quantitatively so small that its further reduction would make little or no difference to Africa ignores the nature of that aid, some of which at least is potentially of considerable long-term significance. Australia, for this reason alone, should be involved in the international discussions designed to improve the effectiveness of aid in Africa, and should also be helping to point the way with appropriately designed projects, small in scale but high in quality. We will develop this point further in a later section, when we move on to a more specific consideration of the potential value of Australian project aid.

The Argument from Australia's Interests

While the Jackson Report frequently states that the major purposes of aid are developmental and humanitarian, it also clearly bases many of its recommendations on what are perceived to be Australia's own foreign-policy and commercial interests in the aid relationship. The report argues that Australia's interests require the proposed geographical concentration of aid on East Asia, the South Pacific and the Indian Ocean islands. Africa's relegation to Category 4 reflects, in part, a judgement that Australia's diplomatic, strategic and commercial interests in the continent are of low priority.

We have questioned earlier whether donor self-interest is a legitimate concern in aid programming. Clearly, however, both the Jackson Committee and the Australian government do regard it thus. Let us, therefore, discuss the issue on the report's own ground.

It can be granted at once that Australia's commercial interests in sub-Saharan Africa are very minor. Although there is a certain amount of quite lucrative trade with the continent's extremes, notably Egypt and South Africa, trade with Black Africa is extremely small-scale: because Australia has little need for the region's output, because the region lacks purchasing power, and because there are no direct shipping links. We cannot, however, agree with the judgement that Africa is of no great diplomatic or strategic significance either. We believe that this view rests on a very narrow perception of Australian foreign-policy interests, and ignores or reduces the full importance of the relationships that have grown up between Australia and the African region. These relationships are evidenced by the growing number of African countries in which Australia has established a diplomatic presence (most recently Zimbabwe, Zambia and Ethiopia) or which have established their own diplomatic missions in Canberra (most recently Zambia, Uganda and Kenya).

There are three main points to be made. First, the African mainland states that border the Indian Ocean, from South Africa to the Horn, are an integral part of the Indian Ocean region, which the Australian government regards as of high importance for Australia's national and economic security and well-being (Department of Foreign Affairs news release, 17 January 1984; Hayden, 1984). The stability and well-being of these states is important for the peace and security of the region itself. The Horn of Africa, which abuts the strategically significant north-western zone of the Indian Ocean, is the scene of much civil conflict and indirect super-power involvement. Seen in terms of these issues, the report's recommendations do not make sense. It recommends major Australian assistance of all kinds for the tiny, Category 1 Indian Ocean islands which almost certainly do not have the capacity to absorb large quantities of aid, but ignores the African littoral states which are experiencing deep economic (and in some cases political) crises. It further ignores the growing links between the mainland states and the island states which must undoubtedly affect the latter and, therefore, affect any assistance program (e.g. the new Preferential Trade Area (PTA) for Eastern and

Southern Africa, which came into operation in July 1984 and which already includes Mauritius and the Comoros, with the Seychelles likely to join soon). In short, from a geopolitical and strategic viewpoint the restriction of Australian assistance as proposed is essentially ridiculous. We would also point out that in the case of the Indian Ocean littoral, Australia's national interests reinforce rather than run counter to her humanitarian and developmental concerns in the two major poverty belts of the globe, Africa and South Asia.

Secondly, it is equally difficult for Australia to avoid recognition of the importance of the Commonwealth connection. Whether Australia likes it or not, fifteen of the member states of the Commonwealth are African. We share institutions, interests and concerns, which have been shown on numerous occasions to be an important asset in our common search for global peace and development. In particular, Australia's membership of the Commonwealth has enabled her to make an important contribution, on successive occasions, to the search for justice and political stability in Southern Africa.

Thirdly, Australia's political commitments regarding Southern Africa in fact go well beyond the Commonwealth involvement. Her commitment to the fight against apartheid, which has already won her considerable respect, calls for a strengthened, rather than reduced, presence in Southern Africa. Her corresponding commitment to the goals of the countries of the Southern African Development Co-ordination Conference (SADCC) -- reaffirmed by Australian representatives at SADCC's annual meetings -- has been important in the evolution of that body. The proposed restrictions on Australian aid must adversely affect relations with those countries. It is relevant here that South Africa's own destabilising activities in the region have contributed directly to the crisis conditions in some states -- conditions which, in turn, increase the need of these states for outside help. Similarly, Australia's commitment to the cause of Namibian independence, reflected in her membership of the Council for Namibia, requires that Australia's Southern African role be maintained. A continuing Australian aid involvement in Southern Africa, in short, is justified not only in terms of assisting very poor countries but also in signalling support for countries under pressure from the apartheid regime. Quite apart from its moral justification, this approach makes good diplomatic sense by helping to improve Australia's standing in the Third World as a whole.

In general, the consequences for Australia of the reduction of assistance, regardless of the amount involved, will include the loss of important goodwill in countries where Australia is known and with which she is closely associated in the Commonwealth. Australian bilateral project aid is, as the report points out, the most highly visible part of the Australian aid program. Even Australian NGO assistance has a 'made in Australia' identity tag (Norris, 1984). It is greatly appreciated at all levels and brings Australia a good deal of warm regard, the loss of which undoubtedly has political implications. It would be a pity if Australia's reputation were affected in this manner, and she should come to be seen (and not only in Africa) as self-interested in an excessively narrow way.

We are, therefore, concerned that the nature and importance of Australia's interests in Africa should be fully appreciated and recognised. Those who wish to set arguments about aid priorities within the framework of a broader political case for Australian involvement in any given region should see that such a case does exist with regard to Africa. This does not mean that we dispute the importance of Australia's interests elsewhere, and especially in East Asia and the Pacific. We do, however, stress the need for a better balance in Australia's foreign investments. The emphasis on East Asia which lies at the heart of the report's proposals ignores the problems and disadvantages for Australia of being drawn so overwhelmingly into what is still a difficult and turbulent region. This applies not least to matters of trade and commerce; in the words of a Canadian observer, 'the new international division of labour will not be centred on the Pacific alone and Australian capitalism may not be able to compete with or become complementary to Japanese, Korean or Taiwanese high technology' (Shaw, 1984, p. 1777). To repeat: this is not to maintain that Australia should regard its East Asian relationships as of anything less than vital importance. It is to say that Australia's expansion into the region will be problematic, to say the least, and that the East Asian and Pacific involvements should be balanced by other interests, including some diversification into Africa (and South Asia). As Eldridge has commented:

> In a world of burgeoning communications and shrinking distances, the emerging geo-political determinism shaping Australia's sense of its place in the world seems myopic ... Indeed, neighbouring countries appear to set no such narrowly regional constraints in their external relations ... the current fixation on countries to our North and East and the near total indifference to those to our West, apart from a few Indian Ocean islands, seems very unbalanced. (Eldridge, 1984, p. 22)

So far we have been commenting on the report's own arguments and indicating why we find them unsatisfactory. It should be apparent that we are concerned not just to criticise the report, but also to present a positive case for the maintenance of Australian aid in Africa. Some further points are now put forward.

The Potential Value of Australian Project Aid

The report suggests that Australian bilateral project aid is not only of minimal size but of minimal value to the African development effort. Yet the report itself points out the crucial difference which aid provided 'at the margins' in small agrarian-based economies may make to the success of local development efforts. This is indeed one of the arguments advanced for assistance to Nepal, Bhutan and Sri Lanka, which are placed in Category 2 (Jackson Report, 1984, pp. 189-90). The same argument applies to the small agrarian economies of Africa. Australia's recognised skills in land and animal husbandry, food production, erosion control, forestry, water conservation, grain storage and pest control are very definitely the sorts of skills these economies need, and they are also the skills which African spokesmen are explicitly asking Australia to provide (see e.g. Kamencu, 1985, pp. 9-12). The report does envisage that Australia should continue to teach these skills to African officials, scientists, extension workers and farmers, and that Australian research in these fields should continue. To some extent this is being done, as we have noted. But it is important that training and research programs should be expanded to embrace more of the very large reservoir of Australian skills identified in the Newton-Turner report, and also that Australian skills should be embodied in small-scale, simple-technology agricultural projects; for such projects have significance well beyond their own boundaries. Essentially, they are 'pilots' which show what can and cannot be achieved in difficult, semi-arid areas. They have important demonstration effects and point the way to wider applications of the lessons learned. The specific ACIAR research efforts noted earlier will prove their value only when they are applied in African conditions. For such a purpose, Australian involvement in project design and implementation is an important requisite. Indeed, work under African drought conditions could greatly enhance Australian experience and expertise to the benefit of the aid program overall, and could well be extremely valuable to Australia herself. Such benefits cannot be derived from the limited 'co-financing' role which the report suggests for Australia; they require an active presence on the ground.

It is arguable that to judge by the major examples, Singida and Magarini, Australia's project aid efforts in Africa so far have not been outstandingly successful. Both these projects have been criticised, largely on cost-effectiveness grounds, and Australia has now withdrawn from Singida. Certainly Singida was problematic, but so are Australian projects in other regions of the world where withdrawal has not been contemplated. That the project itself could not be dismissed as completely non-viable is shown by the fact that withdrawal was only one of three options put to the government by the review mission; and, in fact, the project will continue, under the aegis of the Lutheran Church. The decision to withdraw was basically a political one, reflecting the government's broad preference for downgrading Africa in its scale of priorities. We have argued against this attitude on broad political grounds, and within the framework of our argument would repeat that in relation to particular aid projects, such as Singida, the principles remain clear. This was a project that sought to meet urgent human and agricultural needs, and which drew upon a recognised area of Australian expertise (rural water supply). The mistakes that were made have now been well enough recognised; they included too much high technology and too little appreciation of the role of women in African agriculture. No-one expects African development to be easy, and the aid effort will inevitably entail a good deal of protracted trial and error. But this is all the more reason why a donor country possessing skills that are both relevant and scarce should maintain its commitment.

The case of Magarini is instructive in other ways. Established in 1978, the Magarini settlement project was meant to serve one of the poorest peoples of Kenya, the Giriama, in their home region. In its early years the scheme was over-capitalised and aimed at over-ambitious rural production targets. In addition, the Giriama people were required to change their cultivation patterns from semi-nomadic to sedentary, and were given little responsibility for organising and running the scheme. For these and other reasons results in terms of agricultural output were disappointing. In subsequent years project designs began to be revised and the Giriama people became increasingly involved in project administration and in plans for social and community development. Food aid generated some counterpart funds which were applied specifically to social development. Within severe financial constraints the agronomic research has been good, and the results have been applied (as they could only have been applied within the framework of a project). After the first few years the settlers began to show a high degree of acceptance of the scheme.

But many problems remain. Perhaps the most important are that the Kenyan Government appears increasingly unable to meet the local costs, that there is a shortage of local personnel qualified to run the scheme and cope with such matters as the maintenance of water supply, and that settlers from more powerful social groups elsewhere in Kenya are moving in. It is all too likely that these factors will undermine a good deal of what has been achieved. Their impact might have been lessened, however, if Australian policy had permitted a more flexible approach to project budgeting and if Australia had made a stronger supervisory and monitoring effort.

In fact, Magarini represents in miniature many of the problems, social and cultural as well as economic, which have arisen in foreign-induced rural development schemes all over the developing world, not just in Africa. The point remains that Australian expertise did lead to some effective solutions to technical problems at Magarini -- e.g. in developing appropriate crop packages, planting techniques, and methods of water reticulation -- while at the social and cultural levels a learning experience, and consequent improvements, did take place between the early and middle phases.

The difficulties encountered at both Magarini and Singida have contributed to the widely-held view that there should be no more large-scale, 'one-off' capital projects in agriculturally marginal regions in Africa; too many things can go wrong, and in any case such schemes put too great a strain on the fragile administrative and financial resources of host countries. Certainly this is an arguable view. But it is not an argument for abandoning project aid altogether. Rather, the hard lessons that have been learned in Africa should be seen in positive rather than negative terms; as increasing Australia's stock of experience and understanding, and as enhancing her competence to devise more appropriate projects. In general terms, we feel that Australia should be aiming at smaller-scale, primarily technical-assistance projects directed towards the goal of improved small-farming systems and framed with due awareness of social and cultural factors (such as the sexual division of labour in African farming).

An additional argument for continuing with project aid ties in with the matter of food aid. There seems an illogicality in the report's recommendation that project aid be withdrawn in view of its accompanying recommendation that food aid be continued at present levels 'preferably with developmental objectives' (Jackson Report, 1984, p. 204); for surely the most effective way to make food aid developmental is to incorporate it into carefully managed projects. Indeed, Australian aid officials have themselves spoken of the possibility of 'food security projects' in Africa; projects in which diverse inputs -- food aid, equipment, persons, seeds, fertilisers, vaccines, counterpart funds -- are tied together, in coordination with other donors, on the basis of genuinely long-term (say, fifteen-year) commitments. Once again, it is not for lack of ideas, knowledge and capacity that Australia has as yet done little along these lines; it is for lack of political commitment at top level.

Assistance to African refugees is another area in which Australia has committed herself to a continuing role. So it should be noted that the ICARA II conference of July 1984 adopted the view that a lasting solution to the refugee problem would require, over and above emergency relief, 'the acceptance by donors of long-term development projects ... having a wider social and economic impact on the countries concerned' (Alliband, 1984, p. 3). Various Australian NGOs are actively considering involvement in ten or so of the 128 projects proposed at this conference. There would seem to be every good reason for the Australian Government to think along similar lines, if indeed it wishes to find more 'developmental' solutions to the refugee problem.

All these arguments for project aid apply regardless of the scale of Australia's involvement in Africa. They are arguments about quality, not quantity. We have suggested elsewhere (AFSAAP, 1983) that Australia's African aid program seems, quite recently, to have achieved a sense of direction: investments have been made, experience gained, lessons learned. To withdraw project assistance at this stage would be a thoroughly retrograde step.

The Case for Country Programming for Africa

The report's proposals for country programming are, in general, sensible and to be supported. The omission of African countries from the proposed arrangements must, however, be criticised for the way in which it is bound further to reduce ADAB's capacity to effectively carry out even a modest African program - with or without aid. No provision is made, so far as can be seen, for the provision and maintenance of any specialist expertise for the African states. The result must be the reduction of the professional expertise and knowledge available to the Bureau. Such expertise remains, however, essential. It is proposed that assistance to Africa should be primarily through the multilateral agencies and the Head of Mission Discretionary Aid Funds. It is also proposed to maintain training and technical assistance. Effective decisions and use of Australian skills in all these areas require an increase rather than a decrease in the African specialist focus within ADAB. The report's strictures on multilateral agencies suggest also that if Australian aid through these agencies is to be fully effective, more detailed and specialist monitoring of the programs will be necessary. Placement of students in Australian training institutions, provision of effective technical assistance, expert advice and support for Australian research contributions to Africa, all call for increased knowledge. So does the need to respond effectively and appropriately to emergency situations. The proposal to withdraw bilateral project aid does not remove the need. At the very least, some country programming support remains essential, to ensure the expertise required for an effective contribution of any aid to Africa at all.

Specifically, and in line with the arguments presented above, we would advocate country programming for the major English-speaking states of Southern and Eastern Africa in which Australia already has a diplomatic presence and aid programs of various kinds; and with which Australia can expect to be continuously involved both within the Commonwealth and in dealing with the broader problems of Southern Africa and the Indian Ocean. This means Zimbabwe, Zambia, Botswana, Malawi, Tanzania, Uganda, Kenya and Mauritius (the latter doubling, of course, as an island state). Several of these countries belong to SADCC and the new Preferential Trading Agreement, which offer additional and natural focal points for Australian connections with Africa.

In certain non-Commonwealth countries where the need for help is great but there are as yet few links with Australia, such as Ethiopia, Somalia, and Mozambique, Australian involvement will probably continue to be geared mainly towards emergency relief; and while country programming would still be desirable for these countries in principle, it might lie, for some time yet, beyond the bounds of the practicable.

Training and Education

The Jackson Report, correctly noting the match between Africa's needs and Australia's skills and experience in several areas, proposes that Australian training and educational assistance for Africa be maintained. The question then is not whether Australia should provide assistance, but how; and the related question is how much. The report itself emphasises education within Australian tertiary and training institutions as a means of development assistance, and recommends a major expansion of tertiary educational places for overseas students. The number of African students currently coming to Australian universities, colleges and training institutions for specialised education and training under SCAAP and other schemes is not large, and we would hope that the number could be increased substantially if the report's recommendation is implemented.

At the same time, it must be stressed that education and training within Australia is not always, or necessarily, an effective form of development assistance. This issue is discussed in general terms in Chapter 8 of this volume; here we have space only to point out the major importance of assistance to education and training within Africa. Obviously this should embrace technical education in agriculture, including especially the training of extension officers, veterinarians, soil scientists and water engineers. It should also include the furtherance of extension services by rural broadcasting, a highly cost-effective method of reaching the farmers and an area in which Australia has long experience. At secondary education level Australia has already begun to play a part through the 'teachers for Zimbabwe program', a practical initiative which should be maintained. At tertiary level there is wide scope for Australian participation in the strengthening of African educational institutions, for example, through staff secondments and library development programs. To help achieve this we would advocate an extension of IDPs mandate to include those Commonwealth African states for which we have recommended country programming. As a specific example, a strong case can be made for an Australian contribution to the rebuilding of Makerere University in Uganda, a major educational institution that is still far from recovered from the depredations of the Amin years. Makerere itself has precise ideas on what it would like from Australia in the way of short-term staffing and staff training, equipment, books and the like. These ideas have been discussed in some detail elsewhere (Gertzel, 1984). Without question, some precisely targeted Australian assistance to Makerere, perhaps organised by ADAB, AUIDP and various universities in collaboration, would be of very great practical long-term value to education in Africa.

Financing Aid to Africa

The proposals we have made would obviously require an increased commitment of funds to African aid. We fully recognise that aid money does not come easily. The fact that 60 per cent of the aid budget is locked into multilateral programs and budgetary support for Papua New Guinea makes competition for the remaining funds all the more intense. We would, nevertheless, make the following points. Firstly, as already noted, Australia's bilateral aid to Africa -- other than food aid -- accounts at present for only about 3 per cent of the total aid budget. If, for the sake of argument, we proposed a doubling of this expenditure -- and this could well be sufficient to achieve many of the improvements we have recommended -- the proportion would still be only 6 per cent or so, which would not seem to lie beyond what is financially and politically feasible. Certainly, there is room for alteration of priorities within the broad budgetary framework. Aid to 'upper middle income' countries (to use World Bank terminology) might be progressively replaced by soft loans. The proposed allocations for the Category 1 island states might be reconsidered, since --notwithstanding the diplomatic arguments for giving them such high priority -- the potential benefits from aid to many of the islands are, on the Jackson Report's own analysis, quite marginal, and there would appear to be major physical limits to their absorptive capacity. Such shifts in emphasis could free not only funds but also expertise and resources for increased assistance to Africa, where the need for aid is extreme.

Secondly, Australia remains officially committed to the United Nations' goal of an aid expenditure amounting to 0.7 per cent of GNP. Mr Hayden, when in opposition, declared the Labor Party's commitment to achieving this goal within its first term of office (Hayden, 1983a, p. 117). Had the target been met in 1984/5, the result would have been an aid budget larger by some 40 per cent or $400 million. Growth in the Australian economy, of course, could and should mean an expanding aid budget even if the target figure were not approached. But growth together with a serious effort to approach the target figure in the next few years could mean a quite rapid expansion. In the context of an aid budget which, it is to be hoped, will expand in real terms once the major decisions on the Jackson Report have been taken, Africa could be given the larger share it so clearly deserves without programs elsewhere being seriously affected.

SUMMARY

Africa is in crisis, and urgently needs more and better developmental assistance. Africa looks to Australia for appropriate aid, and the will to help Africa does exist in the Australian community. The Australian Government has been giving mainly emergency relief aid, for the alleviation of food and refugee problems. But Australia is well equipped to provide more developmental forms of aid to Africa in the longer term. As the Jackson Report recognises, Australia has a comparative advantage over other DAC countries in many areas of agriculture, training and research. The quantity of Australian aid to Africa may be small but the quality is potentially very high, with significant demonstration effects. To deliver such aid effectively, it is important that Australia should maintain appropriate projects in Africa and undertake country programming for selected countries. This is within Australia's capacities. Diplomatic arguments relating to the Indian Ocean, the Commonwealth and Southern Africa all point to the same conclusion.

POSTSCRIPT

In its report published in May 1985, the Parliamentary Sub-Committee on the Jackson Report strongly recommends that Australia should join the African Development Bank. This would be an extremely helpful step towards the joint financing of aid schemes. It would also be helpful to Australian consultants in the field, who in the past have been unable to approach the Bank because of Australia's non-membership and have felt this to be a serious constraint on their work. We would certainly support this recommendation.

The Sub-Committee further recommends, contra Jackson, that Africa should continue to be eligible for Development Import Grants. While we do not see DIGs as a major avenue for aid to Africa, we recognise that they can be a useful source of counterpart funds. Accordingly we welcome this recommendation also.

NOTES

1. From a developmentalist point of view this would seem to be a case in which a subsidiary goal is being pursued at the expense of a basic one, since Egypt's heavy importation of cereals from Australia and other countries is doing nothing to help solve the real problems of development in that country. With a different emphasis in its development program (and perhaps in the donor countries' aid programs) it might have been growing more food for itself. As the Jackson Report comments (p. 15), 'Food aid has often undermined economic development by allowing inappropriate agricultural policies in developing countries to be continued'. On food aid to Egypt specifically, see Elias (1984).

2. We are here following the Jackson Report's usage, which includes in the category 'East Asia' the countries commonly described as Southeast Asian. See e.g. Box 12.1 on p. 189 of the report.

ISSUES IN AN AID PROGRAM

8 AUSTRALIAN EDUCATION AID–WHO BENEFITS ?

Chris Duke

THEME AND CONTEXT

> By helping developing countries to grow, aid provides economic opportunities for Australia. Education should be regarded as an export industry... (Jackson Report, 1984, pp. 3, 87)

The Jackson Report takes, in all essentials, an economistic and elitist view of development in the Third World, various qualifying statements and disclaimers notwithstanding. Development means modernisation: participation through production and consumption in a global economy. Such development is, implicitly, uniform and linear. It sits squarely within what has been labelled the old paradigm of development (Rogers, 1976).[1] The Jackson Report differs in its specific recommendations for aid through education from the Goldring Report (1984), which appeared at about the same time. It was concerned only with overseas students, particularly with modes of managing Asians studying in Australia, and in that sense more with tactics than with fundamental purposes. The Jackson Report, so far as it concerns education, makes best sense read as a strategy for promoting an Australian export industry[2] for the benefit of the Australian economy, with beneficial political spin-off in the foreign affairs arena. As such it is well considered and -- accepting certain assumptions --largely convincing.

However, other views of the causes of poverty in the Third World will generate other views of 'development' -- indicated by terms such as 'alternative', 'authentic' or 'people's'. This alternative paradigm, though by no means new, is perhaps more confidently embraced by workers in adult nonformal education in and for the Third World than by educationists embedded in the formal education system. It is much less acceptable still to the economists and planners to whom Australia and aid counterpart governments look for guidance. Recent international adult education literature has highlighted such differences (Hall and Kidd, 1983; P Healey, 1983; Ahmed and Coombs, 1975).

Educational planning and provision logically derive from a view of society, its structure and dynamics. They also largely reflect and depend upon political, economic and cultural forms, rather than education standing apart from these as an independent agent of change. Australian educational aid policy, elaborated by the Jackson Report, well demonstrates this fact. Reflecting the values and views of economists and business leaders, the report proposes changes in aid for education, which would tend further to enhance Australian interests. It stresses modernisation, with capital accumulation, at the expense of the traditional and rural sectors of the economy. This is not surprising, echoing as it does the approach to development currently adopted by both main political parties, in and for Australia.[3] The result, as in Australia, is likely to be a widening of the gap between rich and poor, further depriving the latter of economic and political power as well as of an identity and sense of being or purpose.

Experience of adult nonformal education programs for reflecting the alternative paradigm referred to suggests that educational aid intended to promote equitable economic and social development might be better directed through non-governmental agencies to partner organisations in the Third World. Most aid would be channelled to local- level groups and institutions away from metropolitan areas. Aid for formal education (higher, technical and, perhaps, secondary and primary) would be more heavily concentrated on building up indigenous resources, institutions and capacities within the partner countries of the Third World. Students would be brought to study in Australia mainly as a temporary expedient or as part of a definite plan for building up educational institutions and resources in partner countries. More Australians might accept Third World assignments, on the other hand, toward this end. Realistically, at the least, some modest strengthening of this philosophy and kind of aid would help to compensate for the largely anti-populist approach of the Jackson Report. Even this compromise might, in practice, require an effective program of development education in Australia to prepare the ground. Paradoxically, the logical consequence of a successful program of development education, such as the Jackson Report proposes, could be to discredit many of the assumptions and recommendations of the report itself.

This chapter, then, questions dominant assumptions about development --dominant still in the Jackson Report in 1984 although Rogers (1976) described them as 'passing' eight years earlier. Thought about formal mainstream education, a major function of which is reproduction of the structure and culture of society, is in turn bound up within these same assumptions. The present analysis, informed by the somewhat different perspective of adult nonformal education, adopts a more separate and critical stance. It has been pointed out by one of the authors of the Jackson Report that, as well as being a report of economists and businessmen, it is also a report strongly influenced, through several of its authors' academic status, by the perspectives of the institutionalised Australian higher education lobby.[4] The report clearly adopts the 'trickle-down' view that ultimately all will benefit from enhanced national productivity based upon infrastructure investment and development; this is the proper target, therefore, of aid programs. In this chapter an alternative view is adopted: that there is commonly a choice, and conflict, between equity and economic development objectives. 'Trickle-down' may not be assumed, and frequently does not occur -- a familiar lesson, by now, of the Green Revolution.[5]

Behind these different perceptions may be discerned different philosophies: the benevolent 'hidden hand' of laissez-faire liberals from the time of Adam Smith; or the sceptical, sociologically and historically informed consciousness of conflict of interests and classes. The latter may lead logically to the adoption of State socialism. Intermediate political configurations are, however, also possible, such as participatory social democracy involving affirmative action, 'positive discrimination', and education for raising critical awareness, mobilisation and empowerment.

At the time the Jackson Report appeared other events in Australia were relevant: 'context' in a different sense. The contemporaneous publication of the Goldring Report was important for its contradictory recommendations for action: reportedly, an interdepartmental committee of federal government set up to adjudicate between the two reports split along precisely the lines upon which Jackson and Goldring differed.[6]

The report appeared at a time of commitment by the Labor administration to a Participation and Equity Program (PEP) for Australian education, a central purpose of which is to enhance the upper secondary and tertiary education retention rates of young Australians. This could lead to possible competition between Australian and overseas students for places -- especially in higher education -- and for necessary financial support to take advantage of places where they exist. This potential for conflict was taken up by the Australian media in the course of public discussion following the release of the Jackson Report and was amplified and complicated by a third factor of context and timing: the 'Blainey debate' about Asian immigration to Australia. The lead-up to the federal election in late 1984 reactivated dormant racial prejudices about Asians in Australia. These became in some measure entwined and confused with public discussion about Asian students coming temporarily to this country. The connection is most obviously demonstrated by the concern in the Goldring Report not to allow large concentrations of overseas students in any one department or institution of higher education.

Finally, the Jackson Report appeared at a time when Australians had come to know a highly popular and pragmatic Labor leader and administration seeking to make Labor the 'natural party of government' by winning the political middle ground; promoting economic growth considerations ahead of those of equity; and avoiding unpopularity other than with its own left wing. The contrast with the first year of the previous (Whitlam) Labor administration was sharp, in foreign as well as domestic affairs. An economist's top-down approach to development, and an Australian educational aid approach calculated to favour Australian economic and foreign policy interests, would seem likely to fall on receptive political ears at such a time.

EDUCATION IN THE JACKSON REPORT

> Education is critical to the development of human resources. Although Australia has strengths in this area, it is missing opportunities to make a substantial impact on education in developing countries. A new approach to the education of developing country students in Australia is needed. (Jackson Report, 1984, p. 10)

Thus begins the Jackson Report summary of its advice on 'Education, research and technical assistance'. Later the summary says of development education -- the education of Australians about development issues -- 'The principal deficiencies of development education can only be met within the education system and this deserves high priority ... expenditure on aid information and development education should be substantially increased' (Jackson Report, 1984, p. 12).

All in all, education features prominently in the report -- and its recommendations for education have attracted spirited debate subsequently. One member of the committee observed, speaking about the report at a conference later that year, that education was given a high profile, being seen as one of the best channels for expressing aid purposes relatively non-interferingly. The recommendations, he held, also reflected an idealistic faith in our neighbours' ability to manage their own affairs once they were tooled up for this purpose. The net result, it was claimed, was not revolutionary but it added up to a radically new approach.

The report's opening chapter pointed out the influence of tertiary education institutions as a lobby group: articulate representatives were well connected in government circles, and 'Australian aid for education and research is almost completely tied to Australian sources, so this lobby takes a close interest in aid policy' (Jackson Report, 1984, p. 22). Chapter Three, noting the difference between technical assistance as part of project aid, and other education and research activities, reports that the training and aid program sponsors about 3,600 students and trainees in either formal post-secondary courses or short practical courses. Assistance is given especially to ASEAN universities to upgrade their teaching, research and administration through what was the Australian Universities' International Development Program (AUIDP), but is now IDP, which includes all parts of Australian tertiary education (Jackson Report, 1984, p. 53).

In the committee's main discussion of education in Chapter Six, 'Education, technical assistance and research', the report is unequivocal: noting the close link between these and 'fundamental inputs into the development process', and also Australia's success in some countries and subject areas, it asserts that:

> The share of Australian aid flowing to education and associated areas should be increased. Education should be regarded as an export industry in which institutions are encouraged to compete for students and funds. (Jackson Report, 1984, p. 87)

Adhering to the distinction between formal education and other educative activities outside the formal system (a distinction which sits uncomfortably with those in adult nonformal education):

> Technical assistance provided through the service of consultants and volunteers is an effective and personalised part of the aid program. Its impact is enhanced where associated with educational support and adaptive research. (Jackson Report, 1984, p. 87)

Education then is defined as central to development, although 'spending on education should not be allowed to run ahead of investment in directly productive sectors' (Jackson Report, 1984, p. 88), else the numbers trained will outrun the supply of 'useful and remunerative jobs'. Here is a clear statement of the sense and scope of education in the report, one which echoes a dominant (though by no means uncontested) view of education for the 'development' of Australia. The report considers improved access to education for disadvantaged groups 'one of the most important steps that a government can take towards improving equality of opportunity' (Jackson Report, 1984, p. 88). Rural areas, slum areas and women are specified. While the report states that 'education deserves support from donors on both growth and equity grounds, and is an area where donors have relative strength' (Jackson Report, 1984, p. 88) it is not specified, here or elsewhere, how donors exercise their strength to secure the 'equity ground'. The section on primary and secondary education notes that some 5,500 foreign students attend secondary schools here, without scholarships but with various levels of subsidy; some schools encourage this as enriching home students' experience -- as a form, that is, of experiential development education. This section leans more than the main discussion of post-secondary education towards 'in-country' assistance -- building up expertise in the countries concerned as distinct from bringing people to Australia.

The next section begins with this point: 'there is little doubt that a good indigenous university can make a significant contribution to development'; referring to AUIDP, it goes on to state that:

> Assistance to students from one developing country to undertake tertiary level training in another developing country is appropriate where Australia's technological environment is of limited relevance, or where groups of countries are joining together to provide regional facilities. A 'third country' environment often involves less 'culture shock' for students, and less cultural alienation on longer term courses. (Jackson Report, 1984, p. 90)

The main thrust of the chapter, however, is towards increasing post -secondary education within Australia. Estimating that some 200,000 mainly Asian and Pacific students have graduated in Australia since World War II, and that total 'brain drain' has been small, the report finds (echoing the Goldring Report) a hidden subsidy of around $70 million a year despite the overseas student charge of from $2,150 to $2,900. To this must be added some $12 million for transportation, living allowances and other costs. (A member of the Jackson Committee, explaining the report to a conference subsequently, said the hidden subsidy might be anything from $60 to $120 million, depending on the basis of the estimates.) Most of the students are supported by their families; 80 per cent come from Malaysia, Hong Kong and Singapore. The present system was found to be cumbersome and unsatisfactory in several respects. The report makes various proposals to remove the administrative barriers; it also recommends 'enrichment' of Australian courses to enhance their relevance for Third World students. On the other hand, it is not in favour of specially tailored courses which isolate such students. These 'carry little more recognition than would have been obtained by training at home' (Jackson Report, 1984, p. 93).

If Australia is to develop its educational institutions into 'a major export sector' (Jackson Report, 1984, p. 93) it must compete with the United States and Europe. It does not need the protection it now enjoys. This would mean more jobs for Australians, with multiplier effects on an estimated one-to-one basis -- one town job for every gown job. From this analysis the committee was led to recommend radical changes within the existing system and institutions. The key to these is to increase the present overseas student charge progressively, to reach full cost by the mid-nineties. The present $70 million subsidy would be redirected into 'merit' and 'special' scholarships based respectively on development criteria, and on balancing up representation of disadvantaged groups, and specifically of women to the point of gender parity. Also, scholarships should be increased to some 10,000 student places over the same decade, raising the total subsidy to $150 million. Generally, a free market approach is commended in place of bureaucratic regulation, leaving the educational institutions a free hand to choose the best merit scholars. Institutions would likewise administer the 'special' scholarships within criteria established by ADAB, assisted perhaps by voluntary agencies and other bodies with suitable international networks (Jackson Report, 1984, p. 96).

These changes would free ADAB to concentrate on short-term courses, also on a less regulated basis. These, it is noted, are increasingly designed to support Australian aid projects. Competition for such courses between tertiary institutions should continue. Later, the report calls for technical assistance to reinforce on-the-job training so that local staff can take over. The chapter concludes with a call for more, and professionally better qualified, volunteers.

Apart from the main discussion of education summarised above, the report addresses education in its fifth chapter, on women. The chapter opens with a discussion of the relative disadvantage of women as measured, for example, by their lower level of primary school enrolments and, especially, their significantly lower levels of adult literacy. An extract from the World Bank (Jackson Report, 1984, p. 81) is headed 'Education: a key to unlock women's potential'. The Jackson Report itself sees a need for more women professionals at all levels, and seeks an increase in women among those studying with Australian support until parity is achieved.

Voluntary aid agencies,

> see people as the means to -- not just the recipients of -- development and want to involve them in decisions about how development should take place. Most agencies have been critical of aid programs that seek to assist growth without regard to equity. Prompted partly by what they see as the failure of the 'growth first' approach, the voluntary agencies believe that a proper development strategy demands that basic human needs be met first. (Jackson Report, 1984, p. 104)

It might be deduced, though it is not said, that this would tend to align voluntary agencies with educationists whose interests are also in people's development and who, in the case of adult educators more especially, place high value on participation in this process. Later, the report notes a claim that voluntary agencies 'can go where government aid cannot effectively go' but 'found it difficult to make a judgment' on these claims to grass roots access. Flexibility and local community involvement, it is suggested, might be offset by inexperience and lack of administrative expertise. The chapter concludes with development education which:

> now has wider implications, seeking to explore such fundamental concerns as why people and nations are poor, and how problems of literacy, ill health and unemployment can be overcome ... Ultimately the aim is to increase community understanding of the whole range of development issues rather than merely provide information about aid programs. (Jackson Report, 1984, pp. 111-12)

Although an important role is conceded for voluntary agencies, and although development education is considered in the chapter about these agencies, the report is unequivocal that 'the formal education system remains the primary means of development education. No extraneous activity or informal education can remedy deficiencies in it' (Jackson Report, 1984, pp. 112-13). The report finds the present $50,000 expenditure on information in ADAB's budget 'extremely meagre by international standards', and seeks an initial annual allocation of $1 million for this and development education.

All in all, then, the Jackson Report gives considerable salience to education as a means of development. It recommends changes which are judged to be radical, though not revolutionary, and very much in Australia's own economic and political interests to adopt. It finds the 'Australian tertiary education industry extraordinarily regulated', in the words of one committee member, and believes it must be changed and 'freed up' to meet both foreign aid and equity objectives.

The Goldring Report on Australian educational aid examined how far admission of private overseas students to Australia served Australia's interests and sought changes which would not reduce opportunities for Australian residents or increase public sector spending. In the event the Goldring Committee had its terms of reference widened to consider overseas students generally. It called for a clear, more outward-looking, national policy in the area which balanced conflicting interests, including those of Australian residents. It explicitly rejected the market -based approach (as adopted equally explicitly by the Jackson Committee) which treated education essentially as a commodity to be bought and sold. It opposed the idea of full-fee recovery as being impracticable as well as wrong in principle.

In place of an open door, full-fee approach the Goldring Committee called for a quite modest increase of 6,000 overseas students throughout all tertiary institutions, and for a system of regulation whereby no institution would exceed 10 per cent overseas to total enrolments, and no course would exceed 25 per cent. The Goldring Report was thus much more concerned with the impact and visibility of overseas students within Australian educational institutions, and clearly opposed the free market approach. It also gave somewhat greater prominence than did Jackson to alternative educational approaches, especially to strengthening home country institutions. Coming at the time of the 'Blainey debate' and a new wave of ethnocentrism fed in part by political considerations in an election year, Goldring's more cautious regulated approach to growth was perhaps more acceptable, in a country noted for very high levels of government activity and regulation, than the more swashbuckling free enterprise proposals of the Jackson Committee.[7]

A CRITIQUE OF JACKSON ON EDUCATION

The past decade has been a tough one for education in Australia: loss of faith in its relevance to economic revival and to the reduction of unemployment; falling retention rates into higher education, only reversed when the labour market got so bad that there was nowhere to go but back into more education (CTEC, 1982). From such a perspective the Jackson Report looks very good to those in the education industry. It means a free market expansion and more scholarships to those of particular ability and with special needs. Within its assumptions about the nature of official development assistance as 'an extension of politics by other means'[8] the report is clear, consistent, and very favourably inclined towards education as a form of aid.

A strong concern for the development of institutions and expertise within countries receiving aid, as an end in itself rather than as 'an extension of politics' and a boost to the Australian economy might, however, suggest a very different emphasis and mix as between in-Australia and 'in-country' effort. Brain drain as such may be modest. However, an experienced educational administrator in Thailand holds the view that it takes about as long for a Thai returning from doctoral study overseas to become 'reacculturated' and able to function usefully back in his or her own society and system as it takes to complete doctoral study overseas.[9] Emphasis upon building up Third World institutions would not proscribe study overseas at graduate or even undergraduate level; but it would certainly suggest much clearer specification of objectives, and tighter determination of priorities and selection of students than Jackson's free market approach will permit. The thrust of the report is towards keeping Australian institutions of tertiary education in business and expanding and not towards accelerating an end to dependency on Australian and other Western education systems.

The report seems tokenistic on another important issue. There is some discussion of the needs of different disadvantaged groups, the rural poor, slum dwellers and, in a special chapter, women; and a call to raise to parity the proportion of women coming to Australia for study. Although grounds of equity are cited, emphasis in fact is on the needs and role of professional women. There is no indication of how Australia should or can ensure that its educational aid would be deployed to reduce inequalities, especially those of a socio-economic rather than a gender kind. Important though gender disadvantage is, increasing the number of middle class women educated overseas and moving into professional positions is irrelevant to the huge inequities between rich and poor, metropolis and periphery. These characterise many countries of the region, and concern those who argue for equity. The prominence of women at senior levels in the Philippines, for instance, apparently does nothing to reduce inequity or shift policy towards people's development in that country. There is no indication in the Jackson Report as to how the increased number of scholarships is to find its way to those in real need, and have any relevance to the disparities of wealth and power common throughout the region.[10] The report points out that the majority of those now paying to study in Australia come from families which are not wealthy by Australian standards, but this is still a far cry from showing how education as a form of aid might benefit 'the poorest of the poor'.

Of course, finally, the report does come down unequivocally for a top-down infrastructure approach to 'development', after acknowledging the concerns and claims of the non-governmental organisations about inequality and the basic needs of the very poor. There is no indication that Australian educational aid should promote critical awareness and mobilisation (Kumar and Kidd, 1982). The problem presented by authoritarian and repressive regimes is somewhat coyly touched upon, with recognition that development is slower and takes longer to benefit the masses in such systems. However, political realism naturally asserts itself.

The report subscribes to a false dichotomy between emergency relief and a capital investment model in which western-style growth is both an assumption and a condition. In this context, elite formation and training for capital investment and capital management tend to widen the gap between rich and poor, and to commit Third World countries to a dependent status in a global economy. Incidentally, this rules out the kind of grass-roots or 'trickle-up'[11] approach -- more favoured by those in adult nonformal education -- which takes seriously the empowerment, through education, of those in greatest need, in a direct way.

The Jackson Report's discussion of bureaucratic procedures for selecting and accepting students has a ring of truth in this highly governed country. Indeed, the Goldring Report calls for an end to administrative confusion, duplication and delay while explicitly rejecting the free market approach.

Professor Goldring wrote at length to The Canberra Times criticising the 'Jackson line' in a June 1984 editorial. We conclude this section with part of that letter:

> Even if the whole of the present subsidy for overseas students were devoted to scholarships for students from overseas, our committee was convinced that a very substantial proportion of students from overseas at present in Australia would be forced to return home, as the scholarships would be available to less than half the present number of students...
>
> To relate an education sector's standards of excellence to whether or not it is controlled by market forces is irrelevant. The universities of most of the countries of Europe are free, or charge only nominal fees, yet no reasonable person would argue that their standards are low. Academic excellence does not need to be the result of market forces...
>
> A majority of overseas students in Australia are ethnic Chinese. In some countries, ethnic Chinese are discriminated against on this ground alone, and are denied access to both higher education in their own country and to scholarship schemes in which the home government has a role. As some, at least, of these governments participate in bilateral scholarship schemes only if they have a significant role in the selection process, our committee considered that this presented an unanswerable argument against making aid scholarships the only way in which Australian public funds were available for overseas students in Australia...
>
> Australia has always been a place in which any academically qualified student may study, regardless of race, nationality, gender, or political views, and we consider this something which it is essential for Australia to retain... (The Canberra Times, 4 July 1984)

These extracts highlight some of the value positions which Jackson for practical purposes ignores. They are values widely held, not least within that 'education industry' which the Jackson Report seeks to expand.[12]

ALTERNATIVES

It is all too easy to attack a report like that of the Jackson Committee, attempting to provide practical and realistic proposals which the government of the day might put into effect. It is quite another matter to suggest constructive alternatives which have some chance of being heeded in the same climate and culture. The Australian context in 1984, it has been suggested, was a difficult one: development was placed ahead of equity at home, and 'trickle-down' was assumed to provide an answer to inequities and poverty over the longer haul. The fallacy of this position has been suggested both for Australia and for the Third World; yet this 'old paradigm' remains dominant among Australian economists and planners. On the other hand, the Jackson Committee seems to have underestimated the strength of feeling against introducing full fees for overseas students, as subsequent lobbying by student groups indicates, and so in practical terms to have misjudged the climate, underestimating the strength of the popular belief in 'fair play'.

The committee effectively ends up in favour of development versus equity, despite its own disclaimers on this score. Is it possible to conceive of an Australian government commitment to an alternative, people's form of development; one which does not stave off the educating, equipping and empowering of the mass of people until the economic infrastructure has been fixed? It is one thing to say that people are a country's greatest natural resource and target for investment; quite another to persuade an administration as pragmatic as the present government that another kind of educational aid is better, which does not represent large export earnings for Australia's economy. Both education and aid are dependent on political and economic factors. The idealism which characterises many in adult education, especially,[13] is a far cry from the kind of domestic and foreign policy adopted by the administration to which the Jackson Committee reported. It might indeed be argued not only that the previous (Whitlam) Labor government, with its radical, especially pro-Asian, foreign policy would have been more receptive to a more radical, less self-seeking, approach to overseas aid, but that the intervening conservative (Fraser) administration would also have been more receptive to a more radical report.

Be that as it may, there are countries not very different from Australia which adopt educational and other aid policies more in line with such alternative values. The Scandinavian countries might be thought too socialist for present-day Australians of either major political persuasion. Often they are not shy about taking an overtly political stance, or at least supporting non-governmental organisations which take such a position. Also, Canada and the Federal Republic of Germany, neither of them susceptible to charges of socialism, both give support to adult education agencies and sectors which clearly adopt a Freirean or similarly radical approach to education for 'authentic' development. The pedagogy of Paulo Freire is already practised in small ways by groups outside and even within ASEAN and other neighbouring countries. These could be assisted to address the more fundamental causes of inequality and underdevelopment within the social and political structure, even while the larger programs continue the work of (often unequalising) modernisation. The Canadian development agency CIDA gives substantial core and project funding to the International Council for Adult Education (ICAE). This council commonly adopts a radical approach to adult education for development. It numbers Paulo Freire among its executive members. The West German Ministry for Economic Cooperation similarly supports a large number of foundations and other agencies providing aid for people's development in the Third World. These include the German Adult Education Association (DVV) which funds, inter alia, projects of the regional adult education network ASPBAE (Asian and South Pacific Bureau of Adult Education). ASPBAE works with governments, of very diverse complexion, including many on the authoritarian right which do not obviously hold human rights or popular development very dear. It is nonetheless able to promote critical and radical adult education programs within such countries. ASPBAE sets out explicitly to support innovators working within the government systems of participating countries, like those of ASEAN, and to help them to draw on nongovernmental energies and experiments to shift somewhat the direction of large-scale government programs (ASPBAE, 1981; Duke, 1981). Third World bureaucracies are not uniform monoliths: there is room to manuoevre and to support change so long as the local knowledge and contacts are there. It is one of the weaknesses of the Jackson Report that in its quest for realism it overlooks some of the realities of power and of change in partner countries.

A series of case studies on adult education and the reduction of poverty commissioned by the International Council for Adult Education drew out the different gains which large-scale top-down and small-scale local-level adult education programs could achieve, the former usually governmental in funding and management, the latter usually non-governmental. Distinctions emerged between adult education for (immediate and temporary) relief and for remedy (removing the causes of poverty); for liberalism (with stress on the individual) and for liberation (implying structural transformation and the redistribution of power). National programs have the potential for country-wide impact in a short time, but usually, except in circumstances of a post-revolutionary regime, of a very modest kind. While many projects can 'achieve a close and specific relationship with the unique needs and circumstances of a particular community' and mobilise new sources of energy, there are problems of wide-scale replication (Duke, 1985). A 'Special Session' of ICAE, discussing these findings, resolved that:

> national and local education associations should associate themselves with efforts of governments to meet immediate basic needs of the people, attempting to ensure that such programmes reach those for whom they are intended and are not subverted by middle-men; national and local adult education associations should make every effort to assist the longer term reduction of the causes of poverty, especially through redistribution of powers, by providing adult education which enables the poor to organize and to obtain their rights. (Duke, 1983, p. 80)

These are but pointers to alternatives which might reasonably be sought even in the cautious and capitalist-oriented Australian context. The caution and sensitivity displayed by the Jackson Committee in not appearing, through aid, to interfere in the affairs of other countries is perhaps overplayed, given the forms of interference which countries of the North do in fact employ to influence those in the Third World. As a result, the report is left rather weak in acknowledging the obstacles to people's development created by right-wing governments, yet seeing no way that egalitarianism can be expressed in the aid area -- admittedly a weak point for intervention. Others are less inhibited. Father Brian Gore called on a national conference in November 1984 to stop aid to the Marcos regime, referring to a 'paranoia' of Australian foreign policy which reflected a lack of realism about the situation in the Philippines. 'Criticising a "lack of social conscience" in Australia, he said: "I think we are going to invest in the rope that hangs us"...'. And, in the words of another speaker, 'Withdrawal of Australian aid will not itself force the downfall of his regime. But it will help the people who are fighting for their freedom' (ANU Reporter, November, 1984). One alternative for Australian educational aid would be to restrict what it gives in educational and other ways so as not to reinforce systems which appear clearly committed to repression rather than development of their subjects. Where scholarships go to students from such countries, safeguards might be sought to ensure that they are not equipping those who will continue reinforcing repressive systems of government and inequitable forms of development -- for instance, by allocating at least a proportion of the awards through selected non-governmental organisations.

If such a stance seems hard to imagine, a second alternative would be less unpalatable and scarcely less signifiant. This is to concentrate educational aid on building up the capacities of institutions, and those who staff them, in the countries of the Third World with which Australia has aid relations, so that they may become increasingly independent of Australian and other resources and expertise. This might imply a set of explicit bilateral plans, perhaps building out from and greatly extending the scope and resources of IDP, to identify and support selected institutions. Education and staff development, undergraduate or graduate, credit or short-course, would be calculated to prepare those responsible for such institutions. There would be much more emphasis upon in-country training, of teams of staff rather than of individuals working in isolation. Each institution would be assisted over a specified period to become self-managing. This would help the education and development of underprivileged regions and groups in the partner countries, rather than exacerbate the rural-urban, especially metropolitan, drift which haunts many such countries. In some circumstances third -country training might be supported rather than bringing students to the very different conditions of Australia, on the TCDC (technical cooperation between developing countries) principle. However, since such priorities would be at the expense of building up the Australian 'education industry', and would sharply distinguish aid from trade, they might prove politically unacceptable. Possibly a self-denying clause might be devised whereby for every educational aid dollar spent on overseas students coming to Australia, one dollar would be spent 'in-country' or in third countries on educational development aid.

Another advantage of such a policy would be to reduce the danger of loss of a country's leading educated human resources to the host educating society and, less obvious but still significant, the disorienting effects of a sustained spell of living and studying overseas on young people. An option recently floated by the Prime Minister of Malaysia, whereby the early years of a degree would be taken at home with only the later years to be taken in Australia, deserves serious consideration. It does not, however, avoid the danger of the government concerned exercising political control over access to opportunity to study overseas, especially where ethnic relations are sensitive and highly political, as in Malaysia. Giving institutions a role in selection might help to reduce political bias. A further alternative would be to restrict the numbers of young people coming to higher education straight from secondary studies, and a requirement for most overseas students of several years' post-secondary experience, giving them the maturation and confidence to handle an alien, affluent, culture without turning away from their own.[14]

From an adult education perspective, the Jackson Report appears curiously deficient in these and other respects. The report does look for short-course and on-the-job training to be more closely related to other kinds of development projects; but the case for building applied, nonformal education into all development projects could be made much more forcefully. Learning on-the-job programs engage the interest and commitment of adult learners. The absence of programs may mean the total or partial failure of projects, especially when the project team has gone home.

More generally, an approach to educational aid for development which was committed to people's development would take advantage of those non-governmental organisations which are able to reach 'grass-roots' counterpart organisations and foster development (not emergency relief) from the ground up. Where, as the report hints, experience and managerial skills may be deficient, an effort could be made to remedy these through volunteer training programs. It is unreasonable to suggest that all Australian educational aid should be channelled through the non-governmental sector and take the form of nonformal education of children, adults and their communities. However, a society which claims to value both democracy and pluralism could comfortably support such an approach as a second string to an educational aid bow. If each educational dollar spent in Australia on overseas students were matched by an Australian educational dollar spent in the Third World, a similar ratio might be struck for formal, governmental, top-down and nonformal, non-governmental, local-level educational aid; not dollar for dollar but possibly, over several years, one 'nonformal dollar' for every four spent through formal institutions. Limited absorptive capacity would preclude anything more ambitious. Such a strategy would however allow at least some educational aid effort to be directed specifically to those deprived groups and sectors whose pressing needs Jackson at least acknowledges.

NOTES

1. There is a considerable literature on the nature and meanings of 'development'.

2. A point emphasised by Dr Peter McCawley, a member of the Jackson Committee, in public presentations about the report during 1984.

3. See for example Henderson and Hough (1984); also McQueen (1984).

4. A point stressed by McCawley in addressing the ANU Public Affairs Conference 'Destiny in Asia', November 1984. The Jackson Report itself refers to 'Tertiary education institutions and related research organisations' as an 'influential lobby group' (p. 22).

5. The unintended regressive consequences of economic development is a common theme in contemporary analysis of 'development' and social change. An enterprising British manufacturer has marketed 'The Green Revolution Game' as a means of teaching some of these dynamics of development through role-playing, taking India, home of the original Green Revolution, as the setting.

6. According to press reports e.g. in the The Age, 2 October 1984.

7. Controversy raged in Australia's press through the second half of 1984 both about levels of immigration and about the desirability or otherwise of these, and about Asian students. Asian immigrants were purported to be taking jobs, and Asian students educational places, away from Australians. The Federation of Ethnic Communities' Councils of Australia published during the year The Great Immigration Debate in an effort to foster better informed and less prejudiced discussion of these issues.

8. J.D.B. Miller, quoted by Andrew Selth, 1985.

9. Conversation with Dr Kowit Vorapipatana, Director-General of Nonformal Education, Ministry of Education, Thailand.

10. The fact that education has disappointed social reformers in countries like Australia as a means of reducing inequality does not absolve the committee from the need to show how this is to be achieved, when it states it as an objective in this way.

11. In the sense that the term 'trickle-up' is being employed to characterise some of the local level development projects of Sarvodaya Shramadana in Sri Lanka. The term is also used quite differently on occasion to describe the hi-jacking of basic needs programs by non-poor groups.

12. A news item in The Canberra Times, 5 February 1985, records a very sharp reaction from many educational interests to the rumour that the Federal Government was considering full-fee costs for overseas students.

13. See, for example, the publications of the International Council for Adult Education on participatory research. These display a deep belief in people and their capacity for creating and making intelligent use of knowledge, instead of remaining dependent on the expertise of others: research in the PR mode is of, for and by the people, and its product is community understanding and action rather than remote and scholarly writing (International Council for Adult Education, 1981, 1982a,b).

14. For a study of an analogous problem for Australian Aboriginal students see Sommerlad, 1976.

9 THE JACKSON COMMITTEE AND WOMEN

Helen M. Hill

It has been common at seminars and conferences on the Jackson Report to hear representatives of non-governmental aid agencies criticise the committee for its failure to make a structural analysis of the root causes of underdevelopment. But then they have been partially exempted because of the presence of Chapter Five, 'Women: A Special Concern' in which, it is argued by these critics, the Jackson Committee at last begins to come to grips with some of the structural obstacles to equitable development. For example the Australian Council for Overseas Aid (ACFOA) comments that 'it is a pity the critical analysis of how women have been left out of the development process was not applied to the poor in general' (ACFOA, 1984, p. 1).

Nevertheless, the chapter on women does not offer a new or deeper level of analysis than the rest of the report, despite the fact that it does make a few highly useful and relevant practical suggestions. These include involving women's groups in developing countries in the planning stages of aid projects, contributing to local costs on women's projects and increasing the number of professionally trained women working in Australian aid programming and implementation. The report usefully draws attention to the high percentage of female-headed households in developing countries and to the prevalence of inequitable distribution of incomes within the family in many societies (Jackson Report, 1984, pp. 80-6). It also points to the disadvantageous way in which agricultural modernisation has increased women's workload in a number of countries or taken away opportunities for gainful employment. But, as I argue later, the chapter is superficial in its treatment of women and education, fails to adequately look at women in agriculture or to examine women's role in health care or women's access to land.

WHY A CHAPTER ON WOMEN ?

Given the general economic assumptions as to the nature of socio economic development evident in the rest of the report, it would not appear that the committee would have examined anything so micro-level as the impact of aid on women had they not been so instructed. And indeed it was Foreign Affairs Minister Bill Hayden's press release of 24 June 1983, issued some two months after the original statement of the terms of reference for the review, that informed the committee that they should give attention to the interests of women in their deliberations. But this was by no means the first time that women had come into consideration in the government's development thinking. Hayden noted, in his 24 June press release that 'the ALP platform on development co-operation called for particular attention to be given to programs which raise the status of women'. This policy came into the party's platform at the July 1982 National Conference and followed similar resolutions coming from the ALP Women's Conference and the Conference of Labor Economists the previous November. Nor was this the first time an Australian government had a policy on women in development: the Fraser government had a policy of aiming at 50 per cent of training awards going to women, and a 'Womens' Advisor' had been appointed to the Policy Branch of ADAB in 1979.

Rather than representing a break with the assumptions underlying the rest of the report, an underlying assumption of the chapter appears to be that women are disadvantaged because they cannot raise their level of productivity sufficiently. For example, we read:

> men can seek work in towns, learn skills in the army or go to high schools, while women stay at home or, at best, work as maids or at unskilled tasks in industries. Even the latter occupations are usually preferable to low productivity, low reward, employment or under employment at home and can mean a much higher living standard with some disposable income, but these are jobs without prospects. (Jackson Report, 1984, p. 77, emphasis added)

And later in the report:

> In the cities women look after food stalls and work in modern industries such as clothing, textiles, toy manufacture and electronic assembly. Unfortunately, in most countries the availability of such jobs fall far short of the need. When this is the case, domestic service is often one of the few other options. (Jackson Report, 1984, p. 80)

Is a young peasant woman in Southeast Asia, who moves to the city to take a job on an assembly line for low pay, forced overtime and with the prospect of losing her eyesight within ten years, in a better position than one who remains in the subsistence agricultural sector? This question cannot really be answered on the individual level, but countries are basing development strategies on policies which assume there will always be a steady flow of women coming from the rural areas to take such jobs. How will the rural areas be affected? Who will do the work traditionally done by women, often food production? Is the increasing participation of women in development to be defined simply as the creation of more jobs for women in the cash sector, regardless of the pay and conditions? It would appear that in the development strategies being followed in the fast-industrialising countries, women run the risk of being isolated into low-wage ghettos, and unless they have adequate bargaining power this life might not be much of an improvement over that which they sought to leave behind.

Philip Eldridge (1985, p. 24) claims the chapter on women is the only one where the concept of participation by the intended beneficiaries of Australian assistance is mentioned. Thus it 'contrasts sharply with the rejection in the rest of the report of proposals for targeting programs directly to meet the needs of disadvantaged groups' (Eldridge, 1985, p. 25) when it makes the laudable recommendation that:

> project design guidelines should ensure that there will be adequate analysis of the impact of the proposed changes on women and also ensure that they participate in the benefits that are expected from the project. (Jackson Report, 1984, p. 82)

But the contrast is more apparent than real. For while women in recipient countries can certainly be consulted about the planning of Australian aid projects, it is more likely that they will be senior female public servants, members of national women's councils, women's advisors to governments, or even politician's wives rather than the rural or illiterate women whom one would expect to be the beneficiaries of aid projects.

One of the problems of the chapter on women, like the other chapters in the report, is its failure to treat class as a significant variable in the process of development. This might not matter when dealing with economic abstractions, and national aggregates as in purely economic analysis. But an examination of the role of women in development forces attention to be paid to such aspects as the division of labour between men and women, sharing of income within the family, and differential access to education between men and women. No generalisation can be made about these within one country, let alone for Third World countries as a whole, for they each vary considerably according to class. The inequalities produced over the past decades by differential access to formal education in many countries are greater among girls and women than they are among boys and men, yet women are more often lumped together as if all their needs were the same. Speaking in 1973 on the Papua New Guinea situation, Nahau Rooney (1975, p. 119) emphasised the necessity of considering at least three separate groups of women:

1. traditional village women -- mainly in the rural areas and of great number;
2. urban uneducated or semi-educated women;
3. educated women -- a small minority.

Each of these three groups has particular problems with development. For the traditional village women it is often problems of overwork, due to food growing, water collecting and other responsibilities, often exacerbated by too many pregnancies. The urban uneducated women, often recent arrivals from the rural areas, are commonly the most neglected by government authorities. The educated women, while privileged in relation to the majority of women, still find themselves the victims of sexism in the workplace, their talents and their experience underutilised and under -emunerated.

The Jackson Committee, quite rightly, puts emphasis on education as an important prerequisite for women's advancement in any country of the world. It is somewhat odd, however, that in a report which sees one of the main applications of Australian aid as 'removing major constraints to development' (Jackson Report, 1984, p. 59) that more attention was not paid to the structural reasons for women's failure to benefit from education as much as men. The typical economist's 'black box' approach to education seems to be taken, where education is seen as a significant variable, measured in terms of the number of years spent sitting in a classroom, while no attention is paid to the content or quality of that education.

A 1975 seminar of the American Association for the Advancement of Science identified four sets of obstacles to women gaining an education in Third World countries. These were: the cultural attitudes which militate against women's full participation in educational institutions, the lack of relevance of much of girls' education to the local or the national economy, the language of instruction which often creates a barrier between educated elites and the villagers, and the teaching methods used within classrooms which often encouraged girls to remain passive non-participants in the educational process (Tinker, Bo Bramsen and Buvinic, 1975, pp. 158-60). Unless something can be done to overcome each of these obstacles, merely expanding the number of places available in schools will not assist girls to benefit by them.

Australian aid assistance for education has been almost completely at the tertiary level until now. While the committee does recommend that more 'in-country' training would enable more women to participate in Australian-sponsored training there is no indication given as to what might be the level or content of these courses. Indeed it is likely that the types of recommendations made concerning Australian training aid as a whole, namely concentrating even more on post-graduate and vocational training, will disadvantage women even more. Without improved participation rates in primary and secondary education, women will continue to be less likely than men to qualify for and be selected by their governments for overseas training. A precise strategy is needed by ADAB if the 50 per cent female target is to be reached for those countries where it has not already been achieved, and this must not be done simply by increasing the number of courses in Home Economics or other traditionally female subjects. An obvious area of need, as Eileen Byrne (1983, pp. 54-5) has pointed out, is agricultural education for women in countries where they are the major food producers. She argues that in those few countries which have attempted to include women in agricultural education, along with men, agricultural productivity has been increased.

The question of the impact of development assistance on women remains a somewhat controversial one among ADAB officers, despite the official adherence to a policy which pays particular attention to the needs of women. There appear to be two reasons for this. One is that the promotion of women's rights is seen to be somehow 'Western' and an imposition of our own culture on other countries whose governments might resist it. The other is that many ADAB officers regard it as too difficult to design, staff and implement 'women's components' of projects. On the first point, the 'cultural interventionism' argument, this is quite surprising when one considers how much other areas of life are intervened in by Western aid. Diet, work relationships, dress, agricultural methods, land tenure, language and health practices are all areas in which western culture has imposed itself on indigenous cultures, often with beneficial outcomes but sometimes with disastrous ones. Yet interventions in these fields are rarely halted in the name of cultural integrity, rather they become part of the changing culture of the country concerned, for better or for worse, or are rejected by certain classes. In a capitalist society no culture can isolate itself completely from changing values and attitudes. ADAB officers and consultants rarely think twice about any other aspect of 'Western culture' they import to their posting. Unfortunately, many of them do not have an adequate understanding of cultural change so they become easy prey for reactionary elements in a society which tries to keep women in a dependent and subordinate relationship to men, often in the name of a 'traditional culture'. In some cases this 'tradition' owes as much to the attitudes of former colonial rulers as it does to authentic local culture.

There are unhappily some countries in which traditional authoritarianism and feudalistic values are used to keep women from sharing the benefits of development. In these societies a struggle often exists between women's groups and the ruling party, with sometimes the ruling party's own official women's group taking issue with its prescriptions. In such cases it is particularly important for projects to be carefully evaluated from the point of view of their impact on women. If the impact is likely to be detrimental, the projects should not be funded.

The second argument, that it is difficult and costly to design and implement 'women's components' of bilateral projects has more substance to it. First, there should not generally be a need to have a 'women's component' of a project. The main reasons why 'women's components' of projects are generally included are because the project is often so male-biased, or the project actually disadvantages women by taking away their rights to land, livelihood etc. and thus it is seen as compensation. Many projects will increase the workload of women. This was almost inevitable as long as women's work was undervalued because it was not paid work. Many projects were designed on the assumption that women had 'spare-time' even though surveys showed they often worked many hours longer than men. Some Australian projects have been a total failure in benefiting women because they were designed purely from the technical angle, by engineers or land surveyors. The classic example of this is the Magarini Project in Kenya, which the Jackson Report (1984,

p. 84) refers to as a case where women lost their rights to land. One problem of designing projects properly so that women are not disadvantaged, is that very skilled people are required, with sufficient local knowledge, in addition to capability of sociological analysis. These people must use techniques, such as participatory research (Duke, 1978) which are little known in Australia, for ascertaining the views of all the interested parties on the proposed project. The current methods of recruiting people to ADAB do not encourage such people to join the Bureau and the regular consultancy firms do not have them.

NO TECHNICAL SOLUTIONS TO POLITICAL PROBLEMS

One of the real problems faced by those who are working to expand women's role as participants and beneficiaries of development is that many of the obstacles faced by women in developing countries cannot be solved by aid projects. Often their subordinate role and disadvantageous status arises from lack of political power or having no access to land or credit. In some Pacific islands women even lack the basic right to control their own fertility. Anyone who has attended a meeting of the South Pacific Commission will be aware of the real obstacles women face in the South Pacific region due to their lack of political power. The male delegates at such conferences are able to ignore, ridicule or trivialise any issue related to women which comes up on the agenda, and frequently do, Australians included (Hawkins, 1981). Until women form a substantial part of delegations to regional meetings this will continue to happen. Concerted lobbying on the part of women in all Pacific countries could achieve this, as there are undoubtedly able women in these countries who could make a good contribution, not only to so-called 'women's issues'.

Other problems of women in the development process also require transnational lobbying and political action rather than aid funds, for example, the international efforts which exposed the marketing of breast-milk substitutes in countries with poor hygiene and balance of payments problems. Similar campaigns are desperately needed in the area of dumping of dangerous drugs in Third World markets where they can be sold without prescription and advertised misleadingly. Sex-tourism and other forms of trafficking in women are also a problem in many countries which have a high disparity between rich and poor, and often involve international capital, some of it from Australia. In 1981 former Prime Minister Gough Whitlam suggested that the best way to assist Asian workers, many of whom are women, would be to urge Asian governments to ratify and implement the ILO Conventions on freedom of association, the right to organise, the abolition of forced labour and night work for women (Whitlam, 1983, p. 182).

One of the recommendations which the Jackson Committee makes is for a Women in Development Fund, and the 1984/5 Budget incorporated this recommendation with an allocation for $50,000 to be spent on women's projects. In many ways this is a problematic recommendation. While it's useful for the Women's Advisor in ADAB to have access to some funding for particular projects, once such a fund is announced it becomes flooded with applications so that the role of the Womens' Advisor in ADAB changes from that of a lobbyist throughout the Bureau for improved practices to that of an administrator of a program, with little time left for the other work. For this reason also the Women and Development Network of Australia (WADNA) has resisted becoming a funding body, except in very rare circumstances, partly because it sees the lobbying, advising and awareness-raising role as so much more necessary at this time, and also because to take over the funding of women's projects would be to remove them from the domain of all the other voluntary aid agencies, most of which were set up primarily as funding bodies.

The Jackson Report fails to address the problem of land reform. As Gunnar Myrdal pointed out over a decade ago, monopoly of ownership of land is, together with monopoly of education, the fundamental basis of inequality (Myrdal, 1970, p. 199). The OECD's Development Assistance Committee, in its Guiding Principles for Women in Development, put great emphasis on women's access to productive resources, in particular women's right to own land and their access to credit and banking facilities (OECD, 1984, p. 23). The Jackson Report also fails to address concretely women's productive role in agriculture and how their benefits from it can be improved. While the report points out how women have been disadvantaged by men gaining access to higher level agricultural technologies (Jackson Report, 1984, p. 80), nowhere in the report do we get an idea as to what should be done about this, save that of women moving out of agriculture altogether.

In considering the Jackson Report's relevance to women in developing countries we should look beyond Chapter Five, for many of the other recommendations will have impacts on projects affecting women. The explicit rejection of 'basic needs' strategies, for example, is one which is not in the interests of women generally. Basic needs strategies, as opposed to export-led industrialisation, recognise the differential role of men and women in the economy (Palmer, 1977). It is somewhat odd that the Jackson Committee warns against intervention in domestic affairs in its section on basic-needs approaches only, when many of the other strategies recommended are highly interventionist.

Other recommendations of the committee, such as adopting a more clearly defined sectoral focus, and 'country programming' could be of definite benefit to women in recipient countries (Jackson Report, 1984, p. 65, 134). However, this will only be the case if women are not seen as a sector themselves, but rather as having a contribution to make to all sectors. Similarly, in country programming exercises it is not 'women' as such which should be looked at, but gender relations, division of labour between men and women, relative access to education, employment etc. (bearing in mind also the impact of class as mentioned above). In the process of writing country programs, use can be made of the increasing amount of research being done by female researchers from these countries, many of whom are producing very detailed analyses.

Surely one of the most intractable problems in the development assistance field today is that the beneficiaries of most aid projects are rarely those most in need. Addressing the topic of women in development should, as I have argued elsewhere (Hill, 1983), open up the possibilities for new strategies involving women to enable the needy to play more of a role in improving their own material conditions of life. Unfortunately, this does not seem to have been considered by the Jackson Committee. One example is the section on Health and Nutrition in which it sees the Australian medical profession as making a major contribution (Jackson Report, 1984, p. 62). The majority of health problems in Third World countries require the contribution of local health educators, vaccinations, good food, access to clean water, sanitation and healthy environments more than they need the advice of medical practitioners. The Jackson Committee has adopted a highly bureaucratic and technocratic solution to problems whose long-term solution will only be in mobilising people within the community to meet those in need themselves. What does it mean by saying that 'Australia can provide an integrated health care package aimed at meeting the complete range of primary health care needs in a particular area' (Jackson Report, 1984, p. 63)? It would seem to be a prescription for the committee's own health care needs. This cannot be in the interests of independent development.

But perhaps one should not be too hard on the committee in this respect. The nature of its terms of reference, which were limited to examining the impact of the Australian aid program, and to recommend strategies which can be implemented by a bureaucracy in Canberra, restricted it from looking at development in its broadest sense. The overloading of the committee with economists and businessmen, to the exclusion of any sociologists, health professionals, agriculturalists etc. also clearly clouds its recommendations. Women should be thankful that the report gave such prominence to their needs, as this undoubtedly makes it easier for those within ADAB who see it as a serious and urgent issue to argue their case. Hopefully it will also enable more networking to go on between women in ADAB and women researchers and representative women's organisations within the recipient countries. Everyone must guard against a new 'ghettoism' of womens' projects arising, particularly those which do nothing to assist women to improve their power and status.

CONCLUSION

The issue of women in development is not, as a member of the Jackson Committee quipped to ADAB staff at the launching of the Jackson Report, a 'fashion' in development thinking. It is a logical outcome of individuals and movements working to bring it to the attention of policy -makers. Now that we have gained that attention it is important that more work be done on identifying how to enable women to benefit more from development and to be disadvantaged less. Much more searching analyses remain to be done. For example, during the media publicity which surrounded last year's famine emergency in East Africa, how often did one hear any mention of women's role in agriculture? The fact that 60 - 80 per cent of agricultural workers in Africa are women (Isis, 1983, p. 73) should have started people asking questions about women's work in this vital sphere, for a long-term solution to Africa's food problem will obviously have to involve women at every level. Nor was there much discussion about women's role in, for example, the distribution of emergency food aid and in food preparation. The fact that this did not happen shows that we still have a long way to go even fn getting the basic issues raised.

10 TRADE AND DEVELOPMENT

Steve Keen

AID, TRADE AND INVESTMENT

The aid debate has had more than its fair share of fads. The initial one, in the wake of the Marshall Plan post-war reconstruction of Europe, was that a similar transfer of funds from the First World to the Third World would lead to a similar rapid pace of economic growth there, and the consequent elimination of poverty.

The Jackson Report alludes to this belief in its section on international aid diplomacy:

> The 'two gap' theory of economic development which attracted much attention in the 1960s suggested that development was constrained in poor countries by two factors: the inability to save and the inability to import essential goods and services. It was argued that aid flows, by bridging both gaps, could boost growth in developing countries. Large amounts of economic and military aid evidently contributed to rapid growth in Taiwan and the Republic of Korea and it was expected that these results could be replicated elsewhere. (Jackson Report, 1984, p. 43)

They were not, and a radical creed emerged from the failure of aid to engender development. This was that the true root of poverty was economic oppression. Changes to local economic relations -- and land ownership in particular -- were at least as important as international aid flows if poverty was to be eliminated. With poverty in the Third World primarily the consequence of Dickensian social relations, the Marshall Plan approach amounted to pouring money into Scrooge's coffers.

This case was reinforced by re-examination of the supposed aid success stories of South Korea and Taiwan. In both those countries extensive land reform accompanied the flood of aid dollars. The landlord class was exterminated (in South Korea's case literally so) and a legally enforced system of smallholdings -- which hardly coincides with allowing the free market to operate -- provided a vital base for rural and industrial growth. On this view, social conflict and the redistribution of wealth were unavoidable elements of development.

This was not a case which pleased the proponents of the Third World Marshall Plan. Undaunted, they began to preach an alternative gospel of 'trade not aid'. The moral was that the Third World Marshall Plan had failed because only miniscule amounts of money had been transferred, compared to those which went from the USA to Europe. Since it seemed unlikely that such funds would be donated to our poor Third World cousins, they had to generate them themselves. The only way to generate such amounts of money was by trade.

The development success stories were also reinterpreted. Their growth was attributed to trade, and their obedient enactment of the conventional economics view of how trade should be conducted. The Jackson Report, like its Harries predecessor, is firmly planted in this 'trade not aid' camp:

> The rapid increases in the per capita income of these countries were achieved primarily by pursuing labour-intensive, export -oriented policies in a growth-oriented policy framework. In the two larger countries, the Republic of Korea and Taiwan, the development of a dynamic agricultural sector accompanied industrialisation ... The industrialisation of these countries began with the manufacture for export of labour-intensive and low technology goods. Price distortions through protection were offset in various ways in the Republic of Korea and Taiwan, and Hong Kong and Singapore adopted free trade policies... (Jackson Report, 1984, p. 22)

As for aid's domestic rationale, while the committee acknowledges the humanitarian element, it prefers to see the trade advantages which aid can confer as the key factor:

> Development expands the market for Australian goods and services and increases opportunities for direct investment abroad by Australian companies. Developing countries need to export to be able to import Australian goods and technology. Trade leads to specialisation and efficiency. Aid and trade reinforce each other. (Jackson Report, 1984, p. 22)

THE MARKET RULES OK

The Jackson Committee's edict is that market-based policies will lead to the greatest growth within the Third World and that market principles should rule international trade. Conventional trade theory gives the committee a neat way out of the 'tied aid' dilemma.

The growth power of a market economy cannot be denied. What can be denied is that the countries of the Third World, universally feudal prior to colonisation, then battened upon and manipulated to foreign ends during the colonial period, were capable of demonstrating all the virtues of developed market economies upon independence. More often than not, they demonstrated their vices.

Virtues however are all the committee will countenance. Here is their list of essential ingredients for economic growth:

> A stable economic environment which encourages savings and investment, and the efficient allocation of resources, and which promotes an equitable distribution of the benefits of growth has the following characteristics: Realistic exchange and interest rates which encourage investment, production and exports; taxes which provide avenues to create public infrastructure; and wages which reflect productivity. Health and education receive high priority. Public ownership and private entrepreneurship are balanced, with competitive markets which reflect scarcities. (Jackson Report, 1984, p. 30)

The list continues, but the instructive comment is about wages. In blunter language, the phrase means that one of the reasons for tardy growth in most Third World countries is that the workers are paid too much.

If the typical developing economy were characterised by widely disbursed ownership of resources, and peopled by individuals free to choose between self-sufficiency and working for wages, then that allegation could stand a chance of being true. But the great bulk of the Third World is characterised by concentrated ownership of resources, and peopled by tenants and landless labourers without recourse to self-production.

In these circumstances it is not the wages of workers which exceed productivity, but the rents of landlords and the charges of moneylenders. Though such rates may come as news to drafters of government reports in Australia, people who have worked with Third World peasants are no longer stunned by landlords taking 50-70 per cent of a farm's product as rent, or moneylenders charging 120 per cent interest a year. This situation is a double disincentive to growth. The rural elites make significant returns with little or no need to invest in the land, and the extreme poverty of the vast bulk of the population means there is no 'mass market' to encourage ancillary investment. It is investment, not trade, which is the engine of growth.

Those Third World countries which boomed and sustained their growth either did not face these rural problems in the first place, as with Hong Kong, Singapore and, to a lesser extent, Malaysia and Thailand, or overturned their landlord dominated systems of tenure prior to successful industrialisation, as with South Korea and Taiwan (and even Japan). Landed surpluses which previously went into feudal consumption patterns were turned towards productive rural investment; food production increased, and the rural exodus to the cities slowed. A domestic market began to evolve, providing a base for the eventual development of export-oriented manufacturing behind protective tariffs and regulations. Frequently, these developments also involved a perceived external threat, which overcame the resistance of political rulers to the abolition of old strongholds of privilege. With the sole exception of Hong Kong, all these developments occurred under the strong hand of government policy.

THE INTERNATIONAL FRONT

The reality that the Third World high-flyers more often flaunted than obeyed the edicts of economics creeps uneasily through the committee's otherwise confident championing of free trade. The statement that:

> In general, those developing countries which have promoted trade and have pursued outward looking economic policies have achieved faster growth, fuller employment and higher wages than those which have clung to protection. (Jackson Report, 1984, pp. 118-9)

is followed almost immediately by the admission that the leading lights of development have in fact practised a very circumspect version of 'free trade':

> The more advanced developing countries such as the Republic of Korea must expect that a reduction in aid flows will be followed in due course by a loss of privileged trade access. With the exception of Hong Kong and Singapore, most developing countries are themselves highly protectionist. They, too, would benefit from competitive pressures through increased imports. Reciprocal liberalisation will become increasingly important as their standards of living approach those of the industrial countries. (Jackson Report, 1984, p. 119)

South Korea and Taiwan, like Japan before them, have followed mercantilist trade policies, vigorously promoting exports while reserving the home market for local producers. Their development has resulted not from specialisation inspired by a liberal trade regime, but from an export -oriented manufacturing policy, with corporate investment pushed by the state and underwritten by a protected domestic market. There certainly is a lesson for Australia in their success, but it is not the one the committee has drawn:

> There is a lesson for Australia in this. Despite problems of negotiating reciprocal access in Europe, Japan and the United States for farm products, Australia would be best served by moving steadily and purposefully towards a more open economy. Certainly there would be adjustment problems, but the once and for all cost of adjustment would be less than the continuing cost of inappropriate protection. (Jackson Report, 1984, p. 119)

The performances of the NICs, and Japan and West Germany before them, makes nonsense of this 'lesson', for the simple reason that an analysis which is static and based on full employment cannot possibly explain the reality of dynamic, growing economies which are creating new resources, and frequently do not fully employ their current stock.

The true lesson for Australia in the success of the NICs is two-fold. First, it is investment, not trade, which propels growth. Secondly, trade can play a role in promoting investment, if trade is turned to investment's service through interventionist policies.

These conclusions are diametrically opposed to the strictures of conventional economics which, since the days of Leon Walras, have laid the emphasis on static questions of resource allocation, to the near exclusion of dynamic questions of expanding the stock of resources. Economic theory -- other than that derived from Keynes and Marx — presumes a fully employed economy and does not address itself to the expansion of that economy.

Conventional economics believes in a market which, untampered with, will necessarily tend to full employment. Theoretical disputes over the past 50 years have established that this case is invalid, yet the economics profession continues to follow this gospel in a remarkable display of blind ignorance and ideology. Without interventionist, growth -oriented policies, Australia and the West in general will continue to wallow in what is now the longest recession this century.

Mavericks such as Lord Keynes, Joan Robinson and Sir Roy Harrod have long argued that conventional economic thought is incapable of analysing a growing economy; in recent years the intellectual father of modern economics, Sir John Hicks, has come to reject his offspring for the same reason.

The real lever to lift us out of depression and the Third World out of poverty is not trade and its much vaunted specialisation, but investment and its much neglected impact on productive capacity and aggregate demand. The growth that investment can generate is a far more valid source of mutual gains than the economists' chimera of comparative advantage. The NICs have used trade to propel investment in manufacturing, with myriad incentives to attract overseas investors and with a protection guaranteed domestic market to coax investment out of domestic capitalists. The economics profession holds these countries up to the West as bastions of economic rationality, and it is right to do so: but they are rational because they have ignored the 'lessons' of the neo-classical economists.

TIED AID

The committee was pressed heavily on the question of tying Australian aid to Australian products:

> It has been put strongly to the Committee that Australian business should benefit more from aid, and that Australian goods and services should be used whenever possible within the Australian aid program. This would help expand manufacturing production, promote greater service industry exports and increase the number of jobs within Australia. Participation in aid programs can familiarise Australian firms with business conditions in developing countries and introduce them to new customers. There are various lobbies for bilateral rather than multilateral aid; for food aid (comprised of Australian produce) rather than cash contributions; for project aid tied to Australian procurement

> rather than untied budget support ... Specific proposals include greater tying, an expanded development import finance scheme, and more liberal aid-trade lines of credit. It is said that too little of Australia's aid is in the form of manufactured goods or construction. (Jackson Report, 1984, p. 119)

Given the report's free trade orientation, it is not amazing that it felt inclined to reject such pressures. Due to its prime focus on the impact of aid on the recipients, it was politically uneasy about submissions which laboured the interests of the donor. But the pressure to tailor aid to suit commercial interests was considerable.

The committee fell back on economic theory for a neat way out of this dilemma:

> Although the Australian aid program is closely related to trade, and although aid and trade policies should be complementary, aid policy cannot substitute for export policy. However, Australian business plays an important role in aid delivery, and participation in aid programs provides firms with the experience necessary to compete in export markets. By focussing aid on particular sectors where Australian services and goods have a comparative advantage, a coincidence of aid and commercial interests can be served without sacrificing the integrity of either. (Jackson Report, 1984, p. 115, emphasis added)

The committee sidestepped the issue of the tying of aid with this theoretical ruse. To truly resolve the conflicting interests, the committee should next have indicated precisely where Australia's 'comparative advantage' lay with respect to the Third World, and suggested means by which Australian aid could be focused on these sectors. It did not.

Its recommendations, if anything, will increase the antagonism of commercial interests to aid. Though the committee was not shy in seeing self-interest as a major motivation behind the giving of aid -- 'Development expands the market for Australian goods and services' -- here as everywhere else it preferred to see things done by the textbook. It attacked the expansion of 'mixed credit' schemes, where the financing for an aid project involves a concession to induce the purchase of the donor's goods, and suggested that Australia's Development Import Finance Facility (DIFF) be limited to 5 per cent of the aid budget. Even so, reference to the report's projections indicate that they anticipate a 600-750 per cent increase in DIFF funding up to 1993/4 (Jackson Report, 1984, p. 163).

The committee's case for rejecting the tying of aid rests partly on humanitarian grounds -- that the aid budget should actually assist recipients, and not be a disguised subsidy for domestic industry -- and partly on the veracity of its free trade, non-interventionist case, for both the recipient and the donor of aid.

The humanitarian case matters, but like the gains from free trade itself, it can be grossly overstated. It is true that tied aid can, and in most countries does, amount to little more than a disguised subsidy to domestic industry. But the real issue in development is whether the project into which the tied aid is poured helps or hinders the social change which is needed to let growth commence. If you are going to build your wells on the landlord's property, it matters little which country designed the well.

As I have argued above, the committee's analysis of Third World economies is flawed. Countries which have followed the non-interventionist path --despite its socialist rhetoric, India has done so in the crucial area of rural development -- have yielded stagnant economies with investment limited by mass poverty and the wastefulness of a rural elite. Countries which have broken the economists' creed, initially in rural policy with land reform and land ownership ceilings, subsequently in industrial policy with barriers to trade, state planning and corporate collusion, have yielded dynamic economies with genuine improvements in the living standards of the mass.

Nor does the market of the committee's dreams exist in the international economy. The committee's way out of its tied aid dilemma was to rely on the market in the developing world to decide what products are needed, and on 'comparative advantage' to decide the successful tender. The theory of comparative advantage envisions a homogeneous world where countries differ only in their consumer preferences and endowments of resources: technology and products are similar the world over. In reality the world is diverse, with huge differences in technology, products and tastes. In the theory's rarified world, the only motive force for trade is comparative advantage.

If 'the market' did behave in this way, then tied aid would necessarily diminish the value of aid to recipients. The aid vote would be a dumping ground for Australian produce (which is certainly the way it has been regarded by some who put their barrow before the Jackson Committee), which would burden the Third World with produce which it could get elsewhere at lower cost, and leave Australian manufacturing slightly fatter, though otherwise unaltered.

But in the real world, product innovations are common and differentiation within established product lines the rule rather than the exception. These differentiations are often the prime motivation for trade in manufactures, yet products are normally first developed for the home market -- simply because it would be a prescient capitalist who could foretell the tastes of a different country without first testing a product in his home market.

For this reason, a secure home market is frequently the first requirement for establishing a successful export. Not surprisingly, investment in Australia is frequently stymied by the belief that the Australian market is not big enough to support 'esoteric' developments, and by the inability of potential investors to see beyond the Australian market for unique products.

Frequently products which fail to inspire investment in Australia are ones which would be of considerable use in a Third World environment. Some of the best examples have occurred in the area of decentralised power-generating equipment, designed in part to suit conditions in outback Australia where the distribution costs from conventional centralised power-generation systems are prohibitive.

Evacuated tube solar power generators, which could have found commercial application in the Third World, foundered for lack of interest on the Australian market. These units overcome the usual objection made to solar power that it is incapable of producing temperatures high enough to be of use in industrial processes. At the same time they are suited to decentralised power generation, which is as cost effective in the heavily populated and evenly distributed settlements of the Third World as it is in the sparsely settled (but 'uneconomic') outback. But its university inventors could find no commercial support for it in this country, and it has now been purchased by a Japanese company. If this invention ever assists Third World development, it will be as part of a Japanese aid program.

There are several examples of Australian-designed technologies which have assisted particular Third World communities -- earthquake -proof houses in Afghanistan, micro-hydro power stations in the Pacific. Most have had only limited impact because they have relied entirely on the meagre funds of Australia's voluntary aid organisations. Their impact would have been much greater if funds had been earmarked from the aid vote.

These and other unique contributions to development could have much wider currency with a well administered scheme to develop, promote and subsidise sales of appropriate Australian manufactures. There is a danger that such a scheme might become a palliative to domestic industry, but properly administered and policed by some of the development oriented bodies, such as APACE (Appropriate Technology and Community Awareness), which have pioneered the Australian design of appropriate technology for the Third World, it could underwrite the manufacture of unique Australian products and provide a genuine benefit to the recipients of Australian tied aid.

With the Australian market as it is, products will continue to fail and both Australian manufacturing and Third World communities will be the poorer. But if an institution existed which sought out and sometimes commissioned products for Third World usage, worthwhile Australian innovations would no longer collapse for lack of a perceived market.

THE CASE FOR ECONOMIC NATIONALISM

The Jackson Report is hardly original. Like numerous economist-drafted government reports before it, it pushes the case for internationalism and against economic nationalism. Rarely is a chance missed for a homily on the 'mutual gains from trade', the merits of following Australia's 'comparative advantage', and the evils of 'protectionism' -- the trade policy manifestation of nationalism.

Since Adam Smith and The Wealth of Nations, economists have striven to make nationalism unfashionable. Prior to his fable of the pin factory, where specialisation led to a material bounty, the creed of the day was mercantilism. Its message was distinctly nationalist -- expand your exports, restrict your imports, and build a positive trade balance to finance growth. Economic theory has an impressive arsenal of reasons why mercantilist policies will not work: mercantilism restricts specialisation, and it is specialisation which generates growth; a positive balance of trade simply causes inflation; protection causes the misallocation of resources, and so on.

First amongst these weapons is the theory of comparative advantage, developed by David Ricardo when he supported the calls for the repeal of the Corn Laws (which forbade the importing of European grain into Britain) on behalf of the rising cotton industrialists of Manchester. Comparative advantage asserted that even a country which was technically less efficient at everything than its competitors could benefit from trade. Trade would allow it to concentrate its resources on producing the thing which it was least bad at producing, and by trading a surplus of it for other goods, it would be materially better off.

Ricardo's original analysis simply took as given the fact that one country was better than another at producing a particular product — his example was Portugal for wine and England for cloth. Later economists have seen differences in each country's stock of resources as the origin of country advantages in producing some goods. A country with a relative abundance of capital is expected to be better at producing 'capital-intensive goods', one with a relative abundance of labour is expected to be better at producing 'labour-intensive goods'. Trade enables countries with a relative abundance of capital to produce capital-intensive products, those with a labour abundance to produce labour-intensive products, and overall world production increases.

Seductive as the prospect of mutual gains from trade may be, the theory of comparative advantage fails at both the theoretical and practical levels. As argued above, the countries which have made trade their engine of growth have done so in a distinctly mercantilist fashion (even England's initial development of a cotton manufacturing industry followed decidedly mercantilist policies): they have restricted imports, supported exports with government incentives, and pushed capital intensive industrial development.

Empirical attempts to validate comparative advantage, both in terms of its material benefit and as a predictor of trade flows, have failed. Studies by mainstream economists of the benefits to Europe from

Table 10.1: Comparison between Tariff and Free Trade Alternatives: Key National Account Variables, 1958/9-1968/9

	Tariffs	Free Trade	Percentage difference
Depreciation	1026	1035	0.88
Net Investment	1381	1422	2.97
Consumption (public & private)	7747	7771	0.31
Capital inflow	200	200	0.00
Gross National Product	9952	10028	0.76

Units: m, 1958/9
Source: from Evans, 1972, p. 88

greater specialisation found that it could be worth as little as a twentieth of 1 per cent of GNP: no study predicted gains of more then 1 per cent.

Harry Johnson, a respected proponent of comparative advantage, found that the best England could expect to gain from joining the Common Market in 1960 was an increase of about 1 per cent in GNP over and above estimates for 1970 (Johnson, 1958, p. 255). More detailed studies were done by Janssen (1961) and Skitovsky (1958). Skitovsky derived an 0.05 per cent gain, while Janssen found an 0.1 per cent gain. One study of the benefits Australia could expect from adopting free trade found that, after ten years, our GNP would be larger by 0.76 per cent (Evans, 1972) (Table 10.1).

As one reviewer commented, these gains from specialisation amounted to no more than a few months normal growth during the 1960s -- hardly worth the outpouring of economists on the subject, and certainly not worth the dislocation of industry that such 'specialisation' required. Evans' Australian study predicted that for a gain of 0.76 per cent of GNP, we would have to eliminate all manufacturing other than automobiles (which would shrink by half), processed foods and paper making.

Nor has comparative advantage proved a reliable predictor of trade flows. The Bureau of Industry Economics analysed trade between Australia and Southeast Asia from 1972/3 to 1975/6 (Bureau of Industry Economics, 1978). It expected that (after making allowances for differences in natural resources) Australia's exports to the region would be dominated by capital-intensive goods, while our imports would be dominated by labour-intensive goods.

The results were:

> It does not appear, in 1972-73, that superior export performance was necessarily linked with the more highly capital intensive Australian industries ... Trade flows between Australia and developing Asian countries can be explained only to a limited extent by reference to differences in basic factor endowments. (Bureau of Industry Economics, 1978, p. 49-51)

The BIE's explanation of this failure of fact to comply with theory was perceptive:

> The conventional theoretical model would suggest that the Asian developing economies would not have a comparative advantage in capital intensive goods. Rather, they would give priority to labour intensive manufactures. However, an important qualification to this view is that we observe direct foreign investment from the developed countries in a range of capital intensive industries in developing economies. This foreign investment is often attracted by investment incentives, tax holidays and other fiscal and protective devices. It is not uncommon for such industries to channel a significant share of their production towards export markets. Indeed, the development policies adopted often explicitly encourage this practice. (Bureau of Industry Economics, 1978, p. 51)

A vast number of Free Trade Zones have been established throughout the developing world (even China had three in 1980, and has many more now), attracting foreign corporations with cheap labour, low taxes and numerous other incentives, to relocate their factories in the Third World and export the products back to their developed world markets. The policy has been important to the industrialisation of South Korea, Taiwan and Hong Kong, and nearly as instrumental for Singapore, Malaysia and Mexico. This form of investment breaches all the rules of comparative advantage, since it removes the guarantee that 'labour abundant' countries will focus their energies on labour-intensive goods. Absolute, rather than comparative, advantage rules trade flows, and in such circumstances it is hard to nominate an industry which could not be undertaken more cheaply by a Third World country.

The reason for the failure of comparative advantage is simple: it is a static theory, concerned with the better utilisation of today's resources --which are presumed to be fully employed -- in the production of homogeneous goods. With full employment and no question of increasing the stock of resources, the only way to increase output is to improve the allocation of resources. Since the theory also assumes that resources -- labour and capital -- cannot move between countries, trade in goods provides the only means for specialisation.

The real world is dynamic, growth comes from bringing unemployed resources into production and from increasing the stock of capital and labour, differentiated goods are a major factor in trade, and capital in particular moves with great ease between nations. Though the old mercantilist prescriptions lack a theoretical tapestry, they succeed because they focus attention on the dynamic issues of growth.

The reality that mercantilism works -- when backed with distributive policies, which are common in NICs within Southeast and East Asia -- obliterates the easy answers to the complex problems of trade and development. The seductive appeal of comparative advantage was that everyone could practice it without conflict. Mercantilism by definition involves conflict between trade policies, and particularly during times of recession it will have to be limited by international treaties and bilateral negotiation. Such treaties and negotiations are commonplace today, of course: all that should be dispensed with is the fiction that the dismantling of national barriers to trade will necessarily be to everyone's benefit.

CONCLUSION

In development, the 'trade not aid' case should be seen as a red herring, like the Third World Marshall Plan before it. The requisites for development are social change, in particular the reform of land ownership, investment and planned industrialisation. Those countries which are attempting export-oriented industrialisation without having broken the power of their landed elite will find the effort futile, with mass poverty in the countryside dominating the use of development funds, and the flow of landless to the city swamping any attempt to move industries up market.

In aid policy, the crucial question is whether our interventions assist or prevent the kinds of social change which are required to bring about growth. Large-scale road building projects, for example, which are intended to improve access to markets for peasants, can strengthen the hands of the rural rich if they are not accompanied by improvements in transportation which peasants can actually afford to use. In that circumstance, it matters little whether the trucks involved are made in Australia, or in Sweden.

The Jackson Report may have some impact on the administration of Australia's aid program, and the structure of ADAB. It will not quell demands from the manufacturing sector that the aid program should in part serve Australian trade policy. And, like many similar reports before it, its well intentioned but politically naive and incorrect advice will fail to influence the processes which determine Australia's trade policies.

11 THE JACKSON REPORT AND AGRICULTURAL AID

Brian Chatterton and Lynne Chatterton

INTRODUCTION

The report of the Jackson Committee contains only two paragraphs on agricultural aid (Jackson Report, pp. 63-4) and they add to the record of Australian reviews to produce little else but inconsistent platitudes and to evade any detailed analysis of the subject.

The Jackson Committee is unfamiliar with farming and this is demonstrated by its inability to see the grave inconsistencies between the rhetoric put before it by officials who are responsible for agricultural aid, and the reality of the programs allegedly designed to meet the needs of poor farmers in the developing world. The result is a conflicting series of recommendations on future directions for agricultural aid.

One possible reason for this is that Australia's population distribution is the reverse of that of the developing world. In Australia, 80 per cent of people live and work in cities and have no personal experience of farming for food. In the developing world, 80 per cent of the world's 1000 million poorest people live on peasant holdings and do not eat unless they farm their own food.

The Jackson Committee, having said of developing countries that 'poor performance in agriculture undermines the whole economy' (Jackson Report, p. 63), and having acknowledged the importance of agriculture to Australia's aid program, then recommends expansion into a large number of new areas of expertise it feels Australia should provide including large capital-intensive projects. Given a limited aid budget now and in the foreseeable future, this can only result in a substantial reduction in agricultural aid projects. The committee states that Australia has especially suitable agricultural expertise for developing countries because of our climatic likenesses, and stresses the advantage this provides because our agricultural technology is more easily adapted to the environment of the recipients than exotic techniques from farming systems of other Western donors. This unique expertise, says the committee, should attract the highest priority in projects designed to help the rural poor.

The committee failed to analyse why we have not used it, or guide us towards a future policy that will enable us to do so, but its own recommendation for a geographical focus that effectively creates an incompatible environment for it will ensure that we have little opportunity to test its unique suitability.

The committee recognised the need for integrated rural development and the involvement of local communities in projects, but failed to examine the inadequacies of the present aid programs in meeting these objectives, nor did it provide guidelines for an alternative administration that would do so.

ADAB'S PRESENT AGRICULTURAL AID PROGRAM

The Director of ADAB reported in 1983 that agricultural aid received between 20 and 22 per cent of the bilateral budget for the period 1950 to 1983. In 1983, $34 million was allocated to specific bilateral agricultural projects with 5 per cent being earmarked for research; a further $21 million was allocated to multilateral and regional activities, of which $6 million provided the core budgets of international agricultural research centres. In addition, $7 million annually is allocated to the Australian Centre for International Agricultural Research (ACIAR) to support institution based research programs. A further $17 million for unspecified 'integrated rural development' programs which are 'not entirely for agriculture' padded the total agricultural aid budget out to $79 million (Dunn, 1983). This was the allocation from a total aid budget of $836 million (ADAB, 1984d). The agricultural aid allocation appears to be a 'drop in the bucket' and it indicates that not much regard is held in ADAB for that unique Australian agricultural expertise that could be of such benefit to the developing world. However, the budget for the South Australian Department of Agriculture is $34 million annually (Auditor-General, South Australia, 1984, p. 36) and $79 million, more or less, (given the cost savings in research that the climatic suitability of our agricultural technology should confer) should still enable us to make a significant contribution to the alleviation of the farming problems of the poor peasant.

Yet in 1982, an ex-Director of ADAB (Jim Ingram) wrote that 'despite their need (the rural poor) and our ability, Australia has put much less into agriculture than has been the case with other bilateral aid donors ...'. Ingram put this down to a 'lack of both cohesion and flexibility in Bureau administration ...'. In 1983, the Director of ADAB (Bob Dunn) wrote that the expenditure on bilateral agricultural programs had barely increased and in an update of Ingram's criticisms, Dunn said that 'ADAB has no sectoral program in agriculture in the sense that this is consciously planned and implemented'. He stated that 'ADAB has yet to achieve clear objectives, the definition of country programs, and improved coherence and flexibility in administration. TO ACHIEVE CHANGE, RELIANCE IS BEING PLACED ON THE REVIEW OF AUSTRALIAN AID BEING CARRIED OUT BY THE JACKSON COMMITTEE' (Dunn, 1983). If that was the hope of ADAB's director in 1983, the publication of the Jackson Report in 1984 must have come as a blow. The rhetoric and the reality remained as far apart as ever. Two case studies will suffice to show the questions that should have been addressed by the Committee.

TWO CASE STUDIES

In selecting these case studies to illustrate the actual performance of Australia's agricultural aid program, we have taken them from climatic regions where Australia (because of its own experience of farming in similar conditions) does have uniquely relevant technologies and experience. The regions are the dry tropics of Northern India (similar to much of northern Australia) and the semi-arid cereal zone of Jordan (similar to the Mediterranean climate of southern Australia).

Indo-Australian Livestock Projects

The projects at Hissar in North India consist of two parts. One is a Corriedale sheep breeding program and the other is a dairy cattle project. The project planners were officers from the New South Wales Department of Agriculture who went to Hissar in 1967, chose the land and drew up the requirements. The Indian government agreed to provide land, irrigation water, fencing, buildings and the wages of Indian counterparts. ADAB agreed to provide, through contractors, sheep, cattle, machinery and technical personnel (Indo-Australian Sheep Breeding Project Brochure, 1976, p. 2).

The brochure from the project tells the story of the almost lunatic manner in which this project proceeded. In considering it, one must keep constantly in mind that outside the project fence live villagers who inhabit primitive housing, are fortunate to have one electric light bulb that may shine one or two nights a week for them and who have great difficulty in feeding themselves and their families.

The objective of the sheep project was to use the Corriedale sheep to improve the meat and wool producing capacity of Indian village sheep. The brochure claimed that the difference in wool production from Corriedale and Indian sheep was due to 'density of wool fibres', the difference in body weight of Corriedale and Indian sheep was implied to be 'conformation and body frame' (Indo-Australian Sheep Breeding Project Brochure, 1976, p. 2). In fact, it is more likely that the significant differences in meat producing capacity were due to diet. Breeding will have a large impact on wool production, but local breeds are good meat producers given a good diet.

By 1976 the Australian team had realised that the Corriedale sheep could not breed in the heat of Hissar and they had erected air conditioned sheds in which to house them (Indo-Australian Sheep Breeding Project Brochure, 1976, p. 12). They acknowledged that the Corriedales (developed for the cool, temperate zone of Australia) faced a 'dramatic climatic change' when transferred to the extreme summer temperatures (up to 47,C) and monsoon periods of high humidity and rainfall at Hissar. This would demand 'a completely new set of management techniques which is neither wholly Indian nor wholly Australian' to minimise the effect of these changes. The team also reported that the Corriedales could not produce adequately without 'similar nutritional conditions to that found on high producing Australian sheep farms'. To achieve this they were undertaking a 'massive programme of land reclamation, irrigation and pasture establishment at the site' (Indo-Australian Sheep Breeding Project Brochure, 1976, pp. 5-8). They carried out earthworks and levelling operations with the aid of Australian experts from the Water Conservation and Irrigation Commission of New South Wales and set up a 25-mile long (40 km) Australian-style irrigation system. The description of this undertaking and the variety of pastures that were then planted would make an Australian sheep farmer's eyes pop.

The team reported that lucerne areas would remain productive for three to four years only, and that relevelling of land and resowing of pastures would, therefore, be a continuing process 'even after all farm development is complete' (Indo-Australian Sheep Breeding Project Brochure, 1976, p. 9). A shearing shed was set up with six electrically operated shearing machines. The contrast between the capital affluence of this and the hand-held shears that represented the only form of sheep shearing technology realistically available to the peasant farmer was not recognised.

Problems with disease emerged. The Corriedales were not resistant to local diseases such as pneumonia, screw worm fly, and foot abscesses. In 1975 a Workshop on Exotic Sheep Management was held at the project. This was the 'first opportunity given to managers of other exotic sheep farms to inspect the project and discuss their common problems of management'. The team reported that 'in nearly all regions performance and management problems were the same for all exotic breeds. The... workshop has provided a firm technical base for future training courses' (Indo-Australian Sheep Breeding Project Brochure, 1976, pp. 17-18). For whom? Exotic sheep farm managers?

Even the use of the project as a shop window for Australian -supplied vehicles failed when the lack of spare parts and the astronomical cost of imports finally caused the project team to turn to locally made vehicles as replacements.

The sheep project at Hissar can be criticised on many grounds. In essence it followed the old, arrogant colonial model of agricultural development -import the exotic, spend huge amounts of money attempting to simulate exotic conditions to support it when it cannot cope with climate and conditions, create unreal expectations for the putative recipients and, when it fails, blame them, their country and their 'infrastructure'.

In the 1976 brochure there is a photograph captioned 'Sheep breeders belong to one of the poorest rural groups in India. The project at Hissar gives them hope of a better sheep flock and higher income' (Indo-Australian Sheep Breeding Project Brochure, 1976, p. 1). No account seems to have been taken by the project managers of the social and economic environment of these sheep breeders or of the impossibility of their ever being able to attain the nutritional and other conditions considered necessary for the health of the cross-bred sheep from the project.

We inspected that project ourselves in 1976. There was no sign that the Hissar sheep owners had benefited one iota from the project. They still had their village sheep and they still fed them on scavenged weeds. The project appeared to exist in dream-like isolation while those who lived outside its 33 kilometres of boundary fencing had long since lost any interest in it or its possible role in improving their lot.

An Indian buffalo improvement project was complaining that it was being deprived of land and funds by constant demands made on Indian resources by the expanding sheep and cattle project.

During subsequent visits to India, we followed quite a path looking for signs that the project had 'leaked' into the villages. We came upon an Indian project that was getting some Merino cross-bred sheep out the villagers. They were using Russian merinos, poor quality specimens, but alive and thriving without air conditioning and under Indian management.

The questions that must be asked of ADAB are not just why they agreed to set up such an unrealistic project in the first place; but why it continued to support the use of climatically bizarre Corriedales (not the best meat producer by any means). Why was the Australian-developed technology on the utilisation of urea-treated straw and urea and molasses blocks as a low cost means of improving existing village fodder supplies ignored? Why did investment continue to be made on irrigated pasture development that could never be realistic for poor sheepowners?

On the same site a dairy herd improvement scheme was also set up, using Friesian cows from Victoria. They also need high quality grain and forage feeding to perform well -- a diet far beyond the resources of the Indian peasant farmer.

The villagers can only afford natural pastures and cereal crop residues. Yet, here again, the project developed capital-intensive irrigated pasture and grain supplements for feeding. The Indians who subsequently have benefited from this project are not the poor peasant farmers in need of aid, but well-off merchant farmers who supply socially -desirable cow's milk to the relatively wealthy Indian middle class. Not only are these farmers in a better position to pay for their own imported technology than almost any other group but they are already the recipients of similar aid programs from many European countries. On the negative side, the surplus cross-bred calves from the city milk supply farms leak out into the villages where, because they are fed the normal diet of low quality roughage, they produce less milk than indigenous breeds. They are inferior as draught animals; a matter of great importance to the ordinary Indian village farmer as cattle are kept more to pull the cart and the plough than for milk.

One cannot excuse ADAB on the grounds that the European nations and the USA were at that time undertaking the same sort of program. In the early 1970s the CSIRO was well aware that European breeds, such as the Friesians, are poorly adapted to the tropics and were developing the Australian Milking Zebu which is now considered by most experts as the only 'exotic' breed worth considering for export to the tropical regions. Tropical legume pasture work in Queensland was producing good tough varieties that cost little to establish, and the nutritional value of urea supplements for straw was well established, yet all this knowledge and experience, eminently suited to farming in the dry tropics, was overlooked. Farming in the dry tropics gave Australians a unique experience of the problems of feeding cattle on low-quality roughages and this experience was of particular relevance to peasant farmers in Hissar during the lifetime of the project. Contrast the Hissar approach with an independent program under the direction of an Australian-based expert, which is providing more than one million village cattle with an improved nutritional intake and increasing production by 50 per cent to 100 per cent through the integration of low cost urea/molasses blocks into their ordinary feeding program (Leng, personal communication).

The Indo/Australian Hissar projects demonstrate ADAB's inability to connect useful technology from Australia to the needs of the peasant farmer in the developing world. More disturbingly, the projects reflect an almost callous lack of concern for their social and economic consequences and an inability to learn from mistakes.

By contrast, the Dutch aid organisation only took three years to learn in Sri Lanka that treatment of cereal residues for local cattle provided greater benefits for small farmers than the importation of exotic bulls for cross breeding (Perdok, 1983). The inflexibility in ADAB continues. In Bangladesh in the 1980s ADAB administrators determinedly rejected strong advice to discontinue an exotic breed and feed project and change to a locally desired village program for treated straw and a low-level training program for cattle owners (Davis, 1981), and in 1984 ADAB funds are being used in Burma to develop a dairy cattle project to support a milk plant diverted from Vietnam to a country where cow's milk is not commonly available (ADAB, 1984d, p. 36).

Jordan dryland farming project

The planning of this ADAB project was a complete contrast to the Hissar projects. It was proposed to use an extension program to introduce new dryland farming technology to Jordan. This approach resulted from discussions that took place in Jordan in 1979 between the then South

Australian Minister of Agriculture (Brian Chatterton), the then Jordanian Minister (Salah Jumaa), his Director of Agriculture (Hassan Gharabey), the Chairman of the Jordan (farmers') Cooperative Organisation (Hassan Nabulsi) and the Crown Prince of Jordan (Prince Hassan). They agreed that the aid funds from Australia and equipment and other resources from Jordan should not be put into yet another research monument, but that direct work with Jordanian farmers in a land preparation and seeding program would be the most effective way of adapting the South Australian technology into the existing Jordanian farming system.

Due no doubt to the favour of the Crown Prince that gave extra authority to the project's direction, and the fact that the South Australian Department of Agriculture (under the direction of Chatterton at that time) was to be the contractor for the project, ADAB agreed to the somewhat unusual concept and allowed the project to follow the original intention, in spite of both Ministers and the Director being diverted to other positions by the time the team took up duties in August 1980.

No project headquarters were erected, no elaborate shearing shed was constructed with aid money, no demonstration farm was excised from the local farmers' land, no pre-fabricated project houses were imported and local equipment was used, with the exception of several pieces of agricultural machinery that were not available locally. The very unconventionality of the project -- without a 'monument' and without a colonial model to follow, put great pressure on the contractor to provide clear directions to the team and to ensure it had sufficient support to maintain the extension role of the project.

This direction from both ADAB and the eventual South Australian implementing agent (SAGRIC INTERNATIONAL) did not eventuate and soon began to cause problems for the three-man team (a farm management adviser/economist, a farmer, and an agronomist). Although they were given good access to all levels of Jordanian involvement -- farmers, Ministry and University -- the consultant Australian agronomist reviewing the progress of the project in April 1982 reported that in his opinion the team was floundering in a morass of confused research objectives -- trying to solve every problem that arose by beginning new research programs, thus losing sight of the extension task that was the major plank of the project.

He wrote: 'Given that the agronomist also has an important extension and management role, the ... programs are clearly very ambitious' (Jordan Dryland Farming Project, 1982, No. 8, Appendix 5, p. 3). The agronomist was at that time responsible for extension work with the original twelve farmers involved in the scheme -- a number that eventually grew to 30. He was also expected to liaise with and advise research workers at the University of Jordan. The consultant, in drawing attention to the lack of direction from which the team suffered, warned that 'The benefits should be clearly understood by the extension personnel themselves' (Jordan Dryland Farming Project, 1982, No. 8, Appendix 5, p. 5). He put forward a much simpler applied research program that would tackle adaption problems so that the team could keep on the original course -- the adaptation and teaching of the annual medicago/cereal rotation used by sheep/wheat farmers of southern Australia to farmers of Jordan. This reinforcement of the extension role enabled the team leader to have a film made locally of the newly introduced system in operation vis-a-vis the traditional system, as well as an audio-visual kit showing steps in preparation of land and seeding which was distributed to Jordanian institutions. Australian varieties of medicago were planted and much time and effort was spent on trying to find techniques that would enable them to grow in what turned out to be a difficult eco-niche for them. Towards the end of the five-year program it was recognised that identified local ecotypes which did not suffer the germination and growth problems encountered by Australian varieties should be multiplied so that they could be used in future programs (Jordan Dryland Farming Project, 1984, No. 15, Appendix 1, p. 12).

This cultural blindness, not uncommon to most Australian projects in the region, while it slowed things down, did not prevent the project team, even with its limited resources, from achieving its objective -- that of teaching a group of Jordanian farmers a new farming system and working with them to adapt its operations and technology into their own farming program. The reports constantly stress the problems faced because of the lack of extension and training services and support organisations (Jordan Dryland Farming Project, 1984, No. 15, Appendix 2, pp. 6, 11, and 50).

By July 1983, in the closing stages of the contract, the Jordanian government was anxious to ensure a continuity and expansion of the work. It was difficult to get any firm indication of the intention of ADAB and in order to avoid the loss of a growing season while the indecision continued, a joint Jordanian and Australian team worked to prepare a proposal for an extension of the project. At a meeting of the Coordinating Committee of the project the representative of ADAB in Amman told the Jordanian representatives that 'there is no certainty that the Australian Government would agree to such a proposal', while SAGRIC INTERNATIONAL's head office manager said that 'there was a financial and economic crisis facing Australia and the whole world and therefore a strong request would have to be made on behalf of ... Jordan if they wished for an extension' (Jordan Dryland Farming Project, 1983/4, No. 11, Appendix 5). In September 1984, still with no decision made, the farmer and the agronomist finished up, leaving the team manager to wind-up the project and give the Jordanians a draft program for the new season's planting requirements.

Considerable efforts had been made by the Jordanians and supporters of the project to have it extended and expanded. The team manager had written that 'a decision on the future of the project is urgently required if the interest and cooperation of the Jordanian authorities is to be maintained'. There was 'a certain reluctance of the Jordanian counterparts to become involved in planning the new season because of the uncertainty of the project's future' (Jordan Dryland Farming Project, 1984, No. 15, pp. 1 and 3).

In February 1985, ADAB at last announced its decision to fund the project for a further three years. No expansion of the project appears likely, and composition of the new team appears to indicate that the usual ADAB policy of evading a decision by jumping up and down in the same spot has been followed.

By most criteria, this project has been a success. It has established a valuable record of the development of an extension program for the adaptation of Australian dryland farming experience into small cereal farms and onto range land in a semi-arid region where nomadism exists and where strip ownership of cereal land exists. It officially recommended that local eco-types of annual medicago should be considered for future farming programs in the region -- a cultural breakthrough of significant proportions.

It joins the plethora of experience in the region using annual medicago to develop rangeland and increase livestock production in cereal areas, including the highly successful ten year dryland farming development program in Libya; the problems that have been overcome on the commercial demonstration farms in Iraq; the development strategies successfully used by the Tunisians; the farming and commercial successes achieved through integrating annual medicago pastures on to individual farms in Algeria and Tunisia; and development work in Morocco. In our experience, much of this information is likely to be either lost or ignored unless some effort is made to use it to spread the benefits of the experience gained to countries where it is badly needed.

Yet perhaps because this ADAB project lacked the investment in a research monument, more certainly because of the low place of the Middle East in the categories of aid recommended by the Jackson Committee (i.e. Category 5 -'others'), and possibly because of the lack of status for extension work in the eyes of the powerful research lobby which dominates agricultural programs, this project is left to limp along under a constant cloud of reluctance. In terms of its potential benefit to other semi-arid regions in the developing world it has a great deal to offer. The Australian/Arab experience of integrating legume pastures and shallow cultivation on to cereal farms (in this case very small parcels of land that required a cooperative approach in some instances) and in developing rangeland pasture management strategies have enormous potential in other developing countries where European farming systems and techniques have failed, or caused problems of over-exploitation of fragile soils and limited water resources.

LESSONS TO BE DRAWN FROM THESE CASE STUDIES

The lesson that emerges most strongly from these case studies is that Australia does not make the best use of its unique expertise when undertaking agricultural aid projects to better the conditions of the rural poor. The case studies simply add weight to the claims of Dunn and

Ingram that confusion and lack of direction are the major problems within ADAB. Until that confusion and lack of direction is overcome, Australian aid funds will continue to be used in projects that provide career paths for permanent staff; opportunities for professional consultants to get jobs; funds for agricultural research personnel to carry out exotic research projects; opportunities for department of agriculture personnel to get overseas experience; a subsidised shop window for Australian manufacturers to show their goods to a potential export market; and an avenue for the misguided belief that this sort of agricultural aid will increase our political influence in regions in which we have an interest.

The lack of sensitivity to the actual conditions of the rural community in need, a marked inability to select from Australian agricultural expertise that which could be of relevance to that need, and an entrenching of the mistakes through the uncritical acceptance of their continued funding by administrators responsible for planning decisions are factors one could have expected the Jackson Committee to address.

The Jordan project, while free of many of the faults of the 'research monument' so characteristic of Australia's aid projects, points the lesson of how conflict can occur between the priorities of achieving agricultural and social relevance in a program, and the capricious demands of foreign policy. The actual and potential aid value of the Jordan project to the rural poor in semi-arid regions of the developing world is unquestionable, yet the diminution of the importance of influence in the Middle East to Australia's view of its world role led to it being kept as a 'minor' project with little hope of expansion or use as a source of reference for similar projects. The folie de grandeur implicit in the Australian government's perception of its agricultural aid programs as a source of international influence (reinforced by the Jackson Committee's acceptance of it) provides a stark contrast to countries, such as Denmark, who (with similar budgets for aid) send their agricultural aid to the two countries they consider most in need of it --Tanzania and Bangladesh -- countries well outside any possible sphere of influence that Denmark may conceivably exert (DANIDA, 1983, p. 30).

This sincere altruism does not avoid the multiple difficulties of carrying out agricultural programs in developing communities, but it does free the aid agency from the additional complication of being a pawn in the game of international influence.

OTHER AGRICULTURAL AID

Australian agricultural assistance is not confined to agricultural projects. We also undertake training programs for students and support agricultural research through the Australian Centre for International Agricultural Research (ACIAR).

ACIAR

The establishment of ACIAR 'as a means of encouraging and supporting research into agricultural problems of developing countries in fields in which Australia has special competence' (Jackson Report, 1984, p. 98) is a perfect example of rhetoric unmatched by performance. The Jackson Committee's account of ACIAR says that 'The main emphasis on ACIAR's projects is in South East Asia, Papua New Guinea and the South Pacific...', areas that grow crops largely unknown in Australia (Jackson Report, 1984, p. 98). The ACIAR brochure (Partners in Agricultural Research) reveals a concentration on programs such as paddy rice production using hand planting and buffalo cultivation, an area of agriculture in which Australia has no experience, and which is a duplication of the work of the International Rice Research Centre in the Philippines, a multilateral funded institute which Australia supports anyway -- and plant breeding programs that duplicate the work of at least twelve other international agricultural research centres. In our experience, all the plant improvement in the world will not have much effect in increasing production until general farming skills such as seed bed preparation and weed control are improved. Research centres ablaze with green trial plots of improved plant varieties next door to eroded and badly cultivated peasant farms in the developing world are a graphic illustration of the gap between the work of the pure scientist and the needs of the peasant farmer.

ACIAR's Communication Program is to be devoted to publicising scientific papers, and could be used to provide editorial services to scientists. It is also to include, so we are told, a computerised register of relevant expertise available in Australia (Jackson Report, 1984, p. 83). Such lists proliferate in every aid and finance agency throughout the world, and the direction of more funds to duplicate yet another indicates a poor set of priorities when there is such a shortage of low -cost extension material in every developing country currently in need of assistance to improve the farming of the rural poor.

ACIAR, at this stage anyway, simply reflects yet another face of ADAB —well meaning, but confused and without a clear policy designed to make Australia's agricultural development experience available to countries faced with similar farming problems.

Foreign student training

To make agricultural training effective it should be linked to practical experience of a farming system. Naturally that farming system should relate to the farming system of the students' own country. The Jackson Report expresses concern about the number of submissions complaining of excessive bureaucratic delays in the placing of foreign students in Australia under ADAB's training programs (Jackson Report, 1984, p. 95). We support that concern, but point out that the geographical specificity of agriculture has often been ignored by those who have placed foreign agricultural students in Australia's institutions. The well-designed and highly-successful International Diploma in Dryland Farming set up by Dr Don Williams during his term as Director of Roseworthy Agricultural College was eventually destroyed by the insistence of ADAB in diluting the students from countries with a similar Mediterranean climate to Southern Australia, with students from countries of the dry tropics, such as Kenya, where the South Australian farming system is not climatically compatible.

Similarly, Thai students have been sent to Perth, and North African students sent to New England. Short courses of three months' duration relating to components of dryland farming have been set up in various states, and one can only conclude that these reflect once more the ADAB shotgun approach -- if they produce numbers and do a bit of everything it will deflect specific criticisms. Interviews with numbers of these students in their own countries reveal that the combination of culture shock (coping with a new language and a vastly different culture, as well as a largely unknown farming system), and a highly compacted course leaves them confused and exhausted and little better off than they were before. The lack of any means of expanding or reinforcing the knowledge gained when they return to their own countries is a complaint frequently made.

A CONSTRUCTIVE ALTERNATIVE

There is little doubt that many conflicting objectives for Australian aid are the reason for the chaos that presently characterises our agricultural aid program. We ourselves come down on the side of programs that would help peasants living in similar climates to ours make use of techniques we have found valuable and productive. The hard-nosed pragmatists will no doubt claim this is politically naive because it does not meet the needs of a 'presence' in areas where Australia believes it has political influence and does not provide lucrative contracts to the Australian aid industry of consultants and State Departments of Agriculture.

If an attempt were made to match up the rhetoric of those who vaunt Australia's unique agricultural expertise with programs that reflected it, there would no doubt be short-term problems that would require considerable political will to overcome but, in the long-term, such an approach would not only benefit the poor farmer in the developing world, but also gain for Australia much more prestige than the current mishmash of agricultural projects that are either invisible because they are so detached from reality, or are spectacular failures because they clash with reality.

Besides the climatic similarity we share with much of the developing world -- semi-arid conditions and areas of dry tropics -- we have developed another advantage we should share. In some cases our farmers have been forced by low export returns to develop low-cost farming operations. Climatic similarities and low input costs are the two filters that should be applied to Australian technology to assess its suitability for agricultural aid programs.

If we apply these two filters to Australian agriculture the most obvious candidate for Australian aid is the dryland farming system for semi-arid regions with Mediterranean climates. Shallow cultivation, legume pastures and cereal production that benefits from legume nitrogen all contribute to a lower cost and more productive system than traditional peasant systems or imported European techniques. The system also provides significant advantages in the control of soil erosion. The work in Northern Australia on pasture legumes and the treatment and supplementation of straw with urea and molasses, although not yet so widely adopted as a practical farming system, should be pursued with equal vigour because of its vast potential for improving the lot of the poorest of the poor in villages in the dry tropics of Africa and Asia.

At the other end of the scale, we should accept that Australia has limited experience with wet tropical crops and what experience we do have fails the test of low input costs. We do not grow rubber, oil palms, coconuts or paddy rice on a scale, or using techniques, that are in any way relevant to the rural poor of developing countries. Even our successful sugar cane industry is so highly mechanised that adaptation to poor communities is almost impossible. Our dairying in the tropics has not succeeded and consumers in the north of Australia depend on production from the temperate south.

If such selection of technology was undertaken, Australia could further improve the effectiveness of its agricultural aid if the emphasis of programs was shifted from the laboratory to the farm. In order to do this it is necessary to make a clear distinction between professional agriculture and farming to understand how necessary is this shift of emphasis. In the minds of the peasant, farming equals food; in the minds of the agricultural scientist, agriculture is connected with farming but it equals scientific laboratories and published papers; to the administrator, agriculture is a mystery but it equals a temporary stage in a career path. The simple need of the peasant to grow more food has been lost sight of.

To redirect our agricultural aid program would require an extension aspect to projects that ADAB currently does not provide. It would require a thorough understanding of the practicalities of farming, and personnel with skills in communicating simple lessons, in acquiring the confidence of peasant communities, and in being able to drop their own cultural package and to see the requirements of another.

Identification and feasibility studies

An examination of the 1983/4 list of ADAB's agricultural projects suggests that they were chosen by pin from a list juggled into country programs by a strategist from the political section of the Department of Foreign Affairs (ADAB, 1984d).

The Jackson Committee's recommendation that 'finance management must be seen as a central element of program administration' (Jackson Report, 1984, p. 234) could mean that only bigger, and more, feasibility studies will improve the effectiveness of our agricultural aid programs. The real aim of the feasibility study is to satisfy the bureaucratic desire for uniformity and legitimacy at any cost. There is a fundamental dysfunction between the bureaucratic requirement for ordered legitimacy that rationalises waste but excludes risk, and the real world of farming where expenditure must produce output and where risk is taken as a matter of course. The mechanism of a feasibility study produces nothing real as output. In effect, money is shifted from the account where it is supposed to produce real results, and put into the account where it produces reports.

As feasibility study teams commonly jet into a country for a few weeks, meet senior officials in the head office of the Ministry, but rarely talk to extension workers and local farmers, it is hardly surprising that projects frequently have little local support, especially as studies are only projections, models of the likely outcome for the project, frequently based on imperfect statistics and unreliable estimates.

An added problem with the notion of a feasibility study as an assessment tool is that, in Australia, the feasibility study is frequently carried out by the eventual contractor. The insulation of the resultant project performance against disinterested assessment is reinforced by the fact that all studies and reports are judged by the ADAB staff who approve the feasibility study and administer the project. The current administrative procedures for evaluation are the focus of strong criticism both in the efficiency audit (Auditor-General, 1981, pp. 115-17) and the Joint Parliamentary Committee on Public Accounts Report (JCPA, 1982, pp. 7, 15, 28-30, 59) because of their effect in deflecting criticisms and enabling mistakes to be ignored. We propose that in place of feasibility studies, small pilot projects should be set up and evaluated on the ground in terms of their practical results.

Identification and assessment procedures have been severely criticised by both the Auditor-General's Report, and the JCPA Report, but little constructive advice has been offered on how to establish an assessment mechanism that is rigorous in demanding relevance and accountability from agricultural aid programs. Truly independent assessments of the success or otherwise of projects require a receptive environment for soundly based arguments for change to be put and considered seriously. The open policy of Denmark which relies on independent groups of persons with adequate skills assessing potential projects and their performance during and after operation; the requirement that no contractor shall carry out a feasibility study for a contract for which they intend to tender; the financial support for journalists and others to visit projects and report back openly on their performance; and a vigorous Parliamentary scrutiny of all sectors of its aid program, could well be adopted in Australia (DANIDA, 1983).

Project management

For the most part, agricultural project management is presently undertaken for ADAB by State Departments of Agriculture and private consultants. They have little demonstrated success in adapting Australian technology and delivering it to peasant farmers. They have shown little or no expertise in planning and managing a whole farm development program. The curricula vitae of their staff show how their qualifications build as they move from one project to another. It is the award of the project to them that is counted, not the quality of their performance in carrying it out. State Departments are expert in managing the clerical affairs of their seconded staff -- safeguarding the superannuation, holiday pay and substantive position of the absent staff member, but they have a poor record in selecting staff with relevant expertise, understanding aid objectives and the needs of rural poor. They have been criticised in several studies for using projects as patronage and as an opportunity for overseas trips, rather than as a means of increasing the standing of Australia as a compassionate provider of aid (Nalson, 1982; Thiele, 1982; Ayres and Nalson, 1984; Chatterton and Chatterton, 1984).

The selection criteria and the required qualifications for management positions should be reassessed so as to widen the scope of skills that can be recruited in future. At present these tend to exclude candidates other than those from professional agricultural backgrounds.

It may well be that candidates with a broad experience of the farming world are better equipped to understand the objectives of agricultural aid projects than the present managers supplied by some State Departments and private consultants. ADAB should ensure that internal staff have adequate experience of on the ground project management. A period of service on an ADAB project, or secondment to one run by a contractor, should be an essential part of the training of all senior ADAB personnel. The use of pilot projects, rather than costly and often badly planned feasibility studies, would diminish the risk of bad management being locked into a project.

Project staff

It is the face-to-face project worker who is the critical element in the success or otherwise of a project, although undoubtedly that success will be constrained or expanded by the degree of support and assistance he or she receives from the management to which the project worker is responsible. Currently, Australian aid projects are staffed by scientists carrying out exotic research programs; freelance project personnel who go from project to project, from climatic zone to climatic zone, often learning on the job; and by State Department of Agriculture officers who for one reason or another want some foreign experience. Australian farmers, if employed at all on projects are employed as 'skivvies'.

Their farming systems skills are not recognised. Their role as innovators in their own right is not appreciated. The ease with which they communicate with fellow farmers in spite of vast cultural differences is not valued (Chatterton and Chatterton, 1982, 1985). The adaptation process by which 'raw' technology from research institutions in Australia is translated into practical farming techniques, and its further spread from farmer to farmer is poorly understood. The demonstrated success of Australian farmers transferring the dryland farming system to Jordanian farmers without the aid of feasibility studies, resident scientists, a research centre, and highly paid administrators, has been ignored. Lip service is paid to farming experience when project contractors advertise for 'farming systems experts' whose academic requirements (a PhD is de rigueur) effectively exclude those with the most relevant farming system experience, that of practice. The egocentric scientific perception of the process of technology adaptation is counterproductive to the success of farming aid projects. This view is characterised by a belief that there will be a trickling-down of knowledge from the scientist through the extension worker to the farmer who is seen as a passive receiver of the distilled wisdom of the expert.

The private consultants who take on the development projects for ADAB are no better in their recruitment of project staff. The efficiency audit (Auditor-General, 1981, pp. 115-17) referred to the dangers of the gradual extension of aid work into the hands of private consultants — who, it was pointed out, were not trained in aid work, do not always report satisfactorily on what they have achieved, and often evade the normal tender requirements for such work. The insensitivity of the commercial development approach to aid projects has been criticised by many — including large numbers of staff employed by private consultants. Four State governments (South Australia, Victoria, Western Australia and New South Wales) are now in open competition with commercial consultants for Australia's development projects. The changing role of State government departments from a technical resource for commercial companies tendering for aid projects to strong competitors for those projects themselves, will mean that technical experts available for aid work, whether competent and sensitive or not, will be more thinly stretched than in the past.

There is a large alternative source of staff recruitment available in Australia. There are currently many capable and sensitive persons working within NGOs, in associations such as the South Australian Seedgrowers and other farmers who have performed remarkably in this area, individuals within university faculties, agricultural colleges and semi-professional groups (for example, the Australian Farm Management Society and the Australian Merino Society) who could provide judgement and skills gained through practical experience in adapting Australian farm technology. There are also many people skilled in rural media work, whose skills have not begun to be tapped. Indeed, from the testimony of many who have tried to have their experience used, it seems that Australian government aid programs deliberately exclude them. Nor, as in other countries, are there adequate training programs to help staff develop necessary skills, sensitivity and cultural awareness and enable them to cope with quite different social and physical environments.

Auxiliary services for project support

As we pointed out in the account of the dryland farming project in Jordan, the concept of using pilot projects as proving grounds for adaptation methods and a basis for expanded programs in the wider farming community has not been adequately grasped by ADAB. This is an essential part of a successful aid program but it needs resources not currently available in ADAB's agricultural aid section. For this reason we suggest that ACIAR is less necessary to the Australian agricultural aid program than an Extension Support Service.

Such a service, by collecting information from pilot and other farming projects using Australian expertise and technology, and disseminating it to other project workers confronted with similar problems in similar climates and conditions, could save an enormous amount of time and money now expended in isolated projects that inevitably repeat mistakes and carry out research into problems that have been solved elsewhere. The inclusion of such information and experience in audio-visual kits, charts, films, radio and TV segments (or other suitable teaching aids) for use in training schemes for peasant farmers, local extension workers, officials who need to be familiarised with resource requirements for necessary extension work, and for Australian project staff who are attending familiarisation courses would be invaluable. This dimension of agricultural work is at present largely unrecognised in aid projects. Such a service could also maintain contact with the recipients of Australian farming expertise, at whatever level, and provide an avenue through which its future use could be recorded.

Reports on Australian aid constantly criticise the way in which, once project staff leave a community, their work is no longer monitored and there is no record available of whether it is incorporated into the farming system of the recipient villagers, what changes take place in its further adaptation, or whether it simply fades away and is forgotten. Nor is there any follow up in any constructive way of what foreign students are able to do with their Australian training when they return to work in their own country. This information is necessary if we are to usefully evaluate the little we do in this area at the moment. The German Humboldt Institute provides a useful model of how this can be done.

An effective extension support service could establish a journal, not for more scientific papers, but for adaptation case studies. Conferences could be sponsored, not for Australian scientists, but for exchanges of accounts of local experience at the farmer level preferably in the country concerned -- paying for key local personnel to attend, not adding to the scientific largesse available to Australians. The service should support and provide guidance for the establishment of foreign students' training courses in relevant climatic zones so that the current confusion about climatic relevance so prevalent among those who now direct the placement of foreign agricultural students would be corrected.

Cooperation with other countries and international organisations

Effective agricultural aid is capable of providing Australia with considerable national prestige in foreign countries. To achieve this aim, however, it will be necessary to take a much wider view of what establishing a national presence entails. There is now a growing realisation in Europe that their farming techniques are not suitable for most of Asia and Africa. This belated realisation is being translated into a search for new ideas with a proven record of success in tropical, Mediterranean and semi -arid environments. Australia with its experience in these environments could provide fresh ideas on agricultural development to many European aid organisations and ideally work with them on a joint farming assistance program.

ADAB should be encouraged to cooperate with other small/medium country agencies such as the Danish, Canadian, and Norwegian agencies, to exchange information on adaptation strategies, integrate teams, and amalgamate funds where appropriate. For example, we could set up a pilot farming project, expand it with Australian aid funds, then work with other funding agencies to expand it into a country project. Exchange of information about farmer training aids and continuing contact with trained farmers and students would be exceptionally valuable. Such an approach would dilute the precisely defined national presence but would lead to greatly increased national prestige which we would of course have to share with other members of the group. This approach would make the aid programs of a number of countries more effective, allow our unique contribution to be recognised, and thus avoid the anonymity that comes when Australian aid and expertise is swallowed up in large multilateral agencies such as the World Bank and FAO.

CONCLUSION

ADAB's current agricultural aid program is confused and chaotic. The Jackson Committee did not analyse the reasons for this and, therefore, offers no alternatives. We suggest that our agricultural aid programs should be based on the technology we have that is climatically compatible with the recipient country, and that uses low-cost inputs suitable for a resource-poor community. The emphasis of agricultural aid should change from the laboratory to the farm, and management and project staff should be drawn from a wide range of individuals and organisations with practical farming experience and extension skills. Such a radical change would require strong political will, given the entrenched interests currently dominating agricultural aid programs. The selection of projects to reflect the use of our climatically appropriate technology is in conflict with the priorities of the Department of Foreign Affairs; the change in emphasis from laboratory to farm upsets the special interests of Australian agricultural scientists; and any changes in management and personnel would diminish the access to lucrative contracts enjoyed by private consultants and State government departments. Support for change lies with the majority of NGOs, many disillusioned project staff, many of the recipients, and not a few idealists, some of them within the Labor Party. Given this unequal grouping of forces, and the Hawke government's preference for institutionalised consensus, the chances of there being sufficient political will for a radical change seem unlikely.

ORGANISATION AND PRACTICE OF AID

12 ADAB AND AID ADMINISTRATION

Juliet Hunt

INTRODUCTION

The greatest failure of the Jackson Report on the Australian Overseas Aid Program is its peremptory dismissal of one of the most important current policy issues on aid and development: the role that the principle of equity should play in the programming and implementation of aid. In contrast, the report's greatest strength lies in its discussion of aid administration and management issues, where many of the recommendations are sound and long overdue for implementation.

If adopted, the report's recommendations on aid administration will go a long way towards ridding us of the ad hoc approach which has moulded the present program. In reality however, an aid program can only be effective if it has a clear statement of aid policy, a hierarchy of broad objectives and the capacity to articulate strategies to obtain those objectives. Although the Jackson Report acknowledges the importance of equity as a factor in growth and development, it does not accord it the status of a legitimate objective for the Australian aid program. Consequently, the need for distinct strategies and guidelines for implementing equity-oriented or poverty-focused policies is overlooked -- with the exception of the chapter on women. Similarly, implementation of the report's recommendations on aid administration and management will of themselves do little to ensure that the principle of equity is given any weight in the planning and programming of Australian aid. Equity considerations have been neglected in the implementation of the current aid program, and are likely to be neglected in future unless specific and significant steps are taken to redress the balance.

This paper explores the type of aid administration structure and process which will be most conducive to the implementation of development objectives, as distinct from diplomatic and commercial goals. Development is defined here, as it is in the Jackson Report (Jackson Report, 1984, p. 59) as including aspects of both growth and equity, although the latter will be the focus for discussion. The context is set firstly with a brief administrative history of Australian aid. The findings of two previous reports -- the Auditor-General's report on bilateral aid administration (1981) and the Joint Parliamentary Committee on Public Accounts report which followed it (JCPA, 1982) -- are reviewed according to ADAB's performance in the areas of aid policy formulation, management and organisation, related to a discussion of requirements for an effective aid program. This is followed by a summary and critique of the Jackson Report. Finally, a number of recommendations and principles are proposed with a view to strengthening the implementation of equity goals in the aid administration process.

CONTEXT

Administrative History

Prior to 1973, Australian aid administration was shared between the Departments of Foreign Affairs, External Territories, Education and Treasury. For these first two decades of Australian development assistance, aid policy was under the direct control of the Department of Foreign Affairs and, as a result, was largely conditioned by diplomatic and strategic considerations (Wilkinson, 1976, p. 354). In December 1973, the Whitlam Labor government established an autonomous Australian Development Assistance Agency (ADAA), which was charged with the responsibility of improving the effectiveness of aid administration by:

1. developing an integrated and comprehensive aid policy, less influenced by diplomatic considerations and more attuned to the social and income distribution effects of aid (Millar, 1978, pp. 376-7; Willesee, 1975, pp. 236-9; Viviani and Wilenski, 1979, pp. 91-2). The latter concern reflected doubts prevalent in the international donor community about the ability of traditional development stragegies to improve the lot of the poorest groups in developing countries (Allen, 1975, pp. 1-4; Willesee, 1975, pp. 236-7);

2. upgrading aid management by encouraging innovation and evaluation (Willesee, 1975, p. 239; Viviani and Wilenski, 1979, p. 92);

3. developing a more 'professional' approach by the introduction of a career stream for aid officers (Viviani and Wilenski, 1979, p. 92).

In early 1976 the Fraser Liberal government abolished ADAA and created ADAB, a semi-autonomous bureau within the Department of Foreign Affairs. In 1981, ADAB was reintegrated further into the Department of Foreign Affairs, as a result of the recommendations of the Liberal government Review of Commonwealth Functions (RCF or Lynch Committee). Both of these administrative upheavals were rationalised as cost-saving measures, but in both cases few actual savings can be demonstrated (Viviani and Wilenski, 1979, p. 127; ACOA, 1982, pp. 19-28).

The role of bureaucratic vested interests in the demise of ADAA, particularly from the Departments of Foreign Affairs and Treasury, has been well documented by Viviani and Wilenski (1979). The establishment of an autonomous aid agency and its attempt to develop an independent aid policy, were thwarted at almost every turn. The structure and staffing of ADAA contributed to conflict both within the new agency itself and with its bureaucratic competitors. ADAA lacked the necessary parliamentary and community support to establish a strong position in the bureaucratic hierarchy, and was abolished before it could demonstrate its effectiveness or build upon the public support that did exist.

It is not surprising then that ADAA failed to fulfil the promise of a new approach to aid. What of ADAB? Its record will be assessed in terms of the three aspects outlined above -- aid policy, management and organisation.

Aid Policy Formulation

Most textbooks on overseas aid begin by acknowledging that donors are motivated by three conflicting considerations: diplomatic and strategic concerns; economic and commercial self-interest; and humanitarianism. The conflict generated by these competing concerns needs to be reconciled at all levels of the aid-giving process -- in articulating aid policies and objectives, in the geographical distribution of funds, in choosing modes of aid delivery and in instituting management processes. The reconciliation and resolution of this conflict forms the substance of aid administration.

The Auditor-General's report on Australia's bilateral aid program, published in 1981, presents the most comprehensive assessment available on Australian aid administration. It acknowledges the highly complex nature of implementing a program in foreign environments where final outcomes can only be seen in the long term (Auditor-General, 1981, pp. v, 6). This complexity is compounded by the fact that each of the competing motives mentioned above is represented by a number of domestic lobby groups. The Departments of Foreign Affairs, Treasury, Finance and Trade, and the sectional groups which they represent, each have a strong interest in the way aid policy is formulated and implemented. ADAB's need to accommodate and reflect these various interests has produced an array of potentially conflicting policy principles and priorities (Auditor-General, 1981, pp. 9, 59-62), resulting in ineffective implementation.

For example, ADAB's preference for funding activities of high priority to recipient governments has resulted in cases where projects contributed more to recipient government prestige and national security, than to economic and social development (Auditor-General, 1981, pp. 17, 93). On-the-job training on projects has been a general objective of Australian aid policy for decades, yet the audit report found that these objectives were often ill-defined, played an insufficient role in the criteria for selecting agents to implement projects, and were not adequately monitored (Auditor-General, 1981, p. 21). The same situation applies to officially declared policy 'priorities' relating to equity goals. These are couched in general terms and no strategies have been developed to ensure their implementation. One consequence is that there has been little redistribution of aid towards relevant (basic needs) sectors (Auditor-General, 1981, pp. 8, 52, 66). It is true that ADAB has had some degree of success in introducing new modes of aid delivery over the last decade, but only one of these (support for voluntary aid agencies) makes any substantial contribution to equity goals. Some have been motivated partly by staffing constraints (the need to maximise the amount of aid disbursed per staff member), and others have reflected the growing importance of commercial considerations in government aid policy.[1]

The Auditor-General's most significant finding in the area of aid policy formulation was that ADAB has no clear definition or philosophy of development, and no understanding of the role of aid in promoting development (Auditor-General, 1981, p. 58). In short, ADAB has clearly not succeeded in the task of formulating an integrated and coherent policy. Furthermore, the link between policy-making and aid practice is weak: equity objectives are either ignored or deflected in the current aid administration process; there has been no comprehensive program of staff development designed to close the gap between policy rhetoric and aid practice (this applies particularly to equity goals); and the current organisational structure reinforces this separation between policy and practice, particularly in the administration of bilateral projects (Auditor-General, 1981, pp. 148-9, 157).

This confusion of conflicting motives and interests is characteristic of many Western donors. In his study of the management of aid agencies, George Cunningham points out that such conflicts can easily engender the claim that no clear statement of principle is ever possible in aid policy (Cunningham, 1974, pp. 39-40). This certainly appears true in the Australian case. For example, the JCPA report more or less endorsed ADAB's ad hoc approach to aid policy and practice, claiming that it is impossible to establish absolute policy objectives and retain flexibility (JCPA, 1982, pp. 9-10, 23). This style of pragmatism is also exemplified in the response of one ADAB officer to audit report criticisms regarding ADAB's apparent lack of a philosophy of development, who stated that one ought not expect ADAB to have such a philosophy, because 'development' is what is agreed upon, on a case-by-case basis, between Australia and the recipient government.

However, among the range of competing priorities and interests, two principles have definitely taken precedence in the implementation of Australian aid over the past decade. First, a priority has been given to recipient government requests. This reflects the importance of diplomatic interests in the program. The second principle has been called Australia's 'comparative advantage' in aid and has been a rather vague notion of what Australia is good at providing. This is an expression of the desire to utilise Australian goods and services and a reflection of the importance of commercial interests.

Aid Management

The Auditor-General's report was also highly critical of many aspects of ADAB's current project selection, appraisal, design, monitoring and evaluation practices. It found that project selection criteria did not always reflect Australian aid policy priorities and that a reliance on recipient governments to identify and request proposals had not provided an adequate supply of fundable projects. ADAB's practice of requesting only one option in project feasibility proposals was also criticised (Auditor-General, 1981, pp. 29, 92, 103, 110).

The most serious deficiency in the project monitoring and reporting area arises out of ADAB's excessive concern with meeting expenditure targets. Described by the Auditor-General's report as an 'organisational imperative to disburse funds' (Auditor-General, 1981, p. 132) it has been more aptly labelled by Judith Tendler as a 'money-moving' mentality (Tendler, 1975, pp. 88-90). In the absence of other clear criteria for judging aid performance, and in an environment where administrative resources are at a premium, the ability to move money is elevated above the achievement of other objectives (McNeill, 1981, p. 12; OECD, 1981, p. 10). In Australia's case, this contributes to a clerical rather than professional approach to aid management, characterised by a preoccupation with financial and technical detail and a consequent neglect of a range of other factors such as the likely social impact, project maintenance requirements, the most appropriate mix of labour, technology and capital inputs, and the capacity of recipient government counterparts to fulfil administrative, personnel, financial and technical requirements (Auditor-General, 1981, pp. 11, 18-19, 29, 97-100). These criticisms apply equally to the project appraisal, design and monitoring phases of aid management. They are magnified by evidence of other instances of neglect, such as a failure to follow up problems raised in project reports and a lack of on-site involvement by ADAB officers posted at embassies (Auditor-General, 1981, p. 23). Although the constraints imposed by an annual budgetary cycle certainly encourage such a money-moving attitude to aid management, the root cause of these problems is the absence of a hierarchy of aid objectives.

In the light of this rather perfunctory approach to project management, the Auditor-General's report was also critical of ADAB's practice of devolving substantial responsibility to its agents and consultants. It recognised that the use of private consultants introduces an additional layer of interests into the aid process and it cast doubt on ADAB's ability to assess the performance of consultants, their adherence to their briefs and the effectiveness of their approaches to particular projects (Auditor-General, 1981, pp. 19, 23, 117, 119). The report also noted examples of poor staff selection, a lack of language training and cross-cultural awareness courses, and inadequate pre-departure briefings restricted to technical issues (Auditor-General, 1981, pp. 20, 132).

Finally, the Auditor-General's report highlighted a number of deficiencies in evaluation practices. These included: a neglect of post hoc evaluation, internal auditing and on-site inspection after project completion; little assessment of developmental impact at either the posts or in Canberra; and few efforts to feed back evaluation results into the project identification and policy-making process (Auditor-General, 1981, pp. 23-6, 31, 62, 68, 128-30, 150).

The Auditor-General's report focused primarily on bilateral project aid, but similar criticisms apply to other modes of delivery. Although ADAB has improved its management practices somewhat over the decade, its failures in this regard are considerable. For example, the case for more sophisticated management information systems was first argued in 1976 (Martin, 1981, p. 6) and the achievement of a country programming approach has been a professed aim of aid administrators for even longer (Viviani and Wilenski, 1979, p. 121; ADAA, 1975, p. 7). While there have been some notable achievements, they are isolated and little progress has been made overall.

There appear to be four major reasons for this failure to implement appropriate management practices. First, aid administration has been located, for most of its life, in a department where the principal brief is a diplomatic one, and where administrative requirements are thus vastly different from those of an aid agency. Secondly, with the exception of recent public debate on aid to the Philippines, aid has rarely been subject to consistent and detailed public scrutiny in Australia. Thirdly, without a coherent set of principles to guide it, there is little incentive for an agency to improve its performance. Finally, there is the inadequacy of organisational resources, itself a product of the second-class status of aid within the bureaucracy and the community.

Organisation

Both the Auditor-General's report and the report of the Joint Parliamentary Committee on Public Accounts which followed it, highlighted ADAB's crucial need for more and better organisational resources. The impact of staffing, financial and support service constraints have been well documented and there seems little doubt that ADAB's resources are deficient in comparison to other government departments and other Western donors (Auditor-General, 1981, passim; ACOA, 1982, pp. 5-18). Both reports focused on the need to upgrade and increase the number of overseas staff and the JCPA recommended establishing a development assistance career stream for ADAB officers (JCPA, 1982, pp. vi-vii).

The JCPA also made a number of recommendations designed to increase ADAB's administrative autonomy from the Department of Foreign Affairs and to upgrade its public accountability. These included increasing the rank of ADAB's Director and formalising his/her direct access to the Minister; giving ADAB a separate staff ceiling from Foreign Affairs; the appointment of a Parliamentary Secretary for aid matters; and the introduction of an annual Ministerial statement on aid policy. These recommendations were prompted by the JCPA's concern for the aid program's reputation of impartiality and for the widespread ignorance the committee discovered of all aspects of Australian aid (JCPA, 1982, pp. vi-vii, 15-16).

It is clear that as a Bureau under the patronage of the Department of Foreign Affairs, both prior to and since the Review of Commonwealth Functions, ADAB has been unable to formulate either coherent or independent aid policies and has been frustrated in its attempts to design and implement an effective aid program. Aid must perforce remain a supplementary and secondary activity for the Department, disadvantaged in its competition for administrative resources and repeatedly required to state its claim as a distinct and separate bureaucratic activity.[2] It is reasonable to conclude that this situation will continue for as long as ADAB remains an appendage of the Department. This raises the question of organisational prerequisites for the establishment of independent aid policies.

According to Viviani, all aid donors face the same central problem of aid organisation: 'how to reconcile the interests of the "great triad" (that is, the foreign, finance and trade ministries) with the interests of aid'. In canvassing the arguments for and against the establishment of an aid agency which is autonomous from the foreign ministry, she identifies two opposing factors. On the one hand, an autonomous agency implies that aid policy decisions will be taken at a higher level than when aid functions are integrated into the foreign ministry. On the other hand, the success of this strategy in promoting developmental objectives depends on the agency's strength in defending itself against the incursions of both trade and diplomatic interests (Viviani, 1979, pp. 86-8).

While it is inevitable that trade and foreign policy concerns will influence aid decisions to some extent, George Cunningham argues that an autonomous agency is needed to ensure a 'reasonable balance' between these conflicting interests (Cunningham, 1974, p. 33). The more vexed question is what should be the relationship between the aid agency and the Department of Foreign Affairs: just how much autonomy is needed to ensure an independent aid policy and an effective administrative process, but without antagonising the foreign ministry to the extent that it becomes a staunch bureaucratic enemy of a weak agency? Viviani states the case succinctly:

> The problem is not how to divorce aid objectives from foreign policy and trade policy, but how to ensure that aid objectives predominate over others in aid flows and that these policies take developmental considerations into account. Administrative isolation does not achieve this, and can be totally counterproductive. (Viviani, 1979, p. 88)

Viviani identifies two possible organisational solutions. The first is to have an aid agency which is functionally separate from Foreign Affairs, and directly responsible to the Foreign Minister. The second option is an aid agency within the Foreign Ministry, but under the authority of a junior minister with cabinet rank (Viviani, 1979, p. 89).

Yet Australia's brief experiment with ADAA shows that organisational autonomy of itself does not ensure the development of a set of coherent principles for aid. According to Cunningham, there are two other essential organisational requirements: a strong and unified central planning unit to initiate, articulate and process aid policy; and a management board to overview all implementation, responsible for ensuring that aid policy is actually applied. A third requirement is rigorous legislative scrutiny and general public accountability, features which have also been lacking in Australian aid administration to date (Cunningham, 1974, pp. 40, 53).

Steven Arnold, who reviewed the aid programs of five major European donors in 1982, also stresses the importance of public and political support (Arnold, 1982, pp. 173-4). Many Western donor agencies, including Australia, do not have a strong domestic constituency. As a result, they are ill-equipped to struggle against bureaucratic incursions and are easy prey for interest groups which seek to influence their objectives. Such a domestic political environment may encourage risk aversion behaviour by donor administrators and can reinforce the tendency to avoid explicit articulation of aid objectives (Tendler, 1975, pp. 39, 44; McNeill, 1981, p. 53; White, 1974, p. 79). John White described the British aid organisation in the early 1970s as:

> a Ministry on the run, a ministry which not only saw every hand turned against it but which also has been conditioned to assume that any widening of the debate, unless in the form of undiscriminating and unreserved support for its activities, could only add to this host of hostile hands and thus hasten its destruction. A ministry in this position could not formulate policy; and it could not in any creative sense interpret policy, even if it had had one. (White, 1974, p. 296)

White's words aptly describe ADAB in the early 1980s.

Summary: An Effective Aid Program

In summary, the requirements for an effective aid program which will be conducive to the implementation of equity objectives include the following:

1. a strong and supportive domestic constituency;
2. a clear statement of aid principles which gives explicit recognition to the importance of equity considerations in a hierarchy of aid objectives;
3. legislative scrutiny to ensure public accountability with regard to aid objectives;
4. administrative autonomy from the Department of Foreign Affairs;
5. a strong central planning unit with the capacity to devise <u>strategies</u> for the implementation of aid objectives, particularly those relating to equity;

6. a management process which ensures a strong link between policy-making and aid practice;

7. adequate financial resources and support services;

8. adequate numbers of well-trained personnel.

SUMMARY OF JACKSON REPORT

The Jackson Report concludes that the efficiency, effectiveness, impact and overall quality of Australian aid administration has suffered from a decade of neglect and needs improving. It correctly observes that the current aid program is fragmented, has developed in an ad hoc fashion in response to competing and vested interests and needs to be more focused geographically, sectorally and by mode of delivery (Jackson Report, 1984, pp. 5-6, 15). Its diagnosis of ADAB's shortcomings can be divided into three areas, those of aid policy, management and organisation.

Aid Policy

The committee's analysis of the procedural aspects of policy development is sound. It notes that there is no formal arrangement for seeing policy decisions through to implementation (the weak policy-practice link identified earlier) and acknowledges that the lack of a strong policy and programming capacity has contributed to the fragmentation in the existing aid program (Jackson Report, 1984, pp. 217, 224).

Accordingly it points out the need for a direct link between those sections of ADAB responsible for policy development and review and the planning, design and implementation of aid). It also recommends the establishment of an 'effectiveness review unit' to report independently to senior ADAB management. Its purpose would be to assess the extent to which a program is meeting overall goals, and its findings would be an essential part of ADAB's reporting responsibility to Parliament (Jackson Report, 1984, pp. 232-4).

Aid Management

The report sees aid management as disparate, uncoordinated, concentrated on individual aid activities and thus lacking a country programming approach (Jackson Report, 1984, pp. 216-17). It concurs with the audit report's assessment that program preparation, appraisal, implementation, monitoring and post hoc evaluation are inadequate. It argues that ADAB's practice of funding high priority recipient requests has resulted in projects for which ADAB could not marshal the relevant Australian capability. It also asserts that the present system of financial planning, where the aid budget is divided into a number of functional items, reduces budgetary flexibility (Jackson Report, 1984, pp. 223-5).

Consequently, the report recommends five-year forward-rolling financial planning, with country programming at the core of aid delivery. Country program managers would be responsible for planning, implementing and monitoring all aspects of Australian aid to that country and, as such, would presumably perform a pivotal role in ensuring a strong link between policy and practice. It also recommends increasing the resources devoted to appraisal, monitoring and evaluation, with specific mention of cost-benefit analysis, on-site inspection and the use of specialist sectoral and technical experts (Jackson Report, 1984, pp. 13, 232-3).

Organisation

The Jackson Report endorses both the Auditor-General's and JCPA reports when it describes ADAB as a predominantly clerical rather than professional organisation, having insufficient staff with inadequate training and seniority (Jackson Report, 1984, pp. 15-16). It asserts that the RCF 1981 decision to integrate ADAB's support service functions with those of the Department of Foreign Affairs has been costly and that ADAB's information systems and liaison requirements are deficient (Jackson Report, 1984, pp. 225-7). To overcome these problems the committee recommends a 'Special Program to Upgrade Resources' (SPUR) which includes recruitment of new senior staff and the provision of career development opportunities (Jackson Report, 1984, pp. 230-2). The committee supports an overall increase in administrative spending and recommends some decentralisation measures (including a reference to the deployment of 'regional field groups' outside Canberra) and a reorganised organisation structure (from two divisions to three) (Jackson Report, 1984, pp. 142, 233, 236-7). It identifies five criteria for an effective aid organisation: accountability, management, skills, support services and consultation (Jackson Report, 1984, p. 228).

Finally, the report considers the question of organisational autonomy from the Department of Foreign Affairs (Jackson Report, 1984, pp. 237-42). Its recommendations will be taken up in subsequent discussion.

CRITIQUE OF JACKSON REPORT

While much of the Jackson Committee's analysis on aid administration is sound, there are several major omissions. First, although the report correctly identifies many of the symptoms of ADAB's ineffectiveness, it overlooks one of the major causes: the lack of a clear hierarchy of development assistance objectives. What the report fails to recognise is that the excessive fragmentation of the existing program is a direct result of ADAB's attempts to accommodate itself to a number of disparate policy priorities and sectional interests. The current ad hoc approach to aid management is a direct reflection of this policy confusion. While ADAB's inadequate financial and professional base has certainly had a crippling effect (ACOA, 1982, 1983; DAOA, 1983), the fundamental issue of aid administration is how the three major aid motivations (diplomacy, trade, development) are to be reconciled in practice. The framework offered by the Jackson Report for the resolution of these competing interests amounts, in effect, to a revamping of the two most dominant priorities in the current aid program -- diplomacy and 'comparative advantage'.

With regard to diplomacy, the Jackson Report rightly criticises ADAB for its 'shopping list' approach (Jackson Report, 1984, p. 221), and the recommendations regarding country programming are a significant improvement on the current principle of ad hoc responses to recipient requests. If sufficient resources are allocated and if it receives the necessary in-house support, a country programming strategy can be used successfully as a tool to deflect other pressures on aid and will lead to a more coherent and coordinated aid program. It should be supported as the major programming mechanism for future Australian aid.

On the second priority of comparative advantage, the report deserves applause when it strongly rejects supporting inefficient industries through the aid program (Jackson Report, 1984, pp. 115, 121). The recommendation regarding greater sectoral focus is also sound in principle (Jackson Report, 1984, p. 65). Unfortunately, the committee's application of the principle is perverse in suggesting that Australia's exportable comparative advantage be used as the major criterion shaping the make-up of Australian aid, presumably even where groups in greatest need have no use for such goods and services.

Overall, the report has articulated a more sophisticated way of implementing Australia's diplomatic, strategic and commercial goals in the aid program. Even if not to the full satisfaction of those groups with a vested interest in those goals, these have been articulated, strategies have been formulated for their implementation and they have been reinforced in their status as legitimate and respectable goals for an aid program to pursue. By contrast, the equity objective has been blurred and effectively dismissed. This is the report's second major weakness.

The principal reason for this dismissal is the committee's belief in what is popularly known as the 'trickle-down' theory of development and its particular interpretation of the role of aid in promoting development. Consequently (with the exception of the chapter on women), the report neglects to consider the need to devise strategies and guidelines for the implementation of equity objectives. There is an assumption that if ADAB has its personnel and other administrative resources upgraded, the resulting 'professional' approach will automatically ensure that there is a proper balance between growth, equity and other concerns. The report concedes in passing that 'intergeneration judgements' will need to be made when deciding on the final make-up of country programs (Jackson Report, 1984, p. 136), but gives no clue as to how an appropriate balance between growth and equity objectives is to be decided by senior ADAB management. The Jackson Committee is not alone when it seeks refuge in technical solutions and sees greater professionalism as a panacea for the ills of aid. A number of aid commentators have noted this tendency, which is another outcome of the lack of clear aid objectives and the difficulty of measuring aid outcomes.[3]

Yet there is much evidence that poverty-focused programs require distinct aid management mechanisms. For example, a country programming strategy will only enhance the achievement of equity objectives if it is set within a policy framework which either gives highest priority to equity, or stipulates a percentage of resources which should fulfil these objectives. Unless country profile papers include a structural analysis of the extent and degree of poverty in recipient countries and its relationship to spatial, class, religious, ethnic, gender, or any other relevant variables, there will be no systematic assessment of the particular requirements of disadvantaged groups. Similarly, without a comprehensive analysis of the recipient government's development approach and of the most effective bureaucratic and non-government channels for targeting aid to the poor, there is little chance of Australia developing the required country-specific strategies to achieve equity objectives.

There are many other examples of how equity objectives require distinct aid management strategies. A poverty-focused aid program needs to be targeted. Although this sounds rather obvious, it has not been a strong feature of the existing program, in any of the bilateral modes of delivery, to delineate beneficiary groups (ADAB, 1982, pp. 29-33). The importance of local participation of beneficiaries in all phases of the project cycle is now well recognised as a crucial element in project success,[4] but these factors are ignored by the committee. The Jackson Report claims that cost-benefit techniques can now take into account a variety of financial, economic, social and environmental considerations and recommends a 'blueprint' approach to project design (Jackson Report, 1984, p. 136). This model has long been rejected in the international literature on development administration in favour of a 'process' approach. Poverty-focused projects are not readily amenable to rigid design criteria that are often employed in large physical infrastructure and construction activities. They require a more flexible approach to project management, one that is responsive to unforeseen implementation problems, including the social and economic constraints facing target populations (Sweet and Weisel, 1979; Mickelwait, 1979, p. 187; Honadle, et al., 1980, pp. 42-6).

The Jackson Report acknowledges that projects designed to have a major social impact will need close monitoring (Jackson Report, 1984, p. 137), but omits to mention that all projects and programs should be monitored for social impact. A lack of local and recurrent cost financing presents a crucial constraint on the implementation of equity programs, yet the report recommends that the former be limited to 10 per cent of bilateral aid and gives no guidelines for the application of either of these mechanisms (Jackson Report, 1984, pp. 73-4). Finally, a poverty-focused aid program may require ADAB to diversify its range of managing agents and local recipient counterparts. As a result of all these factors, programs designed to focus on lower-income groups will involve more work, and work of a different nature, from the desk officers who supervise them.

A further omission in the Jackson Report is in the area of ADAB's relationship with its managing agents. The report does little more than note in passing that most aid implementation is contracted out to consultants and experts (Jackson Report, p. 217), although a number of submissions commented on a range of problems evident in current arrange ments.[5] This was also a major issue in both the Auditor-General's and JCPA reports. The latter recommended that Australian consultants on overseas projects receive training from ADAB and stressed the importance of close supervision by experienced ADAB staff overseas (JCPA, 1982, pp. 30, 33, 39). Currently, there are no formal arrangements for briefing consultants beyond the technical tasks that are assigned to them. Senior ADAB management has not addressed the question of whose responsibility it ought to be to arrange and pay for cross-cultural awareness and language training. ADAB has no guidelines for briefing in these areas, nor is any background given on Australian aid policy and the broad social and economic issues of development. In short, ADAB does not see such briefing as essential to the effective implementation of aid and neither does the Jackson Committee. This is despite strong and repeated evidence, both from Australia and overseas (McNeill, 1981, p. 60; Arnold, 1982, p. 94), that contracting out aid work may have detrimental consequences for policy goals. Again there is an assumption in the report that upgrading ADAB's capacity for appraisal, monitoring and evaluation will automatically mean that ADAB's supervision of consultants will improve. However, this will depend on ADAB having sufficient resources to increase its in-house specialist expertise and to place more staff overseas for on-site monitoring. But as the Auditor-General's report shows, it is the content of this monitoring that is important and the Jackson Report omits to address this aspect.

The report's recommendations on ADAB's autonomy from the Department of Foreign Affairs also require some comment. Here the committee's analysis is sound up to a point, although it neglects to consider Viviani's second option of an agency under the authority of a junior minister. It also excludes the option identified by the JCPA report, which is to increase ADAB's administrative autonomy, upgrade the rank of Director and appoint a parliamentary secretary for aid (JCPA, 1982, p. vi). With the exception of the Department of Foreign Affairs, (DFA, 1983) most parties to the debate agree that, at the very least, ADAB needs increased autonomy. The establishment of a career stream, the institution of wide -ranging staff training programs, in-house control over support services and travel arrangements, a separate staff ceiling and increased administrative resources are all essential prerequisites for a more effective aid organisation and the recommendations in these areas deserve support. However the question of exactly how much independence the aid organisation ought to have is more complex. The committee's own analysis clearly favours the option of a statutory authority reporting directly to the Minister. On each of the four criteria proposed -- consistency with aid objectives, appropriateness in aid delivery, accountability, and professionalism and status -- the creation of a statutory authority is the best option. And yet, the committee recommends a Bureau, where the Director's position is a statutory appointment, on the grounds that this will have more bureaucratic staying power. According to the committee's own analysis, this lesser option downgrades the importance of public accountability for aid management and the integrity of aid objectives.

No doubt the final recommendation is based on a correct assessment of the degree of opposition that Foreign Affairs would mount against the re-creation of a more independent aid agency. The importance of bipartisan support for the stability of a future aid organisation is another valid consideration. There is also some evidence of pressure for pieces of the aid program to be splintered off to other departments. For example: the Head of Mission Discretionary Aid Fund to Foreign Affairs; the Development Import Finance Facility to the Export Insurance Finance Corporation or the Department of Trade; and since the 1984/5 Budget there is already over $100 million of calculated education expenditure on private overseas students that is included as Official Development Assistance but beyond ADAB's purview.[6] These contradictions need to be resolved if ADAB is to mount an effective and coordinated aid program. Whether ADAB would be better equipped to ward off future bureaucratic incursions under the protective wing of Foreign Affairs is debatable.

A further argument in favour of a Bureau rather than an independent authority is put forward by some aid administrators who argue that the latter option would institutionalise conflict with the Department, which would then be resolved at a Ministerial level. According to this view, aid would be the loser in such an arrangement, whereas it is more efficient and predictable if conflict is resolved at the bureaucratic rather than the political level. This argument may have some validity in the case of an agency under a junior minister, or that of a totally separate Ministry. But where the head of the agency is directly responsible to the Minister for Foreign Affairs, the argument loses ground, especially when balanced with the history of the department's neglect of ADAB's administrative needs (DAOA, 1983, pp. 6-7; ACOA, 1983, pp. 1-3). Such viewpoints fail to consider the very real possibility, if ADAB remains a Bureau, of a future reintegration into the Department, similar to that which occurred in 1981 as a result of the Review of Commonwealth Functions. It could also be argued that the Department's mettle will be roused almost as much by increasing ADAB's autonomy as a Bureau, as by the creation of a statutory authority.

In any case, the decision on ADAB's future organisational autonomy is a political one. It is salutary to recall that ADAA's demise was facilitated by inadequate community and parliamentary support for the notion of a coherent and developmentally oriented aid policy. In the long term, an independent aid agency will only maintain its bureaucratic autonomy (whatever degree of autonomy that may be) if it has a strong and articulate domestic constituency. This, in turn, will only be created if the organistion has a firm commitment to development objectives and can demonstrate its effectiveness in achieving them. At the moment ADAB can do neither. Public accountability and integrity of aid objectives are precisely the two principles that ought not to be sacrificed if such a task is to be undertaken. This is not to argue that diplomatic and commercial objectives cannot be achieved through an aid program. Rather, the debate is over the precedence that these factors command and how they influence aid choices. Moreover, in their crudest form, there is evidence that strategic and commercial motivations may be more of a hindrance than a help in mobilising long-term public support for aid.[7]

There can be little argument with the case in favour of an overall increase in administrative spending. The report's recommendations regarding the need for internal audits, an effectiveness review, more regular on-site monitoring of aid and upgrading the responsibilities of field officers are all supported (Jackson Report, 1984, pp. 233-4). ADAB should also ensure that its staff are closely involved in aid appraisal, design and evaluation teams. The report's comments on the need for evaluation of completed aid schemes are worthy of strong support (Jackson Report, 1984, p. 138). Without such feedback, assessments of the effectiveness and social impact of Australian aid will continue to be based substantially on faith and hearsay.

RECOMMENDATIONS

The above discussion indicates the general deficiencies in the Jackson Report's coverage of aid administration. What follows are some more specific suggestions for the implementation of the equity objective.

It has been shown that the Jackson Report has sought to institution-alise a particular interpretation of diplomatic, strategic and commercial objectives. Recognising that equity and humanitarianism have long been part of the rhetoric of Australian aid, equity objectives require a similar status in the aid administration process. Without such a status, they will rarely take precedence over other goals. There are a number of ways to achieve the required institutionalisation which are amenable to government administration practices. First, consideration should be given to establishing a special task force to develop guidelines for the implementation of equity-focused aid, within the overall framework of a country programming approach. ADAB offices involved should have a sufficient seniority for their recommendations to carry weight.

There seems to be a tendency in the Australian aid debate to equate equity with anti-infrastructure, relief and purely welfare-oriented programs. Considering this basic misunderstanding of the concept of targeting aid to the poor, the work of the task force should begin with the study and evaluation of relevant literature on implementing bilateral equity-focused aid, with an emphasis on the work of other donors. It would recommend on appropriate modes of delivery, sectoral strategies, management techniques and organisational resources needed for the implementation of an equity program. For example, the Dutch have developed a concept of 'programmatic assistance' which may be a suitable and administratively efficient mode of aid delivery in the Australian context. Following the identification of a specific target group, region, or sector, an appropriate existing recipient implementating agency or institution is identified, with whom the donor enters into a long-term commitment. The approach, still in its early stages, has evolved out of a dissatisfaction with traditional project aid (Arnold, 1982, pp. 94-5, 183). Australia's own, but still very modest, BINGO (Bilateral-Non-Governmental Organisation) program has a similar potential. Equity-focused projects are often smaller and more complex than traditional approaches and the task force would be charged with identifying innovative methods of overcoming existing administrative constraints. Their work should not, however, be restricted to the project aid area.

In addition to the establishment of an equity task force, the government could allocate a specified proportion of the aid budget to equity programs. This is a similar approach to that taken with other special items in the budget: for example, the Women and Development Fund, Development Studies and Research, DIFF, DIGS and co-financing Again the Netherlands aid program serves as a useful comparison where 25 per cent of total aid has been used as a general guideline (Arnold, 1982, p. 84).

Whatever figure is selected, and while it could be argued that 25 per cent is rather low given the history of neglect of equity issues in Australian aid implementation, the allocation of a special equity fund might well be the only way to ensure that policy rhetoric is taken seriously. An equity task force could utilise such a special budget allocation to ensure that innovative pilot projects were funded and supervised appropriately, and to encourage country program managers and desk officers to give due priority to equity issues.

Currently, ADAB is preparing country profile papers in ten areas for a number of major recipients (Indonesia, the Philippines, Burma, China, Thailand and Malaysia). The result will be a policy statement including a set of goals for Australian aid in the particular country, a strategy for future planning and the adaptation of the existing program and a case upon which to base the country's proportional share of aid. It is proposed that the policy and strategy will be negotiated bilaterally and that it will continue to be directed to areas of high priority to the recipient (ADAB, 1984c). It is impossible to comment in detail on ADAB's proposed country programming strategy before the relevant papers become available. The title of only one background paper being prepared by ACFOA has so far been made public. In this period of debate on the report, there can be little reason why the other titles and the general methodology should not be open for discussion.

As the Jackson Report recognised, implementing a country programming strategy will require an organisational restructuring. Two factors need emphasising here. First, this restructuring needs to take account of the weak link that currently exists between stated policy and aid practice recognised by both the Auditor-General's and Jackson Reports and which will require the creation of a strong central planning unit. Second, regional field groups, including seconded and in-house specialist expertise, should be established. This approach is already used in British aid administration, where it is seen as a compromise between the need for specialist field expertise and on- site aid management and the prohibitive cost of establishing this in a large number of recipient countries (Arnold, 1982, pp. 148-9; OECD, 1981, pp. 26-7). Similar cost constraints exist in the Australian program. These regional teams should be staffed by people on long-term appointments, with the relevant language proficiencies and as recommended in the Jackson Report, they should have a close relationship with country managers based in Canberra. An important part of their role would be an upgraded and more intensive ADAB oversight and management of aid activities, including regular on-site visits, particularly for the larger bilateral projects, and provision of guidance to consultants on questions of socio-economic impact. In this context, more systematic briefing is required of consultants in areas such as cross-cultural awareness, foreign language and general communication skills, Australian aid policy, and development issues. ADAB should at least establish guidelines for these briefings and should indicate that such skills are required when calling for tenders on projects so that training costs can be adequately accounted for.

The Jackson Committee noted the need for ADAB to liaise with a range of groups, but did not mention the establishment of an Advisory Board as proposed by both the Development Assistance Officers Association and the APCC. The Organisation for Economic Co-operation and Development (OECD) notes that a number of donor governments have established advisory committees 'in order to introduce an element of non-governmental opinion into aid policy formulation' (OECD, 1981, p. 19). ADAB has already made use of committees in a limited way and a board could have the advantage of increasing the public accountability of the program, especially when combined with the establishment of an effectiveness review unit. Although there are some notable exceptions, ADAB has tended more towards a siege mentality in the past than one of openness. This can again be contrasted with the approach in the Netherlands, where a National Advisory Council for Development Co-operation, through a system of working groups, prepares comprehensive reports which are an important input into policy-making (Arnold, 1982, pp. 77-8). The government should consider the appointment of an Advisory Council on Equity Issues to work with the ADAB task force recommended earlier. Membership would include a senior officer of the task force and representatives from voluntary agencies and academia who have specific expertise and experience in the implementation, research and evaluation of poverty-focused programs. It would be appointed for a limited period, with the specific task of overseeing the institutionalisation of equity objectives into all aspects of aid delivery. Finally, given the importance of an informed constituency to the domestic political environment of an aid program, the committee's recommendation on the need for development education funding and, more particularly, for this to be managed by an independent unit should be heeded by the government (Jackson Report, 1984, p. 236).

NOTES

1. ACOA (1982) p. 4 lists six new schemes introduced since the establishment of ADAA: Development Import Grants (DIGS); Development Import Finance Facility (DIFF); the Australian Science, Technology and Research Co-operation Program (AUSTREC); Australian Executive Service Overseas Program (AESOP); NGO Project Subsidy Scheme; and the Joint Venture Financing Scheme. A co-financing facility was also introduced in the 1982/3 Budget.

2. See the submission to the Jackson Committee by the Secretary of the Department of Foreign Affairs (DFA, 1983) which appears to give little recognition to the notion of aid as a distinct activity.

3. See Jackson Report pp. 192, 221-3. Aid commentators here include McNeill, 1981, p. 15; White, 1974, p. 49; and Tendler, 1975, p. 96.

4. For example: McNeill, 1981, p. 93; Morss et al., 1976, pp. 202-23; Hunter, 1982; Morss and Morss, 1982, p. 99; Yudelman, 1976, pp. 379-80; Morris and Gwyer, 1983, p. 161; and Brandt Report, 1980, pp. 133, 140.

5. For example, submissions by: CAA, 1983, pp. 44-5; ACFOA, 1983, pp. 77-81; DAOA, p 15; Hinton, 1983, pp. 2-3; Hunt, 1983, para 9.1; Hoare, 1983, pp. 2-3; Macdonald, 1983, p.9.

6. See submission to the Jackson committee by the Department of Trade, 1983, p. 9; and the EFIC, 1983, p. 7. For information on the 'hidden subsidy' to private overseas students, included as part of Official Development Assistance in the 1984/5 budget, see Chapter Six of the Jackson Report, and Budget Paper No.9, pp. 10, 22-3.

7. The following authors have compared US and Scandinavian aid programs, highlighting the importance of humanitarian motivations in mobilising public support for aid: Streeten, 1972, pp. 302-11; Myrdal, 1970, pp. 343-56; and Arnold, 1982, pp. 174, 187. See also Frank and Baird, 1975, pp. 162-3.

13 THE NON-GOVERNMENTAL ORGANISATIONS

Kaye Bysouth

The bulk of Australian non-government 'development' agencies were no doubt pleased to endorse the Jackson Committee's recommendation for a doubling of government funding to non-governmental organisations (currently budgeted at $8.8 million or 0.9 per cent of Overseas Development Assistance), with plans for further increases and for the rationalisation of government-funded NGO programs. The critical question, however, is whether or not the implementation of these recommendations will improve the contribution which NGOs can make to Third World development -- either alone or in collaboration with the Australian government.

If we accept the 'articles of faith'[1] about NGOs -- that they work directly with the poorest in Third World countries, respond to need, involve and empower target communities in design and implementation of projects and that they are cost effective, innovative and flexible — then a policy to double the potential impact of such organisations would seem beyond reproach. Indeed, if these 'articles of faith' can be accepted as correct, it is surprising that so little attention was given in the Jackson Committee recommendations to devising practical methods by which government could utilise the skills of NGOs more effectively. If the government's primary goal in giving aid is to 'alleviate poverty through social and economic development' (Jackson Report, 1984, p. 3), and NGOs purport to have specific skills at reaching and working with people in poverty, then, logically, we would have expected the committee to give some priority to devising practical ways of ensuring that these skills are tapped to improve the effectiveness of the official program in achieving its primary development goal.

Insofar as the Jackson Committee did not explore practical methods, nor make recommendations, designed to tap NGO skills, we are presented with a paradox: the quality of NGO development activities apparently justifies a recommendation for large increases in funding but does not justify increased operational involvement in the official development assistance program. We must assume either that the Jackson Committee was not genuine in its concern to alleviate poverty, or that it was not impressed by the quality of NGO development activities or that it has another conception of the way to alleviate poverty.

The committee certainly recognised a number of faults in NGO performance; NGOs have 'inexperienced field officers', there is a 'lack of effective project supervision' and they suffer from an 'inability to properly handle relations with local implementing agencies'. They are 'small by world standards and their range of activities is limited'. They often have 'limited objectives and activities, a limited absorptive capacity and little potential for duplication' (Jackson Report, 1984, p. 110). Surprisingly, however, the committee did not include amongst its criticisms a direct challenge of NGO performance in relation to the 'articles of faith'. Had it chosen to do so, a careful study of NGO projects funded by the Australian Development Assistance Bureau (ADAB) under the ADAB/NGO Project Subsidy Scheme may have provided sufficient evidence.

HISTORY OF THE GOVERNMENT/NGO PROJECT SUBSIDY SCHEME

The ADAB/NGO Project Subsidy Scheme (PSS) was set up in 1974 to encourage the Australian community's involvement in overseas aid programs through support for the activities of Australian NGOs, to support effectively the development of people in the Third World, and to encourage people-to-people contact and strengthen the links between Australian and indigenous NGOs. Under the PSS, the government has subsidised 50 per cent of the total cost of approved projects of NGOs; in the Pacific region (excluding PNG) and in Least Developed Countries (LDCs), subsidies up to 75 per cent of the total cost are given.[2] The PSS has been administered by a Committee for Development Co-operation (CDC), composed of equal numbers of nominees from ADAB and the NGOs.

To be eligible to participate in the program of cooperation, an organisation has to be clearly identifiable as an Australian NGO which is efficiently managed and capable of providing evidence of its competence to implement overseas projects. The extent to which an NGO is able to mobilise community support, its capacity to contribute to overseas development assistance, its past record of performance and its effective links with counterpart organisations in developing countries have also been taken into account. Finally, NGOs participating in the scheme have been divided into three groups:

1. those which are primarily development oriented, have substantial resources and community support and have satisfied the requirements of the scheme over a number of years;

2. NGOs with smaller budgets and smaller programs;

3. NGOs which make infrequent requests or have only recently been granted eligibility.

Organisations in each of these groups have been allocated annually an Indicative Planning Figure (IPF) and thereafter have received grants up to the level of their IPF following consideration of individual project applications.

According to the project selection criteria, projects would be supported by government subsidy if they responded to the needs of the poorest communities, particularly women, and encouraged and facilitated self-help through local participation in the identification of needs and the implementation of development programs. The criteria recognised the importance of innovative approaches to problem solving, as well as the importance of replicability and of strengthening local counterpart organisations to ensure that they could sustain the development projects. Finally, the project was required to have clearly defined objectives and to be administratively, financially, and economically viable.

Since 1974/5, the number of organisations eligible to participate in the scheme has risen from 12 to 87 in 1983/4. In 1974/5 the PSS supported 67 projects in 14 developing countries. This rose to a peak of 422 projects in 74 countries in 1981/2 and fell back to 378 projects in 63 countries in 1983/4. This decrease in the number of projects supported is due to the fact that larger projects have been implemented and is also a reflection of the impact of the 3:1 ratio introduced in 1980. In the period from 1974/5 to 1983/4 government support for NGO projects through PSS has risen from $250,000 (0.8 per cent of ODA) to almost $5 million (0.6 per cent of ODA).[3] Projects supported have concentrated predominantly in South Asia, followed by Africa, the Pacific and PNG and, to a lesser extent, South and Central America and Southeast Asia. NGO programs supported under the scheme have tended to focus on agricultural programs, water supply, health and education and community development (which would include leadership training, youth training, cooperative development).

Decline in the Quality of NGO Projects

Although the contribution made by ADAB to NGO development projects is actually a relatively small part of the budget of most NGOs, it is fair to say that the NGO programs submitted for government funding probably represent the best portion of their development programs.[4] This is because the CDC has developed quite clear developmental criteria governing project selection, and the desire to meet these criteria, coupled with the overall effect of proposing projects in a publicly accountable arena, has encouraged NGOs to submit their best projects for funding. As such, the performance of NGOs under the PSS can be considered as a legitimate indicator of the quality of NGO development programs.

Prior to 1978, when both the number of organisations eligible for funding and the level of funding available were relatively small, the CDC was able to apply its developmental criteria quite strictly to the selection of projects for funding. At that time the CDC did not visit ADAB subsidised projects for purposes of review or evaluation, so there is little documentation available assessing the quality of NGO programs. Nevertheless, it is probably fair to assume that the projects funded under the PSS up to 1978 lived up to the assessment criteria, both because the agencies participating in the scheme at that time had a long history of development work and because the limited availability of funding dictated that only the best among those projects submitted would be funded; two out of three were rejected. This not only produced a quality PSS but also encouraged the NGOs participating in the scheme to constantly assess and improve the quality of their own programs. Unfortunately, while the quality may have been high the size, and therefore the overall impact, of the program was minimal.

After 1978 the funding increased substantially beyond $2 million as did the number of organisations participating in the program. The combined effect of these two changes was to bring about a relaxation in the strict application of assessment criteria such that fulfilment of the criteria in the broadest possible terms was sufficient to warrant financial support. In some respects, virtually anything that was for the benefit of people overseas could get into the program.

In general terms, the self-improving and self-regulating mechanism which had become part of the scheme began to break down as more participating organisations lacked both a long history in development work and the experience of producing good quality programs to meet strict PSS development criteria. Moreover, because the scheme was based on a matched funding arrangement it clearly began to favour those organisations which were large fund raisers, which was no guarantee that the organisation was capable of implementing good development projects in the field. In fact the opposite appeared to be the case.

As experienced NGOs were under greater pressure to increase the number of projects submitted for funding in order to take up available funds, the CDC became increasingly concerned that even organisations which had a long history in development work were not producing good quality projects for support. Indeed, it was suggested that many of those which had been previously rejected were being resubmitted for support.

The result was inevitable. In 1983 members of the CDC conducted a review of government funded NGO projects in Papua New Guinea and were extremely critical of the quality of these projects. In community based programs the team was disappointed to find neither project personnel nor the communities in which they worked were interested in community control of projects and the growth of community development skills and independence among villages. Institution-based programs often ran projects unrelated to local communities and the team found that the contribution of this project development was therefore doubtful. The team was concerned that the ready availability of project funds has lead to an unquestioning acceptance and dependence on outsiders rather than the promotion of self-reliance. The message was clear. Few of the projects visited were considered to be developmentally sound in the terms outlined in the assessment criteria.

The Committee for Development Cooperation outlined the implications of this lack of performance most succinctly:

> In their submissions to the Jackson Aid Review Committee, NGOs have been emphasizing the need for Government aid to be directed to the needs of the poorer sections of the community. The programs to be supported should be based in the community and lead to self-sufficiency in the medium to long term.
>
> CDC has been concerned for some time that a significant number of projects submitted for support have not really met these objectives. The basic criteria for PSS support are so wide that these projects could be supported, however many of these did not meet the preferential criteria as set out in the PSS Guidelines under 3.2.2.
>
> If the NGOs are going to have more influence on Government policy and are to signal to the Jackson Committee that they are serious about improving the quality of aid in their own programs as well as those of the Government then the quality of projects funded under the PSS must improve. (7th Annual ADAB/NGO Consultation, 1984, pp. 31-2)

These criticisms were repeated the following year when it was noted that 'A further common reason for rejecting or deferring projects was that evidence of local involvement was inadequate or unclear' (8th Annual ADAB/NGO Consultation, 1985, p. 7).

The Implications of Decline in NGO Program Quality

The CDC's concerns about the performance of NGOs appeared to directly question the capacity of NGOs to perform in those areas regarded as their particular preserve, namely targetting towards the poorest and development of Third World communities in a manner designed to promote self-sufficiency.

The implications of these criticisms are extremely serious. First, they raise doubts as to whether it is possible for NGOs to consistently promote development of the poorest, based upon principles of self-help and local participation. Secondly, they raise doubts about the feasibility of increasing the developmental impact of NGO programs by channelling more funds through these organisations, since it appears that as the size and number of NGOs and their projects have increased, the quality of their development programs has deteriorated. Thirdly, these criticisms cast doubt upon the credibility of NGO demands (expressed in many submissions to the Jackson Committee) for the development of an official development assistance program which responds to the needs of those in conditions of greatest poverty and is carried out according to principles of self-help and local participation. How could NGOs argue for a broad -scale poverty-oriented program if they are themselves incapable of implementing such a program even on a small scale?

JACKSON COMMITTEE UNCONCERNED WITH NGO QUALITY

It would give credit to the Jackson Committee if we could believe that, as a result of their genuine doubts about the effectiveness of NGOs in reaching the poorest, and stimulating development according to the 'articles of faith', they did not consider it appropriate to recommend greater involvement by NGOs in the official development assistance program.

Unfortunately, the tenor and recommendations contained in the rest of the report, (including the recommended increase in financial assistance to NGOs) gives the lie to this interpretation. On the contrary, the Jackson Committee did not closely scrutinise the performance of NGOs to promote development amongst the poorest communities for the same reasons that it did not seriously consider whether or not it would be possible for ADAB to carry out a development program which made a direct attack on poverty.

The committee believes that the correct role for an aid program in promoting development is to provide financial assistance for capital investment and specialist training in professional skills in order to remove physical and manpower constraints in economic growth in developing countries, thereby facilitating the provision of basic goods and services to whole communities. According to this view it is not really necessary, nor germane to the argument, to be able to establish a direct link between Australia's aid program and the alleviation of poverty. This is the responsibility of recipient governments.

Coupled with the general lack of concern to directly relate the inputs provided under the ODA Program to improving people's living standards, the committee also clearly has little faith in the possibility of actually implementing a program which recognised this as a primary goal. There is little indication that the committee appreciates the existence of any specific or tangible skills, techniques or strategies designed to ensure that people are involved in, and benefit from, development assistance programs which could fruitfully be applied to large scale projects and programs. Their recommendations regarding NGOs therefore are not designed to improve the capacity of these organisations to stimulate grass-roots development, but rather to overcome perceived administrative and managerial inadequacies and help them to become financially and technically competent, perhaps (although by no means necessarily) as a forerunner to their eventual integration into the existing ODA programs as currently conceived and implemented.

The committee's recommendation that all ADAB supported voluntary agency activities (Project Subsidy Scheme, Special Purpose Grants, Bi/NGO Program, Volunteers, Development Education, Food Aid, etc.) should be consolidated under one program could potentially stem the decline in NGO standards by the application of strict development criteria across a range of NGO programs. The committee's motivation in making this recommendation however appeared to be less a concern with quality and more a desire to bring about administrative cohesion and thereby to facilitate channelling of greater funds through NGOs, particularly in those areas complementary to the official program.

The only area where the committee called for an improvement in quality in what may be regarded as NGO traditional activity related to the request to NGOs to build up a capacity to assist women in developing countries. It is difficult to applaud the committee's progressive attitudes in this regard, coming as they do in the context of a general lack of attention to the capacity of NGOs to reach and involve the poorest, most of whom are women. Without such attention the request to involve women cannot be regarded as any more than a pious hope, lacking practical strategies for achievement. Indeed the focus on women in general has a considerable air of piousness about it given that in all other respects 'people' (of which one presumes women are a subset) were not considered to be either the subject or the object of the official aid program.

As regards further areas for ADAB/NGO collaboration, the Jackson Committee does not encourage ADAB to find ways to strengthen the potential of NGOs to work at the grass roots level and to develop creative ways of using NGOs to get official aid through to those in greatest need. Nor does the committee challenge the NGOs to clarify their role and to systematise their thinking and activities in relation to grass roots development and to identify ways of linking these up with government programs.

On the contrary, they have maintained a fairly strict dichotomy between programs aiming at 'providing poor people with basic needs' which are clearly categorised as relief, and the 'real' development assistance program. The former is fit to be carried out by NGOs through small programs, which are limited in scope and potential impact and are essentially non-replicable. The government must get on with the 'real' development assistance program -- that which confronts 'major obstacles' to development, potentially affects far larger numbers of people and is said to have a far greater long-term impact.

It should be noted that in adopting this attitude, the committee was expressing no more nor less than the attitude of successive Australian governments, which have frequently been inclined to use NGOs to provide emergency relief -- the latest example being the response to the famine in Ethiopia -- but not to call upon them to apply their skills to improve the effectiveness of the official development assistance program.

THE FUTURE ROLE AND RESPONSIBILITIES OF NGOS

The non-government sector in Australia cannot afford to embrace the recommendation of the Jackson Committee (no matter how financially palatable), coupled as they are with a blase indifference to the direct impact of Australian aid -- whether government or non-government -- on the development of the poorest Third World communities.

In order to be able to legitimately challenge the Jackson Committee's position in this regard, however, Australian NGOs must demonstrate a willingness and capacity to re-examine the 'articles of faith' regarding both the reasons for, and the nature of, their own work. Only then will they be in a position to improve the effectiveness of their own work and to influence the overall development effort emanating from Australia.

According to the orthodox view of development espoused by Jackson, the improvement of the 'quality of life' of the people in Third World countries ought to be able to be achieved without the assistance of non-government development agencies. If this view is to be believed, increases in the rate of economic growth should allow Third World states to distribute more and better goods and services to the majority of their poor citizens without the aid of NGOs. On the other hand, if the NGO approach is to be taken to its logical conclusion, the poor must ultimately be responsible for developing themselves by becoming more conscious, improving their education and capabilities and organising themselves to participate fully in the development of their countries.

In practice many Third World countries have not been able to distribute sufficient goods and services to the majority of their poor. In India, for example, the World Bank blames a slow historical growth rate (around 3.5 per cent) and agricultural growth rate (2.4 per cent during the 1970s) for the country's failure to have any significant impact on the reduction of poverty since independence (World Bank, 1984, p. 123ff). By contrast, Planning Commission member Raj Krishna suggests:

> It is an established fact of the Indian economy that poverty ratio has no relation to per capita income level. While the income per capita is rising slowly, poverty ratio is constant. This is because the rate of growth at the bottom levels of society does not change. Most of the increases in income is among the top 25 per cent of society and very little trickles to the bottom. (Krishna, 1983, p. 2165)

Either way it has been estimated that over 330 million people are living below the poverty line in India today. The infant mortality rate for the country is still 130 per thousand, less than 15 per cent of children below five years of age could be considered to have a normal state of nutrition; an estimated 30,000 children are becoming blind every year because of Keratomalacia or Vitamin A deficiency, 63 per cent of India's children below three years of age and about 45 per cent of children between three and five years suffer from iron deficiency anaemia.[5]

If it is difficult for macro-developments (no matter how slow) to be automatically converted into improved quality of life for the majority of the poor, there is no conceptual reason why governments should not be able to directly help the poor. In practice, however, there are operational difficulties.

India has developed nationwide programs aimed specifically at the poor. For example the Integrated Rural Development Program (IRDP) — worth Rs 10 billion and reaching 3.3 million families in 1982/3 -- is intended to provide the poorest of the poor with sufficient credit and subsidies to purchase assets in order to generate sufficient income to raise recipients above the poverty line. Unfortunately 'according to the evaluation of the programme by the Programme Evaluation Organisation (PEO) cited in the Mid Term Appraisal of the Planning Commission, the benefits of the programme are being diverted to the non-poor and relatively rich families who have the power and status in the village to do it'. It has been suggested that as little as 10 per cent of the funds allocated to the program in the three years 1980-1 to 1982-3, actually reached the poor families for whom it was intended. The rest was lost on the way from Delhi to the village through various corrupt practices, unauthorised payments and political extortions (Yojana, 1984, p. 17).

A recent World Bank Report on India confirms this estimation and adds 'it appears probable that the net benefits to households, in terms of net incremental consumption, have so far often been inadequate to assist them significantly or to yield a reasonable return on the invested resources'. In fact this report notes that 'poverty alleviation programs are both important and very difficult to implement effectively. There are few countries which have designed, implemented and sustained truly effective poverty alleviation programs' (World Bank, 1984, p. 143, 142).

Why is it that the poor do not use local organisations and political structures to ensure that they are able to gain some shares in the resources (however meagre) offered by the State? A comparative study of the role of local institutions in the rural development process in over a dozen Third World countries notes that whatever local organisations do exist tend to be skewed towards the better off (those who own land) and do not effectively meet the needs of the small or marginal farmers or the landless:

> land ownership is a fairly reliable source and indicator of social and political power. Where this power is skewed in favor of a small minority, that minority will use its power to preempt for its own use the bulk of the scarce and valuable resources provided by central government for agricultural development. This includes not only the scarce (subsidised) credit, fertilizer, processing and marketing facilities provided by government, but also the attention of the limited number of extension agents who bear knowledge of improved practices. They will also tend to dominate whatever organisations function in the countryside and convert them to their own purposes. Seldom will such organisations mobilize resources and organize projects which raise the productive potential of the less-productive members of the community; rather, what is done will be directed toward improvements benefiting the more powerful members ... The more powerful members effectively deny or severely limit access by small farmers, not to mention tenants and

> landless labourers, to the resources and public services provided by the state. Under these conditions, smaller farmers will not find it worth their time or effort to participate in local organisations which have little of value to distribute to them and cannot facilitate their access to goods and services needed to raise their productivity and income. If such organisations become institutionalized, they would be as instruments of the large and middle farmers, while small farmers would be thrown back on traditional links of dependency on patrons or be compelled to rely wholly on their own meager resources. (Uphoff and Esman, 1974, p. 65)

Moreover, the study found no evidence of organisation among the landless or of governmental efforts to promote such organisation:

> without organization, these poorest of the poor have no bargaining power and no capacity to claim public services. If they should become effectively organized, conflict levels in the rural areas would certainly increase with the landless demanding a larger share of the scarce income and public services that characterize the countryside in contemporary Asia. To acquiesce in the continued powerlessness of the landless, because the alternatives seem more threatening, is to lend futility to tragedy. Uphoff and Esman, 1974, p. 92)

Making Happen What Otherwise Would Not Happen

Given that NGOs are essentially groups of people committed to the alleviation of poverty, then clearly their work must be directed to those who are not gaining any benefit from the macro-development process and their strategy must be to overcome those obstacles which are preventing these people from improving their standard of living. The raison d'etre of NGOs is to make happen what otherwise would not happen.

Leaving aside disaster situations which demand specific relief and rehabilitation responses, the primary on-going role and responsibilities of indigenous Third World NGOs would seem to fall into three interrelated categories; a) organisation of the poor to ensure that they can participate in the development of their countries; b) mobilising the financial and human resources of the poor in order to increase their productive capacity and income levels and; c) developing the capacity of the poor to demand and receive from the government an improved share of the nation's goods and services.

In this vein, many NGOs in India are involved in educating and organising the poor to ensure that the potential benefits of the IRDP actually increase the productive capacity of intended beneficiaries. This involves, for example, organising poor communities to select the poorest from their number to be beneficiaries of the program and assisting the beneficiaries to make the right kind of investments which are both within the management capacity of the household or group of households and which are economically viable. This work also involves assistance to beneficiaries in securing bank finance, thereby reducing dependence on the 'development middle men' who take advantage of the lack of knowledge of beneficiaries to reduce their economic gain. Finally NGOs assist the beneficiary to overcome 'unfavourable market forces' which, left unchecked, can destroy productive initiatives.

In Sri Lanka the cooperative movement has tended to be ineffective in meeting the needs of the rural poor due to political manipulation, bureaucratic control and local corruption. The non-government sector has been actively involved with village communities to revitalise village credit cooperatives as genuine people's organisations capable of taking an integrated approach to community development. These village credit societies are capable of satisfying the limited credit needs of the poor rural communities on conditions which are appropriate and acceptable to poor rural farmers. Moreover, these credit cooperatives have been much more successful than the traditional banking institutions in mobilising the savings of the rural poor, thereby increasing the potential for domestic investment.

Finally, a further example can be drawn fom Thailand where non-government workers (often practising middle-level bureaucrats who have despaired at the possibilities of delivering public goods and services to the poorest through the government system) work alongside teachers, monks and village headmen in rural villages to bring poor communities to the first stage of organisation. Once this is achieved it enables these communities to take advantage of the many revolving funds made available by the Thai government for improvements in agricultural productivity, health, sanitation, and other basic needs.

This type of work also educates the people to be able to demand and utilise government services more efficiently. For example, the elaborate Thai health system, which seldom penetrates below the district level, can be made to work if the people know what they should expect from the District Health Team and the Village Health Worker.

Once the community understands what is possible in terms of health care, they can make a better selection of a Village Health Worker and look to the District Health Officials to provide adequate follow-up training and supervision.

By extension, the role of western NGOs supporting grass roots development in the Third World, is also to make happen what otherwise would not happen. Pursuing the examples given above, Australian NGOs might well provide financial assistance to facilitate training of community development workers, community education, provision of seed capital to enable the poorest groups to participate in national government development schemes or provide assistance in expanding the resource base of village credit societies. They might also provide indigenous NGOs with the financial and moral support they require to attempt innovative demonstration and pilot projects based upon knowledge of local resources, needs and potential as examples to the poorest communities themselves, to other NGOs and government of what can be achieved by the poor for themselves.

<u>Building Nations from the Bottom Up</u>

Beyond carrying out activities which would not otherwise be carried out in the short to medium term, NGOs, whether in Australia or in the Third World, also have a responsibility to publicly and practically address questions of justice, equity and the ultimate goals of development. Why is it that some groups have been left out of the development process in the first place? What must be done to ensure that the macro -development process does not leave them out again? How can the autonomous self-development efforts of isolated communities be expanded and linked with regional and national development efforts so that local communities can play a key role in the development of their nations?

In asking these questions, however, NGOs must be aware that the experiences over the past three decades with cooperatives and community development movements has provided some sobering lessons for naive exponents of bottom up development. Rural cooperative movements have been looked upon by many Third World countries as the key to marshalling and increasing the productivity and therefore the incomes of the rural poor, as well as a method of providing training, services, facilities and assistance to rural populations. In practice, rural cooperatives in developing countries have often excluded or brought little benefit to the poor (particularly women); leaders have often been corrupted and abused their power and the cooperatives have ultimately become weak, inactive and unproductive.

One of the major reasons suggested for this is that too often cooperatives have been the creations of government, intended to promote government policies and provide government control over markets, rather than voluntary creations of individuals to increase their collective economic productivity.

The community development 'movement' which may be said to have begun in post-independence India, and spread over 60 nations in Asia, Africa and Latin America during the 1950s, focused on self-help approaches to increasing agricultural production and strengthening rural infrastructure. Over time, the concept of community development was institutionalised and became the basis of major national rural development efforts -- building nations from the bottom up. By 1960 many programs were faltering and by 1965 most had ended. A number of characteristic weaknesses have been identified as being responsible for this:

1. the existing local power structures were accepted as given;

2. 'community development' was institutionalized in a separate bureaucracy which was neither capable of involving and responding to the genuine needs of the community, nor of penetrating the traditional bureaucracy;

3. there was a greater emphasis placed on the expansion of services rather than on increasing rural incomes;

4. little was done to build actual organisational capacity at the local level;

5. little attention was given to the need to link self-governing villages into larger, more economically viable village units. (Korten, 1980; Uphoff and Esman, 1974, pp. 69 ff)

The experiences of the cooperative and community development movements do not demonstrate that bottom-up development is an unachievable ideal. First, the involvement of local communities of poor people in the development of their nations is not merely an ideal but an essential component of national development strategies, if developing countries are to avoid massive waste of resources through unused human and financial potential and wasted poverty programs which do not reach the poor.

Secondly, there is no evidence to suggest that the involvement of the poor majority in national development efforts cannot and should not be achieved. Rather, experience suggests that the State is ill -equipped to orchestrate community development efforts. This requires acceptance of social diversity and relative autonomy, painstaking investment in building community problem-solving ability before investment decisions are made and a willingness to allow organisations of the poor to develop outside traditional power structures if need be.

However, it is not possible to simply devolve power to local communities to carry out autonomous developmental activities. On the one hand, this leads to abuse of power and misappropriation of resources by some, thereby reducing the productive potential of the community as a whole. On the other hand, local community development efforts are economically and politically non-viable and non-sustainable if they remain unconnected with those at district, regional and national level (cf. Uphoff and Esman, 1974).

Having absorbed the lessons of the past, many Third World NGOs have developed a complex and realistic approach to building nations from the bottom up. They now seek to combine their short and medium term responses to the alleviation of poverty with a longer-term strategy for evolution of a society which distributes the benefits of development more evenly. Therefore, they focus not only upon attempting directly to increase the organisational and productive capacities of the poor, which the State cannot and, in many cases, will not do, but also upon helping local communities to change the factors which will lead to abuse of power and inhibition of local productive potential. In an Asian rural context this essentially means tackling the land reform issue.

Hence, in countries with land reform programs NGOs assist at the local level by identifying clandestinely held land, by supporting poor communities to initiate quasi-judicial processes of vesting and distribution of surplus land among the rural poor, and providing a minimal self

-defence mechanism to prevent illegal physical eviction from the assigned land through violence by erstwhile owners. Most importantly, however, NGOs assist in the provision of consumption and production credit and other agricultural inputs to ensure that the initiative will be productive.

So far, what NGOs have generally been unable to resolve, however, is the question of what their role and responsibilities are in linking parallel community development efforts, as well as linking communities vertically with district, regional and national development efforts. Their attempts to date have generally fallen short of evolving a sustained structure of organisational linkages, communications and joint action which is capable of protecting local initiatives as well as linking them in a manner designed to facilitate more extensive and rapid rural change.

Many Third World NGOs are organisationally fragmented, subject to ideological and territorial disputes and, therefore, easily manipulated by political parties and the bureaucracy; above all they are financially vulnerable.

Which Way Australian NGOs?

Insofar as Australian NGOs seek to assist the majority of the poor in Third World countries to play a key role in the development of their nations they must also absorb the lessons of the past. Not only should they assist Third World NGOs to increase the organisational and productive capacities of the poor through financial assistance and technical support, but also help grass-roots organisations to overcome their weaknesses and practically address the question of how to link these local development efforts with the macro-development activities of the State. This would materially benefit poor groups and usher in a process of accelerated rural development.

Apart from financial, moral and intellectual support, NGOs in Australia must also take action to lend legitimacy to the very concept of macro initiatives in community development. They must themselves be prepared to combine to carry out larger scale community development programs; a recent collaborative effort between four Australian NGOs to implement an integrated rural development program in Mozambique is a good example of this type of initiative.

But perhaps the most important way in which Australian NGOs can have an impact is by convincing the Australian people and the government that it is both necessary and possible to implement an official development assistance program which does not in any way hinder, but rather contributes to, the linking of community development initiatives with macro-development processes.

Hence, Australian NGOs should be promoting programs such as the Special Public Works Programmes (SPWP) of the International Labour Organisation (ILO) (Garnier, 1982). These programs, which are developed by the ILO in conjunction with Third World countries and funded by Western donors, involve the implementation of labour intensive development schemes which utilise 'surplus labour' (marginal farmers, the landless and women, etc.) where the absorption of unemployment and underemployment -- and therefore the reduction of poverty -- by conventional development methods is unlikely. The Special Public Works Programmes aim at developing the infrastructure, such as the land and water resources of target communities, as well as achieving expansion of the productive capacity of agricultural and related activities, thereby ensuring durable employment for part of the agricultural labour force or its shift to the secondary or perhaps even the tertiary sector. The SPWP concept, therefore, simultaneously attempts to speed up the take-off of developing countries, while facilitating the increase and redistribution of incomes towards the poorest groups. When closely coordinated with national economic planning, these programs not only bring about a shift in spending priorities towards the poorest in the short term, but also in the long term, as governments gear investments and/or imports towards meeting the foreseeable rise in the purchasing power of the poor. It is the lack of purchasing power of the poor which has often been cited as a key reason for the poorest majority having almost no impact on macro -economic planning and decision-making (cf. Todaro, 1982).

Although the SPWPs can be threatened by abuse and corruption like any other development project, they at least begin from a position of offering direct benefit to the poor in ways which are integrated with national development efforts. As such the SPWP is the type of model which Australian NGOs ought to be developing and submitting to the Australian government as a practical method for contributing to the overall development of Third World countries.

There are many other ways in which Australian NGOs could provide practical assistance to government in carrying out the official development assistance program. Providing information and contacts to bureaucrats carrying out country profile exercises, appraisal missions, etc; studying existing and planned bilateral projects to identify ways in which these could be improved or modified to ensure adequate benefit to the poorest groups; offering personnel to assist; developing proposals for converting food aid to development assistance; or simply by talking to aid officials until they understand that it is possible to plan for macro community development initiatives and that it is their duty to consider the impact of their aid every time they raise a pen to write a proposal.

If the Jackson Committee did not care to explore the practicalities of developing an aid program which focuses upon and takes into account the development initiatives of poor communities, Australian NGOs must do so. This will not be easy. Many NGOs are hampered in their ability to be directly involved in and understand the stage of grass-roots development in Third World countries because they operate through US or European parent bodies and/or simply provide 'solidarity' grants to Third World counterparts. Others have no genuine constituency in the Australian community and are able to keep on providing simple charity without any external pressure to question the value of their work. Still others would prefer to engage in endless intellectual debates about North/South relations and the importance of a new international economic order rather than address fundamental questions about how the mass of the Third World poor can become involved in the domestic development process and how Third World governments can become sufficiently disciplined and organised to prevent the massive waste of human and financial potential which currently occurs.

NGOs are often accused of having an idealistic concept of development and a missionary sense of strategy. If they do not continue to search for more and better practical ways to assist in the development of the poorest people in Third World countries these terms deserve to be used as epithets of derision. If they accept the challenge of promoting development of the poorest people in an increasingly complex world their idealism should be regarded as a source of strength and a unifying theme for action, while their missionary zeal will be a sign to all that they will continue in their work despite negative evidence on every side.

NOTES

1. Judith Tendler (1982) coined this term in a provocative analysis of NGOs in the US.

2. The provision for increased subsidy for programs in the Pacific and the LDCs was introduced in 1980.

3. During the same period total ODA disbursed through NGOs (i.e. PSS, Volunteer Programs, support for the coordinating body for NGOs, the Australian Council for Overseas Aid, support for International NGOs, emergency assistance, etc., has risen over $20 million (approximately 1 per cent of ODA). See 8th Annual ADAB/NGO Consultation Documents, 1985, p. 3.

4. For many agencies disaster relief, refugee work, etc., represents a major proportion of their programs and budget but for the purposes of this article this is not regarded as 'developmental' activity <u>per se</u>.

5. Data from country-wide surveys carried out by National Nutrition Monitoring Bureau and from the National Institute of Nutrition, Hyderabad.

14 DEVELOPMENT COOPERATION AND COMMUNITY GROUPS IN FOOD AND AGRICULTURE

Sarah Sargent

INTRODUCTION

The Jackson Committee's report fails to demonstrate any clear understanding of the role Australian community groups can take in Third World development. This is evident in relation to food and agricultural policy: a crucial subject on which the Jackson Committee's analysis is both scant and weak.

In Third World countries, the largest proportion of the population depends for its livelihood on the rural sector. Since Australia is a major agricultural nation, the ways in which its agricultural policies -- through commerce and aid -- impinge on or influence Third World countries is critical. Yet, unlike the majority of other Northern countries, these linkages are not widely known in Australia.

It is, therefore, important for those sectors of the Australian community which are also involved in the food and agricultural industries to be aware of the linkages that exist. Policies applied to Australia's official aid program (and, as far as possible, in its trade relations) should be derived from such fundamental analysis. At present they are not. The result is that food and agricultural policies are often inappropriate. This should be of concern to involved Australian communities as well as the recipient Third World communities.

By drawing on examples of 'development cooperation' involving farmers, consumers and other community groups in Europe and North America, this chapter highlights the omissions in the current Australian aid program. Furthermore, by reference to recently completed research, it describes some of the linkages that exist between Australia's rural sector and Third World agricultural communities, and then suggests avenues for community cooperation in food and agricultural policies. The latter provide opportunities for non-governmental organisations (NGOs) in their development education program and in answering the frequent public enquiry, 'What can we do'?

AID FOR CHARITY, EDUCATION FOR AID

The premise with which the Jackson Committee begins its report is that there is a strong community tradition for giving aid. This, it observes, has primarily religious origins based on the emotional 'distress at the existence of poverty' and the charitable or neighbourly desire to eradicate that poverty.

More recently, according to Jackson, the community's support for aid has encompassed pragmatic considerations: that Australia has 'particular skills which can be used to assist poorer nations', 'that Australia's economic prospects are enhanced by sustained economic development in the Asian, Pacific and Indian Ocean regions' and 'an increasing awareness of the political importance to Australia of Asian and Indian Ocean nations' (Jackson Report, 1984, p. 20). The report quotes a survey which found that nearly two-thirds of the population 'believe that Australians should assist developing countries', and that one in five people are opposed to aid (Jackson Report, 1984, p. 20).

Later in its report the Jackson Committee investigates the methods for enhancing community understanding of development problems. Known as 'development education' (deved), this area of activity has had a troubled history. Until recently, it has been treated with suspicion because it has often encouraged debate on political issues. It has also been viewed as an unnecessary cost. In fact, the Jackson Report is the first of its type to legitimise 'deved'. It even goes as far as observing that 'Australia's efforts in development education have been poor by international standards' (without giving the reasons) and recommending that a far from insubstantial budget of $1 million should be allocated by the government to 'deved' programs. In this regard the Jackson Committee's conclusions can only be welcomed.

Likewise, the definition given contains the generally accepted sentiments of the nature of development education:

> The concept of development education emerged in the international aid community in the early 1970s as a means of increasing donor understanding of recipient's problems. It now has wider implications, seeking to explore such fundamental concerns as why people and nations are poor, and how problems of literacy sic ill-health and unemployment can be overcome. Links are sought between poverty, aid programs, development, the arms race, economic growth and affluence. Ultimately the aim is to increase community understanding of the whole range of development issues... Development education has several objectives:-
>
> * to enhance community awareness of development issues,
>
> * to encourage a more informed debate on what Australia should do to assist developing countries,

* to counteract community prejudices, including racist and sexist prejudices,

* to educate people on aid and development. (Jackson Report, 1984, p. 112)

However, the committee makes an illuminating concluding comment:

> By educating the wider Australian community on aid and development and by sustaining their interest with more active and effective public information, community understanding of the need for an aid programme would increase. (Jackson Report, 1984, p. 112, Emphasis added)

In summary, the Jackson Report's attitude towards community groups is based on two fundamental assumptions: that aid is an effective antidote for poverty and that community support for Third World development should be channelled through the aid system. Both assumptions are inadequate, certainly in relation to the rural sector, and they lead to a confused understanding of the importance of development education and the role of community groups.

First, food aid and aid to the rural sector of Third World countries is not always the most effective way to eradicate poverty; it is sometimes counter to development. Secondly, it is generally agreed that Western community support for Third World development is essential. But the reasons for this go beyond merely providing a rubber stamp for the official (or voluntary) aid program.

The two issues are linked: if community groups are convinced that the responsibility and expertise for Third World development are confined to the government and the aid agencies, community action is effectively discouraged. The response is to give money to an agency rather than calling for structural reforms or examining avenues for community cooperation.

The committee's assumptions are, therefore, the vestiges of the charity approach to Third World development which prevailed in the sixties. Community groups are viewed as passive participants in (i.e. donors to) the aid program, neither being expected to investigate their links with the Third World nor being encouraged to participate in development cooperation. The former process is a very significant aspect of development education in which Australia has witnessed only limited activity. The latter process is the logical corollary of development education and is arguably the most desirable and effective form of development assistance. A full explanation with examples will be provided below.

The third and related assumption which the committee makes is that 'The formal education system remains the primary means of development education' and that 'no extraneous activity or informal education can remedy deficiencies in it' although 'development education outside the formal system is largely the province of the voluntary agencies' (Jackson Report, 1984, pp. 112-13). As the examples given below illustrate, none of these statements is true and all block out initiatives that are open to community groups. The importance of the linkages between the community groups in the North and South, can be illustrated with an example from the European Economic Community (EEC).

The dairy sector of the EEC has been geared towards maximising its output for a number of social and political reasons. In the winter, herds require fodder since grass is unavailable. In recent years, soya and cassava have been imported from Third World countries for this purpose. These export crops compete with food crops for domestic consumption and, in common with many primary commodities, have a relatively low and variable foreign exchange earning capacity. Growing them is not in the interests of the rural poor who are typically agricultural labourers and landless farmers or small farmers: wage rates for agricultural labourers are low and landless farmers cannot participate in the industry since they own no land. The existence of cash crop industries, often promoted by governments and/or aid advisers, can also increase the cost of land or of rent thus encouraging speculation, land accummulation and the demise of more small farmers. The net result is that less food is grown in the South, where it is needed, and more milk is produced in the North, where massive surpluses consequently accumulate.

While there are many other details and many qualifications, the model as presented gives a general concept of cause/effect, North/South community linkages in agriculture. It should be noted that in this particular example there is also an ironic twist which forms a second link. Because of food shortages, southern governments request food aid and because of food surpluses northern governments are keen to oblige. Alternatively, northern governments try to foist their surpluses on southern countries. When placed on the market as food aid, milk powder tends to depress domestic prices and act as a powerful disincentive to local producers, further reducing food security.

The next step in justifying the earlier claim that aid is not always the most effective method of alleviating rural poverty is to describe the intervention subsequently made by some European dairy farmers. Through a variety of farmers' organisations, members are informed of the chain in which they are involved (development education) and how, in cooperation with 'grass-roots' organisations in the Third World, the links could be broken (development cooperation). Such groups are now continually lobbying for bans on milk aid to the Third World and have attempted to discourage the use of fodder from the Third World.

This cause/effect model is the simplest to understand, both for the northern and southern farmers and for observers. It also can be the most straightforward, although politically difficult, to act upon. Clearly, in the example given above, the farmers' decision to call for a cessation of milk aid has domestic repercussions. The implications of removing an outlet for domestic surpluses are that it might require a reduction in domestic production and a consequent reduction in farm numbers. For this reason, food aid and other agricultural policies of its type are controversial issues in Western agricultural nations. For this reason also, it is hard for development NGOs without a base in the affected community, to lobby successfully on such issues.

In the case of EEC dairy aid, many farmers' groups have extended the investigation to analyse domestic structural anomalies. It is subsequently argued that if farmers were paid a more equitable price for their milk and were confined to quotas they would not be forced to produce surpluses.

However, opportunities for community cooperation do not have to be confined to this model. Two others exist. One of these covers 'areas of common concern' which can be explained with the example of the marketing of infant formula. Consumers in both Western and Third World countries are common targets for these products and by, in a sense, identifying with their problems, northern consumers have campaigned on behalf of Third World consumers to protect them. There are many other similar consumer protection campaigns on medicines, pesticides etc. which span the North/South divide. There has been a considerable amount of activity on these issues in Australia.

Areas of common concern also exist between Australian and Third World farmers. At the simplest level, for example, the livelihoods of Australian dairy farmers are threatened, as are those of Bangladeshi farmers, by the presence of cheap EEC milk. Australian farmers are trying to compete on the world market against EEC milk, and Bangladeshi farmers are trying to compete on the domestic market against EEC milk aid.

Despite the potential scope for using the issues to raise awareness among rural communities (development education) and encourage cooperation to bring about change, there has been less activity on these farmer-oriented issues in Australia. Recommendations for possible avenues are presented in the final section of this chapter.

The third model covers circumstances in which there are no precise links between community groups, when there is neither a cause /effect linkage nor a link due to common concern. This model can be best explained with another example.

In Germany, the Education Officer for the Protestant Farmers' Association had been working for several years among farmers trying to evoke sympathy and support for Third World farmers' organisations. Not being a farmer himself, he was only successful in evoking the charity -level response but could get no further because of the view that 'their technology is archaic and inefficient and they have too many children'. Eventually, the decision was made to organise an exchange visit between a group of German farmers and a group of peasant farmers from South India. Reportedly, the German farmers were so impressed by the skills of the Indian farmers they visited, and the apparent efficiency of their farming methods in terms of energy, fertiliser and pesticide consumption and preservation of the environment, that they described their experiences enthusiastically to their fellow German farmers. According to the Education Officer, more effective education was carried out during a few convivial evenings together than during all his years of work. Linked by a common profession, the farmers of both North and South established the grounds for cooperation.

Unfortunately, in Australia, farmers, farmers' organisations and rural communities have been more or less neglected by the voluntary development agencies.

CULTIVATING UNDERSTANDING AND COOPERATION

The rural sector is important in Australia's North/South community relations. It is, therefore, necessary first to examine our economic relations before giving aid. Development education is most effective if the community groups can identify with the issues covered.

It is important to place a special emphasis on Australia's North /South relations in agriculture because, in Third World countries, the largest proportion of the population depends for its livelihood on the rural sector. In Australia, the proportion of the population involved in the rural sector and food industries is significant. Despite this, very little work has been done to raise this group's awareness of development issues.

Although many of the problems in Third World agriculture have their origins in domestic political, social, economic and technical structures, many are related to damaging northern policies. Since Australia is a major agricultural nation, the ways in which its agricultural policies — through commerce and aid -- impinge on or influence agriculture in Third World countries are critical. Not only is Australia an agricultural nation but it is situated in a Third World region. Since the entry of Britain into the EEC and the increased exports from the EEC, Australia has been looking to the region for compensatory markets. Yet, unlike the majority of other northern countries, these linkages are not widely known in Australia.

A rural development aid program which is developed in isolation from the normal commercial relations can only be deficient — a palliative rather than a long-term development solution. Again, the illustration of the EEC's cassava/soya imports -- where food aid is used to alleviate the hunger caused by export-oriented agriculture -- helps explain the paradox. This is like giving with one hand and taking with another although, as many people have argued, food aid frequently assists the donor country more than the farmers and the rural dwellers in the recipient country.

There is every evidence that the Jackson Committee makes this error of trying to superimpose its aid program onto existing economic relations. Nowhere does it suggest the need to examine whether any of Australia's commercial agricultural policies conflict with the alleviation of rural poverty. Yet such an analysis should be a prerequisite for determining the form in which its aid is given.

Jackson's error is made because the report does not follow a logical methodology in analysing the need for Australia's aid program. Indeed, at times, the committee seems quite confused about the precise qualities of the aid it has to offer. This is illustrated by the comments made in reference to the project aid and technical assistance programs. Thus the report notes with diffidence that 'Australia has not emphasised expertise in any particular sector', yet, in the same breath, in fact in the same sentence, it makes the vacuous observation 'but a good deal of project aid is oriented to agriculture' (Jackson Report, 1984, p. 51). By the following chapter, it has become much more sure of itself:

> Australia has traditionally focused its aid efforts on agriculture, and within that sector on research in rural infrastructure and extension. (Jackson Report, 1984, p. 63)

and,

> Australia ... is the only major donor country with agricultural conditions similar to those in many developing countries. Australia is one of the few industrial countries with practical experience in such areas as tropical crop development, animal husbandry and dryland farming. Agricultural technologies from Australia often need less adaptation than technologies from other donor nations. (Jackson Report, 1984, p. 63)

The inadequate fashion in which the committee investigates Australia's potential to assist in Third World rural development stems, as stated above, from the lack of preparatory analysis. It also derives from the accent on technological aid, for when saying that Australia's 'agricultural conditions' are similar to those of many developing countries, the committee, in fact, means the soil and climatic conditions are similar. In almost every other respect traditional agriculture in arid Third world countries is different. Therefore, if one presupposes that Australia has suitable technology to offer, the risk remains that technology suited for a sparsely populated wealthy country capable of investing large amounts of capital in agriculture will be imposed upon farming communities involved in small-scale, labour-intensive farming.

Considering the volume of literature now published on the disastrous social consequences of introducing inappropriate technology to rural communities, the failure of the Jackson Report even to mention the 'Green Revolution' and Australia's role in it, is indefensible. It also appears hypocritical when contrasted with the committee's treatment of women. In its chapter 'Women: A Special Concern', the committee makes frequent references to the social costs of introduced technology, for example:

> The introduction of new agricultural methods contributing to higher production has often diminished opportunities for women to obtain paid employment. An increased emphasis on cash crops often reduces women's traditional involvement in subsistence farming while increasing their work-load because of food purchases within the family. (Jackson Report, 1984, p. 79)

While the Jackson Report must be commended for making such statements in relation to women, the report must be criticised for failing to extrapolate such observations to society as a whole.

Jackson, in fact, reflects a common belief in Australia. It is based on conservative economic theory and maintains that the Third World needs increased agricultural production (both cash crops and food crops) to be achieved through the application of 'improved' technology. This technology, so the belief goes, is unavailable in the Third World and has to be transferred from western countries or developed in special research institutes which have been established in Third World countries. Australian attitudes are, therefore, reminiscent of those held by the West German farmers mentioned earlier, illustrating the urgent need for development education.

In this context it is important to note the validity of the committee's observation that Australia's agricultural climate is similar to those in many developing countries. This fact alone provides a starting point for a development education program. 'Deved' programs are most successful when the Australian community group can identify with the Third World community group. By focusing on the problems of drought, soil erosion and dryland agriculture, for example, Australian farmers might better be able to understand some of the difficulties that Third World farmers face. In some respects the educative value of the 1984 to 1985 drought in East Africa was not fully used. The Australian community was, once again, approached en masse for funds and no attempt was made to encourage development cooperation among farmers' groups.

One has to go no further than WADNA (Women and Development Network of Australia) and the activities of the NGOs in support of women in the Third World to see how community groups in Australia can identify with Third World communities and instigate effective development cooperation. In this respect, it is interesting to note that one very important reason for the better treatment given to women's issues in the Jackson Report is that the women's lobby in Australia is strong. It can, therefore, be suggested that if other community groups were to develop an interest in their North/South links, an impact could be made on aid and trade policy.

CULTIVATING COOPERATION IN AGRICULTURE

Whereas the Jackson Committee acknowledges the role that voluntary NGOs can take in development, the role of community groups is not explored and there is a strong emphasis on project instead of community co-operation. By using examples from Europe, the concept of development cooperation in agriculture is explained.

The concept of community cooperation for development is not examined by the Jackson Committee. Fundamental to the concept is the belief that the most effective means of bringing about development is when the Third World community helps itself. It is often said of the NGOs that their value lies in their ability to reach the 'grass roots' because they have links with the Third World community and because their projects are geared towards self help. As Jackson says of the NGOs:

> They see people as the means to - not just the recipients of - development and want to involve them in decisions about how development should take place. (Jackson Report, 1984, p. 104)

However, development cooperation needs to be taken one step further if it is to effectively involve the Australian community. If a development policy does not involve the relevant sections of the Australian community, it runs the risk of not being accepted.

Few of the NGOs have a base in the Australian community. Most have evolved from charities and their members are mainly donors with a superficial understanding of development issues: they give money because they feel pity or sympathy. Even some of the NGOs which claim to have a wider community base discover that many of their community groups focus their activities on fund-raising. Also, because they are locked into overseas project funding, NGOs must constantly raise relatively large sums of money. The general public responds best to simplistic images, as the recent Ethiopian 'famine' has illustrated. Both these facts make development education more difficult. Most agencies are reluctant to complicate the process of fund-raising or encourage controversy by alluding to Australia's agricultural links with the Third World, and so accept the public's desire to give food, sponsor children and concentrate on project funding.

Insofar as NGOs attempt to extend their community base by means of their development education programs, for various reasons, they seldom 'break new ground'. Thus, at ACFOA's development education seminar at Little Bay in 1981, an analysis was made of the community groups towards which the development education campaigns of the member voluntary agencies were geared. It was discovered that most of the efforts were clustered around school students and church groups and other 'captive' audiences whose curricula or concerns incorporate the study of Third World issues. Other community groups including those involved in the food system — farmers and food workers — had been neglected. Very little has changed since then.

However, in the last few years, a number of groups with a community base have evolved outside the NGO community. They concentrate on researching economic and other links between Australia and southern communities and are active in various forms of development cooperation. Starting a decade ago with such groups as International Development Action in Melbourne, newer groups include Australia-Asia Workers Links, the consumer Interpol and International Baby Food Action Network campaigns of the Australian Consumers Association, WADNA, Philippines Support Group, Trading Partners etc. These groups are not primarily involved in fund-raising for overseas projects but concentrate on practical means for development cooperation through lobbying, media campaigns, publications, films etc. Recently, also the ACTU (Australian Council of Trade Unions) has established a development agency, APHEDA (Australian People for Health, Education and Development Abroad), whose work includes overseas project funding as well as educating the trade union community.

Despite the growing number of community based Third World support groups, none has yet reached the rural community. The main reason for avoiding the farming communities in urban-centric Australia is that they are perceived as being reactionary and unsympathetic to the problems of the Third world.

However, in 1980 the Australian Freedom From Hunger Campaign initiated a program aimed at reaching farming communities, food workers and consumers on food related issues. Although results have yet to be demonstrated, there are signs that the positive responses which have been discovered in Canada, USA, Europe and, recently, Britain might be seen in Australia. Freedom From Hunger's program began with a study of Australia's domestic agricultural problems and its North/South agricultural links. During the research, contact with a range of farming organisations, agribusiness corporations, food workers' trade unions and agricultural policy makers indicated a substantial interest. Also, in March 1980, during the speaking tour made by Susan George, the National Farmer newspaper published a feature article on the structural issues in Australian agriculture and the implications for Third World agriculture. The interest it evoked among farmers was partly reflected in the 'Letters to the Editor' column in the following issue.

Two examples can help illustrate the types of response seen among communities concerned with food and agriculture in other northern countries. The first is of CRIAD (Centre for International Relations between Farmers for Development) which began its work in 1980 in the dairy producing areas of the Rhone-Alpes in France. Financed by the five traditional large agricultural organisations, CRIAD aims to make local farmers think about the problem of dairy surpluses in relation to the food needs of the Third World.

At the beginning of the campaign, the President of the largest agricultural trade union, which was supporting CRIAD, suggested there was a need to continue producing surpluses due to problems of world hunger. This statement did not fully satisfy the farmers, so CRIAD contacted the Regional Federation of Dairy Producers (FRPL) to study the subject. The FRPL wanted to find out which dairy production policy would both preserve the largest number of dairy farmers in the region and not damage Third World farmers. Thus, with the help of an agricultural research institute, an examination was undertaken and the findings published in a book full of illustrations and cartoons designed to make it accessible to a large number of farmers.

While carrying out the research, CRIAD members had visited Third World countries, such as Peru, and some African countries, to discover the impact of the twin policy of importing livestock feed and dumping milk surpluses. In so doing they established links with local grass-roots organisations and began to campaign for changes in policy, particularly against food aid and against the unbridled importation of livestock feeds. They also had to address the domestic issues entailed. If food aid was to be stopped, milk production would have to be reduced and so, consequently, would farm numbers. Likewise, if cheap livestock feed was not being imported, the farmers' production costs would increase. Thus, the farmers also lobbied for domestic reforms to enable the damaging Third World links to be severed. Clearly, such a campaign would have difficulty in receiving support from all farmers. However, it has helped to influence government policy (the French government is to introduce production quotas for dairy farmers and to reduce milk production while still protecting the majority of peasant farmers), while building links with Third World farmers and educating community groups on development issues.

The second example is also from France. SOLAGRAL (Solidarity Farm and Food) is an association set up in 1980 by Third World activists and militant farmers, which takes an interest in the relations between French food and agriculture and food and agriculture in the Third World. A large part of SOLAGRAL's work is in conducting research and mobilising groups with potentially conflicting interests (e.g. farmers and consumers) to find common ground. For example, it has also worked on the question of dairy aid. Food surpluses generally act in the consumers' interests because they tend to keep prices low. If the farmers were to produce less milk, they would have to receive some financial compensation. Thus there was potential conflict between consumers and producers. SOLAGRAL's role has been in bringing the consumers and producers together to work towards a common policy.

NORTH/SOUTH LINKS IN AUSTRALIAN AGRICULTURE

Recent research (Sargent, 1983) has indicated that many linkages exist between Australia's rural sector and Third World agricultural communities. These provide potential avenues for community development and cooperation in food and agricultural policies.

Periodic campaigns in Australia have focused on food and agricultural issues, although none has apparently succeeded in influencing the farming community. Examples include the campaign organised through the Philippines Support Group and AAWL to reinstate employees of the Australian agribusiness SAFCOL in the Philippines who had been dismissed for being members of a trade union; the campaign to prevent infant formula milks from being marketed in the Third World; campaigns against the patenting of seeds and against unsafe pesticides.

Being an agricultural nation situated in the Asia/Pacific region the links between Australia and the Third World are many. The following is a review of some of these links, although the list is by no means exhaustive and the typology adopted is not necessarily the most adequate.

Commodities which are Competitive with the Third World

Third World countries are in a dire position, dependent on cash crop exports yet with declining incomes from most. Their position is often aggravated by competition from Western agricultural nations such as Australia. This leads to a treadmill effect in which more cash crops have to be produced to earn the same revenue. The net result is that more agricultural land goes to cash crops and less food is grown.

Cotton. Australia has been able to jump from being a net importer to being the world's thirteenth largest producer, and twelfth largest exporter competing on the world market with a number of Third World countries. The implications of the support for such trading competition today, in the light of North/South cooperation, is significant. Although the concept of trade reforms as a means of assisting the Third World is more recent than Australia's cotton industry, the fact remains that Australia is undercutting some extremely poor countries whose economies are highly dependent on cotton as a source of revenue. The cotton industry itself says that Australian cotton is a different quality to Third World cotton and in fact Australia competes largely with American cotton producers for markets.

Rice. Australia's share of the international rice market is between 2 and 3 per cent of the total traded. However, it is considered high in quality and, for regional markets, Australia's proximity also cuts shipping costs. Australia's rice exports are expected to continue increasing. Nonetheless, Australia is a small producer and a price taker on the world rice market; it is not powerful enough to influence world prices. Australia has only recently become a significant rice exporter, particularly in regional (Asia/Pacific) terms. The impact of its rice exports has to be examined in relation to the Third World countries' development objectives.

Sugar. Sugar is another commodity which falls under the umbrella of North/South trade relations. Sugar is one of the legacies from the colonial era and many Third World countries are still dependent upon sugar as a major source of export-earned revenue. However, the crop has been taken over and dominated by the West (Europe in particular, but also Australia which is the world's fourth largest exporter after Cuba, the EEC and Brazil). According to UNCTAD (Clairmonte and Cavanagh, 1981), 60 per cent of the world's $7,500 million sugar exports were controlled by Western transnational agribusinesses in 1978.

Import Substitution

For various reasons -- including the desire to decrease the dependence on overseas suppliers and the attempts to diversify Australian agriculture --assistance has been given to agricultural import substitution. In fact, some of the commodities which are now successfully exported were originally grown either to avoid imports, or during times such as war when imports were cut. By virtue of its varied climate, Australia is able to grow practically anything and has often erected tariffs against imports while heavily assisting new crops to be developed. The crops concerned are frequently the cash crops on which Third World countries are dependent.

It is sometimes argued that since cash crops compete with food crops in Third World countries, Australia, by taking over the role of cash crop production from Third World countries, is enabling them to grow more food. However, such an argument is inadequate justification for Australian agricultural 'import substitution'. Third World economies still depend on their cash crops, they have no other means of earning the foreign exchange they need to buy manufactured goods. Generally, they are being forced to produce more of their cash crops because commodity prices are so low and the low world market prices are partly due to over -production. Thus, Australia partly contributes to the problem by pure competition and partly because it contributes to the commodity surplus in many sectors.

Tea. In recent years, efforts to grow tea in Australia have been encouraged by the Queensland government. Although Australia is by no means a serious competitor with Third World producers, its fledgling industry does raise serious questions within the North/South debate.

Oilseeds. With the development of Australia's oilseed industry the potential exists for import substitution against crops normally imported from the Third World, such as copra.

Jute wool packs. Formerly, Australia imported significant quantities of jute wool packs from Bangladesh and India. Now, synthetic alternatives are used. The synthetic wool packs contaminate the wool and have other undesirable characteristics such as beng slippery and difficult to handle.

Domination in Processing

Many of the agricultural commodities which Australia still imports from the Third World are imported more or less in their raw form. The benefits of manufacturing -- employment and value added -- are thus accrued by Australia at the expense of the Third World. Oilseeds, coffee and cocoa provide examples of this phenomenon since most of the processing is carried out in developed countries such as Australia.

Commodities Which Set Up New Consumption Preferences

These commodities establish new commercial markets both for the product and for processing technology. Since the rise in prominence of the EEC, an agricultural exporter, Australia has lost many of its export markets. As a result it has looked to the populous Asia/Pacific region as compensation. In order to establish these new markets, it has frequently been necessary to alter diets -- not always to good effect.

Wheat. The introduction of wheat to rice-eating Southeast Asia via aid and commerce has established a new consumer demand for these products. In turn, this has required the introduction of milling and further processing technology. The latter then require the further importation of wheat which establishes new commercial openings for Australia.

Milk. The Australian Dairy Corporation was instrumental in establishing milk reconstitution plants in non milk producing Southeast Asia. The plants were designed to make use of Australian milk surpluses and produced exotic (as compared with staple) products such as ice cream and condensed milk. Now that Australia no longer produces such a large surplus, the industries are dependent upon the world market for supplies.

Costly Food Exports That May Not Be Nutritionally Sound

Many of the Third World countries of Asia and the Pacific are an important source of revenue for the Australian food industry. Australia is growing to depend more and more on the neighbouring countries as export markets. And, in the years to come, the volume of food exports to the region is projected to rise.

Whether or not this commercial expansion represents proof of Australia's 'comparative advantage' over its neighbours as a food producer, and whether it represents successful and fair trade are moot points. For although there would appear to be some evidence of inter-dependence between a food-supplying country and food-consuming countries -- illustrated by the fact that the less 'food dependent' and the more prosperous nations take the greater share of Australia's food exports -- there are other issues to take into account.

First, the burden of food imports on many Third World countries' economies is high. Therefore, Australian commercial gain is often draining the poorer countries' economies. Secondly, there is a likelihood that food imports from Australia help accentuate the changing dietary patterns in both Asia and the Pacific. Often this change is to the nutritional detriment of the consumers in these countries. A substantial proportion of the food exports are relatively high economic value processed foods and soft drinks which may have a negative nutritional value. This trend is particularly pronounced in the Pacific countries.

Given the special socioeconomic and nutritional characteristics of Third world populations, both government agencies and agribusiness corporations should, therefore, be questioned about whether this unrestricted commerce is appropriate and responsible.

Technologies That Are Socially Detrimental To Third World Agriculture

Australia's private consultants, the educational institutions and training courses for Third World nationals and agribusiness are influential in determining the types of technology selected and transferred for Third World agriculture. This has led to the export of 'new' food and agricultural products and the impact of agricultural inputs such as seeds, breeding stock, machinery and agrochemicals. The transfer of agricultural technology from an agribusiness-dominated, capital-intensive, export-oriented and expansionist rural economy, such as Australia, to a Third World country can have serious socioeconomic costs. Therefore, to allow the unrestricted transfer of technology (especially through simple commerce) as Australia appears to do, often contravenes the sentiments expressed towards North/South cooperation.

Common Problems

Western technology and agribusiness have often exacerbated the maldistribution of land and agricultural resources in Third World countries, thus worsening the problem of hunger. Although few Australians starve, a large proportion suffer from diet-related diseases. If Australians could better understand the political economy of their own food industries, they might better understand the plight of people in the Third World. They already know about droughts, fickle commodity markets and government bureaucracies that influence the agricultural industries. However, there are many other issues on which community interest could be stimulated.

Exploitive Cash Crops

In its search for remunerative export industries, Asia has been encouraged to develop new export-oriented crops. Ho Kwon Ping has called these luxury crops and has described how Asia has become the kitchen garden for rich Northern countries, of which Australia is one (AFFHC, 1980, pp. 223-4).

Tropical fruits. Despite its own rich soils and tropical climate, Australia has been importing tropical fruits from countries such as the Philippines. These, like other cash crops, compete for precious agricultural land and are cultivated by poorly paid, badly exploited workers.

Cat food from fish. Australia imports fish from Asia to feed its huge domestic pet population. For example, a large proportion of the so-called luxury cat food manufactured by SAFCOL under the 'Snappy Tom' label is produced by the Thailand subsidiary. In 1983, 'Snappy Tom' captured $21 million of the $92.5 million cat food market. Fish that might otherwise have been consumed by Thai people is fed to Australian cats.

CONCLUSION

Community awareness of Australia's North/South links in agriculture is essential. Without it, policies affecting the Third World, whether development assistance or trade (aid or commerce), will be unlikely to achieve community support, especially in areas of industrial competition. In order to bring about such awareness, development education based on cogent research and issues of relevance is important. This can lead to areas in which the community groups will call for policies of community cooperation. The latter can be implemented through numerous channels including aid. Australia could well benefit from examining the examples from other Western agricultural nations.

It should be recognised that development education and development cooperation in agriculture are becoming all the more urgent as Australia develops its commercial links with neighbouring Third World countries. Unless fundamental areas of competition and avenues for cooperation are identified early, serious policy mistakes could be made.

NOTE

1. The term is frequently subject to nebulous definition. Here it is used to cover a hybrid between 'industry' associations that have links (commercial and other) with the Third World and groups with development objectives.

15 PROFESSIONALISM AND TECHNICAL SOPHISTICATION IN AUSTRALIA'S AID PROGRAM

Doug Porter

Two aspects of the Jackson Committee's wide-ranging terms of reference have received much attention: equity, 'particularly whether there is a need to provide a greater proportion of aid for the benefit of lower income groups', and effectiveness, that is, whether 'there is a need for more effective criteria of economic efficiency in the use of our aid' (Jackson Report, 1984, p. 245). Many events lie behind this emphasis, but not the least significant is the Foreign Minister Mr Hayden's personal interest and commitment. Before and since assuming office he has shown an awareness of the thorny issues of aid. 'We must be extremely fussy about who benefits from our aid', he said. It should benefit 'the poorest in developing countries, for whom the infamous "trickle-down" theory is a crude bottleneck in practice that swells the riches of the money lenders and the greedy and the unethical'. Mr Hayden sees a need for a 'judicious mix of grassroots and infrastructural development' or, in broad terms, of equity and growth in Australia's aid strategy (Hayden, 1983a,b).

The Jackson Committee's brief was not just a matter of sorting out the philosophical conundrums of democratic socialism but was pragmatically motivated. Existing projects attempting the 'judicious mix' of grass-roots equity and infrastructure-based growth are consistently facing three problems: 1) they are reaching the poor much less than is hoped, and in some cases adversely affecting them; 2) they are taking extremely long to negotiate, design and implement, frequently getting bogged down and relegated to holding operations; and 3) they are having difficulty in building self-sustaining institutions and programs which function in the interests of target groups.

These points refer to two basic issues in the aid program. To practitioners the first is known as the 'rip-off upwards' problem 'Why is it that the people that tend to benefit most from aid projects are rarely those most in need?'. The second basic issue has been termed the problem of institutionalisation. 'How is it that despite an emphasis on training and technology transfer, most development assistance fails to leave behind self-sustaining development programs?'.

The rip-off upwards problem focuses on the distribution of benefits from Australian aid and was initially popularised by non-governmental aid organisations' criticisms of the Zamboanga del Sur (PADAP) and Northern Samar (NSIRDP) projects which together represent over 90 per cent of Australia's Philippines bilateral program. In a lengthy serial of claims and counterclaims, agencies like Community Aid Abroad and the Catholic Commission for Justice and Peace charge these projects do not serve the poor, but actually bolster the interests of local and national entrepreneurs and the military's counterinsurgency operations at the expense of the poor (cf. Shoesmith, 1982). In the past, government has rejected such criticism. In 1982, Richard Woolcott, Ambassador to the Philippines, vehemently attacked the integrity of 'ill-informed ... arm-chair strategists' (Woolcott, 1982). But such concerns have not been so ill-informed, as ADAB's own evaluations of the Philippine program have largely confirmed (ADAB, 1982, p. 31). During his August 1982 Australian visit, Philippine Defence Minister Enrile reported that Australian aid was indeed 'assisting the eradication of rural insurgency' (Sydney Morning Herald, 14 September 1982). And in Parliament during November 1983, Mr Hayden remarked that 'the economics of the program NSIRDP are highly questionable' (Hansard, 29 November 1983).

By most accounts the rip-off upwards problem is widespread. The Chittagong hill tribes project in Bangladesh and programs in southern Thailand and west Kalimantan draw similar criticism. Even the submission of PADAP's agricultural consultants to the Jackson Committee conveys a dismal mood. 'Analysis shows' it said, 'that the recipient L.D.C. society has ripped off upwards most of the development benefits. The poor are left no better off and sometimes worse off. In other projects the intended benefits were never generated at all' (ACIL Australia Pty Ltd, 1983, p. 3; cf. Leinbach, 1983, p. 26; McCall, 1977).

The problem of institutionalisation is closely related. Increasingly, ADAB's projects have aimed to facilitate self-sustaining development efforts. Reviews have, however, noted severe 'withdrawal problems', citing inadequate local administrative capability, interagency coordination, post-implementation staffing, and intermittent financial commitments (Auditor-General, 1981, pp. 97-100). More candid are practitioners' references to nest-feathering, kick-backs, corruption or inefficiency. The lack of success in creating self-sustaining development is highlighted in other areas as well. Evaluations suggest that many agricultural programs fail to 'institutionalise' the target population. That is, they incorporate very small numbers of farmers. Drop-out rates of those who do participate are high. In PADAP's case for instance, project staff estimate that only 3 per cent of the target population have been involved and that on average, around 40 per cent of participating farmers drop out each season (cf. Richards, 1981). The rip-off upwards and institutionalisation problems go to the heart of Australia's bilateral program, and to the committee's mandate to address its equity, efficiency and effectiveness.

The Jackson Report Response

Given the neo-classical perspective of the committee's most prominent members, it is not surprising that the Jackson Report hardly champions the aid cause at all. Whilst 'in some countries, and at some times, aid has been an important input to development ... in other countries, aid seemed to make little difference' (Jackson Report, 1984, p. 131). Indeed, in the neo-classical view aid is frequently a constraint to growth. Welfare-oriented aid is often self-defeating in that it interferes with the incentive system which promotes productivity. Of more importance from this perspective is the domestic economic policy a country adopts. According to the Jackson Report, development is not a function of a country's resource endowment, climate, location or history, but of its political commitment to 'outward-looking' growth-oriented policy (Jackson Report, 1984, pp. 30, 46, 118-19, cf. Blazic-Metzner and Hughes, 1982, p. 85). 'Appropriate policy' includes 'realistic' exchange and interest rates, wage rates which reflect productivity, stable prices and 'proper weight' to equity considerations. Trade is more important than aid (Jackson Report, 1984, p. 119; Taylor, Chapter 5 this volume). But 'at the margin', the Jackson Report suggests two important roles for Australian aid. First, aid relations provide one means whereby Australia can encourage recipients to adopt appropriate macro-economic policy. Secondly, aid policy can be 'most effective when applied to removing major constraints to development. This often involves capital intensive inputs' (Jackson Report, 1984, p. 4).

Other contributions to this volume address the adequacy and reliability of this view. It is important, as we shall see, to understand its links with three key themes in the report: geographic and sectoral rationalisation; professionalism; and technical sophistication in aid management. The committee's efforts to rationalise the 'big body and long tail' of Australian aid and the 'shopping list' approach is discussed by Forbes in Chapter 6. Rationalisation is closely linked with two further themes.

'Aid programs need to be clearly focused rationalised to ensure a professional approach' (Jackson Report, 1984, p. 131). Professionalism is invoked by the report's authors to accomplish a multitude of tasks. For instance, it is to 'improve effectiveness' (Jackson Report, 1984, p. 228); it is a kind of judgement and control exercised by effective aid managers (Jackson Report, 1984, p. 235); it is what ADAB's library must have (Jackson Report, 1984, p. 235); an 'internationally recognised' ingredient of aid administration (Jackson Report, 1984, p. 228); and something which is necessary to undertake evaluation (Jackson Report, 1984, p. 138). ADAB is to have a different internal structure, a catch-up program and long-term training to 'allow the necessary work to be done in a professional style' (Jackson Report, 1984, p. 16).

Equally important to the efficiency and effectiveness of a program suffering from a 'decade of neglect' is increased sophistication in all facets of program management. This includes policy analysis and programming; project and program selection and preparation; field appraisal, implementation, supervision and monitoring; evaluation and procedures to feed back results across projects, sectors and country programs, to management.[1]

Although the report has been criticised on many points, these two themes receive almost unanimous agreement by critics. This chapter critically examines this consensus in terms of the distributional and institutionalisation problems discussed earlier. This is done in four steps. The first section provides a broader background to professionalism and technical sophistication and considers some of the more obvious criticisms of the Jackson Report in this light. Following this, two sections examine professionalism and technical sophistication in actual practice. Here I conclude that, as they stand, they will do little to alleviate the two major problems of Australian aid projects. Finally, I consider what changes in aid practice must accompany the Jackson Report's professionalism and technical sophistication emphasis.

Two dangers in commentaries of this kind should be dealt with here. In principle one must accept that aid programs should be efficient and effective. The existing program is replete with evidence of this need. And ADAB is grossly understaffed, morale is low; the improved career paths and less idiosyncratic practices implied by professionalism will no doubt be welcomed. Fully appraised and planned projects, each drawing on lessons of evaluation should indeed be more effective than those that are not. The Jackson Report, however, says nothing about what professionalism will mean in practice. Furthermore, techniques like cost-benefit analysis are often invoked as panaceas without considering their potentially adverse unintended consequences in practice. While supportive overall, I argue that practitioners will need to go a good deal further than common -sense appeal to professionalism and technical sophistication.

Another danger is that this focus on professionalism and techniques may suggest that with modification, the Jackson Report's basic philosophical thrust should be left intact. That implication is not intended. Remarks in Section I will indicate my scepticism and basic agreement with Eldridge's contribution in Chapter 1.

Professionalism, Technical Sophistication and Aid Strategies

In important respects, the Jackson Report reflects the resurgence of neo-classical, structural adjustment policies in international agencies like the World Bank and the move from the 'basic human needs' strategy of the mid to late 1970s (Higgott, 1984, p. 61; Sen, 1983, p. 747). But the view of development as a 'policy management problem' — and the professionalism, rationalisation and technical sophistication themes which flow from this view -- was established much earlier. Indeed, the establishment of the World Bank and the IMF (International Monetary Fund) at Bretton Woods in 1944, and later the IFC (International Finance Corporation) and IDA (International Development Agency) have been seen as 'landmarks on the road to a rationalisation of international decision making' (White, 1970, p. 5).

This period spawned two themes which are well represented in the Jackson Report. The first concerns the leadership role of international agencies and by implication, bilateral programs like Australia's, in providing a supportive environment for international private investment, and fostering political order and stability. In particular, this requires strengthening recipient country institutions in which parochial, idiosyncratic or purely 'political' policy is replaced by fairly universal development policy and procedural mechanisms. Alongside the removal of institutional obstacles are efforts to overcome constraints and bottlenecks in the form of capital-intensive infrastructure projects. At the margin, we learn in the Jackson Report, an efficient bilateral program can overcome institutional obstacles and infrastructural constraints to development.

A second theme of the 1950s, also given particular emphasis in the Jackson Report, was the key role afforded to professional experts as 'linch-pins' of development, 'mid-wives' of change, 'builders of order' and 'inducers and stimulators' of social and economic transformation. As a result, professionals have played increasingly significant roles in the definition, design and implementation of development (cf. Moss 1978, p. 114).

All facets of the international development strategy that emerged almost four decades ago have, of course, drawn steady criticism. The Jackson Report's consensus about the neo-classical strategy undoubtedly has its supporters, but there is also a strongly-held view that its basic assumptions are either wrong or open to serious question (Streeten, 1979; Taylor, Chapter 5 and Keen, Chapter 10, this volume). More to the point, the committee's unanimity gives no indication that any other view is worth serious examination. This is hardly an honest appraisal of recent development experience,[2] or of development studies let alone economics, as Cole Cameron and Edward's (1983) excellent book <u>Why Economists Disagree</u> would point out . Similarly, the report provides a clear sense that Mr Hayden's 'judicious mix' has been resolved. While noting 'a general rule that the equitable distribution of income has ... promoted economic growth' and that without 'equity-oriented policies growth is slower and development slower still', the 'maximum impact of the aid dollar' dictates a focus on infrastructure bottlenecks (Jackson Report, 1984, pp. 29, 60-1). The report argues that the latter 'can be shown' to have higher benefits even in the short term than projects seeking to help the poor directly. In respect of the current Australian aid program, this is simply nonsense. None of these projects has received the kind of <u>exposte facto</u> evaluation that would support this. Besides, as the report notes elsewhere, it is 'usually impossible to isolate the effects of aid from the many other influences which affect development' (Jackson Report, 1984, p. 131). Moreover, we learn that 'the World Bank, in particular, in spite of very large research expenditures has done little work on its own impact on development' (Jackson Report, 1984, p. 138, but cf. Bello et al., 1982). One impact of the growth emphasis is clear however. Its capital requirements result in budgetary constraints and cuts in those sectors which have no immediate growth returns but which are the core of basic human needs (Higgott, 1984, p. 66; World Bank, 1981a, p. 98). Inevitably, a growth strategy is de facto an implied policy on equity. I shall return to this later.

The view that development is primarily a 'management problem' underpins the authoritarian tenor of the Jackson Report overall. We are told there is a proper analysis of development. Those countries with the good sense and political will to grasp the necessity for 'outward-looking' policies will succeed, those who do not will fail. Small Pacific island states for instance, have traditional land tenure and decision making processes which may become impediments to change (Jackson Report, 1984, pp. 174-5). By implication these must be replaced with efficient management by those at the top who control macro-economic policy. All efforts should go to supporting these groups. And where they err, 'ministerial discussions about development matters might also be held regularly to stress the emphasis which Australia places on the need for aid to be used to promote growth' (Jackson Report, 1984, p. 164). Adherence must be maintained. Where Australia's 'encouragement is insufficient, international agencies like the World Bank will be called upon to lend leadership and leverage' (Jackson Report, 1984, p. 181). Again, we find no reservations reflecting documentary evidence indicting this authoritarian stance (cf. Payer, 1982, p. 358; Bello et al., 1982; Connell, Chapter 4, this volume) or of the repeated association of this strategy with repressive developmentalism (cf. Stauffer, 1983; Hirschman, 1981).

A number of contributors consider this matter. The following two sections illustrate how this authoritarian tendency is manifested in actual practice. In this vein I am sceptical about the likelihood of professionalism and technical sophistication averting the rip-off upwards and institutionalisation problems, or this tendency in Australian aid practice.

PROFESSIONALISM IN AID PRACTICE

The Jackson Report uses professionalism as a catch-cry to recommend changes in aid practice, but like its predecessors it fails to specify what 'being professional' actually means. What exactly is implied by the word?

There is, of course, a large literature called the 'sociology of professions'. In its crudest sense, 'professional' is simply the opposite of amateur -- work for which one is paid, as in 'professional pest exterminator'. In the case of ADAB's employees, the report goes further. It notes that ADAB must be changed from a clerical to professional organisation, a point regularly made by the Australian Professional Consultants Council (APCC, 1982). The sociological literature offers a series of constructs which specify professional: that is, particular ethical standards, institutional regulation, professional autonomy, intellectual qualifications and an embargo on some methods of practice. Recent studies, however, conclude that most of these constructs based on studies of law and medicine, lack validity in actual practice. In development practice to talk of a homogeneous collection of 'professionals' dedicated to the same norms or practices would be a taxonomic exaggeration, since very little evidence supports general application of the word (cf. Benveniste and Ilchman, 1969; Caiden, 1976). The range of notions, premises and kinds of conduct characteristic of self-styled professionals in development practice is dauntingly large. Sometimes they are related to a coherent framework, but often as not, this is inchoate and inconsistent.

Being Professional in Development Practice

Notions of professional integrity, dedication, a good job, independence and balanced judgement have become swords used to parry critics of Australian practitioners' activities (cf. 'Letters to Editor' in Shoesmith 1982). Two key notions about arms-length advice and objectivity on the one hand, and a sense of purpose and dedication on the other are particularly relevant in understanding what, to date, has been taken as professionalism in Australian aid practice.

The special authority of professionals rests on a distinction between their empirical grasp of the 'facts of the matter' and the kind of knowledge available to laypersons. Professionalism requires special skills, that is, access to sophisticated techniques of appraisal, design, implementation and evaluation, and a particularly disciplined attitude. 'Arms length advice' (APCC, 1982, p. 6) is objective. Professionals, it is said, are able to make decisions based on 'the facts' independent of personal idiosyncracy, interests or subjective beliefs. Being professional is contrasted with woolly amateurism and with politics. Politics is considered the irrational variable which sabotages the smooth flow of development management. Politics is said to be prejudicial to efficiency and effectiveness. As a corollary, the activities of critics, like CAA, reflect theoretical speculation since they are based on political preferences, philosophy or personal sentiment. They interfere with practitioners 'getting on with the job'; debate is simply talk, academic or, in terms of efficient practice, amounts to 'downtime'. Some matters are technical, like the efficiencies of growth; others, like equity and distribution, are political. In response to criticism, the PADAP agriculturalists, argue 'To get a slice of the cake, first bake the cake' (ACIL Australia Pty Ltd, 1983, p. 2; cf. Transfield Pty Ltd, 1983).

Accompanying arms-length advice is a strong sense of purpose amongst professionals. The dedication is striking. Ray Littlejohn, at the time NSIRDP Project Manager, had this to say:

> We are professionals, we are doing a difficult job in arduous, frustrating circumstances ... and the deprivation is probably quite severe ... we have a good team here, hard workers, dedicated to what they're doing, putting in long hours ... and to meet this criticism from armchair critics ... is hurtful and pretty disillusioning. (3LO Frontline Interview, 15 February 1982)

Closely allied is the belief that the problems of development are so technically complex that specialist knowledge is necessary to unravel them. Professionals offer advice that can be taken at face value without fear of hidden agendas. This is said to counter 'politics' while also facilitating democratic processes based on the facts. They see themselves as treading a middle path between 'revolutionary' approaches and 'hands off, let them have it' approaches. The submission of PADAP's professional consultants to the Jackson Committee argues for a 'velvet glove approach' that is, 'inside the velvet glove of aid we must be prepared to place our iron-fist of control' (ACIL Australia Pty Ltd, 1983, p. 6).

The combination of these two notions gives the so-called 'professional promise'. Professionals know how to clear the muddy philosophical waters of the judicious mix. Moreover the promise implies that without professional involvement, development really will not happen at all. Geoff Faithfull, former Chairman of the APCC argues that this professional approach is crucial. 'The dangers of social and political unrest are colossal' he said, it is essential 'that we muster the right combination of professional skills' (Faithfull, 1982).

Previous reviews have been critical of the acitvities of professionals, particularly consultants, in the Australian aid program (Auditor -General, 1981, pp. 117-18, 128). In non-governmental organisations' circles they are frequently dismissed and there is a growing literature critical of development practitioners in general (for example Chambers, 1983). But such criticism is often rhetorical and maligns the intention of those who see professionalism as a way of enhancing the impact and effectiveness of aid. It is of more value to examine some features of professionalism in practice in terms of the two main problems of benefit distribution and institutionalising sustainable development initiatives.

Professionalism and Problems of Practice

These two problems amount to a failure to adapt and integrate project assistance into the social, economic and political circumstances of the area and people concerned. What does professionalism, as conventionally conceived, offer here? Professionalism turns on the view of the practitioner as a problem-solver. He/she is confident about

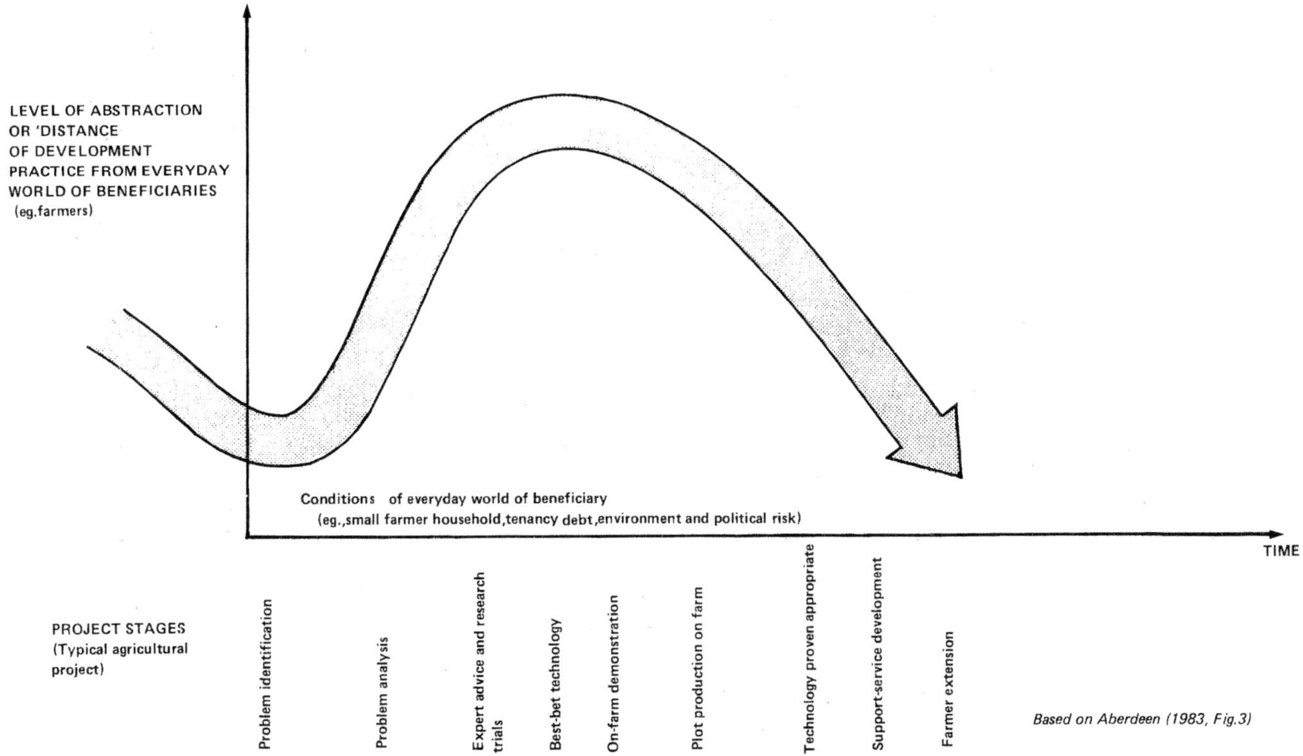

15.1 Agribusiness Methodology in Practice

the nature of these problems, and fairly certain about the appropriate remedies. In agricultural projects, for instance, the problem is a matter of 'yields'; the remedy, broadly, is making the farm system function correctly; that is, efficiently (PADAP, 1980). The horizontal axis on Figure 15.1 illustrates the various stages of a typical agricultural project as identified by an Australian professional. From left to right, a project begins with identification, appraisal and feasibility studies and follows through to the extension of agricultural packages.

Typically, initial problem identification occurs over a short space of time relative to the duration of the project. Two to three week planning missions have not been uncommon in the past. Due to professional training and confidence, the problem has been 'identified' in considerable detail sometime before arrival in the locality. Reflecting the professional's penchant for 'the facts', and specialised interest in agricultural yields, the professional quickly establishes scientific research trials on isolated stations in order to 'get the facts straight'. The vertical axis indicates the consequences of these initial stages. This axis represents the degree of 'distance' created between the professional's activities and the everyday reality of the target group. This example refers to farmers and the various social (household, gender, work patterns), economic (indebtedness, tenancy, landlessness), political (local patronage, dependency relations) and environmental characteristics of their situation.

A number of factors typically keep the professional from appreciating this reality. Robert Chambers' (1983, pp. 13-23) much quoted list of rural development biases is relevant here. Early stages of project development are frequently constrained by time. This reinforces various 'spatial biases' which favour rapid 'wind-screen' surveys of the local situation from vehicles on roads. Where contact is made, 'person biases' lead the practitioner to hear the opinions of officials, local elites, males and innovators. 'Diplomatic biases', politeness and timidity, as well as anxiety about delving into social and political considerations where 'the facts' are blurry and professional authority less certain, decrease the likelihood of contact with the beneficiaries' reality. Specialisation exacerbates the problem. 'Professionals', Chambers notes, 'are trained to look for and see much less. They are programmed by their education and experience to examine what shows up in a bright but slender beam which blinds them to what lies outside' (Chambers, 1983, p. 22).

There are, of course, dangers in overstating these biases. There are exceptions. But the fact that professional advice is frequently inappropriate to the reality of farmers, or the local institutions charged with incorporating the advice within their operations, indicates the pervasiveness of these biases. As the shaded curve on the diagram illustrates, after brief and incomplete contact, the stages of analysis, trials, program design, and technology selection are increasingly distant or scientifically abstracted from the beneficiaries world -- and frequently the day-to-day operation of the relevant line agencies. By 'on-farm' demonstration stages, the professional, armed with the technical wisdom of science, begins to approach this world. Demonstration plots, on-farm trials, all under special conditions and with decisions controlled by the professional, are logically followed by extension stages.

Unfortunately, the institutionalisation problem suggests that the logic does not follow. Farmers are typically reluctant to adhere to professional advice, the technology is rarely appropriate -- save for those sufficiently capitalised to take the risks and absorb the unintended consequences -- and adopter drop-out rates remain high. Ironically, the 'problems' and 'reality' become recognised only at the extension stage.

There are numerous explanations for this state of affairs which go beyond the present discussion. The point here is simply to demonstrate how the usual attributes of professionalism -- arms-length advice, an authoritarian confidence about the causes of poverty, specialisation, a derisive attitude toward the politics of everyday life and a technical focus on the resolution of 'self-evident' problems -- are a far-cry from addressing the most prevalent problems of project practice.

One could respond that these problems will be overcome by improved definition of project objectives and more explicit attention to social and political economy considerations. In one sense this is true. But taken seriously, this implies a quite different understanding of what 'being professional' involves in practice. Clearly the 'professional as problem solver' image will not do. Problems are not self-evident and neither is this broader definition of project objectives amenable to analysis on the research station. Besides, interest in various social and political considerations is not new; as a glance at ADAB project statements for some years will reveal. But unaccompanied by reconsideration of what the professional's role is, this broadening of project scope has merely added new (albeit 'social') inputs, thereby increasing the confusion in practice. Despite a broadened scope, the Chairman of the Joint Parliamentary Committee on Public Accounts was led to conclude that practice was inherently vague and ambiguous. He asked one ADAB officer 'What are the objectives? Toward what end point are you trying efficiently to go? That is probably the most ungrippable part of the whole thing' (JCPA, 1982, p. 456). Nor will this confusion be dispelled by Canberra-based efforts to clarify logframe objectives. As one PADAP employee remarked to me, 'You can look at all the logframes and techniques in the reports, but when you get on the ground, its all bullshit'. The point here is that unless notions like professionalism (or technical sophistication) are closely examined in terms of particular problems, the aid program promises more of the same. After a similar period of 'review', in the mid-1970s one World Bank Director was reported to remark 'I don't know what the hell the goals are, but I'm moving ahead with projects' (Moss 1978, p. 94).

The conventional understanding of professionalism is in keeping with the tenor of the Jackson Report. Basically, it suggests we know what development requires and how to bring about desirable social, economic and political change in a controlled and predictable manner. After close on 40 years' experience, is this assumption warranted? It is true that Australian professionals have the skills to build bridges or to determine the optimum inputs of seeds, fertiliser and credit given soil and climatic conditions. But how 'efficient production' relates to development appears to be another matter altogether. Given this, the certainty of the report is unacceptable, especially since all manner of initiatives are now 'sold' on the basis of their promise to serve the 'poorest of the poor' and thereby reflect their 'real' interests.

TECHNIQUES OF SOPHISTICATED PRACTICE

Professionalism is juxtaposed with increasingly sophisticated techniques of project management; from programming and project identification to evaluation. One aids the other. I argue here in a similar vein: both are essential, and yet each can potentially reinforce the less desirable tendencies of the other.

The Jackson Report gives particular attention to cost-benefit analysis (CBA) which is seen as vital to improved effectiveness. The report makes an important distinction between efficiency, effectiveness and impact. Efficiency refers to cost-effectiveness which is to be assessed by CBA. To help determine which proposals would not 'succeed' and can be weeded out, 'an efficient aid organisation must undertake cost-benefit analysis systematically' in order to determine effectiveness, that is, the project's relevance to broader sectoral and national goals (Jackson Report, 1984, pp. 136, 133). Aid impact is a measure of the project's effects in terms of socio-cultural, institutional and environmental benefits and costs (Jackson Report, 1984, p. 133). 'A professional organisation needs to undertake post-evaluation studies to measure the impact of its aid program' (Jackson Report, 1984, p. 134). Although the role of professional judgement is mentioned, the emphasis, in keeping with the report overall, is on efficiency. CBA is central.

In any event, it is not so much what the report says, but the responses it leads to in practice. The Jackson Report proposes an immediate catch-up program in ADAB 'to remedy the most important deficiencies' (Jackson Report, 1984, p. 16). In practice this has been translated into crash courses in CBA. As Gerhard Hultcrantz remarked about aid agency training manuals, 'SCBA social CBA and related methodologies are sanctioned before us as scientific techniques globally applicable ... as if they were politically and ideologically neutral and theoretically unambiguous (Hultcrantz, 1981, p. 5). Although other techniques to improve management receive mention, there is an important sense in which my comments are not limited to CBA. Some techniques hide the issues of CBA better than others, but none avoid them.

Prior to this, some general remarks about the technical sophistication theme are in order. The fixation on improving ADAB's 'economic analytical strength' goes hand in hand with the belief that aid is one avenue to 'encourage' and 'coordinate' recipient country acceptance of the proper analysis. In the light of the diplomatic interests commonly served by aid, the Jackson Report offers no evidence of the probity of such a venture. It does, however, approvingly cite the UNDP's (United Nations Development Programme) coordinating role in Western Samoa and this provides a case in point. Many will recall the Western Samoan government's expulsion of all UNDP representatives in the mid-1970s. One reason given for this was that the UNDP Head of Mission, a personal friend of the Prime Minister, was not being reappointed. But this exodus would not have happened if there had not been a deep rift between UNDP's 'coordinating role' and Samoan disillusionment with such paternalism. In most places the 'velvet-gloved iron-fist of control' will just not be tolerated -- by either governments or target groups.

On the whole, less dramatic responses to technically sophisticated coordination and management are more prevalent. Many governments adopt an extremely cynical attitude and see sophistication as 'window-dressing' necessary to satisfy the buyer of projects (cf. Morss, 1984). As Ahmad remarks 'the more technical and complex the presentation, the more the use of shadow prices, trade-offs, engineering coefficients, convincing evaluation or investment criteria, the better the chance of funding' (Ahmad 1975, p. 85; cf White, 1976, p. 233). The PADAP employee's remark in the previous section is more candid.

Paradoxically, technical sophistication has been well represented in the two major Philippine projects -- logframe, CBA, institutionalisation action plans, evaluation reviews -- but it is here that the rip-off upwards and institutionalisation problems have been most publicised. The paradox is not limited to ADAB. Denis Rondinelli, after extensive study of the relations between project performance and management techniques across numerous development agencies concluded:

> That 'better' projects will emerge from proposals subjected to highly technical and economic feasibility studies, that optimal choices will emerge from appraisals using an elegant rate of return, s-hadow pricing and social-cost benefit analyses, that projects will be implemented efficiently if planned and controlled through PERT, CPM and systems analysis, that greater impacts can be achieved by integrating projects within sectoral and national development plans, are merely assumed. Little evidence supports the assumptions. (Rondinelli, 1976, p. 596)

This simply underscores the conclusion in the Auditor-General's Report (1981, p. 103) that even where project selection guidelines and techniques exist, their application for 'individual project proposals was not in evidence'. The fact is that by the time sufficient data are available to sensibly apply quantitative techniques a considerable amount of diplomatic time and energy has gone into a project. More frequently, someone decides to go ahead with a project, commissions an engineer to design it, and then brings in an economist to provide justificatory numbers. One Asian Development Bank Evaluation Officer with twenty years experience made the following remark to me about this,

> The text-books tell us that the assessment systems are tools on which to base conclusions -- you know, the Little-Mirrlees and UNIDO systems principle appraisal methods . But the number of projects that have been dropped is very low, and none on the basis that the IRR Internal Rate of Return was too low. The tools are not independent of the practical goal which is to finance projects.

Cost Benefit Analysis in Practice

Much of CBA's appeal is its simplicity. As Layard says:

> The basic notion is very simple. If we have to decide whether to do A or not the rule is; do A if the benefits exceed those of the next best alternative course of action, and not otherwise. If we apply this rule to all possibile choices, we shall generate the largest possible benefits, given the constraints in which we live. And no-one could complain about that. (Layard, 1972, p. 9)

Consequently, the technique is bestowed with the universal dignity of reason which it would be logically perverse and unreasonable to disagree with. But as with most economic techniques, CBA has been castigated for all manner of evils, most of which focus on its conservative political effects. Combined with the consensal view of neo-classical theory, and the tendency to focus on a narrow set of variables regarding technical efficiency, CBA projects the view that certain structural characteristics of society and economy are logical, almost natural necessities. Regardless of whether these natural necessities are deemed so by the public at large, such matters as are 'accounted for' are effectively removed from political debate (cf. Knutsson, 1979; Wynne, 1975, p. 125). The conservative effects ought to be obvious. Governments, even conservative ones, have a broad range of possible actions. Rather than go into this debate, or another concerned with refining the technique, I raise some issues about CBA in practice relevant to the rip-off upwards and institutionalisation problems.[3]

What does CBA typically involve? Practice varies, but CBA takes known data about project inputs (or resources and technology) giving certain outputs (increased yields for instance) and combines these with what is frequently termed the 'planner's objective function'. Theoretically this may be thought of as an expression of certain preferences between alternative states of the economy (Dasgupta, Marglin and Sen, 1972, Chs. 11 and 12). In practice, it is a statement of which political and economic interests should be maximised (for instance, capital intensity, full employment, equity).

This in turn makes it possible to determine the most optimal allocation of resources and to identify the shadow prices to be used in CBA choices.

Practice departs from this ideal in certain respects. Usually the distribution of potential benefits and costs is of interest. CBA by itself attaches no importance to this. An extra dollar for the peasant is accorded the same value (or 'satisfaction') as one for the landlord. Pareto-optimality can be achieved regardless of how unequal the initial resource distribution is. The problems of CBA then are not in ascertaining the 'facts' -- although these are typically imprecise -- but as the authors of the UNIDO Guidelines observe, of obtaining the values to ascertain the meaning of the facts (Dasgupta, Marglin and Sen, 1972, p. 13; cf. Wildavsky, 1967, p. 31). The point is that CBA involves political and ethical judgements at every turn.

Professionals are faced with two alternatives. One is to present equity considerations along with efficiency information so that the appropriate political authority can make its own trade-offs. But as Parrish (1978, p. 307) and others have remarked, the 'conceptual separation of allocative efficiency from distributional equity considerations is ... subject to some difficulties'. Contrary to the consultant's phrase 'first bake the cake', the size of the national cake is not independent of its distribution since the willingness of various groups to pay for its ingredients -- essential to applying CBA --depends on how it is sliced. The second option is to modify the efficiency function to incorporate equity (or any other value) into a single measure. Aside from the quantitative headaches this option creates, CBA offers no guidelines as to how the inevitable political judgements are to be made. For many it is tempting to simplify the problem by ignoring the issue. The prevailing distribution and consumption patterns are subtly transposed into what is best.

Others acknowledge ethical/political judgement is inevitable, but nevertheless claim these are 'subjective judgements of fact' (Parrish, 1978, p. 313; Dasgupta, Marglin and Sen, 1972, p. 135). Ideally these judgements are to be solicited from the political realm. There are two points of contention here. Realistically, politicians are not equipped to provide the kinds of parameters necessary[4] and the simple facts of politics mitigate against this anyway; 'precision is as necessary to economic analysis as vagueness is to politicians' (Self, 1975, p. 152). In this light it is more common for the professional to infer the weights given such things as equity from past government action, like income tax schedules. The view implied here is that governments are above the fray, their action reflects a well-ordered rational preference function -- not inconsistent, contradictory bargaining and conflict between interest groups or classes. In view of the authoritarian character of many Australian bilateral partners, is this a reasonable approach?

The fact is, that these issues are rarely confronted. The professional simply makes these judgements, and justifies this by noting it is impossible and technically frustrating to do otherwise. Practitioners are increasingly asked to reconcile the confusion and ambiguity of aid policy in actual project cases. And when asked 'What should the 'judicious mix' be in this case?', practitioners are rarely able to answer 'Don't ask me, but I can help you design a procedure for bargaining and compromise whereby this decision could be made'. This is reinforced by the attributes of professionalism discussed earlier: the confidence and reluctance to allow the 'pretentious savants' (politicians and public) to interfere and bias judgements. While noting this increases the de facto power of professionals, CBA proponents see advantages in this. It ensures that 'all the relevant variables are considered' and 'forms the basis for deliberate, systematic determination of national parameters when the day finally dawns that these can be specified in advance of project formulation and evaluation' (Dasgupta, Marglin and Sen, 1972, pp. 139-40, 247).

The political problems of techniques are not overcome by 'professionalising' practice in this manner. The techniques and rules of professionalism provide us no value-free or sacrosanct method of avoiding ethical judgements based on individual preferences. This is not remarkable. What is remarkable (and inevitably authoritarian) is that people can be led to believe that such techniques will operationalise the aura of certainty pervading the Jackson Report. The advantages of professional control may be that they have an interest in and access to a variety of information. But the proper authority of professionals does not lie in their insights into other people's preferences. Indeed the biases of professional practice may decrease the likelihood that they have any close association with the people on whose behalf they are said to act.

This is not an argument for rejecting CBA or technical sophistication. Development is about the authoritative allocation of resources. The problems of finding the 'best' way always remain. Such techniques are important in instilling some consistency and discipline and discouraging evasive, vague statements. The issues raised, however, do suggest that CBA provides at best a pretty rocky base for what the Jackson Report presents as an indispensible, hard-headed response to what are essentially political issues in development assistance. Mr Hayden's 'judicious mix' of efficiency and equity considerations can only occur through political processes. CBA can not be independent of or a surrogate for politics in development practice. In the absence of recommendations about how this political process is to be encouraged, professionals need to be extremely modest about what such techniques can contribute. In one sense, a technique which is silent about, or encourages silence about the political nature of development practice has rather little to be said for it. CBA borrows the respect which ordinary opinion accords to economic calculations and professionalism and applies this credibility to what may be fraudulent and politically unaccountable uses (cf. Self, 1975, p. 9).

ACHIEVING THE JUDICIOUS MIX

Professionalism and technical sophistication are logical extensions of the managerial view of development. The committee have said nothing about the potentially adverse tendencies in practice of what seems logically essential in policy. These tendencies are authoritarian; judgements about this are of course matters of personal preference. More significant is the fact that the committee's fixation on professionalism and techniques says very little of relevance to the distributional and institutionalisation problems of project practice. Judgements about this are not just a matter of personal preference, since the problems threaten the probity of the bilateral program overall.

Mr Hayden's comments about the 'judicious mix' implicitly recognises that what appear to be conundrums in policy are in practice conflicts of political interest which are only marginally amenable to managerial solution. The aid program must recognise that questions of local political economy are central to explaining the practitioner's rip-off upwards and institutionalisation problems. They are inherent to the judicious mix. Even if only in token measure, such projects involve the redirection of public sector resources away from those who traditionally control them and who expect to continue to do so. Bilateral projects with basic human needs dimensions will involve the extension of government agencies into areas which in a political sense, were previously unoccupied. The judicious mix has implications for the balance of power between local and national elites and their lines of patronage with the poor.

The Jackson Report ignores this fact. Professionalism and technical sophistication, at least as conventionally practised, maintain and encourage this silence. Quite correctly, the committee notes the conflict among strategic, diplomatic, and commercial interests and between growth and equity. It encourages flexibility and sensitivity to community values (Jackson Report, 1984, p. 24). However, even if we assume that 'community values' provide a good basis for judgement, there is little to suggest they will have great effect. The core of aid policy, at least if the report prevails, will be a modified version of international agency neo-classical analysis. This is clearly the source of proper analysis; hence the coordinating role given to international agencies. Specific judgements about programs will be made by a 'centralised mechanism' of senior ADAB officers (Jackson Report, 1984, pp. 136-7). There is nothing to suggest this will redress the political issues in project practice. Given the absence of constituency pressure and a 'relatively unimpeded arena for the exercise of bureaucratic power' (Viviani, 1979, p. 47) in aid policy, this promises more of the same.

One response is that the report has made provision for consultation with recipient governments. Again we are likely to see a continuation of past trends where recipient government priorities are taken as 'surrogate measures' for the development needs of specific groups

(Auditor-General, 1981, p. 94). It would be naive to assume recipient government priorities necessarily reflect an above-the-fray kind of benevolent rationality -- either in Australia or the Third World. The abstract goals of development often have little meaning in the sense understood by western professionals. On the other hand, the concrete gains for individuals and families are readily appreciated. As Miller (1979, p. 8) has noted they 'will view the business of receiving aid as largely a matter of pecuniary opportunity'. Whereas the domestic recipients of the Australian public purse have some means of scrutiny and redress, this is not usually available to recipients of aid (Viviani, 1979, pp. 85-6).

For professionalism and technical sophistication to begin addressing these features of the Third World, a number of changes are necessary, two of which are briefly considered here: the character of aid policy; and of professional practice.

First, aid policy needs to recognise explicitly some things which are self-evident in practice. Analysis of development trends over the past two decades underscores the importance of economic growth. But experience also reminds us that economic growth is a means to other ends, and that for certain ends, economic growth is not a very efficient means. This has been simply put by Sen (1983, p. 753):

> If the government of a poor developing country is keen to raise the level of wealth and the expectation of life, then it would be pretty daft to try to achieve this through raising its income per head, rather than going directly for these objectives through public policy and social change.

Increased income may improve a farmer's purchasing power of the goods that are available in the market. But increased income may not be able to deal at all adequately with his/her entitlements to education or medical treatment. Rising incomes guarantee no such thing. Indeed a growth emphasis may constrain a country's budgetary capacity to meet these entitlements. Sen (1983, p. 756) writes 'when it comes to health, or freedom from social harassment, income is miles off target'.

This is not a matter of pushing forward the tired old dichotomies of growth versus equity. The report does the aid policy debate a disservice by reinforcing this simplicity. As I have observed, a policy on one is inevitably a policy on another. An immediate result of the Jackson Report has been renewed squaring-off of growth versus equity (top-down/bottom-up, trickle-down/trickle-up, elite-led/community-participatory) protagonists. Most of these polarities can be maintained only by a good deal of selective recall regarding what the other has said and of the evidence from project practice (cf. Arndt, 1983). This last point is crucial; few of the dichotomies reflect systematically substantiated argument. Lest this be taken simply as criticism of the report, a few remarks should illustrate what this means in terms of practical policy.

Aid policy must reflect the peculiar characteristics of task and situation. The themes of participation and community control promoted by some non-governmental organisations are a case in point. There can be no doubt that effective, broad-based participation of intended beneficiaries in projects is essential. This is the only way that the two problems of projects can be addressed and the only effective way of arresting some of the authoritarian tendencies of professionalism and technical sophistication. But there is little systematic knowledge of what participation or local control actually means in practice -- even if it is unambiguously good in policy on normative grounds (cf. Cohen and Uphoff, 1980). Certain things are clear from practical experience. First, the kind of survey/research-based participation that figures in many Australian aid projects will likely reinforce the political alienation of beneficiaries from the kind of participatory control that is essential (Porter, 1984, pp. 137-8). And second, for participation to be effective, the 'community' must have a high degree of control over their assets and production and remain relatively free of broader encapsulating agencies. Again, this is quite at odds with current project practice.

Policy must have other considerations which are begged by single-minded pursuit of the 'maximum-participation' dictates. The question of who the 'community' (or 'poor') are, aside from being handy grist for Australian-based aid debates, is problematic. Policy must also face the fact that participation is closely linked with the scale and purpose of the project. Certain tasks are sometimes frustrated by the 'maximum participation' dictum -- to the ultimate detriment of the poor. Complex technologies (like water purification or pumping stations) necessitate skill and organisational sophistication which may always involve a degree of incompatibility with participant control. In other words, tasks should be the referent for 'judicious' judgement, not the dictates of abstract dichotomies. This does not mean that the tendency for some projects to be intercepted by elites should simply be accepted. It does not imply, for instance, that we should simply accept that agricultural projects are input dependent and therefore support capitalised farmers, or the links between cattle projects, pasture improvement and eviction of share tenants. It does mean that the tendency for control and benefits to be skewed in favour of some groups is not to be averted by 'maximising participation' but by redefining the technology or means whereby the poor will be reached and be able to maintain control.

A further point is that if one has the question of benefit distribution in mind, then the interests of the poor are in some cases better served by more centralised control (for example by state or private corporate agencies) (Hunter, 1981). There are cases, for instance, where a community may be especially adept at controlling some activities -- like sanitation or well use -- but when additional activities are grafted on -- like credit or subsidy control -- jealousies and conflicts surface which undermine both new and traditional patterns of control. Some tasks can only be viable by eliciting elite involvement, and on other occasions, elites acting out of their own self-interest will automatically benefit the poor.[5]

There is a documented relationship between the neo-classical focus on efficiencies of growth and top-down, elite and centralised control. This approach skews the benefits of projects away from intended beneficiaries and is related to their (for example small farmers) reluctance to be 'institutionalised'. But this problem is not to be resolved by invoking professionalism or technical sophistication on the one hand, or participatory 'poor' community articles of faith on the other. Policy based on research and evaluation from specific projects will help here, but in all cases, these issues require much greater sensitivity to and understanding of the political and economic circumstances of the target groups. In turn, this requires basic changes in the conventional understanding of professional practice.

Enough has been said about the tendencies of conventional professionalism to indicate what is implied here. It should go without saying that the self-assured confidence engendered by the Jackson Report will not do in practice. Practitioners need to be extremely modest in their 'professional promise' and about the role of techniques like CBA. Failing this, the urban, commercial, scientific values of development practitioners will tend to discount, disregard and even despise the contributions and interests of the intended beneficiaries and the political processes through which these are articulated (Chambers, 1983, p. 101). This implies some 'reversals' in professional practice. Arms-length advice and other notions will remain important, but mainly in the sense that the professional is forced to relinquish his/her claims to special insight into the 'self-evident problems' and other people's 'real interests'.

The truism that practitioners should start with and pay greater heed to the values and priorities of the target groups has been heard before. Two points should be made about this. First, however much insight professionals gain, they will always project their own values and priorities. The claim to having 'spoken with the people' too often becomes another prop to the professionals' authority. Second, beginning with 'the people's priorities' is often paternalistic. 'Priorities' are rarely simply existent things waiting in the minds of target groups to be extracted by the survey question. Both points lead in the same direction. The practitioners' activities must be accompanied by, and indeed facilitated by, political processes whereby recipient groups learn to establish their priorities and control the strategies that professionals may assist in developing. This of course requires numerous changes in the practitioners' approaches to problem-setting and resolution.

This is not the same as saying that overcoming the rip-off upwards and institutionalisation problems is just a matter of individual will on the practitioners part. It would be daft to suggest this. Practitioners work in an increasingly bureaucratised environment in which their arena of action is often severely circumscribed. This,

> in most countries face(s) inwards and upwards, away from ... clients. Their structure and style are often authoritarian,

> hierarchical and punitive. From the centre and top come targets, commands, exhortations and threats. From the periphery and bottom comes a weaker flow of filtered information that placates and misleads. (Chambers, 1983, pp. 210-11)

But as other contributers point out, the problems of change in policy and practice are frequently exaggerated. There is considerable room to move and for choice. How professionals exercise that choice is affected by their commitments.

This 'new professionalism' popularised by Robert Chambers and others, is summarised by Neil O'Sullivan of CAA,

> Such a professionalism will discount technical expertise and focus much more on the commitment and entrepreneurial skills necessary to negotiate the human, social, and political barriers that inevitably arise when one seeks to assist the poor. (O'Sullivan, 1983, p. 41)

NOTES

I wish to acknowledge the helpful advice of Bill Stent, Bob Richards, Kaye Bysouth, and my fellow editors in preparing this chapter.

1. Although with less assiduity, the themes of professionalism and technical sophistication pre-date the Jackson Report. In 1972, for instance, Mr Morrison, then Chairman of an aid sub-committee of the Parliamentary Joint Committee on Foreign Affairs and Defence, pressed for increased professionalism (Viviani and Wilenski, 1979, pp. 92-3) and it has been a key referent of private consultants' submissions to numerous reviews. Technical sophistication also enjoys wide support, often from unexpected quarters. Bob Whan, then Director of ACFOA, submitted to the JCPA efficiency audit of ADAB that 'we would like to see the technical efficiency of ADAB really honed so that it becomes an ultra-efficient technical organisation in the delivery of aid' (JCPA, 1982, p. 244).

2. Consider for instance two countries, one which largely followed the prescription implicit in the Jackson Report, and another which did not. Chile under Pinochet has followed the monetarist line: government intervention reduced, tariffs dismantled, the exchange rate floated, internal price 'distortions' corrected and the banking system 'freed'. Industrial production has collapsed, unemployment soared, <u>per capita</u> income declined and inequality become more accute. China, on the other hand directly controls the allocation of resources, regulates labour, the capital credit market and intervenes in almost every way imaginable. Exports have grown at the same rate overall as world trade since 1965, infant mortality and life expectancy approach Western standards, malnutrition is insignificant, income equality exceptional and literacy nearly universal among the post-1949 born population (Griffin and Griffin, 1983; Griffin and Saith, 1982).

3. Broader comment on the 'ideology' of CBA is of course relevant. Consider Barnett's (1981, p. 307) remark:

The concepts of investment and profit can be understood in a number of ways. They can be seen as neutral, economic concepts, referring to the inputs and outputs of a productive process as derived from neoclassical production theory ... looked at from another perspective, they are by no means technical and neutral, but deeply ideological. They contain assumptions as to how society operates and ought to operate.

Simply put, CBA sustains the interests of those who plan society from above and whose hands control the economic machinery necessary for the manipulation of social life. This is given only passing attention as is the literature concerned with fine-tuning CBA. That is, debate about the choice of criteria e.g., net present value, benefit-cost ratio or internal rate of return; choice of social opportunity cost or social time preferences for discounting; shadow pricing or the construction of equal welfare curves (e.g., Sinden, 1980).

4. E.g., the relative weights to be attached to different national objectives, the rates of social return on investment, the social rates of discount, the pattern of reinvestment and returns on investment, and the shadow prices of key imports.

5. Cf. Franke and Chasin (1980); Coombs (1981). For example, in programs to eradicate contagious diseases (livestock and human) unless all are vaccinated, poor and elite alike, the elite will remain vulnerable to contagion. Tendler (1982, p. 38) cites the example of elites supporting a health project targetted and controlled by the poor because they expected it would relieve them of patron-client obligations to take care of the poor's health expenditures.

BIBLIOGRAPHY

ACFOA (Australian Council for Overseas Aid) (1984) 'Focusing Australian Aid: Report of the Committee to Review Australia's Overseas Aid Program', A.C.F.O.A. News, June 5/6, pp.1-2

ACIAR (Australian Centre for International Agricultural Research) (1983) 'Major Agricultural Problems and Research Priorities in the Eastern Africa Region', Proceedings of the Eastern Africa-ACIAR Consultation on Agricultural Research, Nairobi, 18-22 July, ACIAR, Canberra

ACIL Australia Pty Ltd (1983) 'Submission to the Jackson Committee', Melbourne

ACOA (Australian Clerical Officers Association Section Committee) (1982) 'Inquiry into the Auditor-General's Report of an Efficiency Audit: Administration of Australia's Bilateral Overseas Aid Program', unpublished submission to the Joint Committee of Public Accounts, Canberra

ACOA (Australian Clerical Officers Association) (1983) Submission to the Committee to Review the Australian Overseas Aid Program', unpublished submission to the Committee to Review the Australian Overseas Aid Program

ADAA (Australian Development Assistance Agency) (1975) Development Assistance Committee Annual Aid Review - Memorandum of Australia, ADAA, Canberra

ADAB (Australian Development Assistance Bureau) (1981) Development Cooperation: Annual Review 1979-80, Australian Government Publishing Service, Canberra

ADAB (Australian Development Assistance Bureau) (1982) Summaries and Review of Ongoing Evaluation Studies 1975-80, Australian Government Publishing Service, Canberra

ADAB (Australian Development Assistance Bureau) (1983) 'ADAB/NGO Project Subsidy Scheme since 1980', Australian Government Publishing Service, Canberra

ADAB (Australian Development Assistance Bureau) (1984a) Australian Bilateral Aid Program 1984-85, Australian Government Publishing Service, Canberra

ADAB (Australian Development Assistance Bureau) (1984b) 'Functional Classification of Australian Development Assistance to Developing Countries. Bilateral Flows by Project and Major Items of Expenditure, 1975/76 to 1982/83', Canberra

ADAB (Australian Development Assistance Bureau) (1984c) 'Country Aid Programming', unpublished ADAB Background Paper to the ADAB/NGO Consultation, 17-18 September, Canberra.

ADAB (Australian Development Assistance Bureau) (1984d) Australian Bilateral Aid Program 1983-84, Australian Government Publishing Service, Canberra.

AFFHC (Australian Freedom From Hunger Campaign) (1980) Trade to Whose Advantage, Australian Freedom from Hunger Campaign, Canberra

AFSAAP (African Studies Association of Australia and the Pacific) (1983) Unpublished Submission to the Committee to Review the Australian Overseas Aid Program

ALP (Australian Labor Party) (1982) Platform, Constitution, Rules, Australian Labor Party, Canberra

ALP (Australian Labor Party) (1984) Platform, Constitution, Rules, Australian Labor Party, Canberra

APCC (Australian Professional Consultants Council) (1982) 'Submission to the Joint Committee of Public Accounts Enquiry into the Administration of Australia's Bilateral Overseas Aid Program', Australian Professional Consultants Council, Sydney

ASPBAE (Asian and South Pacific Bureau of Adult Education) (1981) 'DVV-ASPBAE Partnership-Evaluation Review 1977-1980', Adult Education and Development, 17, 11-21

Aberdeen, I. (1983) Talk to Society for International Development Meeting on the Jackson Review, Australian National University, Canberra, 20 October

Ahmad, Y.J. (1975) 'Project Identification, Analysis, and Preparation in Developing Countries: A Discursive Commentary', Development and Change, 6(3), 83-90

Ahmed, N. and Coombs, P.H. (eds) (1975) Education for Rural Development. Case Studies for Planners, Praeger, New York

Allan, B. and Hinchcliffe, K. (1982) Planning, Policy Analysis and Public Spending, Gower, Aldershot

Allen, B., Brookfield, H., Forbes, D., Howlett, D. and Taylor, M. (1983) Unpublished Submission to the Committee to Review the Australian Development Assistance Program

Allen, K.R. (1975) 'Alternatives for Australian Aid', Congress Papers, ANZAAS Congress 46, Section 21, Paper 492

Alliband, G. (1984a) 'The use of aid as a Political Weapon: a Case Study of Vietnam', in Indochina. The Poverty of Politics, Development Dossier No. 14, Australian Council for Overseas Aid, Canberra, pp.38-45

Alliband, G. (1984b) 'Why Australia should aid Vietnam', in Indochina. The Poverty of Politics, Development Dossier No.14, Australian Council for Overseas Aid, Canberra, pp.46-53

Alliband, G. (1984c) 'Report on ICARA II Conference, Geneva', ACFOA News No. 7, 3

Amin, S., (1978) Imperialism and Unequal Development, Harvester Press, London

Anon. (1982) 'Exporting Reaganomics: The President Wants to do Things Differently at AID', National Journal, May 29, pp.960-4

Arndt, H.W. (1983) 'The 'Trickle-down' Myth', Economic Development and Cultural Change, 32(1), 1-10

Arnold, S.H. (1982) Implementing Development Assistance: European Approaches to Basic Needs, Westview Press, Boulder, Colorado

Auditor General (1981) The Report of the Auditor-General on an Efficiency Audit into the Administration of Australia's Bilateral Overseas Aid Program, Australian Government Publishing Service, Canberra

Auditor General, South Australia (1984) Report of the Auditor-General for the Year Ended 30 June 1984, Government Printer, South Australia

Australia Department of Trade (1983) Unpublished Submission to the Committee to Review the Australian Development Assistance Programme

Ayres, J. and Nalson, J. (1984) 'Development Projects and the Production Responsibility System in China: A Case Study', The Australian Journal of Chinese Affairs, 11, 131-45

Balassa, B. (1982) 'Structural Adjustment Policies in Developing Countries', World Development, 10, 1

Barnett, T. (1981) 'Evaluating the Gezira Scheme: Black Box or Pandora's Box?', in J. Heyer, P. Roberts and G. Williams (eds.), Rural Development in Tropical Africa, St Martin's Press, New York, pp.306-24

Bauer, P.T. (1971) Dissent on Development, Weidenfeld and Nicolson, London

Bauer, P.T. (1981) Equality, the Third World and Economic Delusion, Weidenfeld and Nicolson, London

Beazley, K.C., Elstob, R.C., Fry, K.L., Holding, A.C., Jacobi, R., McIntosh, C.D., Morrison, W.L., Simm, J.P. and Sibraa, K.W. (1981) 'Dissenting report on recommendation 3 - Indo China Report', in Joint Committee on Foreign Affairs and Defence, Power in Indo China Since 1975, Australian Government Publishing Service, Canberra, pp. 93-5

Bellam, M. (1980) A Question of Balance: New Zealand Trade in the South Pacific, New Zealand Coalition for Trade and Development, Wellington

Bello, W., Kinley, D. and Elinson, E. (1982) Development Debacle: The World Bank in the Philippines, Institute for Food and Development Policy, San Francisco

Bennett, R.B., Merchan, J.E. and Metcalfe, J.S. (1981) Motives for Australian Direct Foreign Investment, Working Paper No. 23, Bureau of Industry Economics, Canberra

Benveniste, G. and Ilchman, W.F. (eds.) (1969) Agents of Change: Professions in Developing Countries, Praegar, New York

Blazic-Metzner, B. and Hughes, H. (1982) 'Growth Experiences for Small Economies', in B. Jalan (ed.), Problems and Policies in Small Economies, Croom Helm, London, pp.85-102

Brandt Report (Report of the Independent Commission on International Development Issues) (1980) North-South: A Programme for Survival, Pan, London

Britton, S.G. (1979) 'Tourism in a Peripheral Capitalist Economy: the Case Study of Fiji', unpublished PhD thesis, Australian National University, Canberra

Brookfield, H.C. (ed.) (1973) The Pacific in Transition, Edward Arnold, London

Brookfield, H.C. (1977) 'Australia and the Pacific Islands', in Senate Standing Committee on Foreign Affairs and Defence, Australia and the South Pacific, Australian Government Publishing Service, Canberra, pp.511-16

Brown, W. (1983) Unpublished Submission to the Committee to Review the Australian Development Assistance Programme

Buckley, K. and Klugman, K. (1981) The History of Burns Philp: The Australian Company in the South Pacific, Burns Philp and Co. Ltd, Sydney

1984-85 Budget Paper No. 9 (1984) Australia's Overseas Development Assistance Program 1984-85, Australian Government Publishing Service, Canberra

1985-86 Budget Paper No. 9 (1985) Australia's Overseas Development Assistance Program 1985-86, Australian Government Publishing Service, Canberra

Bureau of Industry Economics (1978) Industrialisation in Asia: Some Implications for Australian Industry, Research Report No. 1, Australian Government Publishing Service, Canberra

Byrne, E. (1983) 'Educating Third World Women for Development - An International and Regional Perspective', in C. Baldock and D. Goodrich (eds.), Women's Participation in the Development Process, School of Social Enquiry, Murdoch University, pp.45-9

CAA (Community Aid Abroad) (1983) Unpublished Submission to the Committee to Review the Australian Overseas Aid Program

CTEC (Commonwealth Tertiary Education Commission) (1982) Learning and Earning, Australian Government Publishing Service, Canberra

Caiden, G.E. (1976) 'International Consultants and Development Administration', International Review of Administrative Sciences, 62(1), 1-7

Campbell, J.R. (1984) Dealing with Disaster: Hurricane Response in Fiji, Pacific Islands Development Program, Honolulu

Carstairs, R.T. and Prasad, R.D. (1981) Impact of Foreign Direct Private Investment in the Fiji Economy, Centre for Applied Studies in Development, University of the South Pacific, Suva.

Chambers, R. (1983) Rural Development: Putting the Last First, Longman, Harlow

Chatterton, B. and Chatterton, L. (1982) 'Failures in Technology Transfer. Are Farmers Overlooked?', Food Policy, 7(2), 141-55

Chatterton, B. and Chatterton, L. (1984) 'The Transfer of Agricultural Technology - the Australian Disconnection', Proceedings of 2nd Australian Middle East Studies Association, Footscray Institute of Technology Library, Victoria

Chatterton, B. and Chatterton, L. (1985) 'Farmers as Extension Agents, a Libyan Case Study', Ceres, 103, 40-2

Chenery, H. (1979) Structural Change and Development Policy, Oxford University Press, London

Chenery, H., Ahluwalia, M.S., Bell, C.L.G., Duloy, J.H. and Jolly, R. (1974) Redistribution with Growth, Oxford University Press, London

Clairmonte, F. and Cavanagh, J. (1981) 'Dynamics of Oligopolistic Power: Fibres and Allied Textiles', Economic and Political Weekly, 16, 529-40

Cohen, J.M. and Uphoff, N.T. (1980) 'Participation's Place in Rural Development: Seeking Clarity Through Specificity', World Development, 8(3), 213-35

Cole, R.V. (1983a) 'Development Assistance in the South Pacific: the Role of Credit', World Review, 22, 70-84

Cole, R.V. (1983b) Unpublished Submission to the Committee to Review the Australian Development Assistance Programme

Cole, K., Cameron, J. and Edwards, C. (1983) Why Economists Disagree: The Political Economy of Economics, Longman, London

Commonwealth of Australia (1978) Australia and the South Pacific: Report of the Senate Standing Committee on Foreign Affairs and Defence, Australian Government Publishing Service, Canberra

Commonwealth Secretariat (1983) Towards a New Bretton Woods, Commonwealth Secretariat, London

Connell, J. (1983) 'Migration, Employment and Development in the South Pacific', Country Report No. 16, Solomon Islands, South Pacific Commission and International Labour Organisation, Noumea

Connell, J. (1984) 'Kiribati and Tuvalu: A Suitable Case for ......?', Pacific Aid Research Newsletter, 5, 8-10

Connell, J. (1985a) 'Islands on the Poverty Line', Pacific Viewpoint (forthcoming)

Connell, J. (1985b) 'Strategies for the South Pacific? A Critique of the Jackson Report on Australian Aid', Working Paper No. 1, Sydney University Development Studies Colloquium, Sydney

Conroy, J. (1982) Essays on the Development Experience in Papua New Guinea, Monograph No. 17, Institute of Applied Social and Economic Research, Port Moresby

Cook Islands (1983) Unpublished Submission to the Committee to Review the Australian Development Assistance Programme

Coombs, P.H. (1981) New Strategies for Improving Rural Family Life, International Council for Educational Development, Essex, Connecticut

Cox, R. (1979) 'Ideologies and the New International Economic Order: Reflections on Some Recent Literature', International Organisation, 32, 2, 257-302

Cunningham, G. (1974) The Management of Aid Agencies, Croom Helm and the Overseas Development Institute, London

Currey, B. (1980) 'Famine in the Pacific: Losing the Chances for Change', Geo Journal, 4, 447-66

DANIDA (1983) Annual Report, Ministry of Foreign Affairs Information Office, Copenhagen, Denmark

DAOA (Development Assistance Officers Association) (1983) 'Submission to the Australian Aid Review from the Development Assistance Officers Association', unpublished submission to the Committee to Review the Australian Overseas Aid Programme

DFA (Department of Foreign Affairs) (1983) 'Should ADAB be Autonomous?' unpublished submission to the Committee to Review the Australian Overseas Aid Program

Dasgupta, P., Marglin, S. and Sen, A. (1972) Guidelines for Project Evaluation, UNIDO Project Formulation and Evaluation Series, New York

Davis, C. (1981) Bangladesh Cattle Development Project, Animal Nutrition Section. Final Report, Dhaka

Davis, E.W. and Yeomans, K.A. (1974) Company Finance and the Capital Market: A Study of the Effects of Firm Size, Cambridge University Press, Cambridge

Demas, W.G. (1975) 'Economic Independence: Conceptual and Policy Issues in the Commonwealth Caribbean', in P. Selwyn (ed.), Development Policy in Small Countries, Croom Helm, London, pp.191-207

Department of Trade (1983) Unpublished Submission to the Committee to Review the Australian Overseas Aid Program

De Vries, B. (1975) 'Development Aid to Small Countries', in P. Selwyn (ed.) Development Policy in Small Countries, Croom Helm, London, pp.164-75

Dommen, E. (1980) 'External Trade Problems of Small Island States in the Pacific and Indian Oceans', in R.T. Shand (ed.) The Island States of the Pacific and Indian Oceans: Anatomy and Development, Monograph No. 23, Development Studies Centre, Australian National University, Canberra, pp.179-99

Donaldson, M. and Turner, D. (1978) 'The Foreign Control of Papua New Guinea's Economy and the Reaction of the Independent State', Political Economy Working Paper 1, University of Papua New Guinea, Port Moresby

Drysdale, P. (1984) Pacific Growth and Economic Interdependence: The Role of Australia, Australian Institute of International Affairs, Perth

Duke, C. (1978) Participatory Research: Collected Papers, Asian and South Pacific Bureau of Adult Education, International Council of Adult Education and A.N.U. Centre for Continuing Education, Canberra

Duke, C. (1981) 'Adult Education and Development: Some Important Issues', Adult Education and Development, 16

Duke, C. (1983) 'Adult Education and Poverty: What are the Connections?', Convergence, XVI, 1, 80

Duke, C. (ed.) (1985) Combatting Poverty Through Adult Education: National Development Strategies, Croom Helm, London

Dunn, R. (1983) 'Australia's Contribution through ADAB to the Improvement of Agriculture in Developing Countries', Australian Foreign Affairs Record, 54, 9, 500-4

EFIC (Export Finance Insurance Corporation) (1983) Unpublished Submission to the Committee to Review the Australian Overseas Aid Program

Eisen, H. (1973) 'Some Factors Affecting Changes in the Geographical Distribution of Aid', IDS Internal Working Paper No. 7, Brighton

Eldridge, P.J. (1983) 'Diplomacy, Development and "Small Government": Conflicting Directions in Australia's Overseas Aid Program', CSAAR Research Paper No. 23, Griffith University, Brisbane

Eldridge, P. (1984) 'Diplomacy and Development: A Preliminary Assessment of the Jackson Committee Report on Australia's Overseas Aid Program', Paper presented to Australian Political Studies Association Conference, University of Melbourne, Melbourne

Eldridge, P. (1985) 'The Jackson Report on Australia's Aid Program: Political Options and Prospects', Australian Outlook: The Australian Journal of International Affairs, 39, 1, 23-32

Elias, D. (1984) 'Aid for Political Aims: Report', The Age, 31 August, p.9

Emmanuel, A. (1972) Unequal Exchange: A Study in the Imperialism of Trade, New Left Books, London

Evans, H.D. (1972) A General Equilibrium Analysis of Protection, North-Holland, Amsterdam

FFH (Freedom from Hunger) (1983) Unpublished Submission to the Committee to Review the Development Assistance Programme

Faithfull, G. (1982) 'Urban Planning and Development Authority', Address to Symposium on Australian Development Practice in Asia and the Pacific: Experience and Issues, Transcript, Planning Research Centre, University of Sydney, Sydney

Feder, E. (1983) 'Plundering the Poor: the Role of the World Bank in the Third World', International Journal of Health Sciences, 13, 649-60

Ferris, W. (1984) Lifting Australia's Performance as an Exporter of Manufactures and Services; Report of the National Export Marketing Strategy Panel, Australian Government Publishing Service, Canberra

Fieldhouse, D.K. (1978) Unilever Overseas: The Anatomy of a Multinational 1895-1965, Croom Helm, London

Fisk, E.K. (1982) 'Subsistence Affluence and Development Policy', Regional Development Dialogue, Special Issue, 1-12

Forbes, D.K. (1985) 'Australian Bilateral Urban Aid, Present and Future', Australian Urban Studies, 12(4), 3-4

Frank, C.R. and Baird, M. (1975) 'Foreign Aid: Its Speckled Past and Future Prospects', in C.F. Bergsten and L.B. Krause (eds.), World Politics and International Economics, The Brookings Institution, pp.133-67

Franke, R.W. and B. Chasin (1980) Seeds of Famine: Ecological Destruction and the Development Dilemma in the West African Sahel, Universe Books, New York

Fröbel, F. Heinrichs, and Kreye, O. (1980) The New International Division of Labour, Cambridge University Press, Cambridge

Fry, G. (1977) 'The Need for an Increased Australian Commitment to the South Pacific', in Senate Standing Committee on Foreign Affairs and Defence, Australia and the South Pacific, Australian Government Publishing Service, Canberra, pp.804-10

Garnaut, R. (1981) 'The Framework of Economic Policy-Making', in J.A. Ballard (ed.), Policy Making in a New State, Papua New Guinea 1972-77, University of Queensland Press, Brisbane, pp.157-211

Garnier, P. (1982) 'Introduction to Special Public Works Programmes', International Labour Office, Geneva

General Foods Corporation (NZ) Ltd (1982) 'General Foods: Inside Gen', General Foods Corporation (NZ) Ltd, Hastings.

Gertzel, C. (1984) 'Makere 1984: The Problems of Reconstruction', AFSAAP Neewsletter, 6(2) 17-23

Goldring Report (Committee of Review of Private Overseas Student Policy) (1984) Mutual Advantage, Australian Government Publishing Service, Canberra

Griffin, K. and Griffin, K. (1983) 'Institutional Change and Income Distribution in the Chinese Countryside', Oxford Bulletin of Economics and Statistics, 45(3), 223-48

Griffin, K. and Saith, A. (1982) 'The Pattern of Income Inequality in Rural China', Oxford Economic Papers, 34(1), 172-206

Hall, B.L. and Kidd, J.R. (eds.) (1983) Adult Learning: a Design for Action, Pergamon, Oxford

Harries Report (Committee on Australia's Relations with the Third World) (1979) Australia and the Third World, Australian Government Publishing Service, Canberra

Harris, S. (1980) 'The Brandt Commission: Objectives, Progress and Issues' unpublished seminar paper, Australian National University, Canberra

Harvey, P. (1982) 'Overview of Nutrition-Related Agricultural Research', in P. Kripps (ed.), Proceedings of the National Nutrition Workshop, Nutrition Section, Health Department, Port Moresby, pp.68-74

Hau'ofa, E. (1983) Tales of the Tikongs, Longman Paul, Auckland

Hau'ofa, E. (1985) 'Aid: a South Pacific Perspective', unpublished paper to South Pacific Planners Seminar, Canberra

Hawkins, R. (1981) 'Strike One for the Pacific Woman', Islands Business, 7(12) 39-41

Hayden, B. (1983a) 'The North-South Dialogue and a Labour Government', in J. Langmore and D. Peetz (eds.), Wealth, Poverty and Survival, Allen and Unwin, Sydney, pp.115-24

Hayden, B. (1983b) 'Address to North-South Seminar', Southern Cross Hotel, Melbourne, 17 June, Minister for Foreign Affairs News Release

Hayden, B. (1984) 'Indian Ocean', Speech to the Western Australian branch of the Australian Institute of International Affairs, 20 June, Department of Foreign Affairs, Backgrounder, No. 436, 27 June

Hayter, T. (1971) Aid as Imperialism, Penguin, Harmondsworth

Hayter, T. (1981) The Creation of World Poverty, Pluto Press, London

Healey, D.T. (1983) Unpublished Submission to the Committee to Review the Australian Development Assistance Programme

Healey, P. (ed.) (1983) Towards an Authentic Development: The Role of Adult Education, ICAE, Toronto

Henderson, R. and Hough, D. (1984) 'Sydney's Poor Get Squeezed', Australian Society, 3 (11), 6-8

Herr, R. (1977) 'On the Need for an Increased Australian Commitment to the Sout Pacific', in Senate Standing Committee on Foreign Affairs and Defence, Australia and the South Pacific, Australian Government Publishing Service, Canberra, pp.1266-75

Herr, R. (1984) 'The Changing Geo-Politics of Anzus: the Place of the South Pacific', World Review, 23, 21-42

Hicks, N. (1980) 'Is There a Trade-Off Between Growth and Basic Needs?', Finance and Development, 17(2), 17-20

Hicks, N. and Streeten, P. (1979) 'Indicators of Development: The Search for a Basic Needs Yardstick', World Development, 7, 567-80

Higgott, R.A. (1981) 'Beyond the Sociology of Underdevelopment: An Historiographical Analysis of Marxist and Dependencia Theories of Underdevelopment', Social Analysis, 7, 72-98

Higgott, R.A. (1983) Political Development Theory; The Contemporary Debate, Croom Helm, London

Higgott, R.A. (1984) 'Export-Oriented Industrialisation, the New International Division of Labour and the Corporate State in the Third World: An Essay in Conceptual Linkage', Australian Geographical Studies, 22, 58-71

Higgott, R.A. (1985a) 'The State in Africa: Some Thoughts on the Future Drawn From the Past', in T. Shaw and O. Aluko (eds.), Africa Projected from Recession to Renaissance by the Year 2000?, Macmillan, London, pp.14-39

Higgott, R.A. (1985b) 'Africa and the New International Division of Labour', in J. Ravenhill (ed.), Africa in Economic Crisis, Macmillan, London

Higgott, R.A. (forthcoming) 'The Dilemmas of Interdependence: Australia and the New International Division of Labour', in J. Caporaso (ed.), The International Political Economy Yearbook, Vol. 2, Westview Press, Boulder

Higgott, R.A., Robison, R., Hewison, K.J. and Rodan, G. (1985) 'Theories of Development and Underdevelopment: Implications for the Study of Southeast Asia', in R.A. Higgot and R. Robison (eds.), Southeast Asia: Essays in the Political Economy of Structural Change, Routledge and Kegan Paul, London,

Hill, H. (1982) 'The Philippine Economy Under Marcos, A Balance Sheet', Australian Outlook; The Australian Journal of International Affairs, 36(3), 32-9

Hill, H. (1983) 'The Impact of Development Policies on Women', in J. Langmore and D. Peetz (eds.), Wealth, Poverty and Survival: Australia in the World, Allen and Unwin, Sydney, pp.67-90

Hinton, P. (1983) Submission to the Committee to Review the Australian Overseas Aid Program

Hirschman, A.O. (1981) Essays in Tresspassing: Economics to Politics and Beyond, Cambridge University Press, Cambridge

Hoadley, J.S. (1981) 'Aid, Politics and Hospitals in Western Samoa', World Development, 8, 433-55

Hoare, P., (1983) Unpublished Submission to the Committee to Review the Australian Overseas Aid Program

Honadle, G., Morss, E.R., Vansant, J. and Gow, D.D. (1980) Integrated Rural Development; Making it Work?, USAID and Development Alternatives, Inc., Washington, DC

Howard, M. and Chand, A. (1984) 'Australian Companies in Fiji', in E. Utrecht (ed.), Fiji: A Client State of Australasia?, Transnational Corporations Research Project, University of Sydney, Sydney, pp.283-305

Howie, I. (1973) 'The Effects of Foreign Investment', in A. Rokotuivuna et al. (eds), Fiji: A Developing Australian Colony, International Development Action, Melbourne, pp.59-70

Howlett, D.R. (1983) 'Aid to the South Pacific Forum Island Countries', unpublished submission to the Committee to Review the Australian Development Assistance Programme

Hughes, A. (1983) 'Independence for Sale: What are the Offers', in R. Crocombe and A. Ali (eds.), Foreign Forces in Pacific Politics, Institute of Pacific Studies, University of the South Pacific, Suva, pp.250-63

Hughes, H. (1983) 'Global Economic Relations', Australian Outlook; The Australian Journal of International Affairs, 37(3), 132-7

Hughes, H. (1984) 'Industrializing Small Countries', Industry and Development, 12, 89-99

Hultcrantz, G. (1981) 'Foreword', in A. Elzinga, Evaluating the Evaluation Game: On the Methodology of Project Evaluation, with Special Reference to Development Cooperation, SAREC Report, R1, Swedish Agency for Research Cooperation with Developing Countries, Berlings, pp.5-7

Hunt, J. (1983) Unpublished submission to the Committee to Review the Australian Overseas Aid Program

Hunter, G. (1981) 'A Hard Look at Directing Benefits to the Rural Poor and at 'Participation'', Discussion Paper No. 6, Agricultural Administration Network, Overseas Development Institute, London

Hunter, G. (ed.) (1982) Enlisting the Small Farmer: The Range of Requirements, Agricultural Administration Unit Occasional Paper No. 4, Overseas Development Institute, London

IMF (International Monetary Fund) (1983) Balance of Payments Statistics, Volume 34, Yearbook, Part 1, International Monetary Fund, Washington, DC

Indo-Australian Sheep Breeding Project Brochure (1976) 'A Story of Cooperation', Produced in collaboration with the Australian Information Service, New Delhi

Indyk, M. (1985) 'The Australian Study of International Relations', in D. Aitkin (ed.), Surveys of Australian Political Science, Allen and Unwin, Sydney, pp.265-311

Ingram, J.C. (1979) 'The Administration of Australian Aid', in R.T. Shand and H.V. Richter (eds.), International Aid: Some Political, Administrative and Technical Realities, Monograph No. 16, Development Studies Centre, Australian National University, pp.129-49

Ingram, J.C. (1980) 'Foreword', in R.T. Shand (ed.), The Island States of the Pacific and Indian Oceans, Monograph No. 23, Development Studies Centre, Australian National University, Canberra, pp.vii-xii

Ingram, J.C. (1983) 'Australian Development Assistance in the South Pacific', in B. O'Dwyer (ed.), Australia and the South Pacific, Centre for Continuing Education, Australian National University, Canberra, pp.103-6

International Council for Adult Education (1981) 'Participatory Research: Development and Issues', Convergence, XIV, 3, Special Issue

International Council for Adult Education (1982a) 'Participation as Pedagogy', Convergence, XV, 1

International Council for Adult Education (1982b) 'Primary Health Care', Convergence, XV, 2

Isis (1983) Women in Development: A Resource Guide for Organization and Action, Isis, Geneva

JCFAD (Parliament of the Commonwealth of Australia, Joint Committee on Foreign Affairs and Defence) (1983) The Provision of Development Assistance and Humanitarian Aid to the Horn of Africa, Australian Government Publishing Service, Canberra

JCFAD (Parliament of the Commonwealth of Australia, Joint Committee on Foreign Affairs and Defence) (1985) The Jackson Report on Australia's Overseas Aid Program, Australian Government Publishing Service, Canberra

JCPA (Joint Parliamentary Committee of Public Accounts) (1982) Efficiency Audit: Administration of Australia's Bilateral Overseas Aid Program, Report 201, Australian Government Publishing Service, Canberra

Jackson Report (Committee to Review the Australian Overseas Aid Program) (1984) Report of the Committee to Review the Australian Overseas Aid Program, Australian Government Publishing Service, Canberra

Jalan, B. (ed.) (1982) Problems and Policies in Small Economies, Croom Helm, London

Janssen, L.H. (1961) Free Trade, Protection and Customs Union, Kroese

Johnson, H. (1958) 'The Gains from Freer Trade with Europe', The Manchester School, 255

Johnson, M. (1984) 'The Search for a New Japanese Locomotive', in B. Catley (ed.), Australia and Asia: Towards New Horizons?, Australian Institute of International Affairs, Adelaide

Jordan Dryland Farming Project (1982) Quarterly Report No. 8

Jordan Dryland Farming Project (1983-4) Quarterly Report No. 11

Jordan Dryland Farming Project (1984) Quarterly Report No. 15

Kamencu, Z. (1985) 'An Overview of Kenya's Hopes and Expectations Regarding Agricultural Development', Paper presented by H.E. The Kenyan High Commissioner to ACFOA Seminar on the Newton-Turner Report, 29 May, Canberra

Keith-Reid, R. (1982) 'How Fiji Lost an Empire', Islands Business, June, 12-15.

Knutsson, K.E. (1979) Food and Nutrition in National Development: An Evaluation of the Tanzania Food and Nutrition Centre (TFNC), Report Submitted to the Government of the United Republic of Tanzania, SIDA

Korten, D.C. (1980) 'Community Organization and Rural Development: A Learning Process Approach', Public Administration Review, 40(5), 480-510

Krause, L.B. (1984) 'Australia's Comparative Advantage in International Trade', in R.E. Caves and L.B. Krause (eds.), The Australian Economy: A View from the North, Allen and Unwin, Sydney, pp.275-311

Kripps, R. (ed.) (1982) Proceedings of the National Nutrition Workshop, Nutrition Section, Health Department, Port Moresby

Krishna, R. (1983) 'Development and Deprivation The Indian Experience', Economic and Political Weekly, 18

Kumar, K. and Kidd, R. (1982) 'Coopting the ideas of Paulo Freire', Ideas and Action, 148/5, 4-8

Lambert, J. (1978) 'National Nutrition Survey', National Planning Office, Port Moresby, mimeo

Langmore, J. (1972) 'A Critical Assessment of Australian Economic Policy for Papua New Guinea Between 1945 and 1970', Discussion Paper No. 1, Department of Economics, University of Papua New Guinea, Port Moresby

Lappé, F.M., Collins, J. and Kinley, D. (1980) Aid as Obstacle, Institute for Food and Development Policy, San Francisco

Layard, R. (ed.) (1972) Cost Benefit Analysis, Penguin, Harmondsworth

Leaver, R. (1985) 'Reformist Capitalist Development and the New International Division of Labour', in R.A. Higgott and R. Robison (eds.), Southeast Asia: Essays in the Political Economy of Structural Change, Routledge and Kegan Paul, London, pp.149-71

Lee, B. (1984) 'The Africa Connection for Agricultural Reserch', AFSAAP Newsletter, 6(2), 10-16

Leinbach, T. (1983) 'Transport Evaluation in Rural Development', Third World Planning Review 6(1), 23-35

Lim, D. (1985) 'The Jackson Report on Australian Aid: The Underlying Framework', Australian Outlook; The Australian Journal of International Affairs, 39(1), 19-22

Lipton, M. (1977) Why Poor People Stay Poor, Temple Smith, London

Love, R.S. (1982) 'Basic Needs in Kiribati', Pacific Perspective, 10, 66-74

McCall, M.K. (1977) 'Political Economy and Rural Transport: A Reappraisal of Transport Impacts', Antipode, 9, 113-25

McCawley, P. (1983) 'Australia's Misconceptions of ASEAN', in P. Dibb (ed.), Australia's External Relations in the 1980s: The Interaction of Economic, Political and Strategic Factors, Croom Helm, Canberra, pp.84-95

McCawley, P. (1984a) 'Economic Prospects for the Southeast Asian Region', Third Australia-Indonesia Seminar, Grifith University Brisbane

McCawley, P. (1984b) 'The Boom in ASEAN: Implications for Australia', in B. Catley (ed.), Australia and Asia: Towards New Horizons?, Australian Institute of International Affairs, Adelaide

Macdonald, A. (1983) Unpublished submission to the Committee to Review the Australian Overseas Aid Program

McDonald, A., Evans, D. and Sevele, F. (1982) 'A Guide to Project Planning and Appraisal in the South Pacific', South Pacific Commission, Noumea

McNeill, D. (1981) The Contradictions of Foreign Aid, Croom Helm, London

McQueen, H. (1984) 'In Search of Equality', Australian Society, 3(10), 12-15

Madigan, R. (1984) 'Australia and Asia in the 1980s', in B. Catley (ed.), Australia and Asia: Towards New Horizons?, Australian Institute of International Affairs, Adelaide

Martin, R.C.G. (1981) 'Development of a Management Information System - Bilateral Programs', unpublished ADAB document, Canberra

Mickelwait, D.R. (1979) 'Information Strategies for Implementing Rural Development', in G. Honadle and R. Klaus (eds.), International Development Administration-Implementation Analysis for Development Projects, Praeger Special Studies, New York, pp.182-202

Mikesell, R.F. (1983) The Economics of Foreign Aid and Self-Sustaining Development, Westview Press, Boulder

Millar, T.B. (1978) Australia in Peace and War: External Relations 1788-1977, Australian National University Press, Canberra

Miller, J.D.B. (1979) 'The Politics of International Aid', in R.T. Shand and H.V. Richter (eds.), International Aid: Some Political, Administrative and Technical Realities, Monograph No. 16, Development Studies Centre, Australian National University, Canberra, pp.1-15

Morris, J. and Gwyer, G. (1983) 'UK Experience with Identifying and Implementing Poverty-related Aid Projects', Development Policy Review, 1, 147-61

Morrison Report (Committee to Review Australian ASEAN Relations) (1984) Australia and ASEAN: Challenge and Opportunities, Report of the Joint Committee on Foreign Affairs and Defence, Australian Government Publishing Service, Canberra

Morss, E.R. (1984) 'Institutional Destruction Resulting from Donor and Project Proliferation in Sub-Saharan Countries', World Development, 12(4), 465-70

Morss, E.R., Hatch, J. Mickelwait, D. and Sweet, C. (1976) Strategies for Small Farmer Development: An Empirical Study of Rural Development Projects, Westview Press, Boulder, Colorado

Morss, E.R. and Morss, V.A. (1982) US Foreign Aid: Assessment of New and Traditional Development Strategies, Westview Press, Boulder, Colorado

Moss, L.A.G. (1978) 'Implementing Site and Services: the Institutional Environment of Comprehensive Development Projects', unpublished PhD dissertation, University of California, Berkeley

Myrdal, G. (1970) The Challenge of World Poverty: A World Anti-Poverty Programme in Outline, Penguin, Middlesex

Nalson, J.S. (1982) 'A Sociological Case Study of an Australian Agricultural Development Project in China', Paper presented to Seminar on China's Farms Today and Tomorrow, organised by the Committee for Australia-China Relations, Victoria College, Malvern, Vic.

Namaliu, R. (1984) 'The Content and Context of the Special Relationship Between PNG and Australia', in Papua New Guinea and Australia: PNG Perspectives, Australian National University, Canberra

Nand, S. (1983) Debate in the Fiji Parliament, 24 Nov 1983 on 1984 Appropriations Bill. Proceedings of Fiji Parliament 1290-1295

Newton-Turner, H. (1985) Australian Agricultural Aid to Africa - Appropriate Expertise, Australian Council for Overseas Aid, Canberra

Norris, K. (1984) 'I Saw Australian Rain in Kenya', Report on Kenya Water Project, Freedom From Hunger, 11 May

OECD (Organisation for Economic Co-operation and Development) (1981) Compendium of Aid Procedures, OECD, Paris

OECD (Organisation for Economic Co-operation and Development) (1984) 'Women in Development - New D.A.C. Guiding Principles', The O.E.C.D. Observer, No. 126, 22-3

Omedei, R. (1984) 'An NGO view of the Jackson Report', Pacific Aid Research Newsletter, No. 5, 4-7

O'Sullivan, N. (1983) 'Reaching the Disadvantaged Users through Project Development: The Elusive Vow', in S. Domicelj and G. Faithful (eds.), Australian Development Practice in Asia and the Pacific: Experience and Issues, Planning Research Center, University of Sydney, Sydney, pp.41-6

PADAP (Philippine-Australian Development Assistance Program) (1980) Second Annual Report, Zamboanga del Sur Development Project, PADAP, Pagadian

Palmer, I. (1977) 'Rural Women and the Basic Needs Approach to Development', International Labor Review, 115(1), 97-107

Papua New Guinea (1974) Strategies for Nationhood, Government of Papua New Guinea, Port Moresby

Papua New Guinea (1976) National Development Strategy, Government of Papua New Guinea, Port Moresby

Parboni, R. (1981) The Dollar and Its Rivals: Inflation and International Finance, Verso Books, London

Parrish, R.M. (1978) 'The Scope of Benefit-Cost Analysis', The Economic Record, 54, 304-14

Payer, C. (1974) The Debt Trap: The IMF and the Third World, Penguin Harmondsworth

Payer, C. (1982) The World Bank, Monthly Review Press, New York

Percival, B. (1981) 'Australian Overseas Development Assistance', unpublished B.A. Hons thesis, University of Sydney

Perdok, H.B. (1983) Handing Over Report, Sri Lanka-Netherlands Livestock Development Programme, Ministry for International Cooperation, Gravenhage, Netherlands

Plasschaert, S.R.F. (1979) Transfer Pricing and Multinational Corporations, Saxon House, Farnborough

Porter, D.J. (1984) 'Australian Aid: How Far Should the Jackson Review Go?', Australian Geographical Studies, 22, 129-41

Ramphal, S. (1984) 'Ten Years of NIEO Debate', Development Forum, 12(9)

Ricci, D. (1977) 'Reading Thomas Kuhn in the Post-Behavioural Era', Western Political Quarterly, 77, 7-34

Richards, R. (1981) The Zamboanga del Sur Development Project: The Impact on the Poor, Community Aid Abroad, Melbourne

Righter, R. (1982) 'World Bank Betrays Poor Says Official', Sunday Times, March 7, 10

Robbins, S. and Stobaugh, R. (1973) Money in the Multinational Enterprise, Basic Books, New York

Robison, D. (forthcoming) Indonesia: The Rise of Capital, Allen and Unwin, Sydney

Rogers, E.M. (1976) 'Communication and Development. The Passing of the Dominant Paradigm', in E.M. Rogers (ed.), Communication and Development - Critical Perspectives, Sage, Beverley Hills

Rokotuivuna, A., Dakuvula, J., Narsey, W., Howie, I., Annear, P., Mahony, D., Fong, A., Slatter, C. and Noone, B. (1973) Fiji: A Developing Australian Colony, International Development Action, Melbourne

Rondinelli, D.A. (1976) 'International Assistance Policy and Development Project Administration: the Impact of Imperious Rationality', International Organization, 30(4), 573-606

Rooney, N. (1975) 'What's a Fair Go for Women?', in S. Toupounvia, R. Crocombe and C. Slatter (eds.), The Pacific Way: Social Issues in National Development, South Pacific Social Sciences Association, Suva, pp.119-21

Roughan, J. (1983) Unpublished Submission to the Committee to Review the Australian Development Assistance Programme

Ruggie, J. (ed.) (1983) The Antimonies of Interdependence: National Welfare and the International Division of Labour, Columbia University Press, New York

SPEC (South Pacific Bureau for Economic Cooperation) (1983) Unpublished Submission to the Committee to Review the Australian Development Assistance Programme

SSCFAD (Senate Standing Committee on Foreign Affairs and Defence) (1977) Australia and the South Pacific, Australian Government Publishing Service, Canberra

SSCFAD (Senate Standing Committee on Foreign Affairs and Defence) (1979) The New International Economic Order - Implications for Australia, Australian Government Publishing Service, Canberra

Samana, U. (1984) 'PNG-Australian Relations as they affect Provincial Government and Decentralisation', in PNG and Australia: PNG Perspectives, Australian National University, Canberra

Sargent, S. (1983) Agribusiness in Australia and Australian Agribusiness in the Third World Countries of Asia and the Pacific, Australian Freedom from Hunger Campaign, Sydney

Scarr, D. (1967) Fragments of Empire: A History of the Western Pacific High Commission 1877-1914, ANU Press, Canberra.

Schuftan, C. (1983) 'Foreign Aid and its Role in Maintaining the Exploitation of the Agricultural Sector: Evidence from a Case Study in Africa', International Journal of Health Sciences, 13, 33-49

Seers, D. (1980) 'North-South: Muddling Morality and Mutuality', Third World Quarterly, 2, 681-92

Self, P. (1975) Econocrats and the Policy Process: The Politics and Philosophy of Cost-Benefit Analysis, Macmillan, London

Selth, A. (1985) 'Australian Aid to Asia: Some Problems of Public Policy', Current Affairs Bulletin, 61(9), 27-35

Selwyn, P. (ed.) (1975) Development Policy in Small Countries, Croom Helm, London

Sen, A. (1983) 'Development: Which Way Now?', The Economics Journal, 93, 745-62

Sevele, F. (1984) 'South Pacific Economies 1981, Statistical Summary', South Pacific Commission, Noumea

Shaw, B. (1982) 'Smallness, Islandness, Remoteness and Resources: an Analytical Framework', Regional Development Dialogue, Special Issue, 95-109

Shaw, T. (1984) 'Aussies to Retreat?', West Africa, 3 September, No.3498, 1777

Shoesmith, D. (1982) The Debate on the Australian Aid Projects in the Philippines: A Guide to the Literature, Asia Bureau Australia, Melbourne

Sinden, J.A. (1980) 'Pangloss, Pandora, and Pareto for the Aspiring Benefit-Cost Analyst', Review of Marketing and Agricultural Economics, 48(2), 99-109

Skitovsky, T. (1958) Economic Theory and Western European Economic Integration, Stanford University Press, Stanford

Sklar, H. (ed.) (1980) Trilateralism, Southend Press, Boston

Sommerlad, E. (1976) Kormilda, the Way to Tomorrow?, ANU Press, Canberra

Stauffer, R.B. (1983) 'The Manila-Washington Connection: Continuities in Transnational Political Economy of Philippine Development', Research Monograph No. 17, Transnational Corporation Research Project, Faculty of Economics, Sydney University, Sydney

Steinfels, P. (1979) The Neoconservatives, Touchstone Press, New York

Stent, W. (1985) 'The Jackson Report: A Critical Review', Australian Outlook: The Australian Journal of International Affairs, 39(1), 33-8

Stewart, F. (1985) 'The Fragile Foundations of the Neoclassical Approach to Development', Journal of Development Studies, 21, 282-92

Streeten, P. (1968) 'A Poor Nations Guide to Getting Aid', New Society, 11, 154-56

Streeten, P. (1972) The Frontiers of Development Studies, Macmillan, London

Streeten, P. (1979) 'From Growth to 'Basic Needs'', Finance and Development, 16(3), 28-31

Streeten, P. and Burki, S.J. (1978) 'Basic Needs: Some Issues', World Development, 6(3), 411-21

Sweet, C.F. and Weisel, P.F. (1979) 'Process vs Blueprint Models for Designing Rural Development Projects', in G. Honadle and R. Klaus (eds.), International Development Administration-Implementation Analysis for Development Projects, Praeger Special Studies, New York, pp.127-44

Taylor, M.J. (1983) Business Organisation Segmentation and the Functioning of the Fiji Economy, Report to the Fiji Employment and Development Mission, Suva, Fiji

Taylor, M.J. (1984a) 'The Changing Pattern of Australian Corporate Investment in the Pacific Islands' in M.J. Taylor (ed.), The Geography of Australian Corporate Power, Croom Helm Australia, Sydney, pp.25-45

Taylor, M.J. (1984b) 'Business Organisations and Transfer of Value: Examples from Fiji', in D.K. Forbes and P.J. Rimmer (eds.), Uneven Development and the Geographical Transfer of Value, Monograph 16, Department of Human Geography, Australian National University, pp.175-97

Taylor, M.J. and Kissling, C.C. (1983) 'Resource Dependence, Power Networks and the Airline System of the South Pacific', Regional Studies, 17, 237-56

Taylor, R. (1983) 'Prevention and Control of Non-Communicable Disease in Pacific Island Nations: Prospects and Constraints', South Pacific Commission, Information Document 15, Noumea

Tendler, J. (1975) Inside Foreign Aid, John Hopkins University Press, London and Baltimore

Tendler, J. (1982) 'Turning Private Voluntary Organizations Into Development Agencies: Questions for Evaluation', A.I.D. Program Evaluation Discussion Paper No. 12, USAID, Washington D.C.

Thaman, R.R. (1982) 'Deterioration of Traditional Food Systems, Increasing Malnutrition and Food Dependency in the Pacific Islands', Journal of Food and Nutrition, 39, 109-21

Thaman, R.R. (1983) 'Food and National Development in the Pacific Islands: an Introduction', in R.R. Thaman and W.C. Clarke, (eds.), Food and National Development in the South Pacific, University of the South Pacific, Suva, pp.1-16

Thiele, S. (1982) Yugul - An Arnhem Land Cattle Station, North Australian Research Unit Monograph, Australian National University, Darwin

Tinker, I., Bo Bramson, M. and Buvinic, M. (eds.) (1975) Women and World Development, American Association for the Advancement of Science, Overseas Development Council and Praeger Publications, New York

Todaro, M.P. (1982) Economic Development in the Third World, Longman, London

Townsend, P. (1982) 'Overview of Social and Economic Research', in P. Kripps (ed.), Proceedings of the National Nutrition Workshop, Nutrition Section, Health Department, Port Moresby, pp.75-80

Transfield Pty Ltd (1983) Unpublished Submission to the Committee to Review the Australian Development Assistance Programme

Tuvalu (1983) Unpublished Submission to the Committee to Review the Australian Development Assistance Programme

Ul Haq, M. (1976) The Poverty Curtain: Choices for the Third World, Columbia University Press, New York

Uphoff, N.T. and Esman, M.J. (1974) Local Organzation for Rural Development: Analysis of Asian Experience, Cornell University Press, Ithaca, New York

Utrecht, E. (1984) 'Fiji: A Client State', in E. Utrecht (ed.), Fiji: A Client State of Australasia?, Transnational Corporations Research Project, University of Sydney, Sydney, pp.1-65

Viviani, N. (1979) 'Problems of Aid Administration and Policy Formulation among Western Countries', in R.T Shand and H.V. Richter (eds.), International Aid: Some Political, Administration and Technical Realities, Development Studies Centre Monograph 16, Australian National University, Canberra, pp.46-90

Viviani, N. and Wilenski, P. (1979) 'Politicians, Bureaucrats and Foreign Aid: A Case Study', in R.T. Shand and H.V. Richter (eds.), International Aid: Some Political, Administrative and Technical Realities, Development Studies Centre Monograph 16, Australian National University, Canberra, pp.91-128

Walsh, C. (1984) 'Australia and Asia: The Economic Dimension', in B. Catley (ed.), Australia and Asia: Towards New Horizons?, Australian Institute of International Affairs, Adelaide

Weeks, S.G. (1984) 'The Poor are Losing out in the 'Rich' Capital', Times of PNG, 9 August

Weeks, S.G. and Guthrie, G. (1982) 'First Level Education: Community Schools', in D. King and S. Ranck (eds.), Papua New Guinea Atlas, Robert Brown, Port Moresby, pp.26-7

Weissman, S. (ed.) (1975) The Trojan Horse: A Radical Look at Foreign Aid, Ramparts Press, Los Angeles

White, J. (1970) Regional Development Banks: A Study of Institutional Style, Overseas Development Institute, London

White, J. (1974) The Politics of Foreign Aid, Bodley Head, London

White, J. (1976) 'The Evaluation of Aid Offers', Development and Change, 7, 233-48

Whitlam, G. (1983) 'Democratic Socialism and International Economics', in J. Langmore and D. Peetz (eds.), Wealth, Poverty and Survival, Australia in the World, Allen and Unwin, Sydney, pp.179-92

Wildavsky, A. (1967) 'The Political Economy of Efficiency', The Public Interest, Summer, 3048

Wilkinson, A.E. (1976) 'The Politics of Australian Foreign Aid Policy 1950-72', unpublished thesis, Department of International Relations, Research School of Pacific Studies, Australian National University, Canberra

Willesee, D.R. (1975) 'New Directions in Australia's Development Assistance', Australian Foreign Affairs Record, 46, 233-43

Winkler, J.E. (1982) Losing Control: Towards an Understanding of Transnational Corporations in the Pacific Island Context, Lotu Pacifika Productions, Suva

Wood, A. and Smith, W. (1984) 'Zambia up for Grabs? The Regionalisation of Agricultural Aid, Area, 16, 3-7

Woolcott, R. (1982) 'Objectives of Australian Assistance to the Philippines', Speech to the Rotary Club of Pasay, Metro Manila, 21 April, Manila

World Bank (1981a) World Development Report, 1981, Oxford University Press, Oxford

World Bank (1981b) Accelerated Development for Africa: An Agenda For Action, World Bank Publications, Washington D.C.

World Bank (1983) World Development Report 1983, Oxford University Press, New York

World Bank (1984) 'Situation and Prospects of the Indian Economy - A Medium Term Perspective', Vol II: Main Report Document of the World Bank, Washington D.C.

Wynne, B. (1975) 'The Rhetoric of Consensus Politics: A Critical Review of Technology Assessment, Research Policy, 4, 108-58

Yojana (1984) 'Testing Voluntary Agencies', Yojana, 28, (20/21)

Yudelman, M. (1976) 'Agriculture in Integrated Rural Development: the Experience of the World Bank', Food Policy, 1, 367-81

Zimmet, P., Raab, R. and Wilson, G. (1983) 'Australian Aid and its Implications on the Social and Health Welfare of Recipient Nations', unpublished submission to the Committee to Review the Australian Development Assistance Programmes

INDEX

For Product Safety Concerns and Information please contact our EU representative GPSR@taylorandfrancis.com Taylor & Francis Verlag GmbH, Kaufingerstraße 24, 80331 München, Germany

Batch number: 10725800

Printed by Printforce, the Netherlands